THE STORYTIME SOURCEBOOK

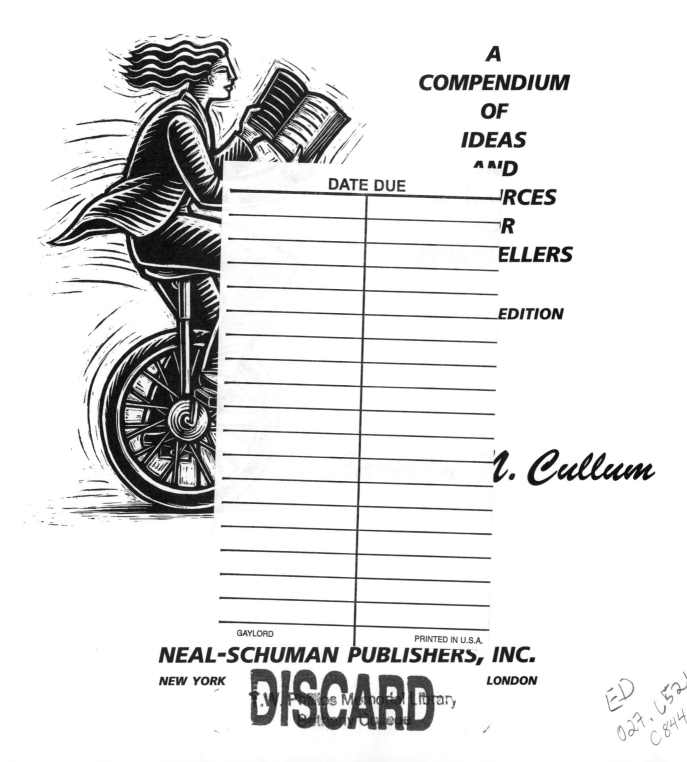

A
COMPENDIUM
OF
IDEAS
AND
RCES
R
ELLERS

EDITION

V. Cullum

NEAL-SCHUMAN PUBLISHERS, INC.

NEW YORK   LONDON

Published by Neal-Schuman Publishers, Inc.
100 Varick Street
New York, NY 10013

The paper used in this publication meets the minimum requirements of American National Standard for Information Sciences—Permanence of Paper for Printed Library Materials, ANSI Z39.48–1992.

Library of Congress Cataloging-in-Publication Data

Cullum, Carolyn N.
    The storytime sourcebook : a compendium of ideas and resources for storytellers / Carolyn N. Cullum.—2nd ed.
        p.   cm.
    Includes bibliographical references and indexes.
    ISBN 1–55570–360–7
    1. Storytelling—United States   2. Children's libraries—Activity programs—United States.   I. Title
Z718.3.C85 1999
027.62'51—dc21   99–046420

This book is dedicated to my family, who have always encouraged me all my life to try new things, and especially to my Mom and Dad, who put up with me during the long hours of research.

When we meet next we'll have a tale to tell.
—Lord Byron
Don Juan

Contents

Preface

Stories and storytelling existed long before the printed page. For thousands of years, both children and adults have gathered around storytellers to hear tales of fancy, myth, or history. With the revival of storytelling in the United States, story hour programs have become a regular feature of children's services in libraries.

Planning and presenting these story programs for young children takes a great deal of the librarian's time. For the past 20 years, I have served as a children's librarian in both public and school libraries. My background in elementary education, educational media, and library service, has helped me introduce children—and their parents or caregivers—to the immense and wonderful body of children's literature.

Over the years, I have prepared and presented a great many story hours featuring a variety of resources (books, flannel stories, films, etc.). When I started telling stories, the libraries I worked in had no prepared programs on file from which I could draw. To give other storytellers a "leg up" in their programming, I compiled the first edition of *The Storytime Sourcebook: A Compendium of Ideas and Resources for Storytellers* in 1990. Now, ten years later, when I began planning this second edition, I had a greatly expanded number of topics and activities from which to select. Thus, while the first edition of *The Storytime Sourcebook* had 100 topics and included 446 picture books (broadly interpreted here to include fiction and nonfiction with a vocabulary level from preschool to second grade), this second edition has 146 topics, ranging from whales to Sherlock Holmes, and includes 2,200 picture books. In recognition of the prevalent technology, I replaced the first edition's filmstrips and 16-mm films with videos; this second edition recommends 147 cassette or CD songs and 564 videocassettes. Instead of one craft, as in the first edition, there are two crafts for each of the 146 topics. Full bibliographic citations to the publishers and distribution information for nonbook materials are included in the bibliography and appendices.

The Storytime Sourcebook is designed to help librarians, teachers, parents, and other caregivers locate the appropriate idea (craft, fingerplay, story, song, etc.) for programs or lessons from the vast number of wonderful books usually available in libraries.

The activities and stories have been selected for use with children three to seven years old. The topics were chosen with three goals in mind:

- to widen the children's experience with literature,
- to formulate programs related to children's physical, emotional, and intellectual concerns; and

- to encourage the sharing of experiences with other children of the same age.

Storytelling can be a rewarding experience for the storyteller, as well as for the child. Some days all the research, preparation time, and expense may seem too overwhelming, but then there will be moments when it will all come together and you will realize that you've meant something in a child's life.

I would like to share with you one such moment for me that occurred just recently. After a particularly frustrating day at the library, I returned to my desk the next day to find a two-page note. My first reaction was "Oh no, not another problem," but to my delight I found the following:

Dear Miss Carolyn,

My name is Christine Laskodi. I am a resident of Edison attending school in PA. I am in my last year of the elementary education program at Millersville University.

Attached you will find a portion of an assignment I completed for my Teaching Reading/Language Arts class. The task was to write a literacy autobiography broken into birth to age five and the elementary school years. Each section contained several vignettes relating to my experiences with learning to read. Take a moment to read what I have highlighted. Thank you for the positive and wonderful experience!

Christine

The following is the vignette she enclosed:

"Story Hour"

She seemed like a giant to me, her lean structure towering over a group of three-year-olds, but her warm voice easily drew us all in. "It is time for storyhour," we heard her say as we let go of our parents' hands and followed Miss Carolyn into the back room of the Edison Public Library. The room seemed huge to me as a tiny three-year-old. It was long and spacious with a very high ceiling. Of course, if I were to go in the same room today it would probably look very small. The surroundings consisted of a table, some chairs, a supply closet, and a screen and film projector, the only essentials for the weekly storyhour. It was probably one of my favorite things to do as a young child. Upon entering the storyhour room, Miss Carolyn would sit in her chair and we would all surround her on the floor. I always liked to be in front so I could better see the pictures of her book. She would read us a story or sometimes show us a film strip. At the end, we always got to make something related to the story. I looked forward to hearing Miss Carolyn's voice lead me to places I had never been before. With my imagination cap on, I felt as though I was a part of the stories she read. The storyhour seemed like another world to me. It was as if all of the story and film strip characters were sitting in the room with us.

Through storytelling, we help children learn about themselves and the world around them, and, best of all, we can be there for the experience. I hope *The Storytime Sourcebook* will make the task of the storyteller a little easier.

How to Use This Book

Book titles, videocassettes, and song cassettes or CDs were selected from searches of actual library collections, published reviews, and media catalogs. Each two-page spread represents one storyhour session on a single subject area of interest to children. By obtaining the books listed on your selected topic you will have complete directions for your activities. (If no source is listed for an activity, the author developed it.) Under each selected topic you will find the following information:

RELATE TO
These programs can be presented at any time during the year, but it's always nice to have them at a specified time that can give the program more meaning to the children. Each topic offers a suggested date during the year when the program can be offered to celebrate a special event (e.g., the "Sign Language" program might be presented during Deaf Awareness Week in September). You may check this under each topic or refer to the Topical Calendar on page xv to view all the dates listed in this resource book.

VIDEOCASSETTES
Where available, videocassettes are listed for each subject; information about the distributor, running time, and whether the videocassettes are animated or live action. Individual users should check to determine whether public performance rights are required for the use they are making of these videocassettes.

BOOKS
Picture books (fiction and nonfiction) related to each topic are listed. The prices indicated in the bibliography are the most recent available for each book.

Although not all the books listed will be in print (children's books go in and out of print quickly), you should be able to find most of them in your local library.

If your local library does not own the book you want, ask the children's librarian to borrow the book from a neighboring library through the Interlibrary Loan. Many public libraries are equipped to offer this service, which locates a book from public libraries throughout the state within a week or two. This service is usually free and will save you time searching from place to place.

FINGERPLAYS
These include short rhyming stories or poems that are very useful for filling in during transition times between activities. Using fingerplay with children helps

them develop their fine motor skills by moving their fingers to act out the rhyme, increases their vocabulary, teaches them new concepts, or may just help them relax after a particularly active game.

Many parents have done simple fingerplay games with their child already by introducing "This Little Piggie" or "Pat-A-Cake." You can expand on these by using the suggested fingerplays. The source for the fingerplay will give you the actual verse along with suggested finger motions to mimic the words.

When teaching a fingerplay to a young child be sure to do the following:

- Begin by teaching the motions alone without the verse.
- Mirror the motions when you are facing the group. If you want the group to wave their right hand—*you* wave the left, etc.
- Add the verse once the motions have become familiar and allow plenty of opportunity for repetition.
- Enjoy it yourself. If you aren't having fun, neither will the children.

CRAFTS

Simple, easy-to-assemble crafts related to the topics are described briefly on each page. Sources for craft ideas are cited, unless they are original. For complete instructions on the craft, you would have to procure the sourcebook. All the crafts suggested use inexpensive materials and do not require skill in art. You will be supplied with two different crafts for each topic so that you can repeat this topic at a later date with a completely new craft.

ACTIVITY

Physical activities of some kind are essential during an hour-long program with preschool children. Attention spans differ and by alternating active and passive periods the leader keeps the children's interest and control of the group.

A general description of each game (two are offered per topic) related to each topic is made available to you. The original source of the game is stated if further clarification is needed.

Fingerplays and games listed for each topic will give you active periods necessary to relieve the children's pent-up energies when their attention wanes.

SONGS

Song titles are listed with a source for the sheet music and lyrics. New in this edition is the listing of songs with an audio source, such as cassette or CD, for those of us who don't play an instrument or read sheet music.

Children enjoy singing and will ask for their favorite song for many days after they learn it. If they ask to repeat a song from a previous session, sing it and then move on to a new one.

Don't be afraid to sing. Young children do not expect a trained voice, and in fact, a little mistake once in a while will only endear you to them.

FINDING AIDS

The Storytime Sourcebook also includes the following features to help you quickly locate resources and ideas:

- Table of Contents (Subject Guide)
- Videocassette Guide
- Book Index
- Craft Index
- Activities Index
- Song Index
- Book Publishers Index
- Videocassette Distributors Index
- Cassette and CD Index
- Topical Calendar

Topical Calendar

NOTE: Dates are based on the 1999 calendar. Since some event dates vary with the yearly calendar, I've included comments on how they move. Right column numbers refer to sequence numbers of activities, not to page numbers.

Numbered Activities

1 Activities: Reading

Relate to:	*Birthday of "The Count" (Oct. 9): Birthday of the famous Sesame Street counting puppet "The Count," whose favorite songs are "Born to Add" and "Count on Me."*

Videos:	*Alexander and the Wind-Up Mouse* (Leo Lionni's Caldecotts) *I Can Read with My Eyes Shut* (Dr. Seuss's ABC video) *Petunia*

Books:	*The Bee Tree*, Patricia Polacco *The Bird, the Frog, and the Light*, Avi *Don't Tease the Guppies*, Pat Lowery Collins *Hog-Eye*, Susan Meddaugh *Johnny Lion's Book*, Edith Hurd *More than Anything Else*, Marie Bradby *Olaf Reads*, Joan Lexau *The Old Woman Who Loved to Read*, John Winch *The Once-Upon-a-Time Dragon*, Jack Kent *Read to Your Bunny*, Rosemary Wells *Secret Code*, Dana Meachen Rau *Silas the Bookstore Cat*, Karen Trella Mather *Storyhour—Starring Megan!*, Julie Brillhart *That's Enough for One Day!*, Susan Pearson *Too Many Books!*, Caroline Bauer *The Wednesday Surprise*, Eve Bunting

Fingerplay:	**Learning.** (Source: *Resource Book for the Kindergarten Teacher*, Virginia H. Lucus and Walter B. Barbe)

Crafts:	**Touch-Me Books.** Many children get their early experience with reading by using books that allow them to touch various textures included in the story. Try having the children make their own "Touch-Me" books. Prepare a small three-page book with one large illustration and word per page for each child. (Suggestion: Use a duck, a rabbit, and a cat.) At the program allow time to color the illustrations, then provide the appropriate textures to glue to the pictures (e.g., feathers, cottonballs for a rabbit's tail, and pieces of fur). Children have a feeling of accomplishment by creating a book of their own for identifying textures as well as animals.

Willie-the-Worm Bookmark.
This decorative bookmark features a tulip with green leaves and Willie the Worm crawling across the stem and behind the leaves. Here you find simple patterns you can easily copy and have precut for the youngest children. What makes this bookmark special is the fact that the bookworm can be moved up and down the page to indicate the line you are reading.
(Source: *Springtime Surprises!: Things to Make and Do*, Judith Conaway)

Activities: **Word Matching.**
Using large flashcards with simple words (e.g., cat, ball, etc.) and illustrations on them, discuss the pictures and words with the children. Next pass out cards with only the words on them, and see how many children can match these to the flashcards. The level of the words will depend on the age level of your group.

The Elephant Story.
Develop a story about an elephant who carries peanuts. Have each child pretend to be an elephant and use a spoon to carry peanuts from one location, past various obstacles, and to the kitchen at the end of the room. As the storyteller tells the story of the elephant named (child's name), he or she will indicate the path the elephant must take to get to the kitchen. Suggested verses are listed in this source. Try peanut butter and cracker snacks to end the game.
(Source: *300 Three Minute Games*, Jackie Silberg)

Song: (Audio) "A Book Is a Wonderful Friend"
(Source: *Peanutbutterjam Incredibly Spreadable*)

2 Adoption/Orphans

Relate to:	*National Adoption Week (week including Thanksgiving): Designated by the National Council for Adoption to celebrate successful adoptions and encourage people to think about adopting wonderful children.*

Videos:	*Madeline* *The Three Robbers*

Books:	*Allison*, Allen Say *The Day We Met You*, Phoebe Koehler *Did My First Mother Love Me?: A Story for an Adopted Child*, Kathryn Ann Miller *A Family for Jamie: An Adoption Story*, Suzanne Bloom *A Forever Family*, Roslyn Banish *Families Are Different*, Nina Pellegrini *Happy Adoption Day*, John McCutcheon *Horace*, Holly Keller *How I Was Adopted*, Joanna Cole *A Koala for Katie: An Adoption Story*, Jonathan London *Let's Talk about It: Adoption*, Fred Rogers *My Real Family*, Emily Arnold McCully *Through Moon and Stars and Night Skies*, Ann Turner *We Adopted You, Benjamin Koo*, Linda Walvoord Girard *When Joel Comes Home*, Susi Gregg Fowler *William Is My Brother*, Jane T. Schnitter

Fingerplay:	**Some Families.** (Source: *1001 Rhymes and Fingerplays*, The Totline Staff)

Crafts:	**The Me Board.** Try making this unique "Me Board" with the children so they can tell everyone how special they are. Their adopted families can add anything they feel is special about the child to the board. Simple instructions are supplied in this book to design this pin-up board. Add a face with the child's special features and trace the child's hands and feet. Using poster board for the body, they can combine all the parts and hang this on their bedroom doors for a very unique display. (Source: *Crafts from Recyclables*, edited by Colleen Van Blaricom)

Picture Magnet.
Adopted children need to know that they are an important part of their new family just as all children do. Picture magnets depicting each important member of the family will help with this goal. Collect jar lids of all different types. Let the children decorate them with construction paper or paints. Place a magnet on the exterior of the lid and a picture of the child on the interior. Do one for each member of the family so the children can place the picture magnets in a prominent place in the home.

(Source: *Rainy Day Projects for Children*, Gerri Jenny and Sherrie Gould)

Activities:

Fuku Wari.
Always try to discuss adoption in a positive manner, letting both the child and parent feel how wonderful it is that they have found each other. With this in mind you can introduce to the group a Chinese game of good fortune called Fuku Wari. A banner is displayed with the outline of a large face representing Otafuku, goddess of fortune. Her features are left off and are given to the children who are then blindfolded and proceed to play this game in the same manner as Pin the Tail on the Donkey. Indicate to the children the different kinds of families that can love each other; introduce Otafuku's motto, which is "laugh and grow fat."

(Source: *Children Are Children Are Children*, Ann Cole, Carolyn Haas, Elizabeth Heller, and Betty Weinberger)

Sardine.
This is a little bit of a stretch for this topic, but it seemed to work well when I used it. After a discussion on what adoption means and how people can feel very special being taken into another's family, we decided to play this game. Relate it to becoming one more member of the family.

The player who is It must go and hide while all the other children close their eyes and count to 100. When they are finished counting, they will all scatter trying to find It. Explain that this is a quiet game and if they find the person hiding they are to join him or her without others noticing. The play continues until all players are crowded in hiding with It. The first to find It becomes the next hider.

(Source: *The Little Witch's Black Magic Book of Games*, Linda Glovach)

Songs:

(Audio) "You Are You"
(Source: *UnBearable Bears*)
(Book) "The Little Orphan Girl"
(Source: *Here's to the Women*, Hilda E. Wenner and Elizabeth Freilcher)

3 Alphabet

Relate to:	*A'PHABET DAY (Dec. 25): This is also called "No-L" Day. It's a time for those who don't want to send Christmas cards but instead send greeting cards listing the Alphabet but leave a space where the L is missing.*

Videos:
Alligators All Around
The Alphabet Dragon
Dr. Seuss's ABC
The Shout It Out Alphabet Film
The Z was Zapped

Books:
A-B-C Discovery, Izhar Cohen
ABC Drive!, Naomi Howland
ABC I Like Me!, Nancy Carlson
The A to Z Beastly Jamboree, Robert Bender
Alfie's ABC, Shirley Hughes
C Is for Circus, Bernice Chardiet
From Anne to Zach, Mary Jane Martin
Goblins in Green, Nicholas Heller
Harold's ABC, Crockett Johnson
The Hollabaloo ABC, Beverly Cleary
I Unpacked My Grandmother's Trunk, Susan Hoguet
Pooh's Alphabet Book, A.A. Milne
The Sesame Street ABC Storybook, Jeffrey Moss
Tomorrow's Alphabet, George Shannon
The War between the Vowels and Consonants, Priscilla Turner

Fingerplay: **ABC Fingers**
(Source: *Rhymes for Learning Times*, Louise Binder Scott)

Crafts: **Pick a Letter.**
Display all the letters of the alphabet somewhere in the room. Some children may know them all while others may recognize only a few. Have each child choose one letter that he or she knows and tell the group what it is. Next have each child take construction paper and in one corner trace the letter with glue and sprinkle with glitter. Design a cover for the new booklet, "My Alphabet Book," to which the child can add letters later as he or she learns them.

Pasta Pencil Holder.
We can find our alphabet all around us in various forms such as alphabet cereal or alphabet pasta. Use either of these to teach the alphabet or spelling, then use them to decorate a container to create your own distinctive alphabet pencil holder.
(Source: *Kids' Holiday Fun*, Penny Warner)

Activities: **The Manual Alphabet.**
Children are fascinated by disabilities. When doing this program discuss the problems of a mute child communicating with his or her friends. Introduce a new type of alphabet, the manual alphabet. Although it would be too difficult and time-consuming to teach the entire alphabet to very young children, try to teach one or two key letters that the children choose themselves.
(Source: *Do a Zoom-Do*, Bernice Chesler)

Headline Bingo.
For this bingo game you will need to collect a large number of newspaper headlines all approximately the same length. Let each child select one or two. The caller will take the remaining headlines in a bag, shake them, and select one. From the selected title the caller will call off one letter at a time and the children will cross off the corresponding letters on their headlines (only one letter per letter called) until someone is done and cries out "Headline!"
(Source: *50 Ways to Have Fun with Old Newspapers*, Bill Severn)

Songs: (Audio)"ABC Song"
(Source: *Six Little Ducks: Classic Children's Songs*)
(Book) "The Alphabet Song"
(Source: *The Reader's Digest Children's Songbook*, William L. Simon)

4 Anatomy: Body Parts

Relate to:	*National Correct Posture Month (May): A month dedicated to the study of the bones of the body and proper posture.*

Videos:

The Foot Book
Mop Top

Books:

Baby's Book of the Body, Roger Priddy
The Boy with Square Eyes: A Tale of Televisionitus, Juliet and Charles Snape
Eyes, Nose, Fingers, Toes, Ruth Krauss
The Growing-up Feet, Beverly Cleary
Hands!, Virginia L. Kroll
Happy Birthday, Sam, Patricia Hutchins
Hello Toes! Hello Feet!, Ann Whitford Paul
I Love My Hair!, Natasha Anastasia Tarpley
I'm Too Small, You're Too Big, Judith Barrett
I've Got Your Nose!, Nancy Bentley
The Littlest Leaguer, Sydney Hoff
Make a Face, Lynn Yudell
The Me I See, Barbara Hazen
My Hands, Aliki
Tail, Toes, Eyes, Ears, Nose, Marilee Robin Burton
Tiny Toes, Donna Jakob
Two Eyes, a Nose, and a Mouth, Roberta Grobel Intrater

Fingerplay:

Where Is Thumbkin?
(Source: *Eye Winker, Tom Tinker, Chin Chopper*, Tom Glazer)

Crafts:

Me-Doll.
Everyone is unique in his or her own way but we also have many similarities, such as where our joints are located. Make a jointed "Me-Doll" just like yourself to show the children where the parts of the body bend. An easy and inexpensive method of construction is the use of paper and brass paper fasteners, among other items listed in the source below. Have the children make their own "Me-Dolls" after seeing themselves in a full-length mirror, then compare the ways in which we are each very special.
(Source: *Purple Cow to the Rescue*, Ann Cole, Carolyn Haas, and Betty Weinberger)

Body Puzzle.
Help children identify different parts of the anatomy by making their own special body puzzle. Have each child lie down and ask someone to trace his or her body (be sure to get hands and fingers traced properly).

Let the child color all the features as well as the clothes. When completed take scissors and cut it into large pieces to create a puzzle.
(Source: *Teaching Terrific Twos and Other Toddlers*, Terry Lynne Graham and Linda Camp)

Activity: **Circus Seals.**
Divide the children into a number of small groups. The goal of each group is to keep their balloon in the air longer than the other groups. If it touches the ground their team will be eliminated. Here's the catch. A caller leads the game by calling out how you may touch the ball. The caller will call out such things as "elbows," "noses," "hips," etc. Only when "flippers" is called may the children use their hands like circus seals.
(Source: *Great Theme Parties for Children*, Irene N. Watts)

**Activity
and Song:**   **Who Has a Nose?**
Done to the tune of "Frere Jacques," this song and activity cover the range of body parts familiar to children including the concept of short and tall. Even the shyest child will participate in a group and with a song that repeats its verses. Additional verses might even be suggested by the children themselves.
(Source: *Dancing Games for Children of All Ages*, Esther L. Nelson)

Song: (Audio)   "Head, Shoulders, Knees, and Toes"
(Source: *Where is Thumbkin?*)

5 Animals

Relate to:	*Be Kind to Animals Week (first full week in May): Declared by the American Humane Society to encourage people to care for animals as we care for ourselves.*

Videos:
The Camel Who Took a Walk
Henny Penny
Sylvester and the Magic Pebble
The Three Little Pigs

Books:
Animals Should Definitely Not Wear Clothing, Judi Barrett
A Bargain for Frances, Russell Hoban
Ducks Like to Swim, Agnes Verboven
Katy No-Pocket, Emmy Payne
Lizard Sees the World, Susan Tews
Mice Twice, Joseph Low
Mrs. Brown Went to Town, Wong Herbert Yee
Peck, Slither, and Slide, Suse MacDonald
Sammy the Seal, Syd Hoff
The Sheep Follow, Monica Wellington
Sitting on the Farm, Bob King
A Snake Is Totally Tail, Judi Barrett
Sylvester and the Magic Pebble, William Steig
Treed by a Pride of Irate Lions, Nathan Zimelman
Who Hops?, Katie Davis

Fingerplay: **Seals.**
(Source: *Finger Frolics—Revised*, Liz Cromwell, Dixie Hibner, and John R. Faitel)

Crafts: **Panda Puppet.**
Hand puppets are always a sure favorite with this age level. Precut pieces or patterns are advisable in large groups. Felt is an easy material to work with. Try constructing a hand panda puppet. Though the source indicated below suggests sewing the edges, a fast-drying material glue (Slomon's Velverette Craft Glue or similar types found in craft stores) would be sufficient to hold the puppet together. A box stage can be used to practice with the new creation.
(Source: *Felt Craft*, Florence Temko)

Percival Porcupine.
Create Percival from construction paper strips. This craft can be made with the youngest of the children. The body is made of construction paper folded into a triangle and the quills from three-inch strips. Let your porcupine display a dash of color by making his quills multiple colors.
(Source: *Easy Does it!*, James Razzi)

Activities:

Foxes and Rabbits.
Divide the players into two teams, the Foxes and the Rabbits. At one end of the room mark an area representing home for the rabbits. Throughout the room designate a few small circles as safe rabbit holes. The rabbits try to get safely from one end of the room to home while the foxes try to tag them. Have the teams change roles and play again. The team with the fewest eliminations wins.
(Source: *500 Games*, Peter L. Cave)

Find the Animals.
Hide a number of animal pictures throughout the room. The children are assigned different animals to find. As they search for their chosen animals they are instructed not to tell other children the animals they are trying to locate or to tell which animals they have already found. This is a good time filler and young children love little secrets.
(Source: *Great Theme Parties for Children*, Irene N. Walls)

Songs:

(Audio) "Animal Quiz"
(Source: *Can a Cherry Pie Wave Goodbye?*)
(Book) "Old MacDonald"
(Source: *Eye Winker, Tom Tinker, Chin Chopper*, Tom Glazer)

6 Animals: Bears

Relate to: *Birth of A. A. Milne (Jan. 18, 1779): Creator of the cuddly and familiar teddy bear, Winnie-the-Pooh.*

Videos: *The Bear and the Fly*
Blueberries for Sal
Paddington Helps Out: Paddington Dines Out (Paddington Bear, vol. 2)
Pierre: A Cautionary Tale
Winnie the Pooh and Tigger, Too!

Books: *Ask Mr. Bear*, Marjorie Flack
Bear, John Schoenher
The Bear That Heard Crying, Natalie Kinsey-Warnock and Helen Kinsey
The Bear under the Stairs, Helen Cooper
Blueberries for Sal, Robert McCloskey
Can't You Sleep, Little Bear?, Martin Waddell
Good Morning, Baby Bear, Eric Hill
The Grizzly Sisters, Cathy Bellows
The Hiccup Cure, Dara Goldman
Maggie's Whopper, Sally Hobart Alexander
Moon Bear, Frank Asch
Mr. Bear Babysits, Debi Gliori
Ralph's Frozen Tale, Elise Primavera
Sody Sallyratus, Teri Sloat
There's a Bear in the Bath!, Nanette Newman
The Three Bears, Margaret Hillert

Fingerplay: **This Little Bear.**
(Source: *Finger Frolics—Revised*, Liz Cromwell, Dixie Hibner and John R. Faitel)

Crafts: **Teddy Bear—Fuzzy Friend.**
Show children how to make a teddy bear character with a soft, furry texture. They begin by cutting a basic bear form from cardboard or poster board. Then they add decorative texture by cutting short lengths of brown yarn and gluing it to the bear form. They finish their fuzzy friends by adding nose, eyes, and the pads of the paws with construction paper or felt.
(Source: *The Fun-to-Make Book*, Colette Lamargue)

Bear Containers.

You will find an attractive container craft available in this source. There is a bear template that can be photocopied and enlarged to hold the size of the tube container you have selected. Have each child decorate the wide tube and glue it to the bear's lap, then simply fold the bear up around the tube where shown. These containers can be used for storing just about anything (e.g., party snacks, paper clips, string, pencils, etc.).

(Source: *Great Paper Craft Projects*, Ingrid Klettenheimer)

Activities:

The Bear Is in His Cave.

Show a group of children a selection of objects on the floor. Have them turn their backs and recite a given verse (see the source listed below). While the others are reciting have another child pretend to be a bear creeping in to carry away one object. The first child to identify the missing object will now become the bear. This game can be played with any number of children and objects. It can also be adjusted to help you introduce specific items to the children, such as the four food groups, animals, toys, or toy trucks for things that go.

(Source: *New Games to Play*, Juel Krisvoy)

Hibernating Bears.

This game is similar to Simon Says. Discuss with the children a bear's experiences with the changes of the seasons. Let the children lie on the floor pretending to be bears hibernating. Continue by calling out various instructions, (e.g., "Mother Nature says the bears are stretching . . . " Remind the children not to fool with Mother Nature. "If she doesn't say what to do, just sleep.").

(Source: *Kids and Seasons*, Kathy Darling)

Songs:

(Audio) "The Bear You Loved"
    (Source: *UnBearable Bears*)
(Book) "The Bear Went Over the Mountain"
    (Source: *The Fireside Book of Birds and Beasts*, Jane Yolen)

7 Animals: Cats

Relate to:	*Adopt-a-Shelter-Animal Month (Oct.): To encourage people to consider selecting their cat or dog from a shelter where many animals need to be adopted and cared for.*

Videos:	*The Cat in the Hat* (Dr. Seuss Showcase II) *Millions of Cats* *Owl and the Pussycat* *The Story of Puss in Boots*

Books:	*Cat among the Cabbages*, Alison Bartlett *Cat and Bear*, Carol Greene *The Cats of Mrs. Calamari*, John Stadler *Cloudy*, Deborah King *Could You Stop Josephine?*, Stephanie Poulin *Easy Peasy!*, Linda Jennings *The Fat Cat*, Jack Kent *Feathers for Lunch*, Lois Ehlert *Have You Seen My Cat?*, Eric Carle *Kitten for a Day*, Ezra Jack Keats *Meow!*, Katya Arnold *Michael and the Cats*, Barbara Abercrombie *Millions of Cats*, Wanda Gag *Orange Oliver*, Robert Lasson *Wanted: Best Friends*, A. M. Monson

Fingerplay:	**A Kitten.** (Source: *Finger Frolics—Revised*, Liz Cromwell, Dixie Hibner, and John R. Faitel)

Crafts:	**Egg Carton Pussycat.** Egg cartons can be transformed into different objects of art. Using this simple, easily obtainable material the children can make a black cat by cutting, painting, and mounting the ears, eyes, and mouth with paper. Try pipe cleaners for whiskers. Other simple characters are also suggested and illustrated in the source listed below. (Source: *Instructor's Artfully Easy!*) **The Cat.** Robyn Supraner's crafts are a delight for teachers because they use easily obtainable and inexpensive materials. This craft is

no exception. The children can become the cat from their favorite story by making their own cat mask from a paper plate. By copying the page from the book and blowing it up you can have a pattern to trace when cutting it out. Add features as desired.

(Source: *Great Masks to Make*, Robyn Supraner)

Activity:

Cat and Rat.

This game can be played by any number of players over six years old. One child, acting as the rat, stands in the center of a circle formed by the other children. Another player, the cat, attempts to break through the circle to tag the rat. If the cat tags the rat, the rat is allowed to choose someone else to be the rat and he or she becomes the cat.

This can be continued as long as desired. It can be used as a fill-in activity when other activities suddenly finish earlier than expected. Another plus is that there are no real losers.

(Source: *Games*, Anne Rockwell)

Songs:

(Audio) "The Cat Came Back"
    (Source: *Singing and Swinging*)
(Book) "Three Little Kittens"
    (Source: *The Fireside Songbook of Birds and Beasts*, Jane Yolen)

8 Animals: Cows

Relate to:	*National Dairy Month (June): Here is a month dedicated to the understanding of the important part milk (and dairy products) plays in our diet and to honor the animal that gives us that important product.*

Videos: *The Cow Who Fell in the Canal*
The Silver Cow

Books: *Calico Cows*, Arlene Dubanevich
Cock-a-Doodle-Moo!, Bernard Most
The Cow that Went Oink, Bernard Most
The Cow Who Wouldn't Come Down, Paul Brett Johnson
Cows Can't Fly, David Milgrim
The Day Veronica Was Nosy, Elizabeth Laird
Donna O'Neeshuck Was Chased by Some Cows, Bill Grossman
Emily and the Crows, Elaine Greenstein
Henry and the Cow Problem, Iona Whishaw
Hunting the White Cow, Tres Seymour
Moonstruck: The True Story of the Cow Who Jumped over the Moon,
      Gennifer Choldenko
Ms. Blanche, the Spotless Cow, Zidrou
Rude Giants, Audrey Wood
There's a Cow in the Road, Reeve Lindbergh
When Cows Come Home, David L. Harrison

Fingerplay: **Slow, Slow Cow.**
      (Source: *Storytime Crafts*, Kathryn Totten)

Crafts: **Over the Moon.**
      Help the cow jump over the moon with this easy paper plate craft. Make a cow from poster board and let the children add the features with markers. Let the moon be designed from a paper plate, then attach the cow with a strip of poster board and paper fasteners. Just move the cow across the top of the plate as the children recite the rhyme.
            (Source: *175 Easy-to-Do Everyday Crafts*, edited by Sharon Dunn Umnik)

      Grazing Cows.
      Supply the children with a sheet of construction paper and permit them to glue a cow shape on the page. After letting the

children color their cow lead them outside so that their cow can go grazing. Give the children glue and let them pull up real grass and attach it under the feet of their cow.
   (Source: *Theme-a-saurus II*, Jean Warren)

Activities: **Fetch the Cows.**
Try Hide and Seek with a farm flavor. Dress one player as the farmer while the remainder of the class are dressed as cows. When the farmer goes to sleep the cows will wander off and hide in the pasture. Ring the bell or have a rooster wake the farmer, the farmer then goes to find the lost herd. The first cow located will be the next farmer.
   (Source: *Party Plans for Tots*, Kate Harris)

Milking Cows.
This activity is a lot of fun for children, as well as being educational. If you can't get your kids to a farm to milk a cow, try it at your own school or library. String a line across an area and tie disposable gloves filled with water to the line. The fingertips can be punctured with very fine pins. Put a bucket below the glove; the children can then sit on a stool and milk that cow (glove) dry.
   (Source: *Theme-a-saurus II*, Jean Warren)

Songs: (Audio) "Old Bell Cow"
   (Source: *Animal Folk Songs for Children [and Other People]*)
(Book) "Bossy Cow"
   (Source: *Cock-a-Doodle Doo! Cock-a-Doodle Dandy!*, Paul Kapp)

9 Animals: Dogs

Relate to:	*National Dog Week (last full week in Sept.): To encourage the proper care and grooming of one of mankind's favorite pets.*

Videos:
Angus Lost
A Boy, a Dog, and a Frog
Harry the Dirty Dog
The Pokey Little Puppy (Best Loved Golden Books)
Whistle for Willie

Books:
The Bookshop Dog, Cynthia Rylant
Buffy's Orange Leash, Stephen Golder and Lise Memling
Claude and Pepper, Dick Gackenbach
Clifford's Good Deeds, Norman Bridwell
A Flea in the Ear, Stephen Wyllie
Freckles and Jane, Margery Cuyler
Harry the Dirty Dog, Gene Zion
Jessica the Blue Streak, Sucie Stevenson
McDuff Comes Home, Rosemary Wells
McSpot's Hidden Spots, Laura L. Seeley
Madeline's Rescue, Ludwig Bemelmans
Martha Walks the Dog, Susan Meddaugh
Oh Where, Oh Where Has My Little Dog Gone?, Iza Trapani
Walter's Tail, Lisa Campbell Ernst
Whistle for Willie, Ezra J. Keats

Fingerplay:
My Doggie Has Fleas.
(Source: *Move Over, Mother Goose!*, Ruth I. Dowell)

Crafts:
Paper Bag Dog.
Paper-bag creations are one of the easiest and least expensive of crafts. They are also great fun for children. Try making a paper-bag dog mask. Use a brown grocery bag, and cut a hole on one side the size of the child's face.

Discuss with the children the parts of a dog's face. You can use construction paper to put long, floppy ears on the side. Get some clown make-up to color the child's nose black.

Dog Bone Parcel.
Man's best friend needs our love and gifts, too. How about showing him how much you love him by giving him a gift of doggie treats in a very special parcel. Fashion and decorate a

bone-shaped board and place little pockets over it where you can store his favorite treats. Hang it where you can reach it for your best friend at all times.
(Source: *Fantastic Paper Holiday Decorations*, Teddy Cameron Long)

Activities:

My Little Dog.
This game is comparable to the well-known Duck, Duck, Goose. This can be played with any number of children in a circle or on opposite ends of the room. Designate a section of the room to be the dog's home. With most of the children at one end of the room and two children (the dog and his master) at the home base, the game can begin. The master walks his dog from the home, down the street past the other children while reciting the verse (text in source listed below) asking someone to take care of his dog. When the master names another player, the new player chases the dog around the room hoping to tag him before he gets home. The new player now can be the new dog.
(Source: *New Games to Play*, Juel Krisvoy)

Hide the Bone.
This is a variation of Hot-Cold with a dog theme. Allow one group to hide a number of dog bones throughout the room. At the end of a given time period the leader will say "bow wow" and all the dogs of the other team may enter and begin their search. The first team can guide the others by calling "bow wow" as they get near, or "arf arf" as they go further away. Add time limits to make it more difficult.
(Source: *Party Plans for Tots*, Kate Harris)

Songs:

(Audio) "Oh Where Has My Little Dog Gone?"
(Source: *Toddlers Sing 'N Learn*)
(Book) "Bingo"
(Source: *The Reader's Digest Children's Songbook*, William L. Simon)

10 Animals: Dolphins/Whales

Relate to:	*International Whale Watching Week (Sunday of the week including Oct. 21): A week dedicated to the preservation of whales as an endangered species.*

Videos:
Burt Dow: Deep-Water Man
How the Whale Got His Throat (Rudyard Kipling classics)
Whales
Willie, the Operatic Whale

Books:
Baby Beluga, Raffi
Big Blue Whale, Nicola Davies
Cimru the Seal, Theresa Radcliffe
D is for Dolphin, Cami Berg
Do the Whales Still Sing?, Dianne Hofmeyr
Henry's Wrong Turn, Harriet Ziefert
I Wonder if I'll See a Whale, Frances Ward Weller
In Dolphin Time, Diane Farris
Rainbow Fish and The Big Blue Whale, Marcus Pfister
The Several Tricks of Edgar Dolphin, Nathaniel Benchley
The Snow Whale, Caroline Pitcher
Story of a Dolphin, Katherine Orr
Whale, Judy Allen
Whale Is Stuck, Karen Hayles and Charles Fuge
The Whales, Cynthia Rylant

Fingerplay: **Whale.**
(Source: *Once Upon a Childhood: Fingerplays, Action Rhymes, and Fun Times for the Very Young*, Dolores Chupela)

Crafts: **Nutshell Families.**
Here's a fun craft that children may create after discussing various types of animal families. Collect as many, intact, walnut-shell halves. If you would like to make a whale family that includes a mother, father, and one baby, you will need two walnut shells and one pistachio shell. Paint the shells gray, add wiggly eyes and a spout, using gray or white paper. Connect them together with a long string and the child can pull the whole family across the table.
(Source: *Crafts from Recyclables*, Colleen Van Blaricom)

A Whale of a Time.
Create a whale of a sea scene with the use of bubbles. Mix blue paint and dish soap with a little water in a bowl. Use a straw to blow bubbles to fill the bowl, then lay a white sheet of paper gently across the top. The bubbles create a beautiful water scene. Frame it with a green seaweed border and add sea creatures of your choice.
(Source: *Making Pictures: Secrets of the Sea*, Penny King and Clare Roundhill)

Activities: **Save the Dolphins.**
This is a variation of an ancient game called Glue. Indicate that the entire play area is the ocean and all the children are now dolphins, except one who is a fisherman. Unfortunately this fisherman fishes with a net. Scatter construction-paper nets throughout the room but leave paths for the children to get around them. The fisherman gets to chase the dolphins through the room to catch (tag) them. If a dolphin steps in a net he is caught until another dolphin who is still free can get to him and tag him to set him free. Any dolphin tagged by the fisherman must go to a net until freed. A great stepping-off game for discussing safe fishing and caring for animals.

Animal Trackers.
Develop a giant-size game that can be played on the floor of your classroom. Although this book suggests using all types of animals, this game can easily be adapted to play as a more specific sea creature game.

Make special flashcards for each sea creature, some whale and a portion of the animal (see the book for exact number of cards and dimensions). Select a player to be the animal keeper, while the others will be the trackers or fisherman. Shuffle the animal cards and place them on the floor to make a path. The animal keeper shuffles the piece cards; when a tracker identifies the piece, he or she can move along the path to the correct animal markers. This huge board game will be a great deal of fun for everyone and can be adapted to a specific family of animals (e.g., farm animals, sea animals, etc.) or just animals in general.
(Source: *Recyclopedia*, Robin Simons)

Songs: (Audio) "Baby Beluga"
(Source: *Raffi in Concert with the Rise and Shine Band*, Raffi)
(Book) "Blow Ye Winds"
(Source: *Proudly We Sing*, Irving Wolfe, Beatrice Krone, and Margaret Fullerton)

11 Animals: Elephants

Relate to: *Elephant Appreciation Day (Sept. 22): A time to honor the largest and most noble endangered land animal.*

Videos: *Circus Baby*
Dumbo
The Elephant's Child
Horton Hatches an Egg
The Saggy Baggy Elephant (Golden Jungle Animal Tales)

Books: *Alistair's Elephant*, Marilyn Sadler
The Ant and the Elephant, Bill Peet
Baashi, The Elephant Baby, Theresa Radcliffe
The Circus Baby, Maud Petersham
Elmer, David McKee
Engelbert the Elephant, Tom Paxton
Little Elephant's Walk, Adrienne Kennaway
Old Noah's Elephants, Warren Ludwig
Oliver, Syd Hoff
Rose and Dorothy, Roslyn Schwartz
Smallest Elephant in the World, Alvin Tresselt
Tabu and the Dancing Elephants, Rene Deetlefs
The Trouble with Elephants, Chris Riddell
The Way Home, Judith Benet Richardson
When the Elephant Walks, Keiko Kasza

Fingerplay: **Five Gray Elephants.**
(Source: *Finger Frolics—Revised*, Liz Cromwell, Dixie Hibner, and John R. Faitel)

Crafts: **A Paper Bag Elephant.**
Your own toy elephant can be formed by stuffing a lunch bag with tissue and tying off one end. Twist the end tied off again to form the nose. Eyes and ears may be made with construction paper or paint. Braid yarn for the elephant's tail; simple clip clothespins are ideal for legs.
(Source: *Simply Fun! Things to Make and Do*, James Razzi)

Elephant Arm Puppet.
With the use of the reproducible elephant face supplied in this source, the children can make a hilarious puppet for acting out stories. The center of the face is cut out to permit the child

to put his or her arm through to simulate the elephant's trunk. A little elephant rhyme and activity are also offered in this source.

(Source: *Pocketful of Puppets*, Tamara Hunt)

Activities:

Zoo Hunt.

Zoo animals are familiar to most children. This simple game of charades allows the children to pretend they are various animals as well as trying to guess what animals others are portraying. Write down the names of familiar zoo animals and distribute them among the group so they know which animal they will pretend to be.

If, as in most storyhour programs, your children are non-readers use simple animal flashcards with illustrations. Avoid breaking the group into teams so that nobody experiences losing.

(Source: *500 Games*, Peter L. Cave)

One Elephant Went Out to Play.

This enjoyable line dance is easy enough to use with any group of 3- to 5-year olds. Choose an adult leader to be the mother elephant or do it yourself. During the singing of the song have the children jump up and down on the selected verse. At the end of each verse call another child into the line, count the elephants, and begin to dance again around the room. Continue until all have joined the group.

(Source: *Dancing Games for Children of all Ages*, Esther L. Nelson)

Songs:

(Audio) "One Elephant"
(Source: *Where Is Thumbkin?*)
(Book) "One Elephant Went Out to Play"
(Source: *Dancing Games for Children of All Ages*, Esther L. Nelson)

12 Animals: Kangaroos

Relate to:	*Australia Day (Jan. 26): Celebrate the founding day of the land of kangaroos, "The Land Down Under," Australia.*

Videos: *Joey Runs Away*
Katy No-Pocket

Books: *Big Talk*, Miriam Schlein
I Love You, Blue Kangaroo, Emma Chichester Clark
It's Not Fair, Anita Harper
Joey, Jack Kent
Joey: The Story of a Baby Kangaroo, Hope Ryden
Kangaroo's Adventure in Alphabet Town, Janet McDonnell
Katy No-Pocket, Emmy Payne
Little New Kangaroo, Bernard Wiseman
Norma Jean, Jumping Bean, Joanna Cole
The Perfect Present, Michael Hague
The Sing-Song of Old Man Kangaroo, Rudyard Kipling
Too Many Kangaroo Things to Do!, Stuart J. Murphy
What Feels Best?, Anita Harper
Will You Take Care of Me?, Margaret Park Bridges

Fingerplay: **Six Down Under.**
(Source: *Ready, Set, Go!: Children's Programming for Bookmobiles and other Small Spaces*, Dolores Chupela)

Crafts: **Katherine the Kangaroo.**
This is a very easy paper plate craft that can be related to *Katy No-Pocket* by Emmy Payne or any of the other kangaroo stories suggested here. All that is required are two paper plates, brown markers, tape, and scissors. The children will make a mother kangaroo with her own pocket holding her baby kangaroo. The children can even use this craft for their desks; you can return the children's papers in the mother kangaroo's pocket, which can also hold handy supplies.
(Source: *Alphabet Art*, Judy Press)

Jumping Joey.
Assemble your own Jumping Joey toy for each child. This is an excellent craft when talking about Australia and the creatures living there. A simple pattern is supplied so you can trace and cut out a kangaroo out of poster board. Punch a hole at

the top and attach a long rubberband and a button to the other end. Now the children can bounce these little creatures all over the room while repeating the verse "Jump, Jump, Kangaroo, Jump."

(Source: *Storytime Crafts*, Kathryn Totten)

Activities:

Kangaroo Tag.
Teach the children the proper way to jump like a kangaroo, then select one child to be the mother kangaroo. The mother is searching for her little joeys by jumping around and tagging them. As one is tagged she becomes the next mother kangaroo. Stress that kangaroos jump but do not run. Other variations of this game are also offered in the source cited here.

(Source: *The Giant Encyclopedia of Theme Activities for Children 2 to 5*, Kathy Charner)

Kangaroo Hop.
This is a team event. Line up your players one behind the other. The children should pass the ball over their heads to the back of the line. The last player will place the ball between his or her knees and hop to the beginning of the line. Continue in this manner until your team is as it orginally began.

(Source: *Making Children's Parties Click*, Virginia W. Musselman)

Songs:

(Audio) "Two Little Snowflakes"
(Source: *Red Pajamas and Purple Shoes*)
(Book) "The Duck and the Kangaroo"
(Source: *Cock-a-Doodle-Doo! Cock-a-Doodle-Dandy!*, Paul Kapp)

13 Animals: Lions and Tigers

Relate to:	*First lion in America exhibited (1716): This first display of a lion in America appeared in Boston.*

Videos:
Andy and the Lion
Happy Lion's Treasure
Leo on Vacation
The Lion and the Mouse (Mr. Know It Owl's Video Tales: Aesop's Fables Vol. 1)
Tawny Scrawny Lion (Golden Jungle Animal Tales)

Books:
Brer Tiger and the Big Wind, William J. Faulkner
Ella and the Naughty Lion, Anne Cottringer
The Happy Lion, Louise Fatio
The Lion and the Mouse, Aesop
A Lion in the Meadow, Margaret Mahy
Little Lions, Jim Arnosky
Little Louie the Baby Bloomer, Robert Kraus
Moon Tiger, Phyllis Root
The Rat and the Tiger, Keiko Kasza
The Sleepy Little Lion, Margaret Brown
The Terrible Tiger, Jack Prelutsky
The Tiger Hunt, Mary Villarejo
The Tiger's Breakfast, Jan Mogensen
Who Is the Beast?, Keith Baker

Fingerplay:
Tiger Walk.
(Source: *Rhymes for Learning Times*, Louise Binder Scott)

Crafts:
Lion Face.
Using a paper plate, have the children draw with markers the eyes, nose, and mouth of a lion. Cut strips of yellow construction paper to be glued all the way around the perimeter of the plate to form the lion's mane. You may curl each strip using scissors.

To turn this into a mask, simply add string to the sides or better yet, put it on a stick to be held in the child's hand.

Larry, the Lion.
Directions are supplied in this source for children to make their own lion sculpture. A cardboard paper tube is used for the body. This body can be covered with brown construction pa-

per; features such as the tail, feet, and face can be added at the end. Uncomplicated assembly instructions are provided with illustrations. This simple sculpture can easily be adapted for a tiger if needed.

(Source: *Alphabet Art*, Judy Press)

Activities: **Lions and Tigers.**
Divide the room with tape or string. One player is chosen to be the tiger and another is chosen to be the lion, each on opposite ends of the room. Other players may move anywhere they want, but the tiger and lion may not cross into the other's den. Any players the lion or tiger can tag must remain in their captor's den. The animal that catches the most victims wins.

(Source: *500 Games*, Peter L. Cave)

Spot the Lion—An African Game.
Divide your class into small groups, each with a home base in separate sections of the room. At a given signal the children scatter and freeze with their eyes closed. The leader will roam and tap each person on the back, but leaving a marker on one person's back to mark him or her as the "lion." When the leader shouts, "The lion is loose," everyone will attempt to discover who is the lion and then run to his home base without telling. If you suspect you're the lion, go to the center of the room and roar for everyone to freeze. The team with the most players in home base when the lion roars wins.

(Source: *Games for Girl Scouts*)

Songs: (Audio) "Tiger Hunt"
(Source: *Bert and Ernie Side by Side*)
(Book) "The Zoo"
(Source: *Music for Ones and Twos*, Tom Glazer)

14 Animals: Mice

Relate to: *Mickey Mouse's Birthday (Nov. 18): The celebration of the first appearance of the most famous mouse in the world.*

Videos: *Abel's Island*
Alexander and the Wind-up Mouse (Leo Lionni's Caldecotts)
Frederick (Leo Lionni's Caldecotts)
Mickey Mouse, The Brave Little Tailor (Cartoon Classics Collection, Vol. 6)
Norman the Doorman

Books: *The Dark at the Top of the Stairs*, Sam McBratney
Do You See Mouse?, Marion Crume
Do You Want to Be My Friend?, Eric Carle
Geraldine, the Music Mouse, Leo Lionni
Max the Mouse, James Cressey
Milo and the Magical Stones, Marcus Pfister
The Perfect Mouse, Dick Gackenbach
Seven Blind Mice, Ed Young
The Story of Jumping Mouse, John Steptoe
The Supermarket Mice, Margaret Gordon
Three Blind Mice, Lorinda Bryan Cauley
Three Kind Mice, Vivian Sathre
Tom's Tail, Arlene Dubanevich
Two Tiny Mice, Alan Baker
Watch Out! Big Bro's Coming!, Jez Alborough

Fingerplay: **Hickory Dickory Dock.**
(Source: *Finger Frolics—Revised*, Liz Cromwell, Dixie Hibner, and John R. Faitel)

Crafts: **Mousie Paperweight.**
The "Pet Rock" craze has allowed us all to have our own little pets by using stones or rocks from our own backyard. To make your own mousie paperweight or pet mouse use a smooth round stone for the basic body. The tail can be added by cutting a small piece of curled wire such as found in a spiral notebook. Cut eyes, ears, nose, and mouth from felt; whiskers can be made from broomstick straw or pipe cleaners.
(Source: *Instructor's Artfully Easy!*)

Photo Mouse.

This photograph holder will delight little children because it's easy to make and also gives the appearance of something difficult accomplished. It is constructed from paper, with a three-demensional mouse head. Add whiskers, a curling tail, and a photo of the child on the mouse's stomach. Any parent would be proud to display this on the family's refrigerator.

(Source: *175 Easy-to-Do Thanksgiving Crafts*, Sharon Dunn Umnik)

Activities: **Three Blind Mice.**

"Three Blind Mice" is a familiar song to children at this age and will create a comfortable foundation for the following game: The children form a circle with one in the center (farmer's wife). As they dance around singing and run for the nearest wall, the farmer's wife tries to catch one person (mouse) who will become the next farmer's wife.

(Source: *500 Games*, Peter L. Cave)

Mousetrap.

This game can be played with any number of children. Let one child be the cat, another the mouse, and the remainder of the group will be the trap. The children form the trap by holding hands in a circle. The cat stands outside facing away. While the mouse goes in and out of the circle the children hold their hands up until the cat yells "trap." If the mouse is outside the trap he can become the next cat. Other interesting modifications are also offered in this source depending on the size and age of the group.

(Source: *The Picture Rulebook of Kids' Games*, Roxanne Henderson)

Songs: (Audio) "The Little Mouse is Creeping"
(Source: *Circle Time*)
(Book) "Three Blind Mice"
(Source: *Sing Hey Diddle Diddle*, Beatrice Harrop)

15 Animals: Monkeys

Relate to:	*Birth of Jane Goodall (April 3, 1934): Celebrate the life and work of the world's foremost authority on chimpanzees.*

Videos:
Caps for Sale
Curious George
Why Monkeys Live in the Trees (Magical Tales from Other Lands)

Books:
Caps for Sale, Esphyr Slobodkina
Curious George Flies a Kite, Margaret Rey
Don't Wake Up Mama, Eileen Christelow
Fifty Red Night-Caps, Inga Moore
Five Little Monkeys Sitting in a Tree, Eileen Christelow
How Mr. Monkey Saw the Whole World, Walter Dean Myers
Last One Home Is a Green Pig, Edith Hurd
Matepo, Angela McAllister
Monkey Do!, Allan Ahlberg
The Monkey that Went to School, Leonard Meshover and Sally Feistel
Monkey Tricks, Camilla Ashforth
Mr. Monkey and the Gotcha Bird, Walter Dean Myers
"Not Me," Said the Monkey, Colin West
Run, Little Monkeys, Run, Run, Run, Charles Kepes
The Turtle and the Monkey, Paul Galdone

Fingerplay:
Two Little Monkeys.
(Source: *Finger Frolics—Revised*, Liz Cromwell, Dixie Hibner, and John R. Faitel)

Crafts:
Silly Salt-Box Monkey.
A salt box can be made into a container for collecting prize possessions. With the youngest children you may wish to have parts precut for this craft. This may be made into a monkey with the use of construction paper and glue. Begin with a collection of salt-box animals.
(Source: *Sticks and Stones and Ice Cream Cones*, Phyllis Fiarotta)

Twirling Monkey.
Monkey see, monkey do. Keep those monkeys twirling through the room with this little craft. Simply made of paper circles and limbs constructed of chenille sticks, our monkey clings

desperately to a drinking straw as the children twirl him around and around.

(Source: *175 Easy-to-Do Everyday Crafts*, edited by Sharon Dunn Umnik)

Activities: **Monkey See, Monkey Do.**

Monkey see, Monkey do
I can————and you can, too.

Children can take turns filling in the blanks with something everyone does (e.g., hopping, clapping), or play this game like Simon Says, substituting the word "monkey" for Simon.

Monkey's Tail.

Let the children pair off to find out who is the top monkey. Add a tail to each child by tying a long string with a crayon on the end around the child's waist. Give it enough length so that it almost touches the floor but not quite. The goal of this game is for the child to be the first to place the end of his monkey tail inside the jar that is located on the floor without using his hands.

(Source: *Child Magazine's Book of Children's Parties*, Angela Wilkes)

Songs: (Audio) "Monkeys"

(Source: *Animal Antics*)

(Books) "Pop! Goes the Weasel"

(Source: *The Golden Song Book*, Katharine Tyler Wessells)

16 Animals: Pigs

Relate to:	*National Pig Day (March 1): To celebrate the pig as one of man's most useful domesticated animals. For further information write to Ellen Stanley, 7006 Miami, Lubbock, TX 79413.*

Videos:
The Amazing Bone
Pig's Picnic
The Pig's Wedding
The Three Little Pigs

Books:
Barnyard Big Top, Jill Kastner
Five Little Piggies, David Martin
Hog-Eye, Susan Meddaugh
If You Give a Pig a Pancake, Laura Numeroff
Mrs. Potter's Pig, Phyllis Root
Peony's Rainbow, Martha Weston
Perfect the Pig, Susan Jeschke
Pigs Aplenty, Pigs Galore!, David McPhail
Pigsty, Mark Teague
A Pile of Pigs, Judith Ross Enderle
The Spotty Pig, Dick King-Smith
Toot and Puddle, Holly Hobbie
A Treeful of Pigs, Arnold Label
Tuck in the Pool, Martha Weston
Wriggly Pig, Jon Blake

Fingerplay:
Two Mother Pigs. Or The Pigs.
(Source: *52 Programs for Preschoolers: The Librarian's Year-Round Planner*, Diane Briggs)

Crafts:
Circle Pig.
After doing a lesson on shapes or farms you can make use of this craft that is easy enough for even two year olds. This pig craft uses three different-size circles for the body to give the appearance of depth and size to your picture. With the addition of floppy ears and a nose made of a toilet paper roll the picture just leaps out at you.
(Source: *Year-Round Crafts for Kids*, Barbara L. Don Diego)

Piggy Bank.
A piggy bank with a little pizzazz will make an enjoyable activity for the children. A plastic bleach bottle or milk bottle,

thoroughly cleaned, gives the pig shape a start. Thread spools make great little legs. Linda Schwartz's book gives you easy-to-follow instructions on how the children can cover the bottle with multicolored tissue paper, then add the final features including its curly tail.

(Source: *Likeable Recyclables*, Linda Schwartz)

Activities: **Oink, Oink, Piggy.**

Have your group sit in a circle with one person in the center as the little pig. Little pig is blindfolded and carries a pillow. He can then roam the circle until he selects a person to sit on his lap on the pillow. Pig says "Oink, Oink" and the child on his lap repeats "Oink, Oink." If pig can identify the child the two are permitted to change places, if not he must continue on.

(Source: *The Penny Whistle Birthday Party Book*, Meredith Brokaw and Annie Gilbar)

Pig Out, Pig Stop.

A slight change from the conventional theme of "Red Light, Green Light" that all the children are familiar with, this game will be a surefire hit with the young children. One child faces the wall while the other children are at the opposite end of the room. As the children move closer, the person who is It calls out "Pig Out" or "Pig Stop." If "Pig Out" is called, the children must walk on all fours like a pig. If "Pig Stop" is called, everyone freezes and It turns around. Anyone caught moving must start all over again.

(Source: *The Penny Whistle Birthday Party Book*, Meredith Brokaw and Annie Gilbar)

Songs: (Audio) "Three Little Pigs"
(Source: *Mommy and Me: Rock-a-Bye Baby*)
(Book) "Eight Piggies in a Row"
(Source: *The Raffi Everything Grows Songbook*, Raffi)

17 Animals: Rabbits

Relate to:	*Birth Anniversary of Beatrix Potter (July 28): Celebrate the life of the children's author who created the famous "Peter Rabbit" books.*

Videos:
The Little Rabbit Who Wanted Red Wings
Morris' Disappearing Bag
Peter Rabbit
The Tortoise and the Hare
Who's in Rabbit's House

Books:
The Brave Little Bunny, Linda Jennings
Carrot Cake, Nonny Hogrogian
Good Job, Oliver, Laurel Molk
The Habits of Rabbits, Virginia Kahl
Hattie Be Quiet, Hattie Be Good, Dick Gackenbach
Hopper's Treetop Adventure, Marcus Pfister
The Hunt for Rabbit's Galosh, Ann Schweninger
Little Rabbit Goes to Sleep, Tony Johnston
Max and Ruby's First Greek Myth: Pandora's Box, Rosemary Wells
Mr. Rabbit and the Lovely Present, Charlotte Zolotow
Rabbits and Raindrops, Jim Arnosky
Rabbit's Good News, Ruth Lercher Bornstein
This for That, Verna Aardema
Zomo the Rabbit, Gerald McDermott

Fingerplay:
A Bunny.
(Source: *Finger Frolics—Revised*, Liz Cromwell, Dixie Hibner, and John R. Faitel)

Crafts:
Silly Salt-Box Bunny.
A salt box can be made into a container for collecting prize possessions. With the youngest children you may wish to have parts precut for this craft. The container can be made into a bunny with the use of construction paper and glue. Begin with a collection of salt-box animals.

If you are using this for an Easter program, you may want to treat the children to an Easter surprise by filling it with paper grass and a special treat.
(Source: *Sticks and Stones and Ice Cream Cones*, Phyllis Fiarotta)

Necktie Bunny Puppet.
Do you have some old-fashioned neckties lying around? Collect these dated fashions and help the children recycle them into puppets. A colorful bunny puppet can be made with the widest section of the tie becoming the face of the bunny. Don't throw anything out. The narrow sections that you cut off can become the ears. Add features as desired. See this source for guidelines and other useful crafts for young children.
(Source: *Crafts for Easter*, Kathy Ross)

Activities:

The Bunny Hop.
This simple dance will allow the children to pretend to be bunnies while moving around the entire room. A good physical activity between nonactive stories.
(Source: *The Reader's Digest Children's Songbook*, William L. Simon)

Hopping Down the Bunny Trail.
Here are two bunny-related activities that children can enjoy and will require little preparation. The first, Hopping Down the Bunny Trail, involves a simple trail marked with taped X's throughout the room, finishing at a cardboard hutch filled with rabbit storybooks for the children to enjoy. The second is the Rabbit Patch Pull. Design a collection of cardboard carrots with paper clips on them. Place the carrots in that same hutch and let your little rabbits hop that trail again and try to fetch the carrots by dropping strings with magnets on them into the hutch.
(Source: *First Time, Circle Time*, Cynthia Holley and Jane Walkup)

Songs:

(Audio) "The Bunny Hop"
(Source: *All-Time Favorite Dances*)
(Book) "Little Rabbit Foo-Foo"
(Source: *Do Your Ears Hang Low?*, Tom Glazer)

18 Art

Relate to:	*Youth Art Month (March): A month to demonstrate the importance of art and creativeness in the development of young people.*

Videos:
Art Dog
Harold and the Purple Crayon
Norman the Doorman
A Picture for Harold's Room
Regina's Big Mistake

Books:
Art Dog, Thacher Hurd
The Art Lesson, Tomie dePaola
Bear Hunt, Anthony Browne
The Bear's Picture, Daniel Pinkwater
Crocodile's Masterpiece, Max Velthuijs
Curious George Goes to School, Margret Rey and Alan J. Shalleck
Daniel's Duck, Clyde Bulla
Emma, Wendy Kesselman
Ernie's Little Lie, Dan Elliott
The Little Painter of Sabana Grande, Patricia Markun
Lucy's Picture, Nicola Moon
Matthew's Dream, Leo Lionni
Mouse Paint, Ellen Walsh
A Painter: How We Work, Douglas Florian
Regina's Big Mistake, Marissa Moss

**Fingerplay
and Activity:**
Draw a Person in the Air.
(Source: *Finger Frolics—Revised*, Liz Cromwell, Dixie Hibner, and John R. Faitel)

Crafts:
Potato or Ink Pad Printing.
Children are fond of working with any type of printing materials. Try potato printing. With this you can arrange any design by cutting it from a potato then using ink pads and paper to design cards, pictures, etc. If time doesn't permit you to use potato printing, try collecting various styles of ink stamps; the children will do the rest.
(Source: *The Fun-to-Make Book*, Colette Lamargue)

Newspaper Snake.
Using old newspapers, wallpaper paste, tape, and paint, chil-

dren can make their own snake sculpture. This is a simple craft that demands minimal skills and time. It also can be used in a program encouraging recycling and the saving of the environment.

(Source: *Great Newspaper Crafts*, F. Virginia Walter)

Activities: **Color Hunt.**
Divide the children into small groups and designate colors for the teams by hanging around each member's neck a string with a piece of colored paper attached to it. Hide different objects in the room that are the same colors as those selected for the groups. The number of objects selected will vary with the size of your group, but each group should have an equal number to locate. At a given signal, allow all to hunt for the items that are the same color as their group. The first group to find them all and return them to its base wins. Repeat the game by changing group colors or mixing up the members of the groups.

Draw-a-Face Relay.
Create two teams and supply them with markers or crayons. The simple goal is for the children to take turns adding the features of a face until it's completed. Find this and other simple games you may have forgotten in this worthwhile book.

(Source: *Pin the Tail on the Donkey and Other Party Games*, Joanna Cole and Stephanie Calmenson)

Song: (Audio) "The Drawing Song"
(Source: *Bert and Ernie Side by Side*)

19 Babies

Relate to:	*The second Thursday in August is a day that usually sees America's oldest Baby Parade held in our very own Ocean City, New Jersey. Try having your own baby parade.*

Videos:
Hush Little Baby
Peter's Chair
Smile for Auntie

Books:
The Baby Book, Ann Morris
Billy and Our New Baby, Helen Arnstein
The Bravest Babysitter, Barbara Greenberg
Couldn't We Have a Turtle Instead?, Judith Vigna
Ellen and Penguin and the New Baby, Clara Vulliamy
Geraldine's Baby Brother, Holly Keller
Go and Hush the Baby, Betsy Byars
How I Named the Baby, Linda Shute
I Wish My Brother Was a Dog, Carol Diggory Shields
McDuff and the Baby, Rosemary Wells
One Up, One Down, Carol Snyder
Starbaby, Frank Asch
That Terrible Baby, Jennifer Armstrong
Twinnies, Eve Bunting
We Got My Brother at the Zoo, John and Ann Hassett

Fingerplay:
Baby.
(Source: *Finger Frolics—Revised*, Liz Cromwell, Dixie Hibner, and John R. Faitel)

Crafts:
Baby Doll Beds.
A small baby-doll cradle can be constructed using an oatmeal box. When a portion is cut away and the box painted and decorated, it will make an ideal rocking cradle for small children to enjoy.
    In case you don't want a cradle, a simple bunk bed can be made by using a shoe box. Decorations for either bed can be made with paint (a material greatly enjoyed by children) and stickers.
(Source: *Just a Box?*, Goldie Taub Chernoff)

Papoose in a Cradle.
Consider the many places mothers put their babies to sleep

each night. The children will probably mention the cradle, crib, a blanket on Mom's bed, and more. Now introduce how Native American mothers used to carry their sleeping babies. Fashion an Indian baby cradle using a cardboard tube and decorate it with original markings from individual tribes. The papoose can be designed using a cork and yarn.
(Source: *Indian Toys You Can Make*, Maurice Gogniat)

Activities: **Hush Little Baby.**
This old American lullaby is an easy piece to sing and act out with a small group. Nelson gives suggestions for different children acting out the parts of the mockingbird, billy goat, etc., as well as music for the song.

Once the children are familiar with the parts they are going to play, repeat the song as many times as the children request. Games that allow the children to sing and move about provide a good outlet for pent-up energy.
(Source: *Dancing Games for Children of All Ages*, Esther L. Nelson)

Baby Bottle Contest.
Here's a contest that takes children back to their infancy. Put an equal amount of water in each baby bottle collected. Distribute them to the children and at a designated signal let them try to be the first to empty it the usual way. Children will love this one and want to do it again and again.
(Source: *The World's Best Party Games*, Sheila Anne Barry)

Songs: (Audio) "Rock-a-Bye Baby"
(Source: *Mommy and Me: Rock-a-Bye Baby*)
(Book) "John Brown's Baby"
(Source: *The Silly Song-book*, Esther L. Nelson)

20 Babysitters and Babysitting

Relate to: *National Professional Pet Sitters Week (March 1–7): Although there does not seem to be a special week for regular babysitters, here's a variation: a week set aside to honor those who take care of people's pets while they are away on vacation.*

Videos: *Arthur Babysits*
The Best Babysitter Ever

Books: *Baby Tamer*, Mark Teague
Baby-sit, Anne Miranda
Babysitting for Benjamin, Valiska Gregory
The Dragon Nanny, C.L.G. Martin
Eleanor and the Babysitter, Susan Hellard
Lemonade Babysitter, Karen Waggoner
Mr. Bear Babysits, Debi Gliori
My Baby-sitter, Ruth Young
Never Babysit the Hippopotamuses!, Doug Johnson
Shy Charles, Rosemary Wells
They Really Like Me!, Anna Grossnickle Hines
Thomas's Sitter, Jean Richardson
Time for Bed, the Babysitter Said, Peggy Perry Anderson
What Alvin Wanted, Holly Keller
What Kind of Baby-sitter Is This?, Dolores Johnson

Fingerplay: **The Family.**
(Source: *Story Programs: A Source Book of Materials*, Carolyn Sue Peterson and Brenny Hall)

Crafts: **Babysitter's Kit.**
Discuss with the children about helping Mom and Dad with smaller siblings. Let the children list what they feel they would need in their special kit in order to help out (e.g., rattles, stuffed toys, etc.). Decorate a special bag for the children to store these tools of the trade.

Since most of the children you are speaking to still need babysitters themselves, why not have them put together a babysitter kit for their own babysitter! Let the children list and collect all the items they would like to see their babysitter bring with her when she comes to watch them for the day.

Oatmeal Box Cradles.
Review with the children the many things babies need for their daily lives. Collect a number of oatmeal boxes and cut a section out of them to form the shape of a baby's cradle. Pass them out to the children and supply them with an assortment of items to decorate with (e.g., lace, stickers, paint, etc.). The children can be encouraged to use their cradle to rock their dolls to sleep or give to a friend who needs one. A good babysitter should know how to rock and sing a baby to sleep when the need arises.
(Source: *Look What I Made!*, Sarah H. Healton)

Activities:

The Babysitter's Lost the Baby.
The babysitter (one of the children or one of the teams) has lost the baby and must go in search of him immediately. Along the way the babysitter encounters a number of other babies who are lost (e.g., calf, duckling, puppy, etc.) along with items that belong to them (e.g., feathers, bone, rattle, etc.).

The teacher has placed boxes with pictures of each baby's mother on it. As you find the babies or their belongings, return them to their moms.

Divide the class into teams and time their search. The team to return all the babies to their moms safely, along with the babies' toys, in the shortest time wins.

Caring for a Baby.
This book suggests gathering the children together for a practice session on caring for babies. Have the children bring in their own baby dolls for this activity so they are motivated to be more careful with them. The leader may wish to supply such items as bath materials, bottles, diapers, clothes, brushes, etc., all the items required in the daily care of a baby.

In addition to this activity, other baby activities and craft ideas are suggested in this book to really develop this unit on baby care.
(Source: *Literature Activities for Young Children*, Dianna Sullivan)

Songs:

(Audio) "The Babysitter"
(Source: *More Music for One's and Two's*)
(Book) "Babysitter's Lullaby"
(Source: *The Fireside Book of Children's Songs*, edited by Marie Winn)

21 Bedtime Stories

Relate to: *First Bookwagon Traveling Library (April 1905): This first bookmobile was started with the Washington County Free Library in Maryland to enable people who normally couldn't get to a library to have stories at night.*

Videos: *Dr. Seuss's Sleep Book*
Ira Sleeps Over
The Napping House
Sweet Dreams, Spot

Books: *The Bed Book*, Sylvia Plath
The Boy Who Wouldn't Go to Bed, Helen Cooper
Can't You Sleep, Little Bear?, Martin Waddell
The Caterpillow Fight, Sam McBratney
Cowboy Baby, Sue Heap
Devin's New Bed, Sally Freedman
Frances, Face-Maker, William Cole
Good Night Dinosaurs, Judy Sierra
Goodnight Max, Hanne Turk
Goodnight, Moon, Margaret Brown
"I'm Not Sleepy," Denys Cazet
Is there Room on the Feather Bed?, Libba Moore Gray
Little Donkey Close Your Eyes, Margaret Wise Brown
No Nap for Benjamin Badger, Nancy White Carlstrom
We Can't Sleep, James Stevenson

Fingerplay: **Little Bear.**
(Source: *Finger Frolics—Revised*, Liz Cromwell, Dixie Hibner, and John R. Faitel)

Crafts: **Night's Nice.**
After discussing what happens at night and asking the children to identify what they see in the sky at night, pass out materials for the children to make their own night sky. This is simple enough for very young children. A piece of black paper, one yellow sticker dot (moon), and star stickers are all that is needed for the youngsters to enjoy themselves.

Bleach Bottle Candle Holders.
Candle holders can make nice Christmas decorations as well as props for familiar fairy tales or nursery rhyme bedtime sto-

ries. The top of a bleach bottle can be cut off, leaving the handle for carrying the candle. Have the children decorate as desired and add a candle in the top opening. Suggested decorations are available in this book.

Now the children can act out some bedtime rhymes such as "Jack Be Nimble" using their newly made candle holders.
(Source: *Scrap Craft for Young Groups*, Gerry Fleming)

Activities: **Ten in a Bed.**
This simple song may be adapted to the size of the group by changing the beginning number of the countdown. It can be a simple fingerplay/song or can be acted out with the children. Tom Glazer's simple-to-follow directions and sheet music for piano and guitar are provided in the source recommended here. Many of his songs can be used with this age group. They are easy and lots of fun for both parents and children.
(Source: *Do Your Ears Hang Low?*, Tom Glazer)

Teddy's Bedtime.
This is a team event that will have the children giggling all the way through it. Supply the children with a pair of adult slippers to wear, a teddy bear to hold in one hand, and an unlit candle to hold in the other hand. Now watch as they race from one end of the room to the other to put teddy to bed. Special phrases for the runner and teammates to call out during the game are also supplied in order to make it a team effort.
(Source: *Giving a Children's Party*, Jane Cable-Alexander)

Songs: (Audio) "Rig-a-Jig-Jig"
(Source: *Toddlers Sing 'N Learn*)
(Book) "Twinkle, Twinkle Little Star"
(Source: *The Golden Song Book*, Katharine Tyler Wessells)

22 Behavior: Growing Up

Relate to:	*Creation of Peter Pan (1906): Originally conceived by J. M. Barrie in his novel* The Little White Bird *and later developed into the play and the movie that children are familiar with today.*

Videos:
The Giving Tree
Leo the Late Bloomer
Owen
Peter's Chair

Books:
Big Like Me, Anna Grossnickle Hines
Bigger than a Baby, Harriet Ziefert
Cleversticks, Bernard Ashley
Devin's New Bed, Sally Freedman
Emily Just in Time, Jan Slepian
Everything Grows, Raffi
Fourth of July, Barbara Joosse
Growing Pains, Jenny Stow
The Growing-up Feet, Beverly Cleary
It's Going to Be Perfect!, Nancy Carlson
Now I'm Big, Margaret Miller
When I Grow Up . . . , Heidi Goennel
When I Was a Baby, Catherine Anholt
Will You Take Care of Me?, Margaret Park Bridges
You'll Soon Grow into Them, Titch, Pat Hutchins

Fingerplay:
Things I Can Be When I Grow Up.
(Source: *Finger Frolics 2*, Liz Cromwell Kobe, Dixie Hibner, and John R. Faitel)

Crafts:
When I Was Young . . .
This is a great follow-up to Cynthia Rylant's *When I Was Young in the Mountains*. After the story help the children to create their own book of when they were young. This is a great keepsake that the children and their families will treasure for a long time.
(Source: *The Best of the Mailbox, Book 1: Preschool/Kindergarten*, Margaret Michel)

Shoelace Bunny Ears.
Tying your shoes has always been a passage in growing up. A fun method to learn has been the Bunny Ear method. This craft can make the practice a little more entertaining and a little less

of a chore. Make a bunny face from a paper plate. Add shoelace ears so that the children can practice tying their laces whenever they want.

(Source: *Glad Rags*, Jan Irving and Robin Currie)

Activities:

When I Grow Up . . .
This is a simple mime game that even the youngest child can participate in with the group. Create a stage area at the front of the room by drawing a circle. One child at a time enters the circle, says "When I grow up I want to be . . . ," and then mimes the occupation he or she is interested in at the time. The remainder of the group will attempt to guess, with the member who guesses correctly getting to go next.

(Source: *Great Theme Parties for Children*, Irene N. Watts)

I Can Do It.
This is a variation of the game King of the Hill, which will help children demonstrate what they are capable of doing. It is a wonderful method of illustrating self-reliance and more while having a great deal of fun and laughter.

Place a large number of papers, each listing activities the children need to perform to show growth in their life (e.g., bounce a ball, tie your shoes, put on your own shirt, etc.), in a bag. These activities can be physical or verbal acts and often change depending on the age of the group playing the game.

Each child sits at the bottom of a flight of stairs. If the child is able to perform the action that the leader announces from the paper drawn from the bag, he or she moves up one step. If unable to do it, the child simply waits for his or her next turn. The first to reach the top of the hill wins. This is a game children will ask for repeatedly.

Songs:

(Audio) "Turn Around"
(Source: *Mail Myself to You*)
(Book) "I Wonder if I'm Growing"
(Source: *The Raffi Singable Songbook*, Raffi)

23 Behavior: Losing Things

Relate to:	*St. Anthony of Padua Feast Day (June 13): A special feast day to celebrate the life of a saint to whom many people pray to help them find lost things.*

Videos:	*Grandfather's Mitten* *Old Bear: Lost and Found* *Picnic* *Spot's Lost Bone* *The Three Little Kittens*
Books:	*Billy's Beetle*, Mick Inkpen *The Blanket*, John Burningham *D.W.'s Lost Blankie*, Marc Brown *Finders Keepers, Losers Weepers*, Joan Lexau *I Lost My Bear*, Jules Feiffer *The Letters Are Lost*, Lisa Campbell Ernst *Little Brown Bear Loses His Clothes*, Elizabeth Upham *Lollopy*, Joyce Dunbar *Losing Things at Mr. Mudd's*, Carolyn Coman *The Lost and Found*, Mark Teague *Nu Dang and His Kite*, Jacqueline Ayer *Small Bear Lost*, Martin Waddell *The Trip*, Marjorie Sharmat *Where Are You, Little Zack?*, Judith Ross Enderle and Stephanie Gordon Tessler *Where Can It Be?*, Ann Jonas
Fingerplay:	**Little Bo-Peep.** (Source: *Finger Frolics—Revised*, Liz Cromwell, Dixie Hibner, and John R. Faitel)
Crafts:	**The Kitten's Mittens.** Using various color construction paper, cut out enough mitten shapes to allow each child to have a matching pair. One method of getting the children more involved in the craft is to give them only one mitten in the color of his choice. Place the matching mittens in the front of the room or hide them around the room, and allow the children to search for the match. Now give the children crayons, glitter (if you don't mind the mess), and sticker dots and stars (an all-time favorite with toddlers). Allow them to decorate the mittens to their own taste.

Finally, give them string to attach one to the other and hang their creations around their necks.

This can also be a nice decoration to hang on the library or classroom windows.

(Source: *101 Easy Art Activities*, Trudy Aarons and Francine Koelsch)

Masking-Tape Covered Containers.
Losing things is a problem for all of us. Now the children can make a special container for themselves where they can keep those special items so they don't get lost. This is an uncomplicated craft for children of any age. Take a bottle, jar, or box and let the children cover it completely with strips of masking tape. This will provide texture. Now take your favorite color shoe polish and paint it over completely. Buff with a rag for the final effect.

(Source: *Gifts Galore!*, Ireene Robbins)

Activities:

Button, Button, Who's Got the Button?
This game is for eight or more players. One player sits in the center of a circle formed by the other players. The players in the circle have a button they pass from hand to hand. They keep their hands moving so the center player thinks the button is still being passed; the center player must then guess who has the button.

(Source: *Games*, Anne Rockwell)

Lost Slippers.
Here's a fun Lost and Found game. Have each child take one shoe off. Collect the shoes and hide them throughout the room. Let the group filter out through the room to locate the shoes and return them to their original owners.

This is a wonderful way to make new friends in the classroom.

(Source: *Happy Birthday Parties!*, Penny Warner)

Songs:

(Audio) "The Missing Parade"
(Source: *Billy the Squid*, Tom Chapin)
(Book) "Three Little Kittens"
(Source: *Singing-Bee!: A Collection of Favorite Children's Songs*, Jane Hart)

24 Behavior: Misbehavior

Relate to:	*Golden Rule Week (April 1–7): The goal of this special week is to remind the children of the importance of that special rule we all need to live by.*

Videos:

It's Mine
Miss Nelson Is Missing
Peter Rabbit
Pierre: A Cautionary Tale
Where the Wild Things Are

Books:

Amy Said, Martin Waddell
Big Black Bear, Wong Herbert Yee
Contrary Bear, Phyllis Root
Ella and the Naughty Lion, Anne Cottringer
The Grizzly Sisters, Cathy Bellows
How to Lose All Your Friends, Nancy Carlson
A Little Touch of Monster, Emily Lampert
Miss Nelson Is Back, Harry Allard
No Biting, Horrible Crocodile!, Jonathan Shipton
The Popcorn Dragon, Jane Thayer
Rooter Remembers, Joanne Oppenheim
Rough Tough Rowdy, William H. Hooks
That Terrible Baby, Jennifer Armstrong
This Is the Bear and the Bad Little Girl, Sarah Hayes
We're in Big Trouble, Blackboard Bear, Martha Alexander

Fingerplay:

Pop! On Your Clothes!
(Source: *Glad Rags*, Jan Irving and Robin Currie)

Crafts:

Monkey Business.
Most children are already familiar with Curious George, the curious monkey that's always getting himself in a load of trouble. Talk about George's behavior and how he could have stayed out of trouble, then follow it up by having the children make their own swinging monkeys out of paper and pipe cleaners.

Another point mentioned in this source is how monkeys are treated differently in other areas of the world. This can lead to another great discussion.
(Source: *Cut-Paper Play!*, Sandi Henry)

Peace Pipe.
Communicate to the children the many ways people in the world try to settle their differences. Native Americans address their various needs with great ceremony. One of their rituals is the smoking of the peace pipe for resolving problems between groups and ending hostilities. This peace pipe is constructed out of a cork, dowell, yarn, and feathers for decoration.
(Source: *Scrap Craft for Youth Groups*, Gerry Fleming)

Activities:

Bad Words.
All children understand the concept of avoiding the use of "bad words." With this in mind, select a child to be It and have him or her leave the room. Choose a word (e.g., hat, nose, etc.) to be the bad word. The object of the game is to get the person who is It to say the chosen word as many times as possible in a given period of time by asking questions.

Once every child has had a chance to be It, the winner is decided by the person who actually said the bad word the least amount of times. Look for little deviations in this game in the source.
(Source: *The World's Best Party Games*, Sheila Anne Barry)

What Should You Do?
This is a great activity to use on Martin Luther King Day. Talk with the class about how Martin Luther King believed in always settling problems peacefully. With this understood, describe or have children act out a difficult situation. Situation: You are playing with blocks and the new kid knocks them over. Now ask the children how they would resolve this situation.
(Source: *Classroom Parties*, Susan Spaete)

Songs:

(Audio) "Sore Loser"
(Source: *Billy the Squid*, Tom Chapin)
(Book) "Pierre"
(Source: *Maurice Sendak's Really Rosie Starring the Nutshell Kids*, Maurice Sendak)

25 Behavior: Sharing

Relate to:	*National Goodwill Week (first Sunday in May): Encourage children to share their old belongings with Goodwill and those who have less.*

Videos:	*Grandfather's Mitten* *Learning to Share* (Sesame Street) *The Rainbow Fish* *The Story of Jumping Mouse* *Wilfrid Gordon McDonald Partridge*
Books:	*Ananse's Feast: An Ashanti Tale*, Tololwa M. Mollel *Bone Button Borscht*, Aubrey Davis *Chubbo's Pool*, Betsy Lewin *Connie Came to Play*, Jill Paton Walsh *Don't Touch My Room*, Patricia Lakin *Doodle Flute*, Daniel Pinkwater *Earthsong*, Sally Rogers *It's Mine*, Leo Lionni *Just Not the Same*, Addie Lacoe *Keep Your Old Hat*, Anna Grossnickle Hines *Mrs. Rose's Garden*, Elaine Greenstein *One of Each*, Mary Ann Hoberman *The Rainbow Fish*, Marcus Pfister *Rosie and the Poor Rabbits*, Maryann MacDonald *What Feels Best?*, Anita Harper
Fingerplay:	**It's Fun to Work Together.** (Source: *1001 Rhymes and Fingerplays*, The Totline Staff)
Crafts:	**Jigsaw Junk.** Don't throw away those pieces of puzzles. When you're finished with them turn them into a beautiful picture frame. Allow the children to share the photograph of their favorite time with a friend or family member by placing it in a frame made of various puzzle pieces. It's simple and economical as well as a good lesson in recycling. (Source: *Incredibly Awesome Crafts for Kids*, edited by Sara Jane Treinen) **Monkey Bank—Job Sharing Jar.** This is a piggy bank craft designed like a monkey face and constructed from a glass jar and paper. It can also be used as a

job-sharing jar. Tell the children they can stop monkeying around and share the chores with the family. The family agrees on jobs everyone should share. The child puts slips of paper—each one with one of the jobs written on it—into the jar. Everyone in the family agrees to pull one slip from the jar every day and do that task for the family.

Activities: **Beanbag Bop.**
Here's a wonderful control mechanism when working with young children in a large group. Have the children sit in a group circling you. As you hold a bean bag toss it to any child in the group who must then respond to whatever question you ask. This, of course, will force everyone to pay attention since they never know when the bean bag will be coming their way.

Use this as a sharing session. Let the child who receives the bean bag share something of himself with the group.
(Source: *The Best of the Mailbox, Book 1: Preschool/Kindergarten edition*, Margaret Michel)

Tug of War.
This type of game requires a team effort. Discuss how many things can be accomplished more easily when we share our strength and cooperate. Tug of War is a physical example of how children can achieve their goal through sharing and cooperation and still have a lot of fun.
(Source: *Sheet Magic*, Peggy Parish)

Songs: (Audio) "Share It"
(Source: *Rosenshontz Share It*)
(Book) "The Sharing Song"
(Source: *The Raffi Singable Songbook*, Raffi)

26 Behavior: Wishing

Relate to:	*Creation of the Make a Wish Foundation (May, 1980) and the fulfillment of wishes of terminally ill children.*

Videos:
The Alphabet Dragon
Dr. Seuss' Pontoffel Pock and His Magic Picnic
The Fisherman and His Wife
King Midas and the Golden Touch
The Little Rabbit Who Wanted Red Wings

Books:
The Big Fish, Klaus Kordon
Don't Ever Wish for a 7 Ft. Bear, Robert Benton
Emily and the Golden Acorn, Ian Beck
I Wish I Could Fly, Ron Maris
Jeanne-Marie Counts Her Sheep, Francoise Seignobosc
Mama, If You Had a Wish, Jeanne Modesitt
Mordant's Wish, Valerie Coursen
Pizza for Breakfast, Maryann Kovalski
Someday, Said Mitchell, Barbara Williams
Three Wishes, Lucille Clifton
The Three Wishes, Margot Zemach
Twinkle, Twinkle, Little Star, Iza Trapani
A Wish for Wings that Work, Berkeley Breathed
The Wishing Hat, Annegert Fuchshuber

Fingerplay:
Birthday Celebration.
(Source: *Finger Frolics—Revised*, Liz Cromwell, Dixie Hibner, and John R. Faitel)

Crafts:
The Wishing Well.
Use salt or oatmeal boxes to design a wishing-well bank. Glue two Popsicle sticks to the sides of the box to support a small tilted roof. Glue red paper to the exterior portion of the box and have the children design the bricks with markers.

The children can use the newly made bank to save their money for other prizes they may be wishing for.

Wishing Pin.
Remember all those wishes you made on those chicken or turkey wishbones? Well, how about keeping them in one piece and making them into a wishing pin that you can wish on for months to come. Here you will locate instructions for drying

and polishing the wishbone, along with suggestions for decorating it to become a special wishing pin for your best friend or other loved ones.
(Source: *The Never-Be-Bored Book*, Judith Logan Lehne)

Activities: **The Wishing Candle.**
Place a large candle in the center of a table. Each player should be blindfolded, then spun around three times near the table. The first child who can blow out the wishing candle is the winner.

This activity can precede a discussion of what each child would wish for if he or she were granted one wish. (Caution: This game must be supervised by an adult because of the open flame!)

Swish, Swish, Make a Wish.
Encourage the children to use their imagination and express their wishes through this simple child's game. Instruct the children to sit in a circle with one child in the center holding a broom. As the child sweeps the floor the other children chant:

Swish, swish, make a wish.
What will you be today?

This chant continues with various refrains until the child is granted his or her wish and he or she jumps on the broom to ride it around the room; then another child sits in the center of the circle. The source provides the full text of the suggested refrains.
(Source: *1–2–3 Games*, by Jean Warren)

Songs: (Audio) "Three Fine Wishes"
(Source: *Camp Sleepy*)
(Book) "When You Wish Upon a Star"
(Source: *The Illustrated Disney Song Book*, David E. Tietyen)

27 Bicycles

Relate to: *National Bike Month (May): A month dedicated to the fun of riding a bicycle and the safety techniques that are important to know before beginning to ride.*

Videos: *Curious George Rides a Bike*
The Remarkable Riderless Runaway Tricycle

Books: *Annie Flies the Birthday Bike*, Crescent Dragonwagon
The Bear's Bicycle, Emilie McLeod
Bicycle Bear, Michaela Muntean
A Bicycle for Rosaura, Daniel Barbot
Bike Trip, Betsy and Giulio Maestro
Charles Tarzan McBiddle, Andrew Glass
Constance Stumbles, Pat and Frederick McKissack
Curious George Rides a Bike, Hans Rey
Dudley Bakes a Cake, Peter Cross
Franklin Rides a Bike, Paulette Bourgeois and Brenda Clark
The Grogg's Day Out, Anne Bently
Let's Go Froggy!, Jonathan London
Mrs. Armitage on Wheels, Quentin Blake
Mrs. Peachtree's Bicycle, Erica Silverman
Shawn's Red Bike, Petronella Breinburg
SuperGrandpa, David M. Schwartz
Ugh!, Arthur Yorinks

Fingerplay: **My Little Tricycle.**
(Source: *Finger Frolics—Revised*, Liz Cromwell, Dixie Hibner, and John R. Faitel)

Crafts: **Wheel Dressings.**
The children are preparing for the big bicycle parade and want their bicycles and tricycles to look their best. Besides washing the bikes and making them shine, adding baskets, etc., how about dressing up those wheels? Provide the children with long strips of crepe paper of many colors. Then show them how to weave the streamers in and out of the spokes of their bicycle wheels. This will add some wonderful colors as their bikes go whizzing by in the parade.
(Source: *Children's Crafts: Fun and Creativity for Ages 5–12*, Sunset)

Activities:

Bicycle Safety Course.
With the cooperation of the local police department you might set up a small obstacle course for the children to ride their bicycles through. It should be emphasized to all that this is a safety course and not a race track.

You will need to close off a portion of your parking lot for this event and might even want to invite older children to attend. Chalk out a course to be followed by arrows. At various key spots in the course place a stop sign, a small ramp, and, if possible, a working traffic light.

Many police departments will send a police officer to speak with the children and will also donate such items as bike reflectors for those children completing the course.

Tricycle Parade.
Along with the bicycle safety course previously suggested, try a tricycle parade for the younger children with the help of their parents. Provide streamers for the children to decorate their bikes and let them ride the bikes around a secure lot or, if permitted, down the hallways of your school to visit the various classes and drop off special bike safety posters they have designed.

Invite an older child or parent to stand at the hallway intersections with a stop sign to direct traffic.

Song:

(Book) "The Doll and the Bike"
(Source: *God's Wonderful World*, Agnes Leckie Mason and Phyllis Brown Ohanian)

28 Birds

Relate to:	*National Wild Bird Feeding Month (Feb.): To bring to people's attention that winter months are the hardest for wildlife and to ask people to provide food, water, and shelter for the birds.*

Videos: *Dorothy and the Ostrich*
Horton Hatches an Egg
The Little Red Hen
The Most Wonderful Egg in the World
The Ugly Duckling

Books: *Condor's Egg*, Jonathan London
Feathers for Lunch, Lois Ehlert
Goose, Molly Bang
Hector Penguin, Louise Fatio
The House I'll Build for the Wrens, Shirley Neitzel
How the Ostrich Got It's Long Neck, Verna Aardema
Moon Bear, Frank Asch
Nicolas, Where Have You Been?, Leo Lionni
The Paper Crane, Molly Bang
Penny Wise, Fun Foolish, Judy Delton
Quiet! There's a Canary in the Library, Don Freeman
Round Robin, Jack Kent
Seasons of Swans, Monica Wellington
Stellaluna, Janell Cannon
Tree of Birds, Susan Meddaugh

Fingerplay: **Fly, Little Bird.**
    (Source: *Rhymes for Learning Times*, Louise Binder Scott)

Crafts: **Feed the Birds.**
Allow the children to make a bird feeder for their backyard.
Use a cardboard milk carton and cut out two opposite sides to
allow birds to move through. Punch holes in the top section
for yarn to tie it to the tree. Decoration of the carton can be
done with available materials. Bird seed can be placed in the
bottom of the feeder every other day.
    (Source: *Lollipop, Grapes, and Clothespin Critters: Quick, On-the-Spot Remedies for Restless Children 2–10*, Robyn Freedman Spizman)

Robin Redbreast Door Hanging.
The robin is the most recognizable of birds for little kids. This paper plate craft results in a large size robin to hang in the child's room for the spring. Place pipe cleaners for feet between two large plates for a body and two small plates for the head. Two large plates are folded in half to create wings for the bird to take flight. Paint the whole bird brown and then add the critical features of eyes, beaks, etc. Don't forget his red breast made out of a paper bowl should be painted red to give it some depth.
(Source: *Crafts to Make in the Spring*, Kathy Ross)

Activities:

Humming Birds.
This is a variation of the game of Hot and Cold. Have one child turn his back while a chosen object is hidden somewhere in the room. The remainder of the group watches where the object is hidden. As the first child looks around the room to find the object, the other children hum. The closer the person gets to finding it, the louder the humming will get; the further away, the softer the children will hum.

This is a game that will need little preparation and can be played as long as the interest is there. Another advantage here is that there are no winners or losers.
(Source: *500 Games*, Peter L. Cave)

Floating Feathers.
This is perfect for playing in rooms with limited space available to you. Can you keep the feather in the air without touching it or it touching you? Find this and other simple games in the source.
(Source: *My Party Book*, Marion Elliot)

Songs:

(Audio) "Percival the Parrot"
(Source: *Sally the Swinging Snake*)
(Book) "Two Little Blackbirds"
(Source: *The Fireside Book of Fun and Game Songs*, Marie Winn)

29 Birds: Ducks

Relate to:	*The Great American Duck Race (Aug. 1980): Usually held the fourth weekend of August in Deming, New Mexico, this charity event raises money for the Special Olympics and the Sunnyfield Association, which provides sheltered workshops for people with disabilities.*

Videos:
Angus and the Ducks
Make Way for Ducklings
Mother Duck and the Big Race
The Story of Ping
The Ugly Duckling

Books:
Arnold of the Ducks, Mordicai Gerstein
Come Along Daisy!, Jane Simmons
Danny's Duck, June Crebbin
Don't Fidget a Feather!, Erica Silverman
Ducks Disappearing, Phyllis Reynolds Naylor
Ducks Like to Swim, Agnes Verboven
Duncan the Dancing Duck, Syd Hoff
Five Little Ducks, Ian Beck
Have You Seen My Duckling?, Nancy Tafuri
Howard, James Stevenson
Last One Home Is a Green Pig, Edith Hurd
A Pet for Duck and Bear, Judy Delton
Quacky Duck, Paul and Emma Rogers
The Surprise Family, Lynn Reiser
Wow!: It's Great Being a Duck, Joan Rankin

Fingerplay:
Mr. Turkey and Mr. Duck.
(Source: *Finger Frolics—Revised*, Liz Cromwell, Dixie Hibner, and John R. Faitel)

Crafts:
A Duck Friend.
An illustration of a duck may be duplicated from the source indicated here. After the children have colored their ducks, distribute feathers and glue so that they can add texture to the illustration. If the picture has been reproduced on cardstock, it can then be cut out and mounted on a Popsicle stick to create a stick puppet.

This craft activity is simple enough for even the two-year-old level. The creations can be used to act out a duck story (*Have You Seen My Duckling?*, Nancy Tafuri) or to sing a song.

(Source: *The Kids' Stuff Book of Patterns, Projects, and Plans*, Imogene Forte)

The Ugly Duckling- Swan Puppet.
After enjoying the traditional story of the ugly duckling becoming a beautiful swan, let the children illustrate the tale through this swan puppet. Use two paper plates for the body; a tube sock makes a great long swan neck. Cover the body with numerous feathers and let the children tell the story again.
(Source: *Crafts from Your Favorite Fairy Tales*, Kathy Ross)

Activities: **Duck, Duck, Goose.**
Have all the children (any number will work here) crouch in a circle in the center of the room. One child will walk around the perimeter of the circle saying, "Duck, Duck, Duck . . ." until he taps another child and says, "Goose." The "goose" must get up and chase the child around the circle and tag him before he reaches the empty spot left in the circle. If the goose fails to reach the child in time, he must go around the circle again.

For a variation of this game, try asking the children to waddle like a duck around the circle instead of running.

Feather Relay.
Mark a game area three or four feet across by placing two pieces of string across the floor. Divide teams A and B in half and line up each half on opposite sides of the string.

Provide one feather to each team. The goal is to get the feather across the game field to their teammates by blowing on it and not letting it touch the ground. The first team to have all their team members complete the task will win.
(Source: *Things to Make and Do for Thanksgiving*, Lorinda Bryan Cauley)

Songs: (Audio) "Six Little Ducks"
(Source: *Kids Silly Song Sing-a-Longs*)
(Book) "The Little White Duck"
(Source: *The Reader's Digest Children's Songbook*, William L. Simon)

30 Birds: Owls

Relate to: *Creation of Woodsy Owl (April 22, 1997): America's original and official environmental icon was created in 1971. On April 22, 1997, Earth Day, the new and improved Woodsy ("Give a Hoot! Don't Pollute!") emerged to encourage children to respect nature.*

Videos: *The Happy Owls*
The Owl and the Pussycat
Owl Moon

Books: *Hoot*, Jane Hissey
Little Owl Leaves the Nest, Marcia Leonard
Oliver's Wood, Sue Hendra
The Owl and the Woodpecker, Brian Wildsmith
Owl at Home, Arnold Lobel
Owl Babies, Martin Waddell
Owl Moon, Jane Yolen
The Owl Scatterer, Howard Norman
Owliver, Robert Kraus
Owly, Mike Thaler
Sleepy Little Owl, Howard Goldsmith
What Game Shall We Play?, Pat Hutchins
Wide-Awake Owl, Louis Slobodkina
Whoo-oo Is It?, Megan McDonald

Fingerplay: **Five Little Girls.**
(Source: *Rhymes for Learning Times*, Louise Binder Scott)

Crafts: **Owl Bank.**
A decorative owl bank will help the children to save their pennies for a rainy day. Use containers easily found in the home, such as bread crumb containers or circular oatmeal boxes. Cover the container with a piece of burlap.
Contrasting colors of burlap can be used to make the eyes, beak, and feathers of the owl. If extra burlap isn't available, try substituting colored construction paper.
(Source: *Make It with Burlap*, Elyse Sommer)

Envelope Owl Wall Hanging.
Turn a simple envelope into a beautiful wall hanging of this bird of the night. Open all the flaps of an envelope, leaving the top flap folded down for the head. On the top flap add eyes

and beak and have the children draw feet on the lower portion of the envelope. Add feathers by folding brown candy wrappers from boxed candy. For a final touch, cut fringes around the wings and tail feathers (left, right, and bottom flaps).
(Source: *Crafts to Make in the Fall*, Kathy Ross)

Activities: **Birds Can Fly.**
This game is a variation of the game Simon Says. All players stand facing the child who is the leader. The leader begins the game by calling out "Birds can fly" and begins flapping his or her arms. Other players copy the leader's actions. The leader continues calling out other flying animals (Butterflies can fly, etc.). At some point he or she can mention an animal that can't fly (Cows can fly). Any children still flapping their wings are out of the game. Continue until one child is left; that child becomes the next leader.
Other variations of this game can be continued with:
• Tigers can growl (everyone growls)
• Fish can swim (make swimming motions)
(Source: *500 Games*, Peter L. Cave)

Whooo Is It?
Help the Mama owl find her baby owlets. Select a child to be the mother and have her leave the room. Upon returning to the room Mama owl discovers all the children with their hands over their mouths. Three of them are hooting for their mother, but because their mouths are covered, she doesn't know which are hooting for her. She must listen carefully to discover which ones are her babies.
(Source: *Theme-a-saurus II*, Jean Warren)

Songs: (Audio) "Owl Lullaby"
(Source: *Sharon, Lois, and Bram Sing A to Z*)
(Book) "Big Old Owl"
(Source: *American Folk Songs for Children in Home, School, and Nursery School*, Ruth Crawford Seeger)

31 Birds: Penguins

Relate to: *Exploration of the South Pole (Dec. 14, 1911): On this date Norwegian explorer Roald Amundsen and his companions reached the South Pole ahead of all others.*

Videos: *The Adventures of Scamper the Penguin*
The Cold Blooded Penguin
Little Penguin's Tale

Books: *Bibi Takes Flight*, Michel Gay
Counting Penguins, Caroline Howe
The Emperor Penguin's New Clothes, Janet Perlman
Little Penguin's Tale, Audrey Wood
Penguin Day, Victoria Winteringham
Penguin Pete, Marcus Pfister
Penguins!, Gail Gibbons
Quickly, Quigley, Jeanne M. Gravois
Solo, Paul Geraghty
Splash!: A Penguin Counting Book, Jonathan Chester and Kirsty Melville
Tacky the Penguin, Helen Lester
Tuxedo Sam, Cathy Nichols
Which Is Willy?, Robert Bright
Winston, Newton, Elton, and Ed, James Stevenson
Your Pet Penguin, Bobbie Hamsa

Fingerplay: **Three Little Penguins.**
(Source: *Rhymes for Learning Times*, Louise Binder Scott)

Crafts: **Egg Carton Penguins.**
An everyday egg carton can easily be transformed into a delightful penguin with the use of only paint and construction paper. Simply cut the egg carton in half and paint it black. Use pieces from the other half to create the eyes, beak, and feet. White construction paper can be used to make the stomach, and then glue it to the front of the egg carton. For an added touch, sit the creation on a pile of cotton to give the effect of snow.
(Source: *Egg Carton Critters*, Donna Miller)

Penguin Pete.
Remember the "Pet Rock" craze? Well, let's bring it back with

this rock design. Penguin Pete is simply two rocks painted black and white but glued so that they stand upright as a penguin night stand. For a base you might want to use white Styrofoam so the rocks can be pressed tightly into it for stability. Add little feet and a beak and your cold creature is ready for display.

(Source: *Fun-to-Make Nature Crafts*, Robyn Supraner)

Activities:

Animal Walks.

This game strengthens children's arms and legs. Select several cards of animal stunts (e.g., penguin walk, seal crawl, etc.) where a large part of your weight is on your arms and legs.

Mark out a path for the children to follow while acting out the animal parts.

(Source: *Teacher's Handbook of Children's Games*, Marian Jenks Wirth)

Peter, Peter Penguin.

This activity requires three or more players. Teach the children about penguin habits and movement; then you can use this activity to move from one room to another. You will find sheet music to go along with the penguin actions.

(Source: *Singing and Dancing Games for the Very Young*, Esther L. Nelson)

Song:

(Audio) "Do the Penguin"

(Source: *Hot! Hot! Hot! Dance Songs*, by Sesame Street)

32 Birthdays

Relate to:	*The song "Happy Birthday to You" (June 27): On this date in 1859 schoolteacher Mildred J. Hill a composed the melody to this familiar song.*
Videos:	*Happy Birthday Moon* *A Letter to Amy* *Princess Scargo and the Birthday Pumpkin* *Winnie the Pooh and a Day for Eeyore*
Books:	*Benjamin's 365 Birthdays*, Judi Barrett *Birthday Blizzard*, Bonnie Pryor *Birthday Presents*, Cynthia Rylant *The Birthday Swap*, Loretta Lopez *The Birthday Thing*, SuAnn and Kevin Kiser *Creepy-Crawly Birthday*, James Howe *Gotcha!*, Gail Jorgensen *Happy Birthday, Sam*, Pat Hutchins *Happy Birthday, Wombat!*, Kerry Argent *Henry's Happy Birthday*, Holly Keller *Hilda Herts Happy Birthday*, Mary Wormell *A Letter to Amy*, Ezra Jack Keats *Secret Birthday Message*, Eric Carle *Some Birthday!*, Patricia Polacco *Veronica and the Birthday Present*, Roger Duvoisin
Fingerplay:	**Look at Me.** (Source: *Finger Frolics—Revised*, Liz Cromwell, Dixie Hibner, and John R. Faitel)
Crafts:	**Add-a-Year Candle.** Birthdays are important events for children. To help them celebrate their birthday every year, construct a birthday cake with a special "add-a-year" candle. Cover a box with construction paper and decorate it with flowers and the child's name as you would a cake. To make the candle, get a cardboard tube (tissue paper roll) and cover it, adding a paper flame to the top. For each year of the child's life, put a strip around the candle with the child's age. This can be added to, year after year. (Source: *Purple Cow to the Rescue*, Ann Cole, Carolyn Haas, and Betty Weinberger)

Styroblock Print Invitations.
The Styrofoam trays from various food products are perfect for using with young children when you want to do prints. Children can sketch their own scene for the front of a birthday invitation by pressing lines into the Styrofoam. Add liquid soap (just a drop) to paints and let the children paint over their scene. Gently place it on paper and rub it into the paper. After lifting it off, let your new scene dry before mounting it on the cards.
(Source: *I Can Make Art So Easy to Make!*, Mary Wallace)

Activities:

Musical Parade.
Choose a small prize, such as a chocolate bar or a small toy, and wrap it in layers of tissue or wrapping paper. Have the children sit in a circle and pass it around the circle. When the music stops, the child who is holding the prize should remove one layer of wrap. Continue until it is completely uncovered. A similar game is Balloon Relay.

Balloon Relay.
Divide the class into two groups, each with a box full of inflated balloons. When the signal is given, each team will attempt to burst all their balloons before the opposing team by sitting on them one at a time.
(Source: *500 Games*, Peter L. Cave)

Chinese Fortune Game.
Try this simple activity that is similar to the Chinese second birthday celebration. Collect a number of objects such as books, cassettes, pens, computer disks, and so forth, and place them on a table. Each child is blindfolded and permitted to select an object that will predict his or her future (e.g., a computer disk may indicate a future computer programmer). For a list of suggestions or other games, crafts, and activities from other cultures, see the source.
(Source: *Happy Birthday Everywhere*, Arlene Erlbach)

Songs:

(Audio) "The Backwards Birthday Party"
    (Source: *ZigZag*)
(Book) "Happy Birthday to You"
    (Source: *Singing Bee!: A Collection of Favorite Children's Songs*, Jane Hart)

33 Boats/Ships

Relate to:	*National Safe Boating Week (May 16–24): Issued by proclamation to encourage safe practices when boating.*

Videos: *The Island of the Skog*
The Little Red Lighthouse and the Great Gray Bridge
Little Tim and the Brave Sea Captain
Little Toot

Books: *Alexander and the Magic Boat*, Katharine Holabird
Baby's Boat, Jeanne Titherington
Benjy's Boat Trip, Margaret Graham
Big City Port, Betsy Maestro
Boats, Anne Rockwell
Emily and the Golden Acorn, Ian Beck
Farmer Enno and His Cow, Jens Rassmus
Harbor, Donald Crews
I Love Boats, Flora McDonnell
Louise Builds a Boat, Louise Pfanner
Maude and Claude Go Abroad, Susan Meddaugh
Mr. Bear's Boat, Thomas Graham
Pigs Ahoy!, David McPhail
Sailboat Lost, Leonard Everett Fisher
Who Sank the Boat?, Pamela Allen

Fingerplay: **Row the Boat.**
(Source: *Little Boy Blue*, Daphne Gogstrom)

Crafts: **Bathtub Boats.**
A simple boat can be built of clay, paper (sails), and toothpicks, with a bottle cap, jar lid, bar of soap, or walnut shell for the base. If you use these items for the base, the boat will be able to float. Don't disappoint the children by using something that won't float.
(Source: *Purple Cow to the Rescue*, Ann Cole, Carolyn Haas, and Betty Weinberger)

Viking Longship.
There is a large variety of ships that can be displayed for the children. This Viking longship can be made from a milk carton. Add the colorful sails and the telltale Viking shields that are always displayed along the sides of the ship. The nice thing

about this one is that it is seaworthy and the class will look forward to the launching.

    (Source: *Cars and Boats*, Vanessa Morgan and David West)

Activities:

Rocking Boat.

While singing Row, Row, Row Your Boat or one of the songs listed below, children get into pairs. Have two children sit on the floor facing each other. Legs should be spread with feet touching their partner's. They may then rock back and forth as a boat would rock. An alternate version can be having the children pretend to row oars and move themselves around the room as if rowing down the river.

Discover the New World.

Here's a way to help children discover the New World just like Columbus. Decorate your room with a maze of large stars taped on the floor. At the end of the maze place a large globe. Lower your lights and let the children be guided by the stars as they row or sail their boats closer to the New World. When they reach the end of their journey you can use the globe to open up any number of discussions.

    (Source: *Classroom Parties*, Susan Spaete)

Songs:

(Audio) "Where Go the Boats"
    (Source: *A Child's Garden of Songs*)
(Book) "Michael Row the Boat Ashore"
    (Source: *Do Your Ears Hang Low?*, Tom Glazer)

34 Careers: Dentist/Teeth

Relate to:	*National Children's Dental Health Month (Feb.): To educate children on proper dental health techniques and stress the importance of regular dental hygiene.*

Videos:	*Dr. DeSoto*

Books:	*Arthur's Loose Tooth*, Lillian Hoban
	At The Dentist: What Did Christopher See?, Sandra Ziegler
	The Berenstain Bears Visit the Dentist, Stan Berenstain
	Calico Cat's Sunny Smile, Donald Charles
	Curious George Goes to the Dentist, Margaret Rey
	The Dentist's Tools, Carolyn Lapp
	Dr. DeSoto Goes to Africa, William Steig
	Dr. Kranner, Dentist with a Smile, Alice K. Flanagan
	Going to the Dentist, Fred Rogers
	Grandpa's Teeth, Rod Clement
	I Have a Loose Tooth, Sally Noll
	Loose Tooth, Steven Kroll
	Michael and the Dentist, Bernard Wolf
	Milo's Toothache, Ida Luttrell
	My Dentist, Harlow Rockwell

Fingerplay:	**Brushing Teeth.**
	(Source: *Finger Frolics—Revised*, Liz Cromwell, Dixie Hibner, and John R. Faitel)

Crafts:	**My Tooth Pouch.**

Using felt, have the children trace and cut out two forms of a tooth. They may then glue on eyes that are easily obtainable at any craft store and put a smile on with markers.

Have the children glue the sides of the tooth together, leaving the upper portion open. (Use fabric glue that can be purchased at a craft store.)

The children now own their own tooth holder, where they may place their tooth and put it under their pillow. The tooth fairy may exchange the tooth for money in the pouch later.

Toothpaste Airplane.
This imaginative craft can be used as a vehicle to begin a lesson on transportation or a classroom discussion on brushing your teeth. A special pattern is made available to check the

dimensions of the toothpaste box to ensure that it will work. Patterns are also made available for propellers, wings, etc.

Let the children use this new airplane to store their own personal toothpaste for brushing each day.

(Source: *Rainy Day Projects for Children*, Gerri Jenny and Sherrie Gould)

Activities:

Good Nutrition.

Prepare flashcards or flannel board pictures of different types of foods. Discuss good nutrition and have the children pick out what foods help to make happy teeth.

You might also be able to borrow a dentist's teeth mold to illustrate proper brushing methods. If this is not available to you, try getting a dentist's aide to visit your group to talk to the children.

Toothbrush Painting.

Cut out large forms of a tooth for each child. Using white tempera paint as toothpaste, have the children practice the proper method of brushing. Dentists can be encouraged to donate real toothbrushes for this activity.

Tile Teeth.

Gather a collection of different foods that stain teeth. Each child can be given white ceramic tiles to paint with the foods and observe how they stain. How do we clean them? Hand out toothpaste and toothbrushes.

(Source: *Theme-a-saurus*, Jean Warren)

Song:

(Audio) "Brush Your Teeth"
(Source: *Singable Songs for the Very Young*)

35 Careers: Firefighters

Relate to:	*Fire Prevention Week (first or second week in Oct.): To make children aware of the safety measures they need to know to keep their families safe from fires.*

Videos:
Curious George
Draghetto
Firehouse Dog
Helpful Little Fireman
Hercules

Books:
Benjamin Rabbit and the Fire Chief, Irene Keller
Clifford's Good Deeds, Norman Bridwell
Fighting Fires, Susan Kuklin
Fire Engines, Anne Rockwell
Fire! Fire!, Gail Gibbons
"Fire! Fire!" said Mrs. McGuire, Bill Martin Jr.
Fire Stations, Jason Cooper
Fire Trucks, Hope Irvin Marston
Firefighters, Norma Simon
Firehouse Dog, Amy and Richard Hutchings
Fireman Jim, Roger Bester
Fireman Small, Wong Herbert Yee
I Want to Be a Firefighter, Edith Kunhardt
The Little Fireman, Margaret Wise Brown
Poinsettia and the Firefighters, Felicia Bond
A Visit to the Sesame Street Firehouse, Dan Elliott

Fingerplays:
Ten Brave Fireman.
(Source: *Finger Frolics—Revised*, Liz Cromwell, Dixie Hibner, and John R. Faitel)

Crafts:
Firefighter's Hat and Ax.
Many children get great enjoyment pretending to be the firemen they see every day on television or in their neighborhood. The source below gives instructions on how to make such things as hats and axes out of cardboard tubes and construction paper. There are many items related to firefighters that can be made from paper and boxes.

Instructions are also available for the construction of a firehose, a fire extinguisher, a fire alarm box, a fire hydrant, an oxygen tank and mask to create an entire unit.
(Source: *Be What You Want to Be!*, Phyllis and Noel Fiarotta)

Five Firefighter Puppets.
Have the children assemble their own five firefighter stick puppets. Cut circles for the faces and attach to craft sticks. The red firefighter hats are formed by tracing the child's closed hand and cutting off the base. Add a little medal to the front with a number and you are ready for your own puppet show.

Try this book for a large collection of crafts that use the child's hand shape.

(Source: *Hand-Shaped Gifts*, Diane Bonica)

Activities: **Firemen's Visit.**
Arrange with the local fire department to have a fire truck visit your school or library so that the firefighters may speak with the children and show them the tools of the trade.

Many fire departments also arrange visits to the firehouse itself and have small coloring books on fire safety that they will give you for the children. Don't forget to make full use of the community services and workers available to your neighborhood.

Occupational Musical Chairs.
Musical Chairs is well known to us all. Tape a picture depicting a different occupation to each chair and begin the music. When it ends let the child without a chair select one and tell the class about the occupation he sees depicted. Once this is done have him remove the chair and begin again.

(Source: *The Giant Encyclopedia of Circle Time and Group Activities for Children 3 to 6*, Kathy Charner)

Song: (Book) "The King and the Fireman"
(Source: *People in My Neighborhood*, Sesame Street Inc.)

36 Careers: Letter Carrier/Post Office

Relate to:	*Benjamin Franklin's Birthday (Jan. 17): To celebrate the birth of the organizer and first postmaster for the Postal System.*

Videos: *Postman Pat*

Books: *Good-bye, Curtis*, Kevin Henkes
Hail to Mail, Samuel Marshak
Here Comes the Mail, Gloria Skurzynski
Katie Morag Delivers the Mail, Mairi Hedderwick
The Post Office Book: Mail and How It Moves, Gail Gibbons
The Post Office Cat, Gail E. Haley
The Postman's Palace, Adrian Henri and Simon Henwood
Snowshoe Thompson, Nancy Smiler Levinson
Somebody Loves You, Mr. Hatch, Eileen Spinelli
To the Post Office with Mama, Sue Farrell
Toddle Creek Post Office, Uri Shulevitz
Tortoise Brings the Mail, Dee Lillegard
A Visit to the Post Office, Sandra Ziegler
What the Mailman Brought, Carolyn Craven

Fingerplay: **The Mail Carrier.**
(Source: *1001 Rhymes and Fingerplays*, The Totline Staff)

Crafts: **Pop-Up Cards.**
After a discussion of the various items that a mail carrier delivers to the children's homes, it's time to create some of these items. Greeting cards are something the children always remember receiving. This source gives samples of various pop-up cards children can create for their friends and family members.
(Source: *Incredibly Awesome Crafts for Kids*, Sara Jane Treinen)

Valentine Mail Vest.
On Valentine's Day children give and receive cards. Try having them delivered by a special mail carrier wearing a mail vest to carry the cards. This simple vest is constructed from brown grocery bags with a special pocket in the front to hold the mail. Although this source illustrates the vest for a Valentine celebration it can easily be adapted for a discussion on careers, specifically on mail carriers.
(Source: *Crafts for Valentine's Day*, Kathy Ross)

Activities: **Postman, Postman.**
This book supplies the music and lyrics to the song Postman, Postman. It's a simple little verse that the whole class can participate in with you. Select one child to be the postman and outfit him or her with the tools of the trade (mailbag and enough letters for everyone). The postman skips around the group until the end of the verse when he or she delivers a letter to each child. Have the children tell you who sent each one or what it says (let them use their imagination).
(Source: *Dancing Games for Children of all Ages*, Esther L. Nelson)

Pony Express Relay Race.
Discuss with the children the early methods of mail delivery, mainly the Pony Express. Once they have grasped this, let the children set up stations for the pony express to stop. Divide the children into two teams with one player from each team waiting at each location. Give the first player the bag with the letters to be passed along. The final child in the relay will place the letter in the box at the end of the race and ring the bell. Add a little western flavor to this by using stick horses and costumes if you like.
(Source: *Party Plans for Tots*, Kate Harris)

Songs: (Audio) "The Mail Must Go Through"
(Source: *Disney's Children's Favorites, Vol. 1*)
(Book) "Mailman"
(Source: *Woody's 20 Grow Big Songs*, Woody Guthrie and Marjorie Mazia Guthrie)

37 Careers: Police Officer

Relate to:	*Police Week (always the week including May 15): This is a week established by Presidential Proclamation to honor those men and women who put their lives on the line for our safety every day.*

Videos:	*I Wanna Be a Police Officer* *Make Way for Ducklings* *Officer Buckle and Gloria* *The Police Station* *Sergeant Murphy's Day Off*
Books:	*Curious George Visits a Police Station*, Margaret and H. A. Rey *I Can Be a Police Officer*, Catherine Mathias *Moon Man*, Tomi Ungerer *My Dog Is Lost!*, Ezra Jack Keats *Officer Brown Keeps Neighborhoods Safe*, Alice K. Flanagan *Officer Buckle and Gloria*, Peggy Rathmann *The Officers' Ball*, Wong Herbert Yee *Police Officers Protect People*, Carol Greene *Police Patrol*, Katherine K. Winkleman *Police Stations*, Jason Cooper *Policeman Small*, Lois Lenski *Sammy, Dog Detective*, Coleen Stanley Bare *Someone Always Needs a Policeman*, David Brown *The Trouble with Granddad*, Babette Cole *Who Blew That Whistle?*, Leone Adelson
Fingerplay:	**Traffic Policeman.** (Source: *Finger Frolics—Revised*, Liz Cromwell, Dixie Hibner, and John R. Faitel)
Crafts:	**The Funny Police Officer.** Police officers are described to children as the people who should look for when they're lost or in need of help. An officer should never be portrayed as someone to be feared. To help the child have a good feeling about police officers, why not make masks and allow them to act out what they believe the police do. In the book below you will find instructions for making just such a mask out of construction paper, oaktag, markers, and glue. This particular policeman sports a beard and a bobby hat. (Source: *Great Masks to Make*, Robyn Supraner)

If you would like to add more to the craft and expand your career unit, try making the badge, policeman's hat, handcuffs, nightstick, ticket book, traffic signs, and traffic lights shown in this source.

(Source: *Be What You Want to Be!*, Phyllis and Noel Fiarotta)

Career Dominoes.
For Career Day or any other time you are working on your community helpers unit, you will find this craft a fun way to pull the unit together. Supply the children with precut cardboard dominoes approximately four inches by six inches with the two sections already marked off. Ask them to look through magazines and cut out illustrations of the different types of careers you have discussed along with pictures of items those professionals would need to do their work (e.g., badge, gun, etc.). Have them paste their pictures randomly on the domino pieces. I suggest laminating them so they will last longer. Now you are ready to play an amusing game of Career Dominoes and see how much the children really remember from the lesson.

Activities: **Police Safety Program.**
Invite the local police department to send representatives to speak to the children about their job and to encourage the children to look to the police for help when they need it. The local police departments can usually be counted on to speak to parents and children at programs on the following topics:
- Strangers
- Bicycle and Traffic Safety
- Dangers of Drugs
- Fingerprinting of Children

Officer for a Day.
Try emphasizing a positive nature when discussing our community helpers. Designate a child as the Officer of the Day. Set up the Officer of the Day with the tools of the trade including a badge, hat, and ticket book. Instruct the child that it is his or her duty to present a ticket as an award to children who do well (e.g., put away toys, take turns, etc.) rather than for doing bad things. Find this and other community helper activities in this source.

(Source: *Kids and Communities*, Kathy Darling)

Songs: (Audio) "I'm a Policeman"
  (Source: *Disney's Children's Favorites, Vol. 1*)
(Book) "The Traffic Cop"
  (Source: *This Is Music: Book 2*, William R. Sur)

38 Character Traits: Cleanliness

Relate to: *National Clean-off-Your-Desk Day (second Monday in Jan.): A special day for desk workers (this may include school students) to clean off their desks to make way for the new year's work.*

Videos: *Alexandria's Clean-up, Fix-up Parade*
The Berenstain Bears and the Messy Room
Clean Your Room, Harvey Moon
Franklin Is Messy
Harry the Dirty Dog

Books: *The Backwards Watch*, Eric Houghton
Bernard's Bath, Joan Elizabeth Goodman
Casey in the Bath, Cynthia DeFelice
Clean Your Room, Harvey Moon!, Pat Cummings
Fritz and the Mess Fairy, Rosemary Wells
The Little Boy Who Loved Dirt and Almost Became a Superslob, Judith Vigna
Messy Bessey's School Desk, Patricia and Frederick McKissack
Mrs. Potter's Pig, Phyllis Root
No More Water in the Tub!, Tedd Arnold
Pigsty, Mark Teague
The Raggly, Scraggly, No-Soap, No-Scrub Girl, David F. Birchman
Soap and Suds, Diane Paterson
Tidy Titch, Pat Hutchins
To the Tub, Peggy Perry Anderson
Tumble Tower, Anne Tyler
When the Fly Flew in . . . , Lisa Westberg Peters

Fingerplay: **Rub-a-Dub-Dub.**
A nice variation on the song with a child in the bathtub washing up for the night.
    (Source: *Storytimes for Two-Year-Olds, 2nd edition*, Judy Nichols)

Crafts: **Bull's Eye.**
Here's a unique way to get your classroom cleaned up quickly and without any complaints. Take a number of large hoops and have some children hold them up. The remainder of the children will begin to put away all supplies used when the music begins but must travel through the bull's eyes (hoops)

to get to where the items belong. Larger items can be carried by two children.

(Source: *The Cooperative Sports and Game Book*, Terry Orlick)

Dirty or Clean Dishwasher Magnet.
This is something that Mom or Dad can use on their dishwasher to remind them that dishes need to be cleaned. Children decorate a simple cardboard circle with fabric scraps or other items of choice. They cut a second circle and write the simple message CLEAN on one side and DIRTY on the other, then fasten this circle to the decorated circle. A magnet on the back will help place the creation in a strategic place on the dishwasher. No dishwasher? Maybe Mom can put it on the child's bedroom door to give a message.

(Source: *Gifts to Make for Your Favorite Grown-up*, Kathy Ross)

Activities:

Bathtime Memory Game.
Try a familiar memory game with the children. Collect a number of items that would be easily recognizable to the children from their bathtime experiences. Display them and discuss their uses. Follow this with a memory exercise by removing one or more objects; ask the children to open their eyes and identify the missing objects and their use.

(Source: *More Picture Book Story Hours: From Parties to Pets*, Paula Gaj Sitarz)

Clothespin Fumble.
Try this game that will train a child to help hang the clean clothes for Mom. It requires some dexterity, especially when the child is blindfolded. With a clothesline spread across the room let the blindfolded child take a clothespin and try to put it on the clothesline with the use of only one hand.

(Source: *Making Children's Parties Click*, Virginia W. Musselman)

Songs:

(Audio) "Soap in My Eye"
(Source: *Meet the Dinner Dogs*)
(Book) "Wash My Hands"
(Source: *The Giant Encyclopedia of Circle Time and Group Activities for Children 3 to 6*, Kathy Charner)

39 Character Traits: Helpfulness

Relate to:	*National Volunteer Week (April 19–25): This is a week planned to honor those people who give of their time and skills to help others.*

Videos:
Alexandria's Clean-up, Fix-up Parade
The Elves and the Shoemaker
Horton Hatches an Egg
The Little Red Hen
Lyle, Lyle Crocodile

Books:
Androcles and the Lion, Janet Stevens
Big Help!, Anna Grossnickle Hines
Can I Help?, Marilyn Janovitz
Chestnut Cove, Tim Egan
Helpful Betty to the Rescue, Michaela Morgan
Helpin' Bugs, Rosemary Lonborg
Hopper's Treetop Adventure, Marcus Pfister
Horton Hatches an Egg, Dr. Seuss
Is Susan Here?, Janice May Udry
It's Your Turn, Roger!, Susanna Gretz
The Little Red Hen, Paul Galdone
One Duck Stuck, Phyllis Root
One Up, One Down, Carol Snyder
Sophie and Jack Help Out, Judy Taylor
You and Me, Little Bear, Martin Waddell

Fingerplay:
Helping is Fun.
(Source: *Everyday Circle Times*, Liz and Dick Wilmes)

Crafts:
Helping Hands Napkin Holder.
Napkin holders are always something a mom can use with pride to the delight of her child. Use the base of a box for the stand. Children can trace their hands out of beautifully designed material for the sides. At every mealtime the children can set the table with a sure sign that they helped, when their own hands are seen holding the napkins.
(Source: *Gifts to Make for Your Favorite Grown-up*, Kathy Ross)

Chore Charts.
Getting children to help around the house or classroom is a chore in itself. Here's an activity that will make children want to help out. Have the children list all the things they can assist

their parents with and then cut out pictures that illustrate these activities. Paste these pictures to the inside lid of an egg carton above each hole. Children can monitor their progress in being helpful by filling the egg carton holes with beans, buttons, or other items for each time they perform that particular activity. Similar chore charts are offered in the source.

(Source: *Purple Cow to the Rescue*, Ann Cole, Carolyn Haas, and Betty Weinberger.)

Activities: **Blizzard.**

This is a great lesson in communication and caring for everyone. Two children at a time are lost in a snowstorm and one is snow-blind. Have the child who can see lead his or her snow-blind friend through the storm to safety. Add some extra challenges such as struggling through a tunnel (hoops) or going under a log (bench).

With older children you may even wish to add another obstacle. Tell the children they can't touch their friend but can only give verbal instructions from their airplane. This is a really enjoyable event for all.

(Source: *The Cooperative Sports and Games Book*, Terry Orlick)

Family Chores.

Initiate a discussion among the children about different types of chores that family members are responsible for in their home. Be sure to steer children into including nontraditional roles in the family also (Dad babysits, Mom does plumbing, etc.).

After the discussion begin a pantomime session where children mimic these chores for the class to guess. An excellent list of suggestions is supplied in the book cited here.

(Source: *More Picture Book Story Hours: From Parties to Pets*, Paula Gaj Sitarz)

Songs: (Audio) "The More We Are Together"
   (Source: *Toddlers Sing 'N Learn*)
(Book) "All Work Together"
   (Source: *Woody's 20 Grow Big Songs*, Woody and Marjorie Mazia Guthrie)

40 Character Traits: Kindness

Relate to:	*Random Acts of Kindness Week (Monday through Sunday including Feb. 14): This is a campaign to use the power of Random Acts of Kindness to counterbalance the violence in this world.*

Videos:
Alejandro's Gifts
Andy and the Lion
Horton Hatches an Egg
Mufaro's Beautiful Daughter
The Story of Jumping Mouse

Books:
Androcles and the Lion, Janet Stevens
The Best Night Out with Dad, Lisa McCourt
Clotilda, Jack Kent
The Happy Hunter, Roger Duvoisin
I Know a Lady, Charlotte Zolotow
If You Give a Mouse a Cookie, Laura Numeroff
Jennie's Hat, Ezra Jack Keats
Red Hen and Sly Fox, Vivian French
Sam and the Lucky Money, Karen Chinn
The Seal and the Slick, Don Freeman
Three Good Blankets, Ida Luttrell
Three Kind Mice, Vivian Sathie
Tree of Birds, Susan Meddaugh
Why Christmas Trees Aren't Perfect, Richard H. Schneider
Wolf's Favor, Fulvio Testa

Fingerplay:
Being Kind.
(Source: *Finger Frolics—Revised*, Liz Cromwell, Dixie Hibner, and John R. Faitel)

Crafts:
Certificates of Kindness.
After a discussion on what services the children can perform to be kind and helpful to their parents, try creating a certificate booklet. Let the children select two or three services they would like to do for their parents (e.g., sweep the floor, make a bed, help Dad wash the car, etc.). Distribute drawing paper and crayons to the children and allow them to draw themselves doing chores for their parents. If the children are of preschool age, you will have to write the accompanying phrase describing the pictures (e.g., wash the dishes, make my bed).

After each drawing is done, design a cover and staple the coupons together along with a note to the parents:

Dear Mom and Dad:

You always help me with so many things. Now it's my turn. Here are some coupons for you to use when you need help. Pick the one you need help with, and give it to me. I promise to help you then.

Love,

Treasure Box.

Ask each child to bring to class a sturdy box such as a shoe box or tissue box to create their treasure box. Supply them with any number of materials (e.g., cloth, paper, buttons, pasta, pictures from magazines, etc.) to decorate the exterior of the box. You may want to encourage the child to work with a particular theme.

Later have the class fill the box with things that they think will make people feel good. Take a class trip and deliver these treasure boxes to a nursing home or similar place where you want to bring some cheer.

(Source: *The Month by Month Treasure Box*, Sally Patrick, Vicky Schwartz, and Pat LoPresti)

Activities:

Come On and Join in the Game.

A physical activity song that allows the children time for movement during the storyhour session.

(Source: *The Fireside Book of Children's Songs*, Marie Winn)

Blizzard.

This is a great lesson in communication and caring for everyone. Two children at a time are lost in a snowstorm and one is snowblind. Have the child who can see lead his or her snowblind friend through the storm to safety. Add some extra challenges, such as a tunnel (loops) or going under a log (bench). With older children you may even wish to add another obstacle. Tell the children they can't touch their friend but can only give verbal instructions from their airplane. This is a really enjoyable event for all.

(Source: *The Cooperative Sports and Games Book*, Terry Orlick)

Songs:

(Audio) "Be Kind to Your Neighborhood Monsters"
(Source: *Monster Melodies*)
(Book) "Be Kind to Your Webfooted Friends"
(Source: *The Fireside Song Book of Birds and Beasts*, Jane Yolen)

41 Character Traits: Laziness

Relate to: *National Relaxation Day (Aug. 15): Although we don't want to be completely lazy, everyone needs some time of the year for total relaxation and rejuvenation. This is a day for just that event.*

Videos: *The Ant and the Grasshopper*
Horton Hatches an Egg
The Little Red Hen
Rip Van Winkle

Books: *The Boy of the Three-Year Nap*, Dianne Snyder
Famous Seaweed Soup, Antoinette Truglio Martin
How Leo Learned to Be King, Marcus Pfister
I Can't Get My Turtle to Move, Elizabeth Lee O'Donnell
Jamie O'Rourke and the Big Potato, Tomie dePaola
Lazy Jack, Tony Ross
Lazy Lion, Mwenye Hadithi
The Little Red Hen, Paul Galdone
The Man Who Was Too Lazy to Fix Things, Phyllis Krasilovsky
The Pixy and the Lazy Housewife, Mary Calhoun
Roses Sing on New Snow: A Delicious Tale, Paul Yee
Shenandoah Noah, Jim Aylesworth
Slobcat, Paul Geraghty
Tom's Tail, Arlene Dubanevich
A Treeful of Pigs, Arnold Lobel

Fingerplay: **The Funny, Fat Walrus.**
(Source: *Too Many Rabbits and Other Fingerplays*, Kay Cooper)

Crafts: **Wacky Door Decree.**
Kids who are feeling a little lazy and want to be alone can make these wacky doorknob hangers to keep people away. Some suggested messages are offered in this delightful craft book. Clip letters from newspapers or magazines for variety.
(Source: *60 Super Simple Crafts*, Holly Herbert)

Jumping Grasshopper.
The class can use this source to make a familiar lazy character from the story *The Grasshopper and the Ants*. The grasshopper is constructed from half of an egg carton and a rubber ball

placed inside it to help it hop across the room. This is a nice craft to do in conjunction with this favorite fairy tale.
(Source: *Crafts for Kids Who Are Wild about Insects*, Kathy Ross)

Activities:

Wake Up, You Lazy Bones (Hunt the Cows).
This source offers a little western dance activity for the children to perform. Words and music are included. One child is selected to be the cowboy or cowgirl and the remainder of the group move slowly around the circle. At selected portions of the song the children will go down on their knees and elbows until they're finally asleep. When the cowboy shouts, "Wake up you lazy bones," they all get up and jump around. Switch places with the cowboy and begin again.
(Source: *What Shall We Do and Allee Galloo!*, Marie Winn)

Story Rhymes—Sleeping Beauty.
Circle games such as this one that include all the children keep the whole class's attention on what they are doing. This is a little rhyme based on the familiar tale of Sleeping Beauty. You will need to select a princess, a wicked fairy, and a prince. The rest of the class will form a circle to be the trees in the forest that grow up around the princess's castle once she has fallen asleep for 100 years.

As the children recite the verse, the characters follow the actions of the song. In the end the prince comes, chops his way through the forest (circle), and takes the princess by the hand and leads her out. The children will like that they don't have to kiss the princess to wake her up. It's a fun action game that will make the children laugh and ask to play it again.
(Source: *The Playtime Treasury*, Pie Corbett)

Songs:

(Audio) "Lazy Lizard"
(Source: *Bananas in Pajamas: Bumping and a-Jumping*)
(Book) "Rebekah"
(Source: *Early in the Morning*, Charles Causley)

42 Circus and Circus Animals

Relate to:	*July 5 is a day to celebrate the birth of one of the greatest showmen of all times, P. T. Barnum, who was responsible for "The Greatest Show on Earth."*

Videos: *Circus Baby*
Curious George Rides a Bike
If I Ran the Circus

Books: *Barnyard Big Top*, Jill Kastner
Bearymore, Don Freeman
The Best Night Out with Dad, Lisa McCourt
The Circus, Heidi Goennel
Clifford at the Circus, Norman Bridwell
Engelbert Joins the Circus, Tom Paxton
Harriet Goes to the Circus, Betsy and Giulio Maestro
Henrietta, Circus Star, Syd Hoff
Henrietta Saves the Show, John Prater
Liverwurst Is Missing, Mercer Mayer
Lottie's Circus, Joan W. Blos
My Mother's Secret Life, Rebecca Emberley
Smallest Elephant in the World, Alvin Tresselt
Zorina Ballerina, Enzo Giannini

Fingerplay: **Ten Circus Wagons.**
(Source: *Finger Frolics—Revised*, Liz Cromwell, Dixie Hibner, and John R. Faitel)

Crafts: **Dancing Clown.**
Precut pieces are suggested for this craft. Pages 46 and 47 of the book listed below can be copied to help make patterns for each of these pieces. A bright and amusing clown can be constructed out of inexpensive materials such as construction paper, tape, markers, glue, and rubberbands. The source will give you instructions along with a full-page, color illustration of how your final product should look. The hands and shoes are connected to the body with rubberbands. A rubberband is also attached to the top of the hat so that you can bounce the clown up and down. I suggest that the top rubberband be connected to a stick for easier handling.
(Source: *Rainy Day Surprises You Can Make*, Robyn Supraner)

Clown Wall Pocket.
A decorative wall hanging for a child to keep his special mementos can be constructed by following the step-by-step illustrations in this source. All that is required are paper plates, crayons, glue, and colored construction paper. An additional page is supplied with nine clown-face pictures that can be enlarged and displayed as examples for the children to follow.
(Source: *Paper Plate Art*, Maxine Kinney)

Activities:

Be a Clown.
As suggested in the source cited, you might wish to connect this song and activity with a session of face painting to make the children look and feel like clowns.

With the use of the music and verses given in the book, the children will get a chance to act like clowns. The song also lends itself easily to further suggestions from the children on what clowns do. Often they can come up with better suggestions than we can, and it makes for a more enjoyable program.
(Source: *Game-Songs with Prof. Dogg's Troupe*, Harriet Powell)

Pin the Nose on the Clowns.
A new twist on an old party game. Make your own party game but give the children five chances to be a winner. Pin the Tail on the Donkey becomes now Pin the Nose on the Clowns when five paper plates are designed as various clown faces and used for targets on a single wall. Have the children help you create the faces for their own circus celebration.
(Source: *Cups and Cans and Paper Plate Fans*, Phyllis Fiarotta and Noel Fiarotta)

Songs:

(Audio) "The Circus Is Coming to Town"
(Source: *Old MacDonald Had a Farm and Other Favorite Animal Songs*)
(Book) "The Man on the Flying Trapeze"
(Source: *The Man on the Flying Trapeze*, Robert Quackenbush)

43 Clocks/Telling Time

Relate to:	*Daylight Savings Time (last Sunday in March): Explain to children the concept of resetting their clocks with "spring" forward and "fall" back.*

Videos:	*Dorothy and the Clock*
Books:	*Around the Clock with Harriet*, Betsy and Giulio Maestro *The Backwards Watch*, Eric Houghton *Bear Child's Book of Hours*, Anne Rockwell *Big Time Bears*, Stephen Krensky *Brown Rabbit's Day*, Alan Baker *The Completed Hickory Dickory Dock*, Jim Aylesworth *Get Up and Go!*, Stuart J. Murphy *Leroy and the Clock*, Juanita Havill *The Oak Tree*, Laura Jane Coats *The Snowman Clock Book*, Raymond Briggs *There's a Cow in the Road*, Reeve Lindbergh *Time*, Carol Thompson *Time to . . .* , Bruce McMillan *Tuesday*, David Wiesner *What Time Is It, Dracula?*, Victor Ambros
Fingerplay:	**Hickory Dickory Dock.** (Source: *Playtime Rhymes*, illustrated by Priscilla Lamont)
Crafts:	**Cookie Sheet Clock.** Using Styrofoam trays from fruit or vegetables and cookie sheets, children can create their own clocks to learn to tell time. Use the clocks for lessons on time as well as for reminding children when something needs to be done. Look for more fun ideas in this great source. (Source: *Creative Fun for 2-to-6 Year Olds: The Little Hands Big Fun Craft Book*, Judy Press) **Tell the Time by the Sun.** Discuss the many ways we can tell time, including the use of a sundial. Have the children make a sundial out of yellow posterboard so it looks like the sun. Cut out a triangle from a three-inch square and paste it standing up on the face of the sundial. To make it into a clock draw a line at the edge of the shadow on the clock as each hour passes. (Source: *The Ultimate Show-Me-How Activity Book*)

Activities: **What's the Time, Mr. Wolf?**
Indicate a safe area for the children. One child is selected to be the wolf, standing with his back to the others. While he wanders through the room the other children follow closely, teasing him by asking "What's the time, Mr. Wolf?" He may say any number of times, until he suddenly turns and growls, "Dinnertime." The children scatter, hoping to get home safely before being tagged. Other variations are also offered.
(Source: *The Picture Rulebook of Kids Games*, Roxanne Henderson)

Tick Tock.
After hiding a ticking alarm clock somewhere in the room, instruct the children to locate it. They may begin when you say "Tick" but must freeze when you say "Tock." Guess what they say when they find it? This game and other related activities can be found in the source.
(Source: *The Giant Encyclopedia of Theme Activities for Children 2 to 5*, Kathy Charner)

Songs: (Audio) "Jolly Clock"
(Source: *Can Cockatoos Count by Twos?*)
(Book) "Ticking Clocks"
(Source: *Flying Around: 88 Rounds and Partner Songs*, David Gadsby and Beatrice Harrop)

44 Clothing

Relate to:	*No Socks Day (May 8): Here's a silly, but fun, day. Give up wearing socks for one day and save Mom some laundry to do.*

Videos:	*Charlie Needs a Cloak* *Corduroy* *The Emperor's New Clothes* *The Hat* *A Pocket for Corduroy*
Books:	*Bird's New Shoes*, Chris Riddell *Bit by Bit*, Steve Sanfield and Susan Gaber *Caps for Sale*, Exphyr Slobodkina *A Fox Got My Socks*, Hilda Offen *The Jacket I Wear in the Snow*, Shirley Neitzel *Jennie's Hat*, Ezra Keats *Jeremy's Muffler*, Laura F. Nielsen *Katy No-Pocket*, Emmy Payne *The Long Red Scarf*, Nette Hilton *Max's New Suit*, Rosemary Wells *The Mitten*, Jan Brett *The Most Beautiful Kid in the World*, Jennifer A. Ericsson *Mrs. Toggle's Beautiful Blue Shoe*, Robin Pulver *My Best Shoes*, Marilee Robin Burton *Tan Tan's Hat*, Kazua Iwamura
Fingerplay:	**My Zipper Suit.** (Source: *Finger Frolics—Revised*, Liz Cromwell, Dixie Hibner, and John R. Faitel)
Crafts:	**String a Necklace or Headbands.** Children enjoy stringing various items. Beaded necklaces can be made by stringing macaroni, paper, or straw beads on kite string. The straw beads can be cut in various lengths from drinking straws and colored with markers. For a better variety of shapes and sizes, try shapes from construction paper and string them through holes in the center. Macaroni also is available in different sizes and shapes. To add color you might try food coloring. Headbands lend themselves to more creative decorations as is illustrated in the book indicated here. (Source: *Sticks and Stones and Ice Cream Cones*, Phyllis Fiarotta)

Stegosaurus Hat.
Here's a hat that children will never want to take off. Dinosaurs are enjoyed by children of all ages. Here they can become a stegosaurus themselves with this paper plate hat that stretches all the way down their backs.
(Source: *Dandy Dinosaurs*, Better Homes and Gardens)

Activities: **The Mulberry Bush.**
The music book listed here will supply you with the sheet music for this song that can be played by piano or guitar. All eight verses are supplied: the basic verse and seven verses pertaining to the days of the week. Have the children repeat the verses you sing. When they are comfortable with the words and music, you can add the body motions for acting out the verse.
(Source: *Singing Bee!: A Collection of Favorite Children's Songs*, Jane Hart)

Marathon Dressing.
Relay races are all the rage with young children. Try this elementary dressing race. With a large collection of oversized shirts piled in the middle of the room, the two teams can race to get on the most clothes properly before the whistle blows.

Older students can use an altered version, with each member passing the shirt down the line after trying it on, then moving to the next shirt, and on and on.

This is a nice game to play after reading *I Can Dress Myself* by Shigeo Watanabe.
(Source: *The Big Book of Kids' Games*, Tracy Stephen Burroughs)

Song: (Audio) "Mary Wore Her Red Dress"
(Source: *American Folk Songs for Children*)

45 Clothing: Hats

Relate to: *Fall Hat Week (Sept. 13–20): A week in which people put away their straw hats for felt or fabric hats. Groups and businesses are challenged to develop hat-related events.*

Videos: *Caps for Sale*
The Cat in the Hat (Dr. Seuss Showcase II)
The Hat
How the Trollusk Got His Hat (Mercer Mayer Stories)
Madeline and the Easter Bonnet

Books: *Casey's New Hat*, Tricia Gardella
Catch That Hat!, Emma Chichester Clark
Felix's Hat, Catherine Bancroft
The 500 Hats of Bartholomew Cubbins, Theodor Geisel
The Horse with the Easter Bonnet, Catherine Wooley
Jennie's Hat, Ezra Keats
Lucy's Summer, Donald Hall
Martin's Hat, Jean Blos
The Purple Hat, Tracey Campbell Pearson
Tan Tan's Hat, Kazuo Iwamura
Ten Cats Have Hats, Jean Marzollo
This Is the Hat, Nancy Van Laan
Uncle Harold and the Green Hat, Judy Hindley
Uncle Lester's Hat, Howie Schneider
Whose Hat?, Margaret Miller

Fingerplay: **Special Hats.**
(Source: *Rhymes for Learning Times*, Louise Binder Scott)

Crafts: **Party Hats.**
Dress-up and pretend are common activities with children at the preschool age level. Party hats can be designed by using paper plates or foil pie plates for the base. Trimmings for the hats can be left largely to the imagination, but you will have to guide some of the children. Use materials you have available, such as crepe paper, stickers, doilies, ribbon, yarn, feathers, or even buttons.
(Source: *I Saw a Purple Cow*, Ann Cole, Carolyn Haas, Faith Bushnell, and Betty Weinberger)

Newspaper Hats.

Make various-style large hats from old newspapers. See the source cited here for illustrations on how to size the hat for each child's head using masking tape. After sizing and designing the hats, send the children to the design table to decorate it themselves. At the design table supply easily obtainable materials such as feathers, buttons, markers, stickers, etc.

(Source: *Making Cool Crafts and Awesome Art*, Roberta Gould)

Activities:

Musical Hats.

This is a variation on Musical Chairs, with all players sitting in a circle. All players are given a hat except one. While the music plays, everyone passes the hats around the circle trying each one on in turn. When the music stops the child without a hat on is out of the game.

The choice of music is left solely to your choice depending on the age of the group. Suggestion: Try nursery songs they are all familiar with so they can sing along.

(Source: *500 Games*, Peter L. Cave)

Hat Grab.

This game is a simple elimination game with the group divided into two teams, the "grabbers" and the "defenders." Have your teams line up on opposite sides of the room with one or more hats placed scattered in the area between them. The goal is for the grabbers to successfully run onto the field, grab a hat, and return to their line before being tagged. If they are tagged they are eliminated. There should only be one grabber and defender on the field at any time.

(Source: *Hopscotch, Hangman, Hot Potato, and HaHaHa*, Jack Maguire)

Songs:

(Audio) "The Mexican Hat Dance"
(Source: *Children's All-Time Rhythm Favorites*)
(Book) "My Tall Silk Hat"
(Source: *Do Your Ears Hang Low?*, Tom Glazer)

46 Concepts: Color

Relate to: *Flag Day (June 14, 1834): The day Congress enacted legislation designating the United States flag to have 13 stars and 13 alternating white and red stripes.*

Videos: *Freight Train*
Harold and the Purple Crayon

Books: *The Big Orange Splot*, Daniel Pinkwater
The Chalk Box Story, Don Freeman
The Color Box, Dayle Ann Dodds
Growing Colors, Bruce McMillan
The Mixed-up Chameleon, Eric Carle
Mr. Pine's Purple House, Leonard Kessler
My Yellow Ball, Dee Lillegard
The Orange Book, Richard McGuire
The Pink Party, Maryann MacDonald
Put Me in the Zoo, Robert Lopshire
Samuel Todd's Book of Great Colors, E. L. Konigsburg
Teeny, Tiny Mouse: A Book about Colors, Laura Leuck
They Thought They Saw Him, Craig Kee Strete
Thinking about Colors, Jessica Jenkins
Tom's Rainbowwalk, Catherine Anholt
What Color Was the Sky Today?, Miela Ford

Fingerplay: **Coat of Many Colors.**
(Source: *Finger Frolics 2*, Liz Cromwell Kobe, Dixie Hibner, and John R. Faitel)

Crafts: **Story Pictures.**
In conjunction with *The Chalk Box Story* by Don Freeman listed above, the children may be given black construction paper and colored chalk to create their own picture as they have seen in the story read to them.

These pictures may later be displayed in the library or classroom.

Color Caterpillar.
Build this special-color caterpillar to help each child identify colors. Using a half strip from an egg carton, children can add the caterpillar features and a pull string to make it a toy. Simply cut a number of circles in assorted colors to glue to each section of the caterpillar.

Also found in this source is a gratifying activity in which the children create a rainbow to a song sung to the tune of "The Farmer in the Dell."

(Source: *The Giant Encyclopedia of Circle Time and Group Activities for Children 3 to 6*, Kathy Charner)

Activities: **Parade of Colors.**
The children identify ten colors (blue, red, black, green, yellow, pink, purple, brown, white, and orange). They are each given a card with a color and instructed to march in a circle until their color is mentioned and they are told to either sit down or stand up.

This is a very basic concept activity that young children can handle easily.

(Source: *Learning Basic Skills through Music, Vol. 2*, Hap Palmer)

Call the Colors.
Lay out placemats on the floor of all the colors the children are familiar with. In the caller's bag place four small squares of each of the colors. While each player gets to stand on a color square, the caller will call out a color drawn from the bag. The first to get all four of the colors wins.

You can add a little variety to this game by having the children change places whenever you put music on. They will collect a variety of colors but can only win if they have four of the same color. Of course the caller will need more squares in the caller bag.

(Source: *I Saw a Purple Cow*, Ann Cole, Carolyn Haas, Faith Bushnell, and Betty Weinberger)

Song: (Audio) "Colors in Motion"
(Source: *Can Cockatoos Count by Two's?*)

47 Concepts: Shapes

Relate to: *Driving Safety Week (June 27–July 4): A week to encourage safe driving practices for all. Use this week to speak to children about safe driving practices and discuss shapes in relation to traffic signs they see every day.*

Videos: *Clifford's Fun with Shapes*
The Village of Round and Square Houses

Books: *A Circle Is Not a Valentine*, H. Werner Zimmermann
Circles, Triangles, and Squares, Tana Hoban
The Emperor's Oblong Pancake, Peter Hughes
It Looked Like Spilt Milk, Charles Shaw
Little Cloud, Eric Carle
The Maid and the Mouse and the Odd-Shaped House, Paul O. Zelinsky
The Missing Piece, Shel Silverstein
Round and Around, James Skofield
Shapes, Gwenda Turner
The Shapes Game, Paul Rogers
The Silly Story of Goldie Locks and the Three Squares, Grace Maccarone
So Many Circles, So Many Squares, Tana Hoban
Ten Black Dots, Donald Crews
There's a Square, Mary Serfozo
When a Line Bends . . . A Shape Begins, Rhonda Gowler Greene

Fingerplay: **Draw a Circle.**
(Source: *Finger Frolics—Revised*, Liz Cromwell, Dixie Hibner, and John R. Faitel)

Crafts: **My Shape Book and Felt Pictures.**
After discussing the basic shapes of circle, square, triangle, and rectangle, help the children develop their own book of shapes. Have precut patterns of the shapes available for the children to trace. Then distribute sheets of rough sandpaper on which the children can trace these shapes and cut them out. Some children will need help with the cutting while others will be able to accomplish this task alone. Have all the sandpaper shapes mounted on colored construction paper and stapled together with a decorative cover to form the child's own shape book. The result is a book in which a child can recognize and

feel the shapes discussed and later learn the terms printed under each shape.

Or, make a felt board for each child by gluing a piece of black felt 9 inches by 12 inches to a piece of cardboard the same size. Give each child various pieces of light-colored felt cut in the basic shapes discussed. Using these pieces, demonstrate how to design a picture with them while the children copy it or design their own.

(Source: *More Beginning Crafts for Beginning Readers*, Alice Gilbreath)

Shape Turkey.
This particular craft can be used around Thanksgiving or simply during a lesson on shapes. This large turkey is constructed of six circles of various colors and sizes and a triangle for his beak. It's easy enough to construct and add dimension to the picture.

(Source: *175 Easy-to-Do Thanksgiving Crafts*, Sharon Dunn Umnik)

Activities: **Hoopla.**
Circular rings may be used here to toss on pegs to score points in this game. Suggestion: To adapt this game, shapes may be placed on the gameboard instead of numbers and children may score by ringing the chosen shapes.

(Source: *Games*, Caroline Pitcher)

Mailbox Shape Sorting.
Set up your own post office with mailboxes corresponding to the different shapes the children have learned. Distribute to the class a number of envelopes with shapes on the outside. Let the children take turns delivering their envelopes to the correct post box.

(Source: *The Giant Encyclopedia of Circle Time and Group Activities for Children 3 to 6*, Kathy Charner)

Songs: (Audios) "Everything Has a Shape"
(Source: *Sally the Swinging Snake*)
"Footprints"
(Source: *Monsters and Monstrous Things*)

48 Concepts: Size

Relate to:	*Pandora's Arrival (June 10, 1902): The arrival of Pandora, a giant Panda, at the Bronx Zoo in New York.*

Videos:	*Thumbelina* *Tom Thumb*
Books:	*Big and Little*, Margaret Miller *Big and Little*, Steve Jenkins *The Big Seed*, Ellen Howard *Bigger*, Daniel Kirk *The Biggest Fish in the Sea*, Dahlov Ipcar *Clifford's Puppy Days*, Norman Bridwell *George Shrinks*, William Joyce *Is It Red? Is It Yellow? Is It Blue?*, Tana Hoban *Little Big Mouse*, Nurit Karlin *Little Elephant and Big Mouse*, Benita Cantieni *The Little Giant*, Robert Kraus *Shrinking Mouse*, Pat Hutchins *Sizes*, Jan Pienkowski *The Smallest Stegosaurus*, Lynn Sweat and Louis Phillips *Watch Out! Big Bro's Coming!*, Jez Alborough
Fingerplay:	**Small and Tall.** (Source: *Rhymes for Learning Times*, Louise Binder Scott)
Crafts:	**The Three Bears Puppets.** Have the children trace ready-made patterns or cookie cutters to make the form of the three bears at different sizes. They may then decorate and cut them out by putting on the eyes, nose, and pads for the paws. If time permits, you may cut short pieces of brown yarn to make the body fuzzy. When completed, put the bears on sticks and have the children act out the story of *The Three Bears*. **Giant Sunflower.** A wonderful way to teach the concept of size to children is to have something tangible that they can relate to easily. If you do this lesson in the spring try bringing in a variety of real flowers and show the kids how they grow to a number of different sizes, then bring out the giant sunflower to surprise them with a really large flower.

End the lesson with this wonderful craft in which the children make their own giant sunflowers with construction paper, paper plate centers, and real sunflower seeds in the center.

(Source: *Cut-Paper Play!*, Sandi Henry)

Activities:

Sometimes I'm Tall.

This is a blindfold game. These types of games can be used to help develop a child's hearing perceptions and awareness of the concepts of small and tall. Select one child to be It. Blindfold the child with his or her back to the group. The remainder of the children can either stand in a circle or scatter loosely across the opposite side of the room.

With the guidance of the teacher, the children can recite the given verse (text in book below) about being small and tall as they squat down or stand tall. At the end of the verse the blindfolded child can guess if everyone is tall or small. If he correctly guesses he may change places with another child.

(Source: *Teacher's Handbook of Children's Games*, Marian Jenks Wirth)

Shadow Hunt.

Take the children on a shadow scavenger hunt. Tell them that they will be looking for different kinds of shadows (e.g., littlest, roundest, biggest, oddest looking, etc.). There are many activities you can perform during this hunt. Measure the shadows and let the children trace and label them. Use a camera to take pictures of various shadows to be used later for identification games.

(Source: *Exploring Summer*, Sandra Harkle)

Song:

(Audio) "Thumbelina"
(Source: *Children's Favorite Songs, Vol. 2*)

49 Counting

Relate to:	*First European adding machine invented (Oct. 11, 1887): Demonstrate various calculators and help children test their adding skills.*

Videos:
Lentil
One Was Johnny
Over in the Meadow
Really Rosie
Shout It Out Numbers from 1 to 10

Books:
Counting on the Woods, George Ella Lyon
Harriet Goes to the Circus, Betsy Maestro
How Many, How Many, How Many, Rick Walton
Let's Count It Out, Jesse Bear, Nancy White Carlstrom
More than One, Miriam Schlein
Moving from One to Ten, Shari Halpern
My Little Sister Ate One Hare, Bill Grossman
One Crow: A Counting Rhyme, Jim Aylesworth
One Hungry Baby, Lucy Coats
One, Two, Three Count with Me, Catherine and Laurence Anholt
Roll Over!, Mordicai Gerstein
Ten Black Dots, Donald Crews
Ten Dogs in the Window, Claire Masurel
Ten, Nine, Eight, Molly Bang
Twenty-two Bears, Claire Bishop
Willy Can Count, Anne Rockwell

Fingerplay:
Tall Fence Posts.
(Source: *Rhymes for Learning Times*, Louise Binder Scott)

Crafts:
I Wonder . . . How Many Petals Do Flowers Have?
This is a simple sponge art craft. Utilize old sponges cut in the shape of flower petals and poster paint to create delightfully colorful flowers for your classroom. Indicate to each child how many petals he or she will need to complete the project. Crayons can be used for making stems and leaves. At the completion of the project go back and count together to see if there are enough petals.
(Source: *Play and Find Out about Math*, Janice Van Cleave)

**Craft and
Activity:**

Dominoes.

Dominoes is a simple enough game to play with children three to five years of age. It has the advantage of being a game that can be played in a quiet area and with as many children as you like. The children can be helped in making their own set of dominoes in numerous ways:

- Use cut pieces of cardstock or cardboard and use colored sticker dots to add color to each.
- Using the same background, cut sandpaper for dots so that they can be felt as well as seen.
- In place of dots cut out numerals in different colored paper to be glued to the dominoes.
- If you don't want the children to make their own set, have them cooperate in making one giant set for the library or classroom using posterboard. Let each domino be one foot by two feet in size. They might wish to paint on the dots or numerals.

Activity:

Number Charades.

Create two bags, one named "Number Bag" and the other "Action Bag." Put numbers on slips of paper for the first bag, and actions to be performed on slips of paper for the second bag. Each child will select one paper from each bag and perform the action the number of times indicated.

(Source: *Math Play! 80 Ways to Count and Learn*, Diane McGowan and Mark Schrooten)

Songs:

(Audio) "On the Count of Five"
(Source: *Sally the Swinging Snake*)
(Book) "One, Two, Three, Four, Five"
(Source: *Sing Hey Diddle, Diddle*, Beatrice Harrop)

50 Days of the Week, Months of the Year

Relate to:	*International Calendar Awareness Month (Dec.): A time to illustrate the importance of the calendar in our life and discover its history.*

Videos:
Chicken Soup with Rice
One Monday Morning
Really Rosie
The Twelve Months

Books:
Bear Child's Book of Special Days, Anne Rockwell
The Cats of Mrs. Calamari, John Stadler
Come Out and Play Little Mouse, Robert Kraus
How Do You Say It Today, Jesse Bear?, Nancy White Carlstrom
January Rides the Wind: A Book of Months, Charlotte F. Otten
Jasper's Beanstalk, Nick Butterworth and Mick Inkpen
Lentil Soup, Joe Lasker
My Best Shoes, Marilee Robin Burton
No Bath Tonight, Jane Yolen
October Smiled Back, Lisa Westberg Peters
The Story of May, Mordicai Gerstein
The Tale of Georgie Grub, Jeanne Willis
The Turning of the Year, Bill Martin, Jr.
The Very Hungry Caterpillar, Eric Carle
When This Box Is Full, Patricia Lillie
Wise Owl's Days of the Week, Jane Belk Moncure

Fingerplay: **During this Week.**
    (Source: *Rhymes for Learning Times*, Louise Binder Scott)

Crafts: **Calendar Bingo.**
Bingo is a favorite game for many people and this simple game can be adapted by using the days of the week. The boards can be made of cardstock or posterboard. Replace the letters B-I-N-G-O with the words for the days of the week. Since you only have five letters in Bingo to be replaced you might want to differentiate between weekdays and weekend days.

For children just learning to recognize the days of the week, have parts made up beforehand and ask them to copy the sample boards. Bingo chips can be any number of objects such as buttons, pebbles, pennies, etc.

Owl Calendar.
Have the children make special calendars as gifts to their parents on a special day in their families. With the use of reproducible patterns in this book the child can design a colorful owl who has a calendar dangling just below the branch he's sitting on. This calendar can be hung anywhere in the home for all to enjoy and make use of every day.
(Source: *Holiday Gifts and Decorations Kids Can Make (for Practically Nothing)*, Jerome C. Brown)

Activities: **Calendar Toss.**
The gameboard for this activity is obviously a page from a calendar. If you feel that the calendars you have available make too small a board, you might want to make a larger version using a piece of large posterboard.

Place the board on the floor and give each child a given number of markers to toss on the board. The markers can be pebbles, buttons, etc. The game can be played any number of ways:
- Have young children try to hit a particular date.
- Have older children try to add up the dates hit for the highest score total.
- Try dividing teams to hit odd or even numbers.

(Source: *I Saw a Purple Cow*, Ann Cole, Carolyn Haas, Faith Bushnell, and Betty Weinberger)

Monday, Tuesday.
This is a British ball game that can be played by seven people at a time in a large area. Each child becomes a part of the week by selecting a name day for himself. The object of the game is to avoid being hit by the ball thrown by the day that's It. Skills include listening skills, catching and throwing if your day is called. For young children I suggest dodge balls or nerf balls.
(Source: *The Marshall Cavendish Illustrated Guide to Games Children Play Around the World: Ball Games*, Ruth Oakley)

Songs: (Audio) "Tell Me in the Morning"
(Source: *Patriotic and Morning Time Songs*)
(Book) "Round the Mulberry Bush"
(Source: *Singing Bee!: A Collection of Favorite Children's Songs*, Jane Hart)

51 Dinosaurs

Relate to: *Month of the Dinosaur (Oct.): To promote the scientific awareness of dinosaurs and our past.*

Videos: *Danny and the Dinosaurs*
Dazzle the Dinosaur
Patrick's Dinosaurs
The Mysterious Tadpole

Books: *Albert Goes Hollywood*, Henry Schwartz
Dad's Dinosaur Day, Diane Dawson Hearn
Daniel's Dinosaurs, Mary Carmine
Derek the Knitting Dinosaur, Mary Blackwood
Dinosaur Island, Max Haynes
Dinosaur Questions, Bernard Most
Dinosaurs Do's and Don'ts, Jean Polhamus
Four and Twenty Dinosaurs, Bernard Most
If the Dinosaurs Came Back, Bernard Most
It's Probably Good Dinosaurs Are Extinct, Ken Raney
Mitchell Is Moving, Marjorie Sharmat
Quiet on Account of Dinosaurs, Catherine Woolley
The Smallest Stegosaurus, Lynn Sweat and Louis Phillips
What Did the Dinosaurs Eat?, Wilda Ross
What Happened to Patrick's Dinosaurs?, Carol Carrick

Fingerplay: **Ten Huge Dinosaurs.**
        (Source: *Rhymes for Learning Times*, Louise Binder Scott)

Crafts: **Scale a Dinosaur.**
There are a number of types of dinosaurs that children can be introduced to with hard shells, scales, or spikes. Choose one of these types and have a form run off on cardstock for the children. Give them paper to cut out scales that can then be glued to the body. If time permits, you might want to do a variety of dinosaurs and staple them together for a dinosaur book.

You can also trace the figure of a dinosaur on paper large enough to cover a wall or window. Have the children trace and cut out different colored scales to decorate the creature and then write their names on the scales. Creating a dinosaur could be a project for the whole school or community.

Plate Stegosaurus.
Paper plate crafts can be some of the easiest and cheapest of crafts to deal with in large groups. By using three heavy paper plates, some medium size shells for scales, and toothpicks for tail spikes, children can make a delightful stegosaurus model. It can lead to an exciting unit and this source has a number of crafts for a variety of dinosaurs.
(Source: *Crafts for Kids Who Are Wild about Dinosaurs*, Kathy Ross)

Activity:

Dizzy Dinosaurs.
This game is similar to Musical Chairs but with a slight twist. Again have one less chair than players in a single group, but there are a couple of groups this time. The class can be divided into groups of their favorite dinosaurs. When the person who is It calls out the name of the dinosaur all (including It) scramble for the chairs. Obviously one will be left standing. Many more activities, crafts, and foods related to dinosaurs can be found in this source.
(Source: *The Children's Party Handbook*, Alison Boteler)

Activity and Song:

When a Dinosaur's Feeling Hungry.
This is a simple acting-out song. Dinosaurs are an ever popular topic with children of all ages. Here you will find the source for the music and verses to the song "When a Dinosaur's Feeling Hungry." Begin with a discussion on what the children think dinosaurs would like to eat and what they wouldn't like. At this point you might talk about meat-eaters versus plant-eaters.

Insert the children's suggestions in the appropriate spaces in the song, and let the children act as if they are the dinosaurs while they sing the song.
(Source: *Game-Songs with Prof. Dogg's Troupe*, Harriet Powell)

Song:

(Audio) "If I Had a Dinosaur"
(Source: *More Singable Songs*)

52 Dragons

Relate to:	*St. George's Day (April 23): To honor the patron saint of England and the hero of the "George and the Dragon" legend.*

Videos:	*Draghetto* *Dragon Stew* *Frog and Toad Together: Dragons & Giants* (Arnold Lobel Video Showcase) *Pete's Dragon* *Puff the Magic Dragon*
Books:	*The Dragon Pack Snack Attack,* Joel E. Tanis and Jeff Grooters *The Dragon Who Lived Downstairs,* Burr Tillstrom *Elvira,* Margaret Shannon *Everyone Knows What a Dragon Looks Like,* Jay Williams *The Funny Thing,* Wanda Gag *The Glitter Dragon,* Caroline Repchuk *The Last Dragon,* Susan Miho Nunes *The Library Dragon,* Carmen Agra Deedy *The Little Girl and the Dragon,* Else Holmelund Minarik *The Once-Upon-a-Time Dragon,* Jack Kent *The Popcorn Dragon,* Jane Thayer *Raising Dragons,* Jerdine Nolen *The Tale of Custard the Dragon,* Ogden Nash *There's a Dragon in My Sleeping Bag,* James Howe *There's No Such Thing as a Dragon,* Jack Kent *Turnip Soup,* Lynne Born Myers
Fingerplay:	**Little Huey Dragon.** (Source: *Finger Frolics—Revised,* Liz Cromwell, Dixie Hibner, and John R. Faitel)
Crafts:	**All in a Row Fire Breathing Dragon.** Connect a number of paper plates, painted green, to design a dragon body. Check this useful source for suggestions on adding purple paper scales and legs. For a realistic effect use yellow, red, and orange paper flames emitting high out of your dragon's mouth. Children will love to use their new puppets to tell any number of dragon stories to friends and family that visit the class. (Source: *Look What You Can Make with Paper Plates,* Margie Hayes Richmond)

The Dragon Mask.
Children love to pretend they are large, mythical creatures, and dragons are right up there at the top of the list with dinosaurs. Let the children develop their own dragon masks using a large, brown (paper) grocery bag.

Use construction paper to make the dragon's eyes, ears, scales, mouth, and a tongue that hangs out of the mouth. The book by Robyn Supraner gives you two full-page illustrations of how this mask could look.

Upon completion of this craft have the children wear the masks while they play Dragon Tag (described below).
(Source: *Great Masks to Make*, Robyn Supraner)

Activity: **Dragon Tag.**
This game requires at least ten players or more. While four form a chain to become the dragon, they attempt to capture the other players without losing the chain. As each player is tagged (captured), he or she links up with the chain to become part of the dragon.
(Source: *Games*, Anne Rockwell)

Songs: (Audio) "Puff the Magic Dragon"
       (Source: *Car Songs*)
(Book) "Puff the Magic Dragon"
       (Source: *The Reader's Digest Children's Songbook*, William L. Simon)

53 Ecology

Relate to: *World Rainforest Week (Oct. 17–25): Sponsor events to bring public awareness of rainforest destruction and how we can stop its advancement.*

Videos:
Garbage Day!
Giving Thanks
Recycle Rex
Sing-Along Earth Songs
Where the Garbage Goes

Books:
Andy and the Wild Ducks, Mayo Short
The Brave Little Parrot, Rafe Martin
The Caboose Who Got Loose, Bill Peet
Earthsong, Sally Rogers
Edith and the Little Bear Lend a Hand, Dare Wright
Grizzwold, Sydney Hoff
Happy Hunter, Roger Duvoisin
A Most Unusual Lunch, Robert Bender
A Possible Tree, Josephine Haskell Aldridge
The Salamander Room, Anne Mazer
Whale, Judy Allen
What We Can Do About: Litter, Donna Bailey
Where Does the Garbage Go?, Paul Showers
Wild in the City, Jan Thornhill
The World that Jack Built, Ruth Brown

Fingerplay:
Fire, Earth, Water, and Air.
(Source: *Finger Frolics—Revised*, Liz Cromwell, Dixie Hibner, and John R. Faitel)

Crafts:
Egg Carton Wastebasket.
Collect egg cartons (Styrofoam ones, if possible) to make a small wastebasket for the child's room. These can be used as the sides of the basket and can be painted unless you are able to obtain the egg cartons that are already in colors. An aluminum foil pan (the bottom), a plastic bag, and yarn will also be needed. This craft could be followed by having the children go on a walking tour of the grounds to beautify their school, library, or township.
(Source: *Do a Zoom-Do*, Bernice Chesler)

Eco-Envelopes.

Here's a unique idea to help the earth. Recycle old junk mail, calendars, catalogs, etc., by making them into envelopes. These colorful envelopes can actually be used for mail as long as they are not smaller than $3^1/_2" \times 5"$. For exact size, children can trace old envelopes.

(Source: *Ecology Crafts for Kids*, Bobbe Needham)

Activities: **The Litterbug.**

This game is a variation of Duck, Duck, Goose and should be preceded by a discussion on how we are all responsible for keeping our community clean. Have all the children stand in a circle facing inward except one, the Litterbug. The Litterbug walks around the exterior of the circle until he drops a piece of paper, can, or other item behind one child.

The child in the circle who has the "garbage" dropped behind him picks it up and attempts to return it to the Litterbug by tagging him with it before the Litterbug gets around the circle and back to the empty spot. If he succeeds, he returns to the circle; if not, he becomes the Litterbug.

Recycling Relay.

Form two teams, each with a large pile of trash in front of them consisting of paper, plastic, and aluminum items. At the other side of the room are boxes labeled in the same three categories. Each child takes one piece of trash and places it in the appropriate container. The first team to get all the trash in the correct containers wins.

(Source: *Great Parties for Kids*, Nancy Fyke, Lynn Nejam, and Vicki Overstreet)

Song: (Audio) "Stinky Smelly Garbage"
(Source: *Call Me Mr. Kurt*)

54 Emotions

Relate to:	*National Hugging Day (Jan. 21): Hugging is considered very therapeutic. Take this day to encourage hugging instead of hitting.*

Videos:
Disney Presents Mickey Loves Minnie
Jim's Dog Muffins
The Mountains of Love
Owen
There's Something in My Attic

Books:
A Baby Sister for Frances, Russell Hoban
The Bear under the Stairs, Helen Cooper
The Bravest Babysitter, Barbara Greenberg
Even if I Spill My Milk?, Anna Hines
The Frog Who Wanted to Be a Singer, Linda Goss
I Love My Mother, Paul Zindel
I Love You So Much, Carl Norac
I Love You with All My Heart, Noris Kern
I Was So Mad, Norma Simon
The Lady Who Saw the Good Side of Everything, Pat Tap
Let's Talk about Being Shy, Marianne Johnston
Pip's Magic, Ellen Stoll Walsh
The Quarreling Book, Charlotte Zolotow
Sam's Worries, Mary Ann MacDonald
Shy Charles, Rosemary Wells

Crafts:

Candied Heart.
Children enjoy fingerpainting. Imagine how they would enjoy themselves when they can paint using their whole hand. Have the children press both hands into white paint and then onto sheets of red felt. Once the sheets are dry they can easily cut around the hands in the shape of a heart. Back it with vinyl. For a final touch they can glue candied hearts with messages across their creation. Suggest that they present the work to someone they love.
  (Source: *Hand-Shaped Gifts*, Diane Bonica)

Happy/Sad Face Stick Puppets.
The children can construct reversible face puppets to help them display the emotions they feel. Have the children draw a sad face on one side of a paper plate with crayons or markers and a happy face on the opposite side. Give them some yarn to

glue to the top and sides of the paper plate to form the hair. Mount the plate on a Popsicle stick for ease of handling.

Activities: **Feelings.**
During a discussion of how children feel about different situations, the children may use their new mask puppets to demonstrate their answers by holding the puppets up to their faces. As you read some of the books listed on the previous page to the children, let them use their masks to express the feelings of the characters in the tales.

Heart Match-ups.
This is a joyful game that can be played after a lesson on emotions. You will need a number of paper hearts, each cut in two pieces at different angles. Hide them throughout the room so that the children can search and try to match them. Have exactly the same number of parts as children participating, they can find their partner for the next activity by matching their half of the heart with the other person.
        (Source: *Theme-a-saurus*, Jean Warren)

Songs: (Audio) "Magic Penny"
        (Source: *Circle Around*)
    (Book) If You're Happy and You Know it . . . "
        (Source: *The Reader's Digest Children's Songbook*, William L. Simon)

55 Endangered Animals

Relate to: *Save the Rhino Day (May 1): Help stop the slaughter of this pachy-derm who is on the verge of extinction along with many other crea-tures of the world.*

Videos: *Hot Hippo*
               How the Elephant Got His Trunk
               How the Rhinoceros Got His Skin
               Whales
               The White Seal

Books: *Condor's Egg*, Jonathan London
               Do the Whales Still Sing?, Dianne Hofmeyr
               A Garden of Whales, Maggie S. Davis
               Going on a Whale Watch, Bruce McMillan
               Henry's Wrong Turn, Harriet Ziefert
               Hey! Get Off the Train, John Burningham
               Hungry Hyena, Mwenye Hadithi and Adrienne Kennaway
               In Search of the Last Dodo, Ann and Reg Cartwright
               Jaguar, Helen Cowcher
               Jaguar in the Rainforest, Joanne Ryder
               No DoDos: A Counting Book of Endangered Animals, Amanda
                   Wallwork
               Otters under Water, Jim Arnosky
               Rhinoceros Mother, Toshi Yoshida
               A Safe Home for Manatees, Priscilla Belz Jenkins
               Swim the Silver Sea, Joshie Otter, Nancy White Carlstrom
               Tilly and the Rhinoceros, Sheila White Samton

Fingerplay: **Humpback.**
                   (Source: *Move Over, Mother Goose!*, Ruth I. Dowell)

Crafts: **Eagle.**
               This book aids the children in making a picture of the majestic
               eagle. Using paints and handprints they will be able to show
               the eagle with his feathers spread wide and proud. Parents
               may be squeamish about painting the children's palms for this
               craft but the kids will be delighted.
                   (Source: *Hand-Print Animal Art*, Carolyn Carreiro)

               Foot and Hands Macaw.
               Macaws are beautiful parrots who live in the humid rainforests.

They are gradually becoming rare due to habitat loss and hunting and trapping.

Design your own colorful macaw using various colored construction paper, your foot and your hands. Trace your foot for the body, then your hands several times in a selection of colors to develop the bird's beautiful plumage.

(Source: *Crafts for Kids Who Are Wild about Rainforests*, Kathy Ross)

Activities: **The Ocean Is Storm—A Danish Game.**
Mark a number of circles throughout your room and have the children pair off; each pair then stands in a circle. One pair, however, does not stand in a circle; this pair begins the game by becoming the "whale." Each group of children will pretend to be sea animals, and the whale will swim around naming each animal. As the whale does this, the other sea animals will follow behind him. When the whale finally yells, "The ocean is stormy," all scatter for a circle. The remaining pair will be the next whale.

(Source: *Games for Girl Scouts*)

What's My Sign?
Children enjoy playing guessing games and this one is sure to be a hit with all ages. It can be played with many variations, but for this lesson it can be centered around endangered animals. The children have pictures of different animals taped to their backs. By asking their classmates Yes or No questions they can attempt to determine which animal they are. Continue in this manner until they all discover their identity.

(Source: *Charles the Clown's Guide to Children's Parties*, Charles and Linda Kraus)

Songs: (Audio) "Bye Bye Dodo"
(Source: *Billy the Squid*)
(Book) "Big and Little Whale"
(Source: *Circle Time Activities for Young Children*, Deya Brashears and Sharron Werlin Krull)

56 Environment

Relate to:	*Earth Day (April 22): Planned with the express purpose of purifying the oceans, land, and air of this earth for future generations.*

Videos: *Alexandria's Clean-up, Fix-up Parade*
Aunt Ippy's Museum of Junk
Giving Thanks
The Lorax
Sing-Along Earth Songs

Books: *The Air We Breathe!*, Enid Bloome
And Still the Turtle Watched, Sheila MacGill-Callahan
The Berenstain Bears Don't Pollute (Anymore), Stan and Jan Berenstain
Celebrating Earth Day, Janet McDonnell
The Great Trash Bash, Loreen Leedy
It's My Earth, Too, Kathleen Krull
Mother Earth, Nancy Luenn
Mousekin's Lost Woodland, Edna Miller
Rainforest, Helen Cowcher
The Seal and the Slick, Don Freeman
Ten Tall Oak Trees, Richard Edwards
Welcome to the Greenhouse, Jane Yolen
What to Do about Pollution . . . , Anne Shelby
Where Once There Was a Wood, Denise Fleming

Fingerplay: **Recycle.**
(Source: *Finger Frolics 2*, Liz Cromwell Kobe, Dixie Hibner, and John R. Faitel)

Crafts: **Bag Saver.**
Save old tissue boxes (or encourage the children to save them) and recycle them into storage space for Mom's grocery bags. They can paint and decorate them however they wish, but be sure to see this source for an adorable look that's easy to create.
(Source: *Every Day Is Earth Day*, Kathy Ross)

Pebble Jewelry.
With the use of barrettes, old flat bracelets or hair combs, pebbles, and some paint, children can design their own jew-

elry with materials that are recycled. They don't need to add more trash to the environment.

Shell Butterfly Magnets.
Bring or ask children to collect shells and twigs or pipe cleaners to use to make beautiful butterflies when glued together. Each one can be painted differently and magnets put on the back so they can be placed on their refrigerators.

You can even find recipes and other ideas in this source for making your own natural dyes, recycled paper, natural clay and dough, pastes and glues, finger paints, and homemade yarn.

(Source: *EcoArt!*, Laurie Carlson)

Activities:

Three Rs Rangers.
Duplicate and have the children color the recycling reminder notification provided in this source. Next, lead the children in a tour of the school, library, or other location in search of violations; and have the children leave their notices to encourage everyone to reduce, reuse, and recycle.

(Source: *The Best of the Mailbox, Book 1: Preschool/Kindergarten edition*, Margaret Michel)

Nature Bingo.
Distribute to every child a sheet of construction paper folded into nine squares. If possible take the children out of doors so that they can see the many wonders of nature. Ask them to draw a picture of something they see in each of the squares on their paper. Now you are ready to play Nature Bingo!

(Source: *Sunny Days and Starry Nights*, Nancy Fusco Castaldo)

Songs:

(Audio) "Happy Earth Day"
  (Source: *Billy the Squid*)
(Book) "A Monkey in a Great Kapok Tree"
  (Source: *Library Storyhour from A to Z*, Ellen K. Hasbrouck)

57 Ethnic Groups: Native Americans

Relate to: *Native Americans' Day (Oct. 12): Observed in South Dakota in honor of the great Native American leaders of our country. Have your own celebration to honor the Native American tribes of your state.*

Videos: *Dancing with the Indians*
Giving Thanks
Hiawatha
Knots on a Counting Rope
Princess Scargo and the Birthday Pumpkin

Books: *And Still the Turtle Watched*, Sheila MacGill-Callahan
Dancing with the Indians, Angela Shelf Medearis
Dreamcatcher, Audrey Osofsky
Giving Thanks: A Native American Good Morning Message, Chief Jake Swamp
Grandmother's Dreamcatcher, Becky Ray McCain
Green Snake Ceremony, Sherrin Watkins
How the Indians Bought the Farm, Craig Kee Strete and Michelle Netten Chacon
Indian Bunny, Ruth Bornstein
Knots on a Counting Rope, Bill Martin, Jr. and John Archambault
The Legend of Bluebonnet, Tomie dePaola
Little Indian, Peggy Parish
Little Owl Indian, Hetty Beatty
My Navajo Sister, Eleanor Schick
One Little Indian, Grace Moon
Red Fox and His Canoe, Nathaniel Benchley

Fingerplay: **Ten Little Indians.**
(Source: *Games for the Very Young*, Elizabeth Matterson)

Crafts: **Shield Decorations.**
Shields are a special part of the American Indian culture. A simple shield can be made by cutting two large circles (one smaller than the other) out of colored posterboard. Glue the smaller one to the center of the larger, and add string to the back for holding the shield.

Additional ornaments can be added to the inner and outer circles by drawing and cutting out paper arrows, suns, tepees, etc. Feathers can be glued to the bottom to hang below the shield. Have the children make one for each nation you study.

(Source: *Confetti: The Kids' Make-It-Yourself, Do-It-Yourself Party Book*, Phyllis and Noel Fiarotta)

Navajo Hogan.
This is a simple craft that can be completed with very young children. Use one egg cup off an egg carton for the base of your hogan. Leaving one space clear for the entrance, cover the rest of the cup with strips of masking tape overlapping for a bark appearance. Now the children can use brown markers to color the tape. This can lead to an entire Navajo village if you like. Instructions for simple Plains Indian teepees are also available in this source.
(Source: *Kids Celebrate!*, Maria Bonfanti Esche and Clare Bonfanti Braham)

Activities: **Indian Chief.**
Players sit in a circle, facing one another. One child must leave the room or be blindfolded. Another child is made chief. The chief will perform actions (clap hands, etc.) that the tribe must repeat quickly. The first child returns and must determine who the chief is while the group performs.
(Source: *500 Games*, Peter L. Cave)

Warm Up.
Here's a source of Inuit games that are over hundreds of years old. They were part of survival training for Inuit children and can be survival games now for your children as well. Included in this source you will find:
  • Naukah: Sam's Jumping Game
  • Tu Nu Miu: The Backpush
  • Tiliraginik Qiriqtagtut: Jump through Stick
(Source: *Outdoor Fun*, Catherine Ripley)

Songs: (Audio) "Native American Names"
    (Source: *Joining Hands with Other Lands: Multicultural Songs and Games*)
(Book) "Ten Little Indians"
    (Source: *Eye Winker, Tom Tinker, Chin Chopper*, Tom Glazer)

58 Exercise/Physical Fitness

Relate to: *International Walk Days (April 30 and Dec. 26): Walking is believed to be one of the best exercises available to us. This day it is suggested that you leave bikes, cars, etc., at home. Save the environment and get exercise at the same time.*

Videos: *Chicken Fat: The Youth Fitness Video*
Curious George at the Mini Marathon
Elmocize
Fitness Fun with Goofy
How to Exercise
Kids Can Jump!

Books: *Albert the Running Bear's Exercise Book*, Barbara Isenberg and Marjorie Jaffe
Bearobics: A Hip-Hop Counting Book, Vic Parker and Emily Bolam
Bend and Stretch, Jan Ormerod
Bunnies and their Sports, Nancy Carlson
Calico Cat's Exercise Book, Donald Charles
Dinosaurs Alive and Well!, Laurie Krasny Brown and Marc Brown
Norma Jean, Jumping Bean, Joanna Cole
Old Mother Hubbard's Dog Needs a Doctor, John Yeoman and Quentin Blake
Olympics!, B. G. Hennessy
Tiffany Dino Works Out, Marjorie Sharmat
Toddlerobics, Zita Newcome
A Yoga Parade of Animals, Pauline Mainland

Fingerplay: **On My Head.**
(Source: *The Eensy Weensy Spider: Fingerplays and Action Rhymes*, Joanna Cole and Stephanie Calmenson)

Crafts: **Ice Skater.**
There are many forms of exercise that we can introduce to children. Here's one winter sport that many may like. Discuss how ice skating became an Olympic event and how everyone wishes to look good when they perform.
Construct Olympic ice skaters from layers of folded paper plates, chenille sticks, etc. These graceful skaters are bendable and make a great bulletin board display also.
(Source: *Look What You Can Make with Paper Plates*, Margie Hayes Richmond)

Beanbag Ollie.
There are innumerable games you can enjoy with the use of a simple bean bag. Races, tosses, balancing events, and more are all easy enough for young children. Make the events even more fun with bean bags the children have made themselves. Ollie the Owl beanbag is a little different because you can see the beans inside. He is constructed of a plastic sandwich bag, uncooked beans, and paper eyes and nose.
(Source: *Bag of Tricks!*, James Razzi)

Activities:

Run, Run as Fast as You Can.
You will need a large area for this event. Read *The Gingerbread Man* to the children and follow this with acting out the story. Let each child take a part in the story and get to chase the Gingerbread Man throughout the room.

You may even want to have the children do some preliminary limbering-up exercises in anticipation of the great chase.
(Source: *A Piece of Cake*, Gwenn Boechler, Shirley Charlton, and Alice Traer Wayne)

Warm Up.
Here's a source of Inuit games that are over hundreds of years old. They were part of survival training for Inuit children and can now be survival games for your children, too. Included in this source you will find:

- Nauktah: Sam's Jumping Game
- Tu Nu Miu: The Backpush
- Tiliraginik Qiriqtagtut: Jump through Stick

(Source: *Outdoor Fun*, Catherine Ripley)

Songs:

(Audio) "Who's Got the Bean Bag" or "Bean Bag Catch"
(Source: *Bean Bag Activities and Coordination Skills*)
"Chicken Fat"
(Source: *Children's All-Time Rhythm Favorites*)
(Book) "Walk, Walk, Walk"
(Source: *The 2nd Raffi Songbook*, Raffi)

59 Fairy Tales and Nursery Rhymes

Relate to: *Mother Goose Day (May 1): Declared by the Mother Goose Society of Pennsylvania.*

Videos:
The Gingerbread Boy
Harold's Fairy Tale
Henny Penny
Little Red Riding Hood
Rumpelstiltskin
The Ugly Duckling
Wynken, Blynken, and Nod

Books:
Babushka's Mother Goose, Patricia Polacco
Dragon Kites and Dragonflies: A Collection of Chinese Nursery Rhymes, Demi
Frederick's Fables, Leo Lionni
Grandmother's Nursery Rhymes, Nelly Palacio Jaramillo
The Hare and the Tortoise, Jean de LaFontaine
The Hat, Jan Brett
The House that Jack Built, Rodney Peppe
Joe Giant's Missing Boot: A Mothergooseville Story, Toni Goffe
Mama Goose: A New Mother Goose, Liz Rosenberg
Mother Hubbard's Cupboard: A Mother Goose Surprise Book, illustrated by Laura Rader
Once Upon a Time, John Prater
Puss in Boots, Charles Perrault
The Three Bears, Paul Galdone
The Three Billy Goats Gruff, Peter Asbjørnsen
The Three Little Pigs, Paul Galdone

Fingerplay: **Little Jack Horner.**
(Source: *Finger Frolics—Revised*, Liz Cromwell, Dixie Hibner, and John R. Faitel)

Crafts: **The Gingerbread Man.**
Following the readings of *The Gingerbread Man*, let the children make their own man out of construction paper. Distribute brown construction paper and precut patterns or use large cookie cutters of the gingerbread man to be traced. After tracing and cutting these forms out, you can decorate the cookie in one of two suggested ways:
- Use colored chalk as icing to draw clothes on and sticker dots for eyes, nose, and buttons.

- Cut clothes out of paper and glue it on. Use real raisins or small hard candies for eyes, nose, and buttons.

(Note: Emphasize that the food is decorative and not edible.)

Candlestick Craft.
After you teach the children the nursery rhyme "Jack Be Nimble," they can create their own candlestick to jump over. Paper plates and toilet paper rolls make up the main materials needed to develop this craft. Have the children practice the rhyme again, this time acting it out.

(Source: *The Giant Encyclopedia of Circle Time and Group Activities for Children 3 to 6*, Kathy Charner)

Activities:

The Trolls and the Kids.
Read the story of *The Three Billy Boats Gruff* to the children. Discuss key points in the story, such as the rickety bridge, the cave, the troll, etc. You can then prepare to act out the story by constructing a bridge of chairs with poles across them (some low and some high). A cave can be made of a small barrel or a sheet thrown over a table. Use a drum to make the sounds of the trolls. The children may cross the bridge by crawling under the high bars and stepping over the low ones only when the drum sounds. They must freeze in mid-air when the drum stops.

Be careful to avoid awakening the trolls by rattling the poles and then being captured.

(Source: *Teacher's Handbook of Children's Games*, Marian Jenks Wirth)

Blackbirds in a Pie Game.
You can build your own four-and-twenty blackbirds baked in a pie for this nursery rhyme game. Cut 24 little blackbirds out of paper and place in a pie tin. Create the top of the pie from another tin but cut out the pie air holes first. With your pie complete have each child role a die to determine how many birds they may remove from the pie on their turn. If the player forgets to say "May I?" he or she must return the birds. The winner is the person with the most birds.

(Source: *Music Crafts for Kids*, Noel Fiarotta and Phyllis Fiarotta)

Songs:

(Audio) "Nursery Rhyme Medley"
(Source: *Children's Favorite Songs, Vol. 3*)
(Book) "Baa, Baa, Black Sheep"
(Source: *A Collection of Favorite Children's Songs*, Jane Hart)

60 Family Life

Relate to:	*National Family Week (first Sunday and first full week in May): A week to venerate and value the family unit. Spend time with the whole family and remember the importance of each member individually and as part of the family as a whole.*

Videos:
Alexander and the Terrible, Horrible, No Good, Very Bad Day
A Chair for My Mother
I'll Fix Anthony
Peter's Chair
The Relatives Came

Books:
Beware of the Aunts!, Pat Thomson
I Want a Brother or Sister, Astrid Lindgren
Lots of Dads, Shelley Rotner and Sheila M. Kelly
My Baby Brother, Harriet Hains
My Little Sister Ate One Hare, Bill Grossman
The Not-So-Wicked Stepmother, Lizi Boyd
Octopus Hug, Laurence Pringle
Once There Were Giants, Martin Waddell
Sam Is My Half Brother, Lizi Boyd
The Surprise Family, Lynn Reiser
Take Time to Relax, Nancy Carlson
There's a Dragon in My Sleeping Bag, James Howe
What Did Mommy Do before You?, Abby Levine
What Mommies Do Best/What Daddies Do Best, Laura Numeroff
When Daddy Took Us Camping, Julie Brillhart

Fingerplay: **See My Family.**
(Source: *Rhymes for Fingers and Flannel Boards*, Louise Binder Scott and J. J. Thompson)

Crafts: **Nutshell Families.**
Here's a fun craft that children may create after discussing various types of animal families. Collect as many intact walnut shell halves as you are able. If you would like to make a whale family that includes a mother, father, and one baby you will need two walnut shells and one pistachio shell. Paint them gray and add wiggly eyes and a spout using gray or white paper. Connect them together with a long string and the child can pull them across the table. This same setup can be used to make ladybug and other families as well.
(Source: *Crafts from Recyclables*, Colleen van Blaricom)

Prayer Bundle.
This Navajo craft is considered to be a special charm that offers up prayers to watch over the family. Specially shaped hard clay can be used to form sticks representing each member of the child's family. These are wrapped tightly together along with cut lengths of colorful yarn to make the prayer bundle. It makes a colorful and unique family gift.
(Source: *Festival Decorations*, Anne Civardi and Penny King)

Activities:

Sisters.
This game is like a combination of Musical Chairs and Square Dance. Have the children pair off in teams of "sisters" or "brothers." They will form two circles, one inside the other, each facing the opposite direction. When music is played they will begin to move around their respective circles until the music ends, at which time they will try to find each other as quickly as possible, join hands, and squat. The last to squat is out, and of course the final remaining couple is the winner.
(Source: *Games for Girl Scouts, 2nd edition*, Joan McEniry)

Pass in Order.
Select a player to be the "mother" of the group. She calls out to all her children "Pass in order." When the children do not obey but give other responses (see source for responses) the mother says "All of you rush and bring me ____." The children scatter to find the object the mother has requested. The first to do this remains with the mother and the game continues until all have given her a gift.

This would be a wonderful game for Mother's Day activities, too. You might even wish to have mothers visit your classroom that day to help play the game or use this game as a way of presenting to the mothers the gifts the children have made for them.
(Source: *Games the World Around*, Sarah Ethridge Hunt)

Songs:

(Audio) "Five People in My Family"
(Source: *A Sesame Street Celebration*)
(Book) "What Do You Do with a Dirty Family?"
(Source: *A Prairie Home Companion Folk Song Book*, Marcia and Jon Pankake)

61 Family Life: Mothers

Relate to:	*Mother's Day (second Sunday in May): In honor of that wonderful woman who cares for us each and every day.*

Videos: *Are You My Mother?*
                 Monster Mama

Books: *Ask Mr. Bear*, Marjorie Flack
                 Bread and Honey, Frank Asch
                 Earthsong, Sally Rogers
                 Five Minutes Peace, Jill Murphy
                 I Love My Mother, Paul Zindel
                 I Love You, Little One, Nancy Tafuri
                 Joey, Jack Kent
                 Meredith's Mother Takes the Train, Deborah Lee Rose
                 Mommy's Office, Barbara Shook Hazen
                 A Mother for Choco, Keiko Kasza
                 Mother, Mother I Want Another, Maria Polushkin
                 The Way Mothers Are, Miriam Schlein
                 We're Making Breakfast for Mother, Shirley Neitzel
                 What Mommies Do Best, Laura Numeroff
                 When Mama Gets Home, Marisabina Russo

Fingerplay: **My Whole Family.**
                  (Source: *Finger Frolics—Revised*, Liz Cromwell, Dixie Hibner, and John R. Faitel)

Crafts: **Seeded Pencil Holder.**
                  Use any small can to make a beautiful pencil holder for Mom on Mother's Day. Collect various types of seeds (melon, bird, sunflower, etc.) to add variety to the design. Rather than trying to glue the seeds directly to the can itself, Phyllis Fiarotta, in her book, suggests cutting a piece of paper to fit the exterior of the can, then laying the paper flat to add the seeds.

                  A decorated can of this sort can be used for crayons, or even Mom's or Dad's pencils, needles, or more. For step-by-step illustrated directions take a look at Fiarotta's book listed here.

                  (Source: *Snips and Snails and Walnut Whales*, Phyllis Fiarotta)

About Our "Mums."
This cute spring craft will make every Mom smile when she receives it. A large paper flower can be designed with its center having Mom's facial features. On each petal have the child write (or you can write for them) something the child thinks is special about his or her mom.
(Source: *The Best of the Mailbox, Book 2: Preschool/Kindergarten edition*, Margaret Michel)

Activities:

Mother May I?
This simple game can be played with any number of children. One player (Mother) stands at one side of the room while the other players stand at the other side. The leader states how many steps the children may take to try to reach her. The players must ask her, "Mother, may I?" *before* moving or they return to the beginning of their trip.

My Mother's Purse.
This can be played as an alternative to My Grandmother's Trunk. Arrange the children in a circle with a purse in the center. Recite the verse given in the source and let the children complete it by naming an item found in Mom's purse. Other methods of playing this game are supplied here also for the older children in your group.
(Source: *Glad Rags*, Jan Irving and Robin Currie)

Songs:
(Audio) "Furry Blue Mommy of Mine"
(Source: *Put Down that Duckie!*)
(Book) "Mother's Day"
(Source: *God's Wonderful World*, Agnes Leckie Mason and Phyllis Brown Ohanian)
"Mother Hen"
(Source: *Singing Time: A Book of Songs for Little Children*, Satis N. Coleman and Alice G. Thorn)

62 Farms

Relate to:	*National Farm Safety Week (third week in Sept.): Determined by Presidential Proclamation since 1982 to promote safe methods of farming.*

Videos:	*Big Red Barn* *Henny Penny* *The Little Red Hen* *The Little Rooster Who Made the Sun Rise* *Rosie's Walk*
Books:	*Barnyard Lullaby*, Frank Asch *Big Red Barn*, Margaret Wise Brown *Crocus*, Roger Duvoisin *Emmett's Pig*, Mary Stolz *Farmer Duck*, Martin Waddell *Hamilton*, Robert Peck *Heatwave*, Helen Ketteman *Holly's Farm Animals*, Jill Krementz *Inside a Barn in the Country*, Alyssa Satin Capucilli *Over on the Farm*, Christopher Gunson *Rock-a-Bye Farm*, Diane Johnston Hamm *The Rooster Who Lost His Crow*, Wendy Cheyette Lewison *This Is the Farmer*, Nancy Tafuri *When the Rooster Crowed*, Patricia Lillie *Who Took the Farmer's Hat?*, Joan Lexau
Fingerplay:	**The Scarecrow.** (Source: *Little Boy Blue*, Daphne Hogstrom)
Crafts:	**Farm Animals—Sheep.** Discuss different animals that can be found on a farm with the children. In the source below, a large full-page illustration (8^1/$_2$″ × 11″) of a sheep may be duplicated onto cardstock. The children can be given cotton balls to glue to the sheep to give it the soft texture it should have. (Source: *The Kid's Stuff Book of Patterns, Projects, and Plans*, Imogene Forte) **Farm Collage.** Young children love the cutting and pasting that's needed to make collages. Cut a barn out of red construction paper for the

base of your creation. Let the children search for pictures of various farm animals in magazines and other sources and then paste them on the barn frame.

Activities:

Feathers, Feathers.
This game requires a minimum of five players (there is no maximum). The chosen leader begins by saying the name of the game and an animal with feathers (e.g., duck, turkey, etc.). He or she also begins flapping around like a chicken. Other players also flap their arms. The leader continues to call out naming animals with feathers until suddenly including one that doesn't have feathers (e.g., pig, cow, sheep, etc.). Any players still flapping at this point are out of the game.
(Source: *Games*, Anne Rockwell)

Tape the Fleece on the Sheep.
This is a switch on the familiar Pin the Tail on the Donkey game. With a large outline of a sheep on your bulletin board the children can use cottonballs to replace its fleece. Depending on the size of your sheep there should be enough room for all the children to have several chances. Locate this and other active games on farm animals in this source.
(Source: *Everyday Circle Times*, Liz and Dick Wilmes)

Songs:

(Audio) "The Chicken"
     (Source: *All-Time Favorite Dances*)
(Book) "Old MacDonald Had a Farm"
     (Source: *Eye Winker, Tom Tinker, Chin Chopper*, Tom Glazer)

63 Fish

Relate to:	*National Catfish Month (Aug.): To increase awareness of farm-raised catfish. Use this event as a stepping-stone to discussing how fish reproduce.*

Videos:	*The Fisherman and his Wife* *Fish Is Fish* (5 Lionni Classics) *Jonah and the Great Fish* *One Fish, Two Fish, Red Fish, Blue Fish* *Swimmy* (Leo Lionni's Caldecotts)
Books:	*The Biggest Fish in the Sea*, Dahlov Ipcar *Brian Wildsmith's Fishes*, Brian Wildsmith *Carl Caught a Flying Fish*, Kevin O'Malley *Fish and Flamingo*, Nancy White Carlstrom *A Fish Hatches*, Joanna Cole *A Fish in His Pocket*, Denys Cazet *A Fish Out of Water*, Helen Palmer *Flood Fish*, Robyn Eversole *The Fool and the Fish*, Alexander Nikolayevich Afanasyev *Little Fish, Lost*, Nancy VanLaan *Lorenzo*, Bernard Waber *Louis the Fish*, Arthur Yorinks *The Rainbow Fish*, Marcus Pfister *Rosie's Fishing Trip*, Amy Hest *What's It Like to Be a Fish?*, Wendy Pfeffer
Fingerplay:	**Three Little Fish.** (Source: *Finger Frolics—Revised*, Liz Cromwell, Dixie Hibner, and John R. Faitel)
Crafts:	**Paper-Bag Fish.** A small lunch bag, crayons, and colored paper can easily be made into a stuffed fish-one end closed and spread for the tail. Then add scales and fins to the bag. Scales can be made of large stickers or small fins cut out of construction paper and glued on. For an added touch, attach the fish to a string and a stick to form a fishing pole. (Source: *Easy Art Lessons, K–6*, Tyyne Straatviel and Carolyn K. Corl)

Aquarium Collage.

Paper plate crafts are my favorite because they are easy to make and inexpensive. If you work in an area where the money you spend on supplies is a top concern (and who doesn't?), these crafts are the ones to look for.

Here the children can create their own undersea scene on a paper plate using shell macaroni, small pebbles, yarn, and undersea animal stickers. When complete, staple another plate to it with the center removed and then replaced with blue plastic wrap. The effect is astonishing. Don't stop there; see what else this author has to offer for an "Undersea" program.

(Source: *Hit of the Party*, Amy Vangsgard)

Activities:

Catching a Fish.

Divide the room with the use of a rope or tape. Children stand in half of the room (the river) and the leader is the farmer trying to catch fish to stock his or her pond (other half of the room). The leader will give the fish actions to perform while the tom-tom beats, but when it stops everyone must freeze. The last two to freeze must cross the room to the pond and be added to the farmer's stock.

This game can help develop the children's ability to follow directions as well as balance and reactions.

(Source: *Teacher's Handbook of Children's Games*, Marian Jenks Wirth)

Stone Games.

This uncomplicated stone-tossing game will please children. Cut out a number of fish shapes and set them out on the floor in a fish pond. Distribute small stones to the children to toss and try to land on any fish. Make it a little more difficult by painting the stones and telling the children they need to get their stone on the fish with the matching color.

(Source: *Things I Can Make with Stones*, Sabine Lohf)

Songs:

(Audio) "At the Codfish Ball"
(Source: *Whale Watching*)
(Book) "Three Little Fishes"
(Source: *The Reader's Digest Children's Songbook*, William L. Simon)

64 Folktales and Legends

Relate to: *Boone Day (June 7): This is a day to celebrate the day that Daniel Boone, an American frontiersman, first spotted Kentucky, where later he was to live. Use this day to discuss the legend around his life and other American legends.*

Videos: *American Tall Tale Heroes*
Annie Oakley
John Henry
Pecos Bill
Stone Soup

Books: *The Badger and the Magic Fan*, Tony Johnston
The Great Ball Game, Joseph Bruchac
How Snowshoe Hare Rescued the Sun: A Tale from the Arctic, Emery and Durga Bernhard
How the Ostrich Got Its Long Neck, Verna Aardema
In a Dark, Dark Room and Other Scary Stories, Alvin Schwartz
John Henry, Julius Lester
Johnny Appleseed, Jan Gleiter and Kathleen Thompson
Nathaniel Willy, Scared Silly, Judith Mathews and Fay Robinson
Paul Bunyan, Steven Kellogg
Pecos Bill, Steven Kellogg
People of Corn, Mary-Joan Gerson
The Pied Piper of Hamelin, Michele Lemieux
The Talking Pot, Virginia Haviland
William Tell, Leonard Everett Fisher
Zzzng! Zzzng! Zzzng!: A Yoruba Tale, Phillis Gershator

Fingerplay: **There Was a Princess Long Ago . . .**
(Source: *The Playtime Treasury*, Pie Corbett)

Crafts: **Robin Hood's Quiver.**
Travel to merry old England and romp through Sherwood Forest and to the castles of Maid Marian and Prince John with your own quiver and arrows reminiscent of the days of Robin Hood. Excellent craft for lessons on legends or medieval times. Expensive materials are not needed. You can use simple paper towel tubes and other cheap items easily found around the house.
(Source: *Cups and Cans and Paper Plate Fans*, Phyllis and Noel Fiarotta)

Big Mouth.
Folktales are a lot of fun for everyone. Frogs play a large part in folktales and legends of many countries. Two of my favorite stories are "The Frog Prince" and "The Foolish Frog."

This craft helps the child create a wide-mouthed frog sitting on a lily pad. Add long jumping legs from accordion-folded paper strips. Now try "The Foolish Frog" with this delightful creation.

(Source: *Cut-Paper Play!*, Sandi Henry)

Activities:

Name That Tale.
Let the children sit in a circle and listen carefully as you quote a line from a familiar folktale. The first child to name the story may give the next quote. With preschoolers you can try a variation: The teacher gives the quote and the first child to raise his or her hand gets to select the picture from those displayed that depicts the story and then tells the class the title.

(Source: *The Gingerbread Guide*, Linda K. Garrity)

Charades.
Design a collection of flashcards illustrating a scene from a folktale or just a character from the story. Begin the familiar game of charades with each child getting to act out the card selected. With young children you will first have to determine which tales they are familiar with.

(Source: *The Gingerbread Guide*, Linda K. Garrity)

Songs:

(Audio) "Pecos Bill"
(Source: *Harmony Ranch*)
(Book) "John Henry"
(Source: *Gonna Sing My Head Off!*, Kathleen Krull)

65 Food and Eating

Relate to:	*World Food Day (Oct. 16): A special day designated to help make people aware that there is hunger in the world and to try help those who do not have as much as we do.*

Videos:
Dragon Stew
Frog Goes to Dinner
Green Eggs and Ham (The Cat in the Hat/Dr. Seuss on the Loose)
Let's Eat! Funny Food Songs
Stone Soup

Books:
The Beastly Feast, Bruce Goldstone
A Chef: How We Work, Douglas Florian
Cloudy with a Chance of Meatballs, Judi Barrett
The Fat Cat, Jack Kent
The Gingerbread Boy, Paul Galdone
The Hungry Thing Returns, Jan Slepian and Ann Seidler
Lunch, Denise Fleming
The Magic Porridge Pot, Paul Galdone
Mouse Mess, Linnea Riley
Pete's a Pizza, William Steig
Pickles to Pittsburgh, Ron Barrett
Sheep Out to Eat, Nancy Shaw
Sweet Dream Pie, Audrey Wood
The Turnip, Janina Domanska
Turnip Soup, Lynne Born Myers

Fingerplay:
Pancake.
(Source: *Children's Counting-out Rhymes, Fingerplays, Jump-Rope and Bounce-Ball Chants and Other Rhythms*, Gloria T. Delamar)

Crafts:
Decorative Boxes and Pretty Jewelry.
With the use of the great variety of grains and pasta available, the children can make their own jewelry or decorate a colorful box to be used for almost anything. Instructions and illustrations for these crafts can be found in the source below. Suggested grains to use include maize, rice, lentils, pearl barley, macaroni, spaghetti, butterfly pasta, and vermicelli.
(Source: *The Fun-To-Make Book*, Colette Lamargue)

Bubble Wrap Dried Corn.
This simple art work can be utilized in many lessons on such topics as Thanksgiving, Sukkah, Kwanzaa displays and much, much more. Seal the end of a cardboard towel tube and wrap it with bubble wrap (bubbles outward). Roll the entire thing in a mixture of glue and water; wrap in a couple of layers of yellow tissue paper, tucking the ends inside. Use brown tissue to form the brown husks. For more details and illustrations see this source.
(Source: *Crafts to Make in the Fall*, Kathy Ross)

Activities: **The Fat Cat.**
After reading Jack Kent's *The Fat Cat*, have the children join in acting out the story. The teacher or librarian may drape a long sheet or blanket around herself. As the story progresses and the children take their parts, they will go under the blanket as they are eaten by the cat.

Who's Got the Bread?
Present a variety of breads (bagels, white bread, muffins, etc.) in clean plastic bags to the group. After helping the group identify the types of bread, have them sit in a circle with one child in the center. With everyone's eyes closed, the children can pass the bags around. When they stop, the child in the center can try to guess who has what bread.
Of course, since they were in sealed containers, these breads will make a special treat after the games are all completed.
(Source: *Everyday Circle Times*, Liz and Dick Wilmes)

Songs: (Audio) "Healthy Food"
(Source: *Sesame Road*)
(Book) "Making Pizza"
(Source: *Story Hour: 55 Preschool Programs for Public Libraries*, Jeri Kladder)
"On Top of Spaghetti"
(Source: *Glory, Glory, How Peculiar*, Charles Keller)

66 Foreign Lands: Africa

Relate to: *Afro-American History Month (Feb.): A special month to celebrate the historical and literary contributions of famous African-Americans.*

Videos: *Hot Hippo*
Joshua's Masai Mask
Mufaro's Beautiful Daughters
A Story, A Story
Why Mosquitoes Buzz in People's Ears

Books: *Anansi the Spider*, Gerald McDermott
Dr. DeSoto Goes to Africa, William Steig
The Happy Lion in Africa, Louise Fatio
Kente Colors, Debbi Chocolate
King of Another Country, Fiona French
Lazy Lion, Mwenye Hadithi
Little Elephant's Walk, Adrienne Kennaway
Masai and I, Virginia Kroll
Mother Crocodile, Rosa Guy
Mufaro's Beautiful Daughter, John Steptoe
Rosebud, Ludwig Bemelmans
A South African Night, Rachel Isadora
The Tale of a Crocodile, Ann Kirn
The Talking Cloth, Rhonda Mitchell
When Africa Was Home, Karen Williams

Fingerplay: **This Little Tiger.**
(Source: *Finger Frolics—Revised*, Liz Cromwell, Dixie Hibner, and John R. Faitel)

Crafts: **African Drum.**
Have the children use any cylinder-shaped box (e.g., an oatmeal box)—cut the top and bottom out to make the sides of the drum. These parts will be replaced with pieces of felt and sewn on with yarn.
Decorative designs can be added by using poster paints, crayons, and feathers. This produces workable musical instruments.
(Source: *101 Easy Art Activities*, Trudy Aarons and Francine Doelsch, *Sticks and Stones and Ice Cream Cones*, Phyllis Fiarotta)

Beaded Bracelet.
The people of Zimbabwe, South Africa, are well known for their colorful beaded bracelets. Help the children make their own colorful bracelets using string and cereal loops of various colors.

For school-age children you can use plastic beads, but the cereal loops are advisable for preschoolers. This source also provides you with some wonderful rhymes and games to go along with this craft.
(Source: *Storytime Crafts*, Kathryn Totten)

Activities: **Kasha Mu Bukondi (Antelope in the Net).**
One player is selected to be the antelope and is surrounded by a net (circle) of children. Everyone holds hands and shouts "Kasha Mu Bukondi" and the antelope will try to break through the net. When he successfully escapes, he is chased and the one who captures him becomes the new antelope.
(Source: *This Way to Books*, Caroline Feller Bauer)

Drie Blikkies.
This is a popular South African children's street game. Try this with two teams of at least four members each. Mark four posts with a circle in the center of the four posts (like the dots on a 5 die). At one post, stack three tin cans (blikkies). Team A places people behind each post and Team B lines up at the center circle. Team B members, one at a time, will attempt to topple all the blikkies with a tennis ball. If they are successful they try to run and tag each post before the other team tags them with the ball. The player of Team A that is posted behind the blikkies tries to get the ball and throw it to each post, in order, to allow teammates to tag the runners out. The team with the most points wins.
(Source: *Sidewalk Games around the World*, Arlene Erlbach)

Songs: (Audio) "African Bread Song"
(Source: *Jambalaya! And Other Tasty Food Songs around the World*)
(Book) "Walking through the Jungle"
(Source: *Game-Songs with Prof. Dogg's Troupe*, Harriet Powell)

67 Foreign Lands: China

Relate to:	*Chinese New Year (between Jan. 21 and Feb. 19): Generally celebrated until the Lantern Festival fifteen days later.*

Videos:
The Five Chinese Brothers
Ming Lo Moves the Mountain
Sam and the Lucky Money
A Story of Ping
Tikki Tikki Tembo

Books:
Beautiful Warrior: The Legend of the Nun's Kung Fu, Emily Arnold McCully
Chinatown, William Low
The Cricket's Cage, Stefan Czernecki
The Dragon's Tale: And Other Animal Fables of the Chinese Zodiac, Demi
The Emperor and the Kite, Jane Yolen
The Emperor and the Nightingale, Meilo So
The Emperor's Garden, Ferida Wolff
Everyone Knows What a Dragon Looks Like, Jay Williams
The Last Dragon, Susan Miho Nunes
Ming Lo Moves the Mountain, Arnold Lobel
Roses Sing on New Snow: A Delicious Tale, Paul Yee
Teddy Bear and the Chinese Dragon, Jan Mogensen
Tubby and the Lantern, Al Perkins
The Waiting Day, Harriett Diller
Wan Hu Is in the Stars, Jennifer Armstrong

Fingerplay: **This Is Baby's Trumpet.**
(Source: *Dragon Kites and Dragonflies: A Collection of Chinese Nursery Rhymes*, Demi)

Crafts: **Bing-Banger Noisemaker.**
This small Chinese toy is constructed of corrugated cardboard, string, crayons, metal washers or beads, and a pencil. It is a simple toy that can be held in small hands and spun back-and-forth to make the desired noise.

A circular piece of corrugated cardboard can be painted or colored in any pattern desired, and then mounted on a pencil. With a bead on a string attached to two sides of the circle, you can spin the pencil to make the beads bounce off the cardboard.

This toy was made popular again in the film *Karate Kid II*, which many children have seen.

(Source: *Confetti: The Kids' Make-It-Yourself, Do-It-Yourself Party Book*, Phyllis and Noel Fiarotta)

Feather Tossers.
This is a game played by children in China. This is an ancient game and the exact rules have been lost over time, but it's believed that the game may have been similar to badminton. Instruct the children in making their own feather tossers using a square of heavy cloth filled with a small amount of dried beans. Fold it up and close the top with a rubberband. Decorate with feathers stuck in the band. This is now your ball to be thrown and tossed numerous ways back and forth to other children.

(Source: *City Crafts from Secret Cities*, Judith Conaway)

Activities:

Clapping Hands.
This clapping game is played like Pease Porridge Hot. It may take some practice with the group but this is a game they will enjoy and practice long after the storyhour program has ended. A description of Pease Porridge Hot can be located on page 31 of Vinton's book.

(Source: *The Folkways Omnibus of Children's Games*, Iris Vinton)

Confucius Relay.
Set up two teams for a relay race of a different type. Each team will be inflating balloons and given a pair of chopsticks. The children need to get the balloons from one point to another with the use of the chopsticks only. (Sorry, no hands or body contact.) Depending on the age of your group, try going around obstacles, too.

(Source: *The Penny Whistle Party Planner*, Meredith Brokaw and Annie Gilbar)

Song:

(Audio) "Chinese New Year"
(Source: *Joining Hands with Other Lands: Multicultural Songs and Games*)

68 Fractured Fairy Tales

Relate to:	*Once Upon a Time Day (Feb. 24): On the day of the birth of Wilhelm Grimm read your favorite fairy tales to the children.*

Videos:	*Cinder-Elly* *Prince Cinders* *The Truth about Mother Goose*
Books:	*Cinderella and Cinderella: The Untold Story*, Russell Shorto *Cinderella's Rat*, Susan Meddaugh *The Cowboy and the Black-Eyed Pea*, Tony Johnston *Fables Aesop Never Wrote*, Robert Kraus *The Frog Prince Continued*, Jon Scieszka *Jack and the Beanstalk and the Beanstalk Incident*, Tim Paulson *Jack and the Meanstalk*, Brian and Rebecca Wildsmith *Moonstruck: The True Story of the Cow Who Jumped over the Moon*, Gennifer Choldenko *The Principal's New Clothes*, Stephanie Calmenson *Ruby*, Michael Emberley *Rumpelstiltskin's Daughter*, Diane Stanley *Sleeping Ugly*, Jane Yolen *Somebody and the Three Blairs*, Marilyn Tolhurst *The Three Little Wolves and the Big Bad Pig*, Eugene Triviza *The True Story of the Three Little Pigs*, Jon Scieszka
Fingerplay/ Rhymes:	**Little Rap Riding Hood.** A delightfully modern version of the Little Red Riding Hood story done in rap with audience participation. It will take some practice on your part as a leader but it adds a wonderful touch to the program. Try getting some high school students to help you present this story. (Source: *Crazy Gibberish and Other Storyhour Stretches*, Naomi Baltuck)
Crafts:	**Jack and the Beanstalk.** In this source you will find a wonderfully imaginative craft for your program on fairy tales. Here it centers on *Jack and the Beanstalk* by creating a beanstalk and the giant's castle. All are made of toilet paper tubes connected together. Placed one on top of each other we make the beanstalk; when the tubes are placed in a group we get the effect of castle turrets. With cot-

ton placed under the castle you will get the appearance of a castle floating in the clouds. A wonderful fairy tale effect.
(Source: *175 Easy-to-Do Everyday Crafts*, Sharon Dunn Umnik)

Unique Version of the Classic Tale.
Let the children make their own version of the Gingerbread Man tale. Duplicate on the lower portion of a number of pages the familiar refrain, "Run, run, as fast as your can! You can't catch me, I'm the Gingerbread Man." Reserve the upper portion for illustrating animals the children wish to introduce into the story chasing the Gingerbread Man.
(Source: *The Best of the Mailbox, Book 1: Preschool/Kindergarten edition*, Margaret Michel)

Activities:

Cinderella Dressed in Yella.
Jump rope rhymes are popular with children. Here the entire class recites this little fractured Cinderella rhyme while one child at a time jumps rope or any other activity you designate (bounce a ball, play catch, etc.) to determine the number you need to complete the rhyme. The group can count it out. What I like about this activity is that there are no losers and everyone can participate.
(Source: *Storytime Crafts*, Kathryn Totten)

Mystery Story.
This activity requires that the children have some familiarity with a selection of common fairy tales. With this in mind the leader poses a particular crime from a fairy tale, for example "Who broke a promise and stayed out late? (Cinderella)"

Whoever guesses the answer can explain the story to the class and ask the next question.
(Source: *Games to Learn By: 101 Best Educational Games*, Muriel Mandell)

Songs:

(Audio) "Rapunzel Got a Mohawk"
(Source: *Ants*)
(Book) "Mary Had a William Goat"
(Source: *Jane Yolen's Old MacDonald Songbook*, Jane Yolen)

69 Friendship

Relate to:	*Friendship Day (first Sunday in Aug.): A day to make new friendships and attempt to repair broken ones.*

Videos:
Frog and Toad Are Friends: The Story
Happy Lion
Ira Sleeps Over
Peter's Chair
Petunia

Books:
Alex Is My Friend, Marisabina Russo
Andrew Jessup, Nette Hilton
Discovering Friendship, Sharon Kadish
Do You Want to Be My Friend?, Eric Carle
Harry and Willy and Carrothead, Judith Caseley
How to Be a Friend: A Guide to Making Friends and Keeping Them,
    Laurie Krasny Brown and Marc Brown
Little Bear's Friend, Else Minarik
Little Blue and Little Yellow, Leo Lionni
Little Chick's Friend Duckling, Mary DeBall Kwitz
Mary Ann, Betsy James
May I Bring a Friend?, Beatrice deRegniers
My Best Friend, Pat Hutchins
Timothy Turtle, Al Graham
Wanted: Best Friend, A. M. Monson
You're Not My Best Friend Anymore, Charlotte Pomerantz

Fingerplay:
Five Friends.
(Source: *Children's Counting-out Rhymes, Fingerplays, Jump-Rope and Bounce-Ball Chants and Other Rhythms*, Gloria T. Delamar)

Crafts:
A Friendship Chain.
Have each child cut a strip of construction paper (2″ × 8″ long). To this strip have them glue or draw three pictures of things they like to do with others. All the links designed may be connected to form a friendship chain with each child's name to display in the library during Brotherhood Week.

Friendship Paper Quilt.
Create a classroom friendship quilt using construction paper and yarn. The children can create their own section depicting

their family friends or whatever theme the group decides. Connect the sections with yarn and display in your classroom during Parents Visitation Day, or during Friendship Day if your group meets then.

   (Source: *Creative Fun for 2- to 6-Year-Olds: The Little Hands Big Fun Craft Book*, Judy Press)

Activities: **A Lonely Little Ghost.**
Choose one child to be the lonely ghost. Mark an area with tape on the floor for the ghost's home. The other children will try to sneak into the area to tease the ghost while reciting a simple verse about the ghost friend. (Text found on page 71 of the book.) Any child tagged will become the ghost's friend and will help to catch the others. The last one tagged wins the game.

   (Source: *New Games to Play*, Juel Krisvoy)

Unpack Your Bag.
This is a wonderful activity to help a new child feel welcome to the class. Ask the new child and parent to bring to class a bag labeled "All About Me" and to place in the bag various items that are important to the child. In the class each item can be removed and the child can help the teacher explain its importance. You can also have each child in the class show the new child an item they have brought into the class. This is a terrific ice breaker and way to make new friends.

   (Source: *The Giant Encyclopedia of Theme Activities for Children 2 to 5*, Kathy Charner)

Songs: (Audio) "Say, Say Little Playmate"
   (Source: *Toddlers Sing 'N Learn*)
(Book) "Buddies and Pals"
   (Source: *Do Your Ears Hang Low?*, Tom Glazer)

70 Frogs and Toads

Relate to:	*Preakness Frog Hop (May 13): This event decides Maryland's frog entry in the international frog jumping contest in California. Try having your own human frog jump.*

Videos:
A Boy, A Dog, and a Frog
Frog and Toad Are Friends: The Story (Arnold Lobel Video Showcase)
The Frog Prince
The Frog Princess
Frog Went A-Courtin'

Books:
Better Move On, Frog!, Ron Maris
The Bird, the Frog, and the Light, Avi
The Caterpillar and the Polliwog, Jack Kent
An Extraordinary Egg, Leo Lionni
Felix's Hat, Catherine Bancroft
Frog Odyssey, Juliet and Charles Snape
The Frog Who Wanted to Be a Singer, Linda Goss
Grandpa Toad's Secrets, Keiko Kasza
Green Wilma, Tedd Arnold
Jump, Frog, Jump, Robert Kalan
The Mysterious Tadpole , Steven Kellogg
Periwinkle, Roger Duvoisin
Possum and the Peeper, Anne Hunter
Seven Froggies Went to School, Kate Duke
Toad, Ruth Brown

Fingerplay:
Tadpoles.
(Source: *Finger Frolics—Revised*, Liz Cromwell, Dixie Hibner, and John R. Faitel)

Crafts:
Egg Carton Frog.
Construct a frog on a lily pad with the use of paint, paper, and cardboard egg cartons. These materials are readily available and easy for young children to handle. This craft requires no more than one egg carton for each child. Add little paper legs. Flowers on the lily pad can be made from the cups of the egg carton and painted to add a bright touch.
(Source: *Egg Carton Critters*, Donna Miller)

Frog Puppet.
A manageable craft for someone who works with very young children and has a tight budget for supplies. Fold over a paper plate to make a wide-mouthed frog, but don't forget his tongue for catching flies. A simple party noisemaker that expands forward when blown makes a perfect tongue. Check for further instructions and other enjoyable crafts in the source.
(Source: *Crafts from Your Favorite Fairy Tales*, Kathy Ross)

Activities: **Leap Frog.**
Children love to pretend they are animals. This activity allows them great physical movements within the capabilities of children ages four and up. This game can also be played indoors and outdoors.
(Source: *Games*, Anne Rockwell)

Froggie in the Puddle.
Practice with the children pretending to be jumping frogs and discuss where frogs reside. To set up a pond, designate certain areas as lily pads for the frogs to sit on. While some children sit on the lily pads the remainder join hands and circle them as they sing the verse supplied for the game. At the last verse the frogs hop to the children, who drop their arms to permit the frogs to leave the pond. Select new frogs and begin again.
(Source: *Amazing Alligators and Other Story Hour Friends*, Maxine Riggers)

Songs: (Audio) "The Hippity Hop . . . Hop"
(Source: *Meet the Dinner Dogs*)
(Book) "Froggie Went A-Courtin'"
(Source: *The Fireside Book of Birds and Beasts*, Jane Yolen)

71 Fruit

Relate to:	*Johnny Appleseed's Birthday (Sept. 26): Many people don't know that Johnny was a real person named John Chapman, who got his nickname by planting apple trees across the country.*

Videos:	*Fruit: Close Up and Very Personal* *The Grey Lady and the Strawberry Snatcher*
Books:	*Albert's Field Trip*, Leslie Tryon *The Apple Pie Tree*, Zoe Hall *Apple Pigs*, Ruth Orbach *A Book of Fruit*, Barbara Hirsch Lember *Chestnut Cove*, Tim Egan *Cider Apples*, Sandy Nightingale *A Fruit and Vegetable Man*, Roni Schotter *Good Job, Oliver!*, Laurel Molk *Growing Colors*, Bruce McMillan *Mr. Putter and Tabby Pick the Pears*, Cynthia Rylant *Oliver's Fruit Salad*, Vivian French *The Perfect Orange*, Frank P. Fraujo *Watermelon Day*, Kathi Appelt *What's So Terrible about Swallowing an Apple Seed?*, Harriet Lerner and Susan Goldhor *The Wild Bunch*, Dee Lillegard
Fingerplays:	**My Apple or Two Red Apples.** (Source: *Toddle on Over*, Robin Works Davis)
Crafts:	**Printing with Fruit.** Pieces of firm fruit are ideal for making prints on shirts, cloth towels, etc. Slice an apple in half and add generous amounts of paint to the flat surface. Now you can decorate various items that can be given as gifts by pressing the fruit to the surface of the item. (Source: *Exciting Things to Do with Color*, Janet Allen) **Paper Weave Fruit Basket.** Help the children make their own picture of a fruit basket containing their favorite fruit. Weave the base of the basket with various colored strips of paper, then paste on the handle. Fill the basket with pictures of fruit or cut the shapes from colored paper. (Source: *Cut-Paper Play!*, Sandi Henry)

Activities: **The Fruit Song.**
Using the special fruit song found in the source, have the children identify and gather various types of fruit. Keep singing until all the fruits are gathered into a fruit salad for the final verse.
(Source: *300 Three Minute Games*, Jackie Silberg)

Fruit Pin-Up.
Cut out or color pictures of various fruits to be used in this game. The pictures are taped to the children's backs. Play a simple guessing game where the children give each other clues about the fruit that they have. As the children guess their fruit they hold it up and join the other children. For additional crafts, games, and fingerplays on various fruit see the source.
(Source: *Everyday Circle Times*, Liz and Dick Wilmes)

Songs: (Audio) "Blackberry Pickin'"
(Source: *Cookin'*)
(Book) "Apples and Bananas"
(Source: *The 2nd Raffi Songbook*, Raffi)

72 Gender Roles: Nontraditional

Relate to:	*Take Our Daughters to Work Day (April 23): A special event day sponsored by the Ms. Foundation for women to show young girls the many ways a woman can work in traditional and nontraditional ways.*

Videos: *Mommy's Office*
William's Doll

Books: *Allie's Basketball Dream*, Barbara E. Barber
Beautiful Warrior: The Legend of the Nun's Kung Fu, Emily Arnold McCully
Daddy Makes the Best Spaghetti, Anna Grossnickle Hines
Derek the Knitting Dinosaur, Mary Blackwood
Dulcie Dando, Soccer Star, Sue Stops
Henry's Baby, Mary Hoffman
The Long Red Scarf, Nette Hilton
Mama Is a Miner, George Ella Lyons
My Daddy Is a Nurse, Mark Wandro and Joani Blank
Poor Monty, Anne Fine
Sam Johnson and the Blue Ribbon Quilt, Lisa Campbell Ernst
Thomas's Sitter, Jean Richardson
To Capture the Wind, Sheila MacGill-Callahan
Tough Eddie, Elizabeth Winthrop
What Daddies Do Best/What Mommies Do Best, Laura Numeroff

Fingerplay: **Father Bought a Feather Duster.**
(Source: *Move Over, Mother Goose*, Ruth I. Dowell)

Crafts: **Tissue Box Coupon Holder.**
These days not only Mom does the grocery shopping for the family. Many fathers help with the shopping as well as the cooking. After a discussion of various duties family members perform, try creating a special gift for Dad. Here you will find useful instructions, along with reproducible patterns, to make a coupon holder for Dad's next shopping trip.
(Source: *Holiday Gifts and Decorations Kids Can Make (for Practically Nothing)*, Jerome C. Brown)

Bear Containers.
An attractive container craft is available in this source. A bear template is provided that can be photocopied and enlarged to hold the size of the tube container you have selected. Have the

child decorate the wide tube and glue it to the bear's lap, then simply fold the bear up around the tube where shown. These containers can be used to store just about anything (party snacks, paper clips, string, pencils, etc.). This would be a great little gift for Mom's desk at work. Let her have a bear hug from you every day.

(Source: *Great Paper Crafts*, Ingrid Klettenheimer)

Activities: **Family Chores.**

Initiate a discussion among the children about different types of chores that family members are responsible for in their home. Be sure to steer children into including nontraditional roles in the family also (e.g., Dad babysits, Mom does plumbing, etc.). After the discussion begin a pantomime session where children mimic these chores for the class to guess. An excellent list of suggestions is supplied in the book listed here for you.

(Source: *More Picture Book Story Hours: From Parties to Pets*, Paula Gaj Sitarz)

This Is What Daddy Does.

This activity can really relate to any member of the family. Children have curiosity about the types of jobs parents do outside the home. Here's a game to help them describe those jobs or lead to a discussion of each occupation. The children begin with "This is what my daddy (or mother, uncle, etc.) does." They then act it out until someone guesses and becomes the next pantomimist.

(Source: *Games to Learn By: 101 Best Educational Games*, Muriel Mandell)

Songs: (Audio) "Daddy Does the Dishes"
    (Source: *Family Vacation*)
(Book) "Ride, Sally, Ride"
    (Source: *Here's to Women*, Hilda E. Wenner and Elizabeth Freilicher)

73 Ghosts

Relate to:	*People's Republic of China's Festival of Hungry Ghosts: (Aug.11– Sept.9): Also known as Ghost Month; according to legend, ghosts roam the earth. Many items, such as prayers, food, or "ghost money" are offered to appease the spirits and ensure a prosperous year.*

Videos:
Georgie
The Ghost with the Halloween Hiccups
The Legend of Sleepy Hollow
Tailypo
Winnie the Witch and the Frightened Ghost (Fran Allison's *Autumn Tales of Winnie the Witch*)

Books:
Babar and the Ghost, Laurent de Brunhoff
The Boo Baby Girl Meets the Ghost of Mable's Gable, Jim May
Bumps in the Night, Harry Allard
Georgie and the Magician, Robert Bright
A Ghost Named Fred, Nathaniel Benchley
The Ghost's Dinner, Jacques Duquennoy
Gus Was a Friendly Ghost, Catherine Thayer
Hank the Clank, Michael Coleman
Hubknuckles, Emily Herman
I'm Not Frightened of Ghosts, Julie and Charles Snape
Little Ghost, Kate Khdir and Sue Nash
Martin and the Pumpkin Ghost, Ingrid Ostheeren
Mrs. Gaddy and the Ghost, Wilson Gage
Old Devil Wind, Bill Martin Jr.
The Teeny Tiny Ghost, Kay Winters

Fingerplay:
Five Little Ghosts.
(Source: *Finger Frolics—Revised*, Liz Cromwell, Dixie Hibner, and John R. Faitel)

Crafts:
Ghost Friend.
The children can make their own ghosts and stand them on their windowsills or use them as centerpieces. Napkins, a pencil, rubberband, and a cup are all that is required for this simple craft.

To make it extra sweet try using a lollipop for the inside instead of a pencil.

(Source: *Beginning Crafts for Beginning Readers*, Alice Gilbreath)

Ghost Prints.
Here's a craft that can be enjoyed by even the youngest of your group. Just place a scoop of white paint on a surface easily cleaned later and let them have the time of their lives fingerpainting. When this activity has exhausted their energies smooth the paint out and create eyes and a mouth. Place a black paper on the mess to lift off their own ghost print. You think this is simple and fun? Try the many other preschool arts and crafts offered in this source.
(Source: *Crafts: Early Learning Activities*, Jean Warren)

Activities:

A Lonely Little Ghost.
Choose one child to be the lonely ghost. Mark an area with tape on the floor for the ghost's home. The other children will try to sneak into the area to tease the ghost while reciting a simple verse about the ghost friend. (Text found on page 71 of the book.) Any child tagged will become the ghost's friend and will help to catch the others. The last one tagged wins the game.
(Source: *New Games to Play*, Juel Krisvoy)

A Ghostly Game.
This ghostly game can be played with any number of people over two. It is a word game that requires that the child at least be able to spell the simple words used. The object of the game is for each player to add a letter to the word to continue the spelling without finishing the word. If a player ends the word on the third letter he becomes a half ghost. Any player that gets three half-ghost penalties is eliminated.
(Source: *Halloween Holiday Grab Bag*, Judith Stamper)

Songs:

(Audio) "Ghostbuster's Theme"
(Source: *Halloween Fun*)
(Book) "Casper, the Friendly Ghost"
(Source: *The Reader's Digest Children's Songbook*, William L. Simon)

74 Giants

Relate to:	*Festival of the Giants (4th Sunday in Aug.): A colorful Belgium pageant with a parade honoring the legendary giants Goliath (and his bride), Samson, a warrior named Ambiorix, and several others.*

Videos:
Frog and Toad Together: Dragons and Giants (Arnold Lobel Video Showcase)
The Giant Devil-Dingo
Jack and the Beanstalk
Mickey Mouse: The Brave Little Tailor (Cartoon Classics Collection, Vol. 6)
The Selfish Giant

Books:
Fin M'Coul, Tomie dePaola
The Foolish Giant, Bruce Coville
The Giant, Nicholas Heller
Giant John, Arnold Lobel
His Royal Buckliness, Kevin Hawkes
Joe Giant's Missing Boot: A Mothergooseville Story, Toni Goffe
Kate's Giants, Valiska Gregory
The Little Hen and the Giant, Maria Polushkin
Mary, Mary, Sarah Hayes
The Mysterious Giant of Barletta, Tomie dePaola
The Pumpkin Giant, Ellin Greene
Ribtickle Town, Alan Benjamin
Rude Giants, Audrey Wood
The Selfish Giant, Oscar Wilde
What Can a Giant Do?, Mary Louise Cuneo

Fingerplay:
The Giant and the Leprechaun.
(Source: *Finger Frolics—Revised*, Liz Cromwell, Dixie Hibner, and John R. Faitel)

Crafts:
Tin Can Stilts.
Let the children try to be giants themselves by designing stilts of tin cans and heavy cord. The exterior of the cans may be decorated to taste.
(Source: *Do a Zoom-Do*, Bernice Chesler)

Stick Figures.
Giants are very popular characters in children's literature. In this book you will find some interesting illustrations and sug-

gestions for making your own giant stick puppets. Some are made using paper plates, pieces of cloth, or just construction paper, but all are amusing. Make them as large as possible, then place them on long sticks so the children can make them even bigger by holding them high above their heads while telling their favorite giant stories.

(Source: *Great Paper Craft Projects*, Ingrid Klettenheimer)

Activities:

Giant's Treasure.
One child is chosen to be the sleeping giant who lies guarding a pile of cookies and candies (or other treasures). While the giant pretends to be asleep the other children attempt to steal the treasure. When the giant sits up everyone freezes. Anyone caught moving is out of the game. First to reach the treasure wins and becomes the next giant.

(Source: *500 Games*, Peter L. Cave)

Giant Steps.
A basic game familiar to most children and can be played with three or more people. Remember "Mother, may I?" This is the same type of activity.

(Source: *Rain or Shine Activity Book: Fun Things to Make and Do*, Joanna Cole and Stephanie Calmenson)

75 Glasses

Relate to:	*Children's Vision and Learning Month (Aug.): A month to encourage parents to have their children's eyesight checked by a professional.*

Videos: *Arthur's Eyes*
                Goggles

Books: *All the Better to See You With!*, Margaret Wild
                Arthur's Eyes, Marc Brown
                Baby Duck and the Bad Eyeglasses, Amy Hest
                Cromwell's Glasses, Holly Keller
                Dogs Don't Wear Glasses, Adrienne Geoghegan
                Glasses for D. W., Marc Brown
                Glasses, Who Needs 'Em?, Lane Smith
                Goggles, Ezra Jack Keats
                Hooray for Grandma Jo!, Thomas McKean
                Jennifer Jean, the Cross-Eyed Queen, Phyllis Reynolds Naylor
                Libby's New Glasses, Tricia Tusa
                Little Hippo Gets Glasses, Maryann MacDonald
                Tracks, David Galef
                What Can Rabbit See?, Lucy Cousins
                Willis, James Marshall

Fingerplay: **Grandma's Glasses.**
                (Source: *Mother Goose Time*, Jane Marino)

Crafts: **Sunglasses.**
                If you prefer using environmentally conscious crafts, here's one for you. A simple pattern is provided in this source for children to create their own sunglasses out of scrap cardboard. Decorate them to each individual's preference.
                (Source: *Earth-Friendly Wearables*, George Pfiffner)

                Magic Spectacles.
                Try looking at the world with rose-colored glasses. With the use of posterboard, red cellophane, and Popsicle sticks, children can make their magic spectacles. Let the children look at various things to see what a difference color can make.
                (Source: *Never-Be-Bored Book*, Judith Logan Lobne)

Activities: **A Collection of Goggles.**
                Gather a collection of eyeglasses that people wear (reading

glasses, swimming goggles, sunglasses, motorcycle goggles, etc.) and place them in a location where children can try them on for size. Children love to pretend. You might supply a mirror and drawing paper and let the children draw a self-portrait of themselves in their favorite glasses.

Peripheral Vision Game.
Discuss with the children how there are many ways that people check their eyesight to be sure it is all right. One method is the eye chart that we usually find in the eye doctor's office. Another test that can be given is to check your side vision (peripheral). Tell the children you will try a little game with them to see how well they do and if they can identify the objects that are shown to them.

Let the children sit in a chair and instruct them that they must sit perfectly still and NEVER move their head from facing front as it is at the start of the game. They may move their eyes but not their head.

Select a colorful object (scarf, ball, feather, etc.) and slowly begin to move it forward from behind the children to their side. When they identify the object drop it where it is. Children should be encouraged no matter how well they do. This is a good eye exercise for any child.

(Source: *Teacher's Handbook of Children's Games*, Marian Jenks Wirth)

Song: (Audio) "Harry's Glasses"
(Source: *Nobody Else Like Me*)

76 Grandparents

Relate to:	*National Grandparents Day (first Sunday in Sept. after Labor Day): A day in honor of grandparents, who help and love their families every day.*

Videos:
Grandpa
Song and Dance Man
Spot Visits His Grandparents
What's under the Bed?

Books:
The Berenstain Bears and the Week at Grandma's, Stan Berenstain
A Busy Day for a Good Grandmother, Margaret Mahy
Eleanor, Arthur, and Claire, Diana Engel
Grandfather's Dream, Holly Keller
Grandma according to Me, Karen M. Beil
Grandpa's Garden Lunch, Judith Caseley
Grandpa's Teeth, Rod Clement
Granny and Me, Robin Ballard
My Grandma's Chair, Maggie Smith
My Grandpa Is Amazing, Nick Butterworth
Punky Spends the Day, Sally G. Ward
Supergrandpa, David M. Schwartz
Trouble, Helen Cresswell
Valerie and the Silver Pear, Benjamin Darling
Visitors for Edward, Michaela Morgan

Fingerplay: **Grandma's Going to the Grocery Store.**
A nice rhyme that requires audience response to the leader's queries.
(Source: *Crazy Gibberish and Other Storyhour Stretches*, Naomi Baltuck)

Crafts: **Puzzle Picture.**
Grandparents love receiving and showing pictures of the children and grandchildren. Here's a special treat. Have the children draw their own pictures of themselves or other loved ones. Draw lines on the illustrations for the children to cut along to create a family puzzle. Send it off for a special surprise on Grandparents Day.
(Source: *Kids' Holiday Fun*, Penny Warner)

Personalized Shopping Bag.
Children love to shop with their grandparents, and most grandparents love to spoil their grandchildren when in the stores. In this little craft the children can show their appreciation to their grandparents for everything by making a personalized shopping bag to be carried on their special outings together.
(Source: *Gifts Galore!*, Ireene Robbins)

Activities:

Grandmother's Footsteps.
This is a well-known game for us all but with a different title. Have "Grandma" stand with her back to the class facing a wall. The rest of the class is at the other end of the room and will attempt to make their way to her in small steps. Grandma will turn around quickly, trying to catch someone moving. If she does, that player must go back to the beginning. Of course, the first to reach and tag Grandma wins.
Try variations where children must hop, crawl, or skip to get to Grandma.
(Source: *The Kids' Encyclopedia of Things to Make and Do*, Richard and Ronda Rasmussen)

My Grandmother.
Begin your game by saying, "My grandmother doesn't like tea, but she likes coffee." The next player repeats the phrase but changes what Grandma likes. If the child names anything with the letter "t" in it the caller will say, "No she doesn't like that" and the child will try again. It may take the children a while to discover what is wrong with the words they chose.
You can try it again with different parameters. Maybe Grandma doesn't like sweet things or yellow things, etc.
(Source: *The Fun Encyclopedia*, E. O. Habrin)

Song:

(Audio) "Grandma Slid Down the Mountain"
(Source: *Grandma Slid Down the Mountain*)

77 Handicaps

Relate to: *National Rehabilitation Week (Sept. 19–25): A time to honor those people with handicaps who continue the fight to live full lives, and also to honor those professionals who assist in this endeavor.*

Videos: *Apt. 3*
The Play

Books: *Alex Is My Friend*, Marisabina Russo
Arnie and the New Kid, Nancy Carlson
Cakes and Miracles: A Purim Tale, Barbara Diamond Goldin
Dad and Me in the Morning, Pat Lakin
Discovering Friendship, Sharona Kadish
Harry and Willy and Carrothead, Judith Caseley
Jenny's Magic Wand, Helen and Bill Hermann
Listen for the Bus: David's Story, Patricia McMahan
The Little Lame Prince, Rosemary Wells
Lucy's Picture, Nicola Moon
My Buddy, Audrey Osofsky
Our Teacher's in a Wheelchair, Mary Ellen Powers
Silent Lotus, Jeanne M. Lee
A Story of Courage, Joel Vecere
With the Wind, Liz Damrell

**Fingerplay/
Rhyme:**   **My Friend.**
    (Source: *1001 Rhymes and Fingerplays*, The Totline Staff)

Crafts: **Blind Artist.**
Children can be taught that people with disabilities are very capable people who learn to rely on the senses available to them. Give the children a large piece of paper and blindfold them. Call out an item for the children to draw, or simply give them an item to taste or smell and ask them to draw what they think it is.

Texture Pictures.
After reading *Lucy's Picture* by Nicola Moon, the children will be excited to create their own pictures, using scraps, twigs, sand, and other items that add texture to their creations. Have the children close their eyes and tell you what each scrap feels like to them before adding it to their own illustrations.

Activities: **Hearing-Whispering down the Lane.**
This is the ever popular telephone game. Tell children they must whisper only. The first child begins by whispering a statement that is passed along until the last child calls out the final result. You may not repeat the statement. At the end discuss how hearing-impaired people have difficulty even hearing loud voices, just as the children had a hard time in Whispering down the Lane.
(Source: *Kids' Celebrate!*, Maria Bonfanti Esche and Clare Bonfanti Braham)

Steal the Treasure.
Children can get an understanding of needing to rely closely on their sense of hearing when their vision is taken away from them in this game. A child is placed in a chair and blindfolded. Treasure coins are scattered on the floor around the child. One to three thieves at a time are instructed to try to steal the coins without being heard. If the Great Detective in the chair can accurately point to a thief, that thief is eliminated.
(Source: *Great Theme Parties for Children*, Irene N. Watts)

Songs: (Audio) "Walking on My Wheels"
(Source: *Nobody Else Like Me*)
(Book) "Deaf Woman's Courtship"
(Source: *Songs to Grow On*, Beatrice Landek)

78 Holidays: Chanukah

Relate to: *Chanukah (Dec. 14–21): Feast of Lights, a festival of eight days celebrating the victory of the Maccabees over the Syrians and the dedication of the Temple of Jerusalem.*

Videos:
Hanukkah
In the Month of Kislev
Lamb Chop's Special Chanukah
Liar, Liar, Pants on Fire
Shalom Sesame: Chanukah

Books:
Beni's First Chanukah, Jane Breskin Zalben
The Borrowed Hanukkah Latkes, Linda Glaser
By the Hanukkah Light, Sheldon Oberman
The Chanukkah Guest, Eric A. Kimmel
Hanukkah Lights, Hanukkah Nights, Leslie Kimmelman
Hanukkah Money, Sholom Aleichem
I Love Hanukkah, Marilyn Hirsh
Inside-Out Grandma: A Hanukkah Story, Joan Rothenberg
Laughing Latkes, M. B. Goffstein
The Miracle of the Potato Latkes, Malka Penn
The Odd Potato, Eileen Sherman
A Picture Book of Hanukkah, David Adler
Potato Pancakes all Around, Marilyn Hirsh
The Trees of the Dancing Goats, Patricia Polacco
The Ugly Menorah, Marissa Moss
What Is Hanukkah?, Harriet Ziefert

Fingerplay: **The Candle.**
(Source: *Finger Frolics—Revised*, Liz Cromwell, Dixie Hibner, and John R. Faitel)

Crafts: **Macaroni Star of David.**
Using lightweight cardboard, string, uncooked macaroni, gold spray paint, and other easily attainable items, a large Star of David can be designed and hung as a mobile.

Select various types of macaroni and glue them to both sides of the cardboard star. When this is completed, spray the entire thing with gold paint. This Star of David can be hung in the window for the holiday celebrations. This book contains many other suitable crafts.
(Source: *Hanukkah Crafts*, Joyce Becker)

Dreidel Gift Bag.

A simple Chanukah holiday gift bag can be made for the children using shopping bags, poster paint, and basic decorations. This one can be made to look like a simple dreidel. Need crafts for other Jewish holidays? Look in this great source.

(Source: *The Jewish Holiday Craft Book*, Kathy Ross)

Activities: **Chanukah Game.**

One player, Judah Maccabee, stands in his camp (a circle) while the other players (the Syrians) run in and out of the circle trying not to get tagged. Judah may not leave the camp, but the first player tagged must exchange places with him.

You may also find a delightful recipe for potato latkes in the source below to give the children a treat when the game is complete.

(Source: *A Pumpkin in a Pear Tree*, Ann Cole, Carolyn Haas, Elizabeth Heller, and Betty Weinberger)

Live Dreidel Game.

Add a little variety to the holidays with this live Dreidel game. Follow the instructions to create a belt for a child to wear. This is a special belt with pockets to hold the Hebrew letters. The child wearing the belt is the dreidel and is unaware of which letter is in each pocket. Turn on your music and the human dreidel will begin to spin and collapse onto one of the letters. Keep score as you would when playing with a toy driedel.

(Source: *Crafts for Hanukkah*, by Kathy Ross)

Songs: "Chanukkah, Oh Chanukkah"

(Source: *Hap Palmer's Holiday Magic*)

"My Dreydl"

(Source: *The Holiday Song Book*, Robert Quackenbush)

79 Holidays: Christmas

Relate to:	*Christmas (Dec. 25): A Christian festival commemorating the birth of Jesus Christ.*

Videos:
Arthur's Christmas Cookies (Arthur Celebrates the Holidays)
The Bear Who Slept through Christmas
The Elves and the Shoemaker
The Little Drummer Boy
The Mole and the Christmas Tree
Morris' Disappearing Bag
The Twelve Days of Christmas
A Visit from St. Nicholas

Books:
A Christmas Star Called Hannah, Vivian French
Christmas Trolls, Jan Brett
Claude the Dog, Dick Gackenbach
How Santa Got His Job, Stephen Krensky
Katie and the Sad Noise, Ruth Gannett
Little Bear's Christmas, Janice
Lyle at Christmas, Bernard Waber
Merry Christmas Geraldine, Holly Keller
The Oldest Elf, James Stevenson
Paddington Bear and the Christmas Surprise, Michael Bond
The Perfect Present, Michael Hagu
Petunia's Christmas, Roger Duvoisin
Teddy's First Christmas, Amanda Davidson
Tree of Cranes, Allen Say
What Could Be Keeping Santa?, Marilyn Janovitz

Fingerplay:
Let's Build a Snowman.
(Source: *Little Boy Blue*, Daphne Hogstrom)

Crafts:
Snowmobile.
Winter snowmobiles can be constructed out of easily obtainable egg cartons. The children can paint and decorate the snowmobiles with available materials (crayons, paint, sticker, glitter, etc.). With construction paper or Popsicle sticks they can add skis to the bottom. The simple step-by-step instructions are illustrated.
(Source: *Making Toys that Crawl and Slide*, Alice Gilbreath)

Pine Cone Wreath.
A beautiful and simple Christmas wreath can be constructed using very inexpensive materials such as mat board (or cardboard), glue, pine cones, and ribbon. Put out a box of various beads and glitter and children will be delighted with the variety of wreaths they will produce.
(Source: *One-Hour Holiday Crafts for Kids*, Cindy Groom Harry and staff)

Activities:

Christmas Is Coming.
This old English song includes a delightful dance that children can do. Props required here are pennies and an old hat. The children are only required to sit or skip while singing the short song and placing the pennies in the old man's hat. Actual sheet music is also provided.
(Source: *Dancing Games for Children of all Ages*, Esther L. Nelson)

What Did Santa Bring?
Let the children pair off and sit back to back. One child gets to pull an object from the Christmas stocking and describe the object Santa brought to his or her partner. The partner will try to draw the object. At the end of the activity see if the class can guess the objects that have been drawn by the group.
(Source: *A Pumpkin in a Pear Tree*, Ann Cole, Carolyn Haas, Elizabeth Heller, and Betty Weinberger)

Songs:

(Audio) "Must Be Santa"
(Source: *Raffi the Singable Songs Collection*)
(Book) "Jolly Old Saint Nicholas"
(Source: *The Holiday Song Book*, Robert Quackenbush)

80 Holidays: Easter

Relate to:	*Easter Sunday (first Sunday following the first full moon on or after the vernal equinox, March 20): To commemorate the Resurrection of Jesus Christ.*

Videos: *The Beginner's Bible: The Story of Easter*
The First Easter Rabbit
Funny Little Bunnies
Madeline and the Easter Bonnet
Max's Chocolate Chicken

Books: *The Bunny Who Found Easter*, Charlotte Zolotow
The Candy Egg Bunny, Lisl Weil
Coriander's Easter Adventure, Ingrid Ostheeren
Danny and the Easter Egg, Edith Kunhardt
The Easter Bear, John Barrett
The Easter Bunny, Agnes Mathieu
The Easter Bunny that Overslept, Priscilla and Otto Friedrich
The Easter Egg Artists, Adrienne Adams
Easter Surprise, Catherine Stock
The Funny Bunny Factory, Leonard Weisgard
Happy Easter Day!, Wendy Watson
The Horse with the Easter Bonnet, Catherine Woolley
Humbug Rabbit, Lorna Balian
Max's Chocolate Chicken, Rosemary Wells
Where Is It?, Tana Hoban

Fingerplay: **Robbie the Rabbit.**
(Source: *Finger Frolics—Revised*, Liz Cromwell, Dixie Hibner, and John R. Faitel)

Crafts: **Easter Bunny Mobile.**
Little stand-up ears and whiskers that don't droop are featured on this smiling bunny face mobile constructed of paper plates. By putting the bunny face on both sides of the plate it can be hung as a mobile near a window or in a corner of the room.
(Source: *Craft Fun*, Jane R. McCarty and Betty J. Peterson)

A Most Magnificent Easter Egg.
On a stiff background such as cardboard or cardstock draw a large shape of an egg and divide it into sections with pencil marks. Now the children can let their imaginations go and fill

in the sections by using such materials as glitter, lentils, crushed and colored egg shells, etc. Let them go wild with materials and watch the variations appear and the excitement mount as the children work.

(Source: *The Pre-School Craft Book*, Toy Martin)

Activities: **The Easter Bunny.**
This game and song allows the children to move around quickly, using their entire bodies. While singing this delightful song they pretend to be rabbits thumping their feet, jumping, etc.

(Source: *Singing Bee!: A Collection of Favorite Children's Songs*, Jane Hart)

Easter Egg Hockey.
This is a game that will require a larger area such as a gym or outdoor area. The class can be divided into two teams. Use boxes for your goal areas and a large plastic Easter egg for the ball. Here's the twist, though; the children may not touch the egg with any part of their body. They must move the egg only with the cardboard Easter eggs they have previously decorated. If anyone touches it the other team gains a point. A surefire hit for any group.

(Source: *Creative Games for Young Children*, Annetta Dellinger)

Songs: (Audio) "Easter Time is Here Again"
(Source: *Holiday Songs and Rhythms*)
(Book) "Peter Cottontail"; "The Bunny Hop"
(Source: *The Reader's Digest Children's Songbook*, William L. Simon)

81 Holidays: Fourth of July

Relate to: *Fourth of July Celebration (July 4): A day of family events to celebrate the independence of our country.*

Videos: *Star Spangled Banner*
Independence Day
Yankee Doodle

Books: *Festivals*, Ruth Manning-Sanders
Fourth of July, Barbara Joosse
Fourth of July, Janet McDonnell
Fourth of July Bear, Kathryn Lasky
A Fourth of July on the Plains, Jean VanLeeuwen
The Fourth of July Story, Alice Dalgliesh
Henrietta's Fourth of July, Syd Hoff
Henry's Fourth of July, Holly Keller
Hurray for the Fourth of July, Wendy Watson
One Way: A Trip with Traffic Signs, Leonard Shortall
Phoebe's Parade, Claudia Mills
The Star Spangled Banner, Peter Spier
The Summer Snowman, Gene Zion

Fingerplay: **The Flag.**
(Source: *Finger Frolics—Revised*, Liz Cromwell, Dixie Hibner, and John R. Faitel)

Crafts: **Firecracker Banks.**
Firecrackers are familiar items to children around this holiday. A safe firecracker that the children can use is a firecracker bank. This bank can be made using small cans, paint, or construction paper coverings, and gold and red glitter pipe cleaners coming out of the lid.
(Source: *Beginning Crafts for Beginning Readers*, Alice Gilbreath)

Fiery Fireworks.
These colorful fireworks are a perfect craft for the very young child. Made out of painted toilet paper rolls and colored tissue paper, the child can decorate it with a world of sticker stars. These paper firecrackers are good for decorations or hiding special treats at Fourth of July picnics.
(Source: *My Party Book*, Marion Elliot)

Activity: **Happy Birthday USA.**
Small carnival-like games may be set up for the children to test their skills. Games may include: Happy Birthday Ring Toss, Uncle Sam's Fish Pond, and the Liberty Bell Bean Bag Toss.
(Source: *A Pumpkin in a Pear Tree*, Ann Cole, Carolyn Haas, Elizabeth Heller, and Betty Weinberger)

Songs: (Audio) "Lady of the Light"
(Source: *Joining Hands with Other Lands: Multicultural Songs and Games*)
(Book) "Yankee Doodle"
(Source: *Singing Bee!: A Collection of Favorite Children's Songs*, Jane Hart)

82 Holidays: Groundhog's Day/Shadows

Relate to: *Groundhog's Day (Feb. 2): Discuss the ancient belief that if the groundhog sees his shadow we will have six more weeks of winter.*

Videos: *The Boy with Two Shadows*
The Spirit of Punxsutawney: Groundhog Day
Tale of the Groundhog's Shadow

Books: *The Boy with Two Shadows*, Margaret Mahy
A Garden for a Groundhog, Lorna Balian
Geoffrey Groundhog Predicts the Weather, Brice Koscielniak
Gretchen Groundhog, It's Your Day!, Abby Levine
Groundhog's Day at the Doctor, Judy Delton
It's Groundhog Day!, Steven Kroll
My Shadow, Robert Louis Stevenson
Nothing Sticks Like a Shadow, Ann Tompert
Return of the Shadows, Norma Farber
The Shadow Book, Beatrice deRegniers
Shadows Are About, Ann Whitford Paul
Shadowville, Michel Bartalos
Time for Jody, Wendy Kesselman
Wake Up, Groundhog!, Carol Cohen
What Happened Today, Freddy Groundhog?, Marvin Glass

Fingerplay: **Groundhog Day.**
(Source: *Rhymes for Learning Times*, Louise Binder Scott)

Crafts: **Silhouette Pictures.**
Tracing is something that many children practice a lot during the young years. Try having them trace shadows of plants, toy animals, or other still objects and then frame the pictures. They may also try tracing their friends' shadows on the sidewalks with chalk.
(Source: *Do a Zoom-Do*, Bernice Chesler)

Paperbag Groundhog.
Help your groundhog predict an early spring or a long winter. After discussing this with the children have them make their own groundhog on a hill to make their own predictions. Fold a paper plate in half, color it brown, and cut a small hole in the bottom. This will be the hill. Add a sun to the topside, then cut a groundhog shape out of a paper bag. With your groundhog

attached to a straw, he can now pop in and out of the hill you created to make his predictions. For more details and illustrations of this craft see the source.

(Source: *Kids' Celebrate*, Maria Bonfanti Esche and Clare Bonfanti Braham)

Activities:

Whose Little Shadow Are You?
Each child has a partner who plays the shadow and must do whatever the first child does. After reciting and performing the acts stated, the child joins hands with the shadow and all race to see which pair reaches the door first.

(Source: *New Games to Play*, Juel Krisvoy)

The Shadow Game.
This simple activity has the children bend, stretch, and jump according to the rhyme being sung to the tune of "The Muffin Man." The children watch as their shadows move along with them. For a delightful array of verses to use see the source listed here.

(Source: *Games to Play with Toddlers*, Jackie Silberg)

Songs:

(Audio) "Here's a Little Groundhog"
(Source: *Holiday Piggyback Songs*)
(Book) "A Shadow and a Smile"
(Source: *God's Wonderful World*, Agnes Leckie Mason and Phyllis Brown Ohanian)

83 Holidays: Halloween

Relate to: *Trick or Treat, or Beggar's Night (Oct. 31): Enjoy a day of costumes, treats, and fun on this annual children's event.*

Videos: *Arthur's Halloween* (Arthur Celebrates the Holidays)
Georgie
The Ghost with the Halloween Hiccups
Halloween
The Pumpkin Who Couldn't Smile

Books: *The Best Halloween of All*, Susan Wojciechowski
Five Little Pumpkins, Iris Van Rynbach
Georgie's Halloween, Robert Bright
Halloween Mice!, Bethany Roberts
Humbug Witch, Lorna Balian
In the Haunted House, Eve Bunting
Let's Celebrate Halloween, Peter and Connie Roop
Popcorn, Frank Asch
Rattlebone Rock, Sylvia Andrews
Sheep Trick or Treat, Nancy Shaw
This Is the Pumpkin, Abby Levine
The Trip, Ezra Jack Keats
When the Goblins Came Knocking, Anna Grossnickle Hines
Witch Bazooza, Dennis Nolan
Witch Mama, Judith Caseley

Fingerplay: **Halloween Surprise.**
(Source: *Finger Frolics—Revised*, Liz Cromwell, Dixie Hibner, and John R. Faitel)

Crafts: **Wanda Witch Puppet.**
Children enjoy puppets and having their own shows. Large Wanda, the witch puppet, can be made using paper plates, paper, and markers. This may be used as a puppet or as a mask held in front of a child's face.
(Source: *Happy Halloween: Things to Make and Do*, Robyn Supraner)

A Haunted Woods.
Halloween's a time when children enjoy spooky events and stories. Let them create their own eerie scene by designing a haunted woods as a background for a story they want to tell

later. With the use of black crepe paper for trees and cotton stretched across the scene for clouds you get the effect of trees at night. Add eyes to the trees for a "spooktacular" effect.
(Source: *Making Pictures: Spooky Things*, Penny King and Clare Roundhill)

Activities:

Spider Web.
Give each child a different color ball of string. At a signal each child will unwind the ball while wrapping it around a chair or some other specified object, forming a spider web before the other children.

Reverse it for the next game by having the children wind the ball back up.
(Source: *A Pumpkin in a Pear Tree*, Ann Cole, Carolyn Haas, Elizabeth Heller, and Betty Weinberger)

Headless Horseman.
One child at a time can pretend to be the famed Headless Horseman of Halloween fame. Have the child hide under a blanket and hold a pumpkin pillow. The other children walk silently in a circle around the Headless Horseman, who tosses his head in an attempt to hit and eliminate them from the game. A great game to play after the children have heard the story or seen the film of the same story.
(Source: *The Children's Party Handbook*, Alison Boteler)

Songs:

(Audio) "Are You Ready for Halloween"
(Source: *Halloween Fun*)
(Book) "Have You Seen the Ghost of John?"
(Source: *The Fireside Book of Children's Songs*, Marie Winn)

84 Holidays: Kwanzaa

Relate to: *Kwanzaa, the holiday (Dec. 26–Jan.1): Recognition of the traditional African harvest festivals. Stresses unity of the black family, with a communitywide harvest feast (Karamu) on the seventh day. This holiday was started by Dr. Maulana Karenga in 1966.*

Videos: *Holidays for Children: Kwanzaa*
Seven Candles for Kwanzaa

Books: *Celebrating Kwanzaa*, Diane Hoyt-Goldsmith
The Gifts of Kwanzaa, Synthia Saint-James
Habari Gani? What's the News?, Sundaira Morninghouse
Iwani's Gift at Kwanzaa, Denis Burden-Patmon
K is for Kwanzaa: A Kwanzaa Alphabet Book, Juwanda G. Ford
Kente Colors, Debbi Chocolate
Kwanzaa, Janet Riehecky
Kwanzaa, A. P. Porter
Kwanzaa, Deborah M. Newton Chocolate
Kwanzaa, Dorothy Rhodes Freeman and Dianne M. Macmillan
A Kwanzaa Celebration, Nancy Williams
My First Kwanzaa Book, Debra M. Chocolate
Seven Candles for Kwanzaa, Andrea Davis Pinkney
Seven Days of Kwanzaa, Ella Grier
The Story of Kwanzaa, Donna L. Washington

Fingerplays: **Holiday Candles All in a Row; Kwanzaa Today.**
(Source: *Toddle on Over*, Robin Works Davis)

Crafts: **Pumpkin Trivet.**
Since Kwanzaa is a harvest festival, any fruit or vegetable shape can be used to create a delightful trivet for Mom. Pack in a supply of old bottle caps, cardboard, and orange spray paint and you will see some wonderful results from even the youngest child with this craft.
(Source: *Crafts for Kwanzaa*, Kathy Ross)

Kwanzaa Hug Card.
Here's an item that is simple and can be adapted to any season or situation. Using simple construction paper and yarn, children can create a beautiful greeting card with hands folded over. Open them wide to get a big hug from the friend that sent this lovely card to you for this holiday.
(Source: *Crafts for Kwanzaa*, Kathy Ross)

Kinara.
Let the children make their own paper Kinaras (or candle holders) to help celebrate this family holiday. The Kinara is similar to the Menorah in shape but holds only seven candles. The center candle, higher than the others, is black. Three places are made on either side of this candle to hold six other candles (three green to the left and three red to the right). It's an African custom to make these things by hand.

Activity: **Togetherness Kwanzaa Meal.**
Have the children plan a gathering where elders (not just parents) are invited to share and exchange stories, pictures, and memories. The children can prepare special meals to be served from recipes found in the two books listed here.
(Source: *Let's Celebrate Kwanzaa: An Activity Book for Young Readers*, Helen Davis Thompson; *Kwanzaa: An African-American Celebration of Culture and Cooking*, Eric V. Copage)

Songs: (Audio) "First Fruit"
(Source: *Kwanzaa Songs*)
(Book) "It's Kwanzaa Time" or "The Little Light"
(Source: *It's Kwanzaa Time!*, Linda and Clay Goss)

85 Holidays: St. Patrick's Day
(also includes Elves and Little People)

Relate to:	*St. Patrick's Day (March 17): To commemorate the patron saint of Ireland.*

Videos:	*Holidays for Children: St. Patrick's Day* *Snow White and the Seven Dwarfs*

Books:	*Daniel O'Rourke*, Gerald McDermott *The Hungry Leprechaun*, Mary Calhoun *Jeremy Bean's St. Patrick's Day*, Alice Schertle *Leprechaun Gold*, Teresa Bateman *The Leprechaun in the Basement*, Kathy Tucker *Leprechauns Never Lie*, Lorna Balian *The Leprechaun's Story*, Richard Kennedy *Little Bear Marches in the St. Patrick's Day Parade*, Janice Brustlein *Mary McLean and the St. Patrick's Day Parade*, Steven Kroll *Patrick's Day*, Elizabeth Lee O'Donnell *Seeing Is Believing*, Elizabeth Shub *St. Patrick's Day*, Gail Gibbons *St. Patrick's Day in the Morning*, Eve Bunting *Tim O'Toole and the Wee Folk*, Gerald McDermott

Fingerplay:	**The Giant and the Leprechaun.** (Source: *Finger Frolics—Revised*, Liz Cromwell, Dixie Hibner, and John R. Faitel)

Crafts:	**Leprechaun's Clay Pipe.** Although a clay pipe would be difficult and time-consuming to make, how about one made of small drinking cups, straws, and ribbons? This book will give you short, simple instructions with an illustration for making a shillelagh and a leprechaun family. (Source: *Pin It, Tack It, Hang It*, Phyllis and Noel Fiarotta)
	St. Pat's Harp. Harps are a well-known symbol in Ireland and are used to accompany Irish ballads. Trace and precut the shape of a harp from posterboard. Cut a bar long enough to lay across the top of the harp. Punch five holes on the bar and an equal amount on the lower portion of the harp. Decorate the bottom of the harp with a green shamrock. Give each child some long, green

yarn to weave through the holes to create the strings of the harp.

(Source: *Music Crafts for Kids*, Noel and Phyllis Fiarotta)

Activities: **Shamrock Hunt.**

Make several shamrocks with green construction paper. Put each child's name on different shamrocks, and hide them in the room. Have each child try to find his or her own. This can be played in teams with each team trying to find their names first.

For those who can't read, put special pictures on the shamrocks for them to locate. After the game, let the children make St. Patrick's Day hats and use their shamrocks as a decoration at the top of each.

Beep Bop the Shamrock.

Allow the children to bring in their own lunch bags and they can decorate them with pictures of shamrocks for this special holiday. Blow the bags up (or actually use balloons) and have them practice batting them up in the air. Put music on and tell the children when you yell "Beep Bop the Shamrock" everyone should begin. The one to keep it in the air the longest wins.

(Source: *Creative Games for Young Children*, Annetta Dellinger)

Songs: (Audio) "St. Patrick's Day Is Here"

(Source: *Holiday Songs for all Occasions*)

(Book) "The Galway Piper"

(Source: *The Rhythm Band Book*, Ruth Etkin)

86 Holidays: St. Valentine's Day

Relate to:	*St. Valentine's Day (Feb. 14): A day for sharing your feelings with the one you love or simply making new friends.*

Videos:
Bee My Valentine
The Best Valentine in the World
A Goofy Look at Valentine's Day
Little Mouse's Big Valentine
One Zillion Valentines

Books:
Bee My Valentine!, Miriam Cohen
The Best Valentine in the World, Marjorie Sharmat
A Circle Is Not a Valentine, H. Werner Zimmermann
Froggy's First Kiss, Jonathan London
The Great Valentine's Day Balloon Race, Adrienne Adams
Heart to Heart, George Shannon
The Hunt for Rabbit's Galosh, Ann Schweninger
Little Mouse's Big Valentine, Thacher Hurd
Roses Are Pink, Your Feet Really Stink, Diane deGroat
Valentine, Carol Carrick
The Valentine Bears, Eve Bunting
Valentine Mice!, Bethany Roberts
Valentine's Day, Miriam Nerlove
Valentine's Day: Stories and Poems, Caroline Feller Bauer
Will You Be My Valentine?, Steven Kroll

Fingerplay: **A Day for Love.**
(Source: *Finger Frolics—Revised*, Liz Cromwell, Dixie Hibner, and John R. Faitel)

Crafts: **Valentine Mobile.**
Allow the children to trace and cut out various size hearts for the mobiles they will make. To add a touch of variety let them decorate the mobles differently, using stickers, stars, crayon, and glitter.
Cut four strings of different lengths, and tape the hearts to these. Cut a wide strip of paper and staple it to form a circle. Each of the four strings of hearts can now be attached to this. Precut hearts can be used if time is short.
(Source: *Let's Celebrate: Holiday Decorations You Can Make*, Peggy Parish)

Valentine Bear.
Make your own huggable Valentine Bear with the patterns supplied in this book. Children will be able to put together this simple bear, and add paw prints and a large heart on his stomach.

This book supplies a large number of holiday patterns that children can enjoy.

(Source: *Cut and Create! Holidays*, Kim Rankin)

Activities:

Throne Game.
The Queen of Hearts sits on her throne while the knave tries to steal a tart. The other guests stand on paper squares (the tarts). When the Queen says all change places, each guest tries to get to a new tart with the knave trying to steal one. If one is stolen, the person left out becomes the knave.

(Source: *A Pumpkin in a Pear Tree*, Ann Cole, Carolyn Haas, Elizabeth Heller, and Betty Weinberger)

Cupid Chase.
Here's a game of tag that's played in reverse. Select one child to be Cupid in this game and place a small bell around his or her neck. The remainder of the group are all blindfolded and will attempt to locate Cupid by the sound of the bell. You can also find other activities similar to this one for the Valentine's holiday in this source.

(Source: *February Holidays Handbook*, Ruth Shannon Odor and others)

Songs:

(Audio) "Skinnamarink"
(Source: *Car Songs*)
(Book) "Valentines"
(Source: *God's Wonderful World*, Agnes Leckie Mason and Phyllis Brown Ohanian)

87 Holidays: Thanksgiving

Relate to: *Thanksgiving Day (fourth Thursday in Nov.): A day to give thanks for our friends, family, and everything else in our lives.*

Videos: *Giving Thanks*
The Pilgrims of Plimoth
Thanksgiving Day

Books: *1,2,3 Thanksgiving!*, W. Nikola-Lisa
Clifford's Thanksgiving Visit, Norman Bridwell
Giving Thanks: A Native American Good Morning Message, Chief Jake Swamp
Gracias, The Thanksgiving Turkey, Joy Cowley
Little Bear's Thanksgiving, Janice
Oh, What a Thanksgiving!, Steven Kroll
One Tough Turkey, Steven Kroll
Silly Tilly's Thanksgiving Dinner, Lillian Hoban
Sometimes It's Turkey, Lorna Balian
The Squirrels' Thanksgiving, Steven Kroll
Thanksgiving at the Tappletons, Eileen Spinelli
Thanksgiving Day, Gail Gibbons
Thanksgiving with Me, Margaret Willey
A Turkey for Thanksgiving, Eve Bunting
'Twas the Night before Thanksgiving, Dav Pilkey

Fingerplay: **Five Little Turkeys.**
(Source: *Finger Frolics—Revised*, Liz Cromwell, Dixie Hibner, and John R. Faitel)

Crafts: **Paper Plate Turkey.**
There are many suggestions out there on how to make these brightly colored gobblers, and this is one of the easiest. Paper plates can be purchased rather cheaply and form the major part of the turkey with two plates glued to each other.

The tail feathers are created from looped construction paper. McCarty and Peterson's book will even give you full-size patterns for making the feet and head so they look realistic. A simple and enjoyable craft.
(Source: *Craft Fun: Easy-to-Do with Simple Materials*, Janet R. McCarty and Betty J. Peterson)

Here Come the Turkeys Napkin Rings.
Children can make attractive turkey napkin rings for their familys' holiday tables. On a strip of construction paper six inches long they glue turkey feathers created by strips of colored paper formed in a loop. When finished, they take the entire strip, wrap it around a toilet paper tube, and bend the feathers up to form the turkey tail. The turkey's head is made out of curled strips of brown paper. Don't let them forget his face. This will make an attractive addition to any family's Thanksgiving table and the children can view it with pride.
(Source: *My Very Own Thanksgiving: A Book of Cooking and Crafts*, Robin West)

Activities:

The Turkey Talk.
While the children sing the song "Five Fat Turkeys Are We" they may take the roles of the turkey or the cooks. Piano music for the song is available for use in this source. Children enjoy depicting how animals will behave, and this dance will be enjoyed and asked for again and again.
(Source: *Dancing Games for Children of All Ages*, Esther L. Nelson)

A Thanksgiving Mix-up.
Children sit in chairs in a circle with one person It, standing in the center. Give the children names that identify them as something on a Thanksgiving Day dinner table. The person who is It calls out two items and those two children exchange seats. The caller can continue in this manner until he or she calls, "the dinner table is tipped over," at which time everyone scatters for a different seat, including the caller. The person left out is the next caller.
(Source: *It's Time for Thanksgiving*, Elizabeth Hough Sechrist and Janette Woolsey)

Songs:

(Audio) "Turkey Wobble"
(Source: *Holiday Songs for All Occasions*)
(Book) "Five Fat Turkeys Are We"
(Source: *Dancing Games for Children of All Ages*, Esther L. Nelson)

88 Hospitals/Doctors

Relate to: *Doctor's Day (March 30): In honor of American doctors and the anniversary of the first time Dr. Crawford W. Long used ether in surgery.*

Videos: *Curious George Goes to the Hospital*
The Hospital
Madeline
Sesame Street Home Video Visits the Hospital

Books: *Barney Is Best*, Nancy Carlstrom
The Best Present, Holly Keller
Betsy and the Doctor, Gunilla Wolde
Doctors, Dee Ready
Emergency Mouse, Bernard Stone
A Hospital Story, Sara Bonnett Stein
Maggie and the Emergency Room, Martine Davison
Max's Daddy Goes to the Hospital, Danielle Steel
Miffy in the Hospital, Dick Bruna
One Bear in the Hospital, Caroline Buchnall
Poor Monty, Anne Fine
Robby Visits the Doctor, Martine Davison
This Is a Hospital, Not a Zoo!, Roberta Karim
A Trip to the Doctor, Margot Linn
A Visit to the Sesame Street Hospital, Deborah Hautzig

Fingerplay: **Five Little Monkeys.**
(Source: *Finger Frolics—Revised*, Liz Cromwell, Dixie Hibner, and John R. Faitel)

Crafts: **Postage and Pill Boxes.**
Remember all those small boxes that seem to collect and you don't know what to do with them? Well, here's a great idea for them. Let the children decorate them with various objects (stickers, stamps, paint, etc.) and label them "My Pills." There are many people out there who now take some kind of vitamins on a regular basis, and now the children can give them their own special "Pill Box" to carry those vitamins easily. This source also has some unique ideas of how to use some special boxes in a different way (e.g., a ring box with foam in it can be turned upside down and you can moisten the foam with water to create a good stamp sealer).
(Source: *Let's Make It from Junk*, Eileen Mercer)

**Craft and
Activity:**

Stethoscope and Otoscope.
Help the children learn about a doctor's instruments by constructing these familiar items from cups, paper, and string. Later allow the children to practice with their paper instruments as you show real ones that you have obtained.

When children become familiar with these tools they will not become so frightened when they are used in the doctor's office. If you wish to extend this program into a full-unit lesson, this source also provides detailed instructions for making the following doctor's tools:

- jar-of-pills signs
- doctor's bag
- thermometer
- hypodermic syringe
- blood pressure cuff
- health posters

These items can be made simply and easily out of construction paper and boxes.
(Source: *Be What You Want to Be!*, Phyllis and Noel Fiarotta)

Activity:

Dr. Knots.
Select one child to be Dr. Knots and have him or her leave the room. The remainder of the children will form a circle. Explain that they must try to knot themselves up without letting go of anyone's hands. They will then yell out, "Help! Dr. Knots! We need you!" Dr. Knots enters and attempts to untangle the mess without anyone breaking the chain. If Dr. Knots needs help, the children can give hints. Keep it light and humorous.
(Source: *Everyone Wins!: Non-Competitive Party Games and Activities for Children*, Jody L. Blosser)

Songs:

(Audio) "Doctor, Doctor"
(Source: *People in Our Neighborhood*)
(Book) "My Doctor"
(Source: *God's Wonderful World*, Agnes Leckie Mason and Phyllis Brown Ohanian)

89 Houses/Homes

Relate to: *New Homeowner's Day (May 1): A time when new homeowners can sit back and enjoy their new home and the people who will be sharing it with them.*

Videos: *The Little House*
Madeline and the New House
The Old Mill
The Village of Round and Square Houses

Books: *Better Move On, Frog!*, Ron Maris
Duncan's Tree House, Amanda Vesey
The Halloween House, Erica Silverman
A House by the Sea, Joanne Ryder
I Can Build a House!, Shigeo Watanabe
The Magic House, Robyn Harbert Eversole
The Maid and the Mouse and the Odd-Shaped House, Paul O. Zelinsky
The Mouse in My House, Catherine Chase
My House, Lisa Desimini
A New House for the Morrisons, Penny Carter
Pigs in the House, Steven Kroll
The Someday House, Anne Shelby
Sunflower House, Eve Bunting
This Is Our House, Michael Rosen
Where Does the Teacher Live?, Paula Feder

Fingerplay: **My Home.**
(Source: *Finger Frolics—Revised*, Liz Cromwell, Dixie Hibner, and John R. Faitel)

Crafts: **A Doll House.**
A large cardboard carton can be transformed into a usable doll house. Leaving the flaps open, set the box on end and cut (or paint) windows in the front and sides. Dividers can be glued in to add a second floor.
    The interior and exterior of the box can be painted to taste. Add a roof by folding posterboard in half and placing it on the top. The interior can be designed by marker or by adding the children's toys.
    (Source: *Just a Box?*, Goldie Taub Chernoff)

Cottage Collage.
Fashion a snug little house with smoke billowing from the chimney. Use a number of unique items for this collage, such as a stamp with a face on it on the top of the door to give the illusion of someone being at home. This craft even incorporates things like paper clips, newspaper, Popsicle sticks, and more. Collages allow the children a chance to be different.
(Source: *Papercrafts*, Judith Hoffman Corwin)

Activities:

Sweep the House.
This is a simple team game that requires only the use of two brooms and two pieces of paper. Mark a circle at the center of the room and have the teams stand on opposite ends of the room. The goal is for the teams to try to sweep their garbage into the circle first.
(Source: *New Games to Play*, Juel Krisvoy)

House Sounds Guessing Game.
A house with a family in it is a very busy place. Have you ever stopped to just listen and count how many different sounds you hear in your home? Make a recording of sounds from your house and see if the children can guess what they are. For a list of suggestions see this source.
(Source: *More Picture Book Story Hours: From Parties to Pets*, Paula Gaj Sitarz)

Songs:

(Audio) "Tree House"
(Source: *Ants*)
(Book) "Home"
(Source: *God's Wonderful World*, Agnes Leckie Mason and Phyllis Brown Ohanian)

90 Humor

Relate to:	*April Fool's Day (April 1): This day is set aside to trick people by sending them on nonsensical errands or conning them into doing silly, but unharmful acts; then the prankster says, "April Fool." A time for tricks when all, including the one tricked, can laugh.*

Videos:
Caps for Sale
The Day Jimmy's Boa Ate the Wash
The Emperor's New Clothes
Harold and the Purple Crayon
Rosie's Walk

Books:
Ants Can't Dance, Ellen Jackson
April Fools, Fernando Krahn
The Cats of Mrs. Calamari, John Stadler
The Day the Teacher Went Bananas, James Howe
The Lady with the Alligator Purse, Nadine Bernard Westcott
Miss Nelson Has a Field Day, Harry Allard
My First Picture Joke Book, Shoo Rayner
My First Riddles, Judith Hoffman Corwin
My Mom and Dad Make Me Laugh, Nick Sharratt
Never Ride Your Elephant to School, Doug Johnson
No More Water in the Tub!, Tedd Arnold
Shenandoah Noah, Jim Aylesworth
Sody Sallyratus, Teri Sloat
Too Much Noise, Ann McGovern
Turtle Tale, Frank Asch

Fingerplay: **Who Feels Happy Today?**
(Source: *Rhymes for Learning Times*, Louise Binder Scott)

Crafts: **Joke Box.**
Monkey see, monkey do/Where's the monkey in the zoo?
Open the box and you will see/The only place the monkey can be.

Decorate a box using any available materials such as colored construction paper, stickers, and markers. Allow the children to use their imagination. Inside glue a small mirror to the bottom of the box. Across the open section of the box bottom tape or glue black yarn to form a cage. Design and replace the box cover and you're set for a delightful joke with your friends.

Egg-heads from Mars.
Break out your collection of egg cartons again for this humorous craft from outer space. Open the cartons and let the children decorate the interior of the tops with stars and planets to illustrate a space scene. Then they decorate each center spike as a creature from Mars, Venus, or a planet they make up. They can give one paper antennae, another cotton hair, etc. The stranger the better.
(Source: *Bag of Tricks!*, James Razzi)

Activities: **I Saw a Purple Cow.**
This is a word game for two or more players. The first player says, " I saw a purple cow on the road. I ONE it." The next player says, "I TWO it" and so on until the eighth player says his line.
   You can continue this game by changing the animals. It's lots of fun and no one loses.
(Source: *I Saw a Purple Cow*, Ann Cole, Carolyn Haas, Faith Bushnell, and Betty Weinberger)

The No Laugh Race.
This game pairs children off in an elimination game. The children must face each other and follow the humorous instructions given to them in the song that accompanies this game. The first to laugh is eliminated and everyone pairs up with new partners. Included in this source are the music you can use and suggestions for actions. Add your own as needed.
(Source: *The Cat in the Hat Songbook*, Dr. Seuss)

Songs: (Audio) "Shake My Sillies Out"
   (Source: *Raffi in Concert with the Rise and Shine Band*)
(Book) "A Bear Climbed over the Mountain"
   (Source: *The Silly Songbook*, Esther L. Nelson)

91 Imagination and Pretending

Relate to:	*National New Idea Day (Feb. 16): Develop the idea of brainstorming with children while acting out various events. All ideas should be encouraged.*

Videos:
The Emperor's New Clothes
Harold and the Purple Crayon
In the Night Kitchen
One Monday Morning
A Picture for Harold's Room

Books:
Amazing Grace, Mary Hoffman
And to Think I Saw It on Mulberry Street, Dr. Seuss
The Bear under the Stairs, Helen Cooper
Chimps Don't Wear Glasses, Laura Numeroff
Cloudy with a Chance of Meatballs, Judi Barrett
Dragon Scales and Willow Leaves, Terryl Givens
Harry and the Terrible Whatzit, Dick Gackenbach
I Wish I Had Duck Feet, Theo LeSieg
If I Were Queen of the World, Fred Hiatt
I'm a Jolly Farmer, Julie Lacome
Kate's Giants, Valiska Gregory
Magic Beach, Alison Lester
Pete's a Pizza, William Steig
The Pirates of Bedford Street, Rachel Isadora
Quiet! There's a Canary in the Library, Don Freeman

Fingerplay: **If.**
(Source: *Little Boy Blue*, Daphne Hogstrom)

Crafts: **Boogie Woogie Creatures.**
Have the children bring an old glove from home. With this give them each five medium size pom-poms of various colors to glue to the top of the glove's fingers. To each of these pom-poms, glue felt or craft-store eyes. After the eyes have dried the children may don the gloves and make the creatures dance to music by wiggling their fingers.

Butterfly Finger-Play Puppet.
As you can probably tell as you flip through my book, I love to do crafts with paper plates. They're inexpensive and usually uncomplicated. This is another of my favorites that brought smiles to children's faces.

With the use of a single paper plate, precut small triangles in the four locations shown in the *Easter Handbook* to form butterfly wings. Have the children draw a butterfly body and color in the beautiful wings. Use the remaining cutouts to form finger rings for the back of the plate so the children can make their butterfly flutter around the room.

Enjoy letting the children recite the rhyme provided and pretend they, too, are the butterfly opening up and flying through the room.

(Source: *Easter Handbook*, Ramona Warren and others)

Activities:

Let's Pretend We're Giants.
This simple game requires the children to pretend they're giants. A rope is laid on the ground (rope river) and children must hop back and forth over it to reach the land of the little people. Those that step on the rope or fall have fallen into the river and are out of the game.

(Source: *New Games to Play*, Juel Krisvoy)

The Magician.
This is a noisy game but one that young children can relate to easily. Give one child a wand to be the magician. Let the magician wander through the crowd tapping each child while naming an animal. Each child in turn gets to become that animal. When the entire room fills with noisy animals you may select a child to be the next magician. This is a very flexible type of activity that can fit in with any theme you are currently working on. You may next want a whole room of transportation vehicles.

(Source: *500 Games*, Peter L. Cave)

Songs:

(Audio) "Copycat"
(Source: *Cookin'*)
(Book) "I'm a Little Teapot"
(Source: *Eye Winker, Tom Tinker, Chin Chopper*, Tom Glazer)

93 Insects: Bees

Relate to:	*National Honey Month (Sept.): A time to honor beekeepers and the colonies of bees that make the honey we eat.*

Videos: *Bea's Own Good*
The Berenstain Bears Save the Bees (The Berenstain Bears on the Truth)
The Little Dog and the Bees

Books: *The Bee,* Lisa Campbell Ernst
The Bee and the Dream, Jan Freeman Long
"Buzz, Buzz, Buzz," Went Bumblebee, Colin West
Fiona's Bee, Beverly Keller
The Flower of Sheba, Doris Orgel and Ellen Schecter
"Follow Me," Cried Bee, Jan Wahl
Gran's Bees, Mary Thompson
Harry's Bee, Peter Campbell
The Honey Makers, Gail Gibbons
The Honeybee, Paula Z. Hogan
Honeybee's Party, Joanna and Paul Galdone
King Solomon and the Bee, Dalia Hardof Renberg
The Magic Schoollbus: Inside the Beehive, Joanna Cole
Mr. Bumble, Kim Kennedy
The Rose in My Garden, Arnold Lobel

Fingerplay: **Here Is the Beehive.**
(Source: *Mother Goose Time,* Jane Marino)

Crafts: **Bumble Bee.**
A simple bumble bee can be constructed using folded black construction paper for wings, and pipe cleaners and yellow pom-poms for its body. This engaging little craft will have the children buzzing all over your room.
(Source: *The Giant Encyclopedia of Theme Activities for Children 2 to 5,* Kathy Charner)

Cylinder Bee.
If you would like a bumble bee that's a little more three dimensional try looking up this craft. With the use of the old standby, toilet paper roll, and some construction paper you can make a colorful bee with a little more depth to hang from a string. Patterns for wings and stinger are also included here.
(Source: *Year Round Crafts for Kids,* Barbara L. DonDiego)

Activities:

Buzzing Game.
Select a couple of children from your group to leave the room while selected items are hidden in the classroom. On their return these children will begin their search for the missing objects while all the remaining bumblebees tell them if they are close or not by the intensity of their buzzzzing.
(Source: *Theme-a-saurus*, Jean Warren)

Buzzing Bees.
This is a unique variation of musical chairs. Have the children make a large flower of their own choice. Place the flowers randomly throughout the room. Next instruct the children to act as bees buzzing around the room until they land on any flower when the music stops. Of course, remove one flower with each new round.
(Source: *Kids and Seasons*, Kathy Darling)

Songs:

(Audio) "There Was a Bee-I-EE-I-EE"
(Source: *Kids Silly Song Sing-a-longs*)
(Book) "Baby Bumble Bee"
(Source: *The Funny Songbook*, Esther L. Nelson)

94 Insects: Ladybugs

Relate to:	*Freeing the Insects Day (May 28): Also known as Insect-Hearing Festival, this Japanese festival has vendors selling insects in tiny bamboo cages. These pets are kept near the house so that their music can be heard during the night. Then on a day late in August, people gather in a park to release them and listen to the freed insects burst into their individual sounds.*

Videos: *Ladybug, Ladybug, Winter Is Coming*

Books:
Bubba and Trixie, Lisa Campbell Ernst
Eye Spy a Ladybug!, Melinda Lilly
The Grouch Ladybug, Eric Carle
How Spider Saved Halloween, Robert Kraus
Ladybug, Emery Bernhard
Ladybug, Barrie Watts
The Ladybug and Other Insects, Pascale deBourgoing and Gallimard Jeunesse
Ladybug, Ladybug, Robert Kraus
Ladybug, Ladybug, Ruth Brown
Ladybug, Ladybug, Fly Away Home, Judy Hawes
A Ladybug's Life, John Himmelman
Lucky Ladybugs, Gladys Conklin
My Ladybug, Herbert H. Wong and Matthew F. Vesse

Fingerplay: **Ladybug.**
A new slant on the old "Ladybug" rhyme.
> (Source: *Once Upon a Childhood: Fingerplays, Action Rhymes, and Fun Times for the Very Young*, Dolores Chupela)

Crafts: **Ladybug and Buggy Riddles.**
This refreshing source for library storyhour programs includes a pattern for making a ladybug with movable wings. Patterns are easily photocopied so that the children can decorate them with sticker dots or use crayons. This will make a great prop when reciting the rhyme "Ladybug" or answering the "buggy riddles" supplied in the same source.
> (Source: *Library Storyhour from A to Z*, Ellen K. Hasbrouck)

The Ladybug.
Hand art is a fun way for children to create colorful animals or insects. Have them paint the palm of their hand and imprint it

on the paper to create a bug body. Use black thumbprints to create the spots on the ladybug's back.

A palm print done with green paint can be placed below the bug for a leaf. When all is dry children can add outlines and such features as antennae and legs. Try this source for many animal art creations done in this way.

(Source: *Hand-Print Animal Art*, Carolyn Carreiro)

Activities: **Ladybug Bingo.**
The source cited here provides full-page bingo cards with ladybugs, each with different dots on the card instead of just numbers. Cut the card in half and have the children color their ladybugs. One half of the board is cut up to create markers that match the ladybugs on their board. Now you're ready to play. Children roll dice to determine which ladybug to cover.

(Source: *Kids Celebrate!*, Maria Bonfanti Esche and Clare Bonfanti Braham)

Ladybug Game.
This is an uncomplicated game that even the youngest children can handle. The children can partner with another child or a parent to begin. As they recite the rhyme they perform the actions, first facing each other, then back to back until they fly away to find another partner and begin again.

The children will love moving from one person to the next until they end up finally with their original partner.

(Source: *Storytime Crafts*, Kathryn Totten)

Songs: (Audio) "Hello Ladybug"
(Source: *Piggyback Planet Songs for a Whole Earth*)
(Book) "Ladybug, Ladybug"
(Source: *A Creepy, Crawly Song Book*, Carl Davis and Hiawyn Oram)

95 Kindergarten

Relate to:	*Kindergarten Day (April 21): A special day to show the role of play and creative work in a child's education.*

Videos:	*Everybody Knows That* *Mister Rogers' Neighborhood: Going to School* *Morris Goes to School* *Richard Scarry's: Sally's First Day at School*
Books:	*Amanda Pig, Schoolgirl*, Jean Van Leeuwen *Benjamin Bigfoot*, Mary Serfozo *Big David, Little David*, S. E. Hinton *Boomer Goes to School*, Constance McGeorge *Born in the Gravy*, Denys Cazet *First Grade Can Wait*, Lorraine Aseltine *Harry and Tuck*, Holly Keller *Jessica*, Kevin Henkes *Miss Bindergarten Celebrates the 100th Day of Kindergarten*, Joseph Slate *My Mom Made Me Go to School*, Judy Delton *Rachel Parker, Kindergarten Show-off*, Ann Martin *Red Day, Green Day*, Edith Kunhardt *School Isn't Fair!*, Patricia Baehr *Show and Tell*, Elvira Woodruff *What Will Mommy Do When I'm at School?*, Dolores Johnson
Fingerplay:	**School Days.** (Source: *More Picture Book Story Hours: From Parties to Pets*, Paula Gaj Sitarz)
Crafts:	**First Day Poster.** Let the children show their parents what they accomplished on their first week or month of kindergarten. Each day supply the children with a two-inch white square and ask them to illustrate something they did today. If they did fingerpainting they might just want to put a thumbprint on it. If they cut out things let them draw a picture of scissors, etc. At the end of the week or month give them a large, colored poster board to glue on these squares. Label it "My Kindergarten Accomplishments." **First-Day-of-School Cone.** The first day of school for children can be a great adventure or

a fearsome event. Here's a little tradition from Germany that makes that first day a joyful remembrance. Many parents in Germany try to sweeten the first day of school for the children by giving them a large paper cone filled with candies or cookies in honor of the event.

Why not follow this unique tradition with a little change? Let the children make and decorate their own cones from poster board and crepe paper. When they have completed it, surprise them by helping them fill their cones with special treats.

(Source: *Folk Crafts for World Friendship*, Florence Temko)

Activities:

Unpack Your Bag.
This is a wonderful activity to help a new child feel welcome to the class. Ask the new child and parent to bring to class a bag labeled "All About Me" and to place in the bag various items that are important to the child. In the class each item can be removed and the child can help the teacher explain its importance. You can also have the children in the class show the new child items they have brought into the class. This is a terrific ice breaker.

(Source: *The Giant Encyclopedia of Theme Activities for Children 2 to 5*, Kathy Charner)

Stone School.
This activity gives the children a chance to practice social skills such as taking turns, accepting small problems, and more that are usually worked on in the kindergarten year. The only item needed is a small pebble or such object and a row of chairs.

Each child will sit in front of a row of chairs, which is the preschool class. As the teacher approaches each student she will have in one clenched fist the pebble. The student must decide which fist has the pebble in it. If the child guesses correctly he gets to move to the kindergarten (seated on the chair). Continue in this method with each child going around and around and having each child move through the grades (1st grade standing on the chair, 2nd grade standing behind the chair, etc.) until all children have graduated.

Comments on encouraging sportsmanship in this game are also offered in this source.

(Source: *Teacher's Handbook of Children's Games*, Marian Jenks Wirth)

Songs:

(Audio) "Kindergarten Wall"
    (Source: *Mail Myself to You*)
(Book) "Ms. McDonald Has a Class"
    (Source: *Ms. McDonald Has a Class*, Jan Ormerod)

96 Kites

Relate to:	*National "Let's Go Fly a Kite" Month (March): A month to enjoy the art of kite flying.*

Videos:	*Dorothy and the Kite* *Spot's Windy Day* (Spot Goes to the Farm)
Books:	*Anatole over Paris*, Eve Titus *Angel's Kite*, Alberto Blanco *A Carp for Kimiko*, Virginia Kroll *Catch the Wind!: All about Kites*, Gail Gibbons *Curious George Flies a Kite*, Margaret Rey *The Emperor and the Kite*, Jane Yolen *Hamlet and the Enormous Chinese Dragon Kite*, Brian Lies *The Kite*, Mary Packard *Lucky Song*, Vera B. Williams *Mike's Kite*, Elizabeth MacDonald *Moonlight Kite*, Helen E. Buckley *Nu Dang and His Kite*, Jacqueline Ayer *Rabbit's Birthday Kite*, Maryann MacDonald *The Sea-Breeze Hotel*, Marcia Vaughan and Patricia Mullins
Fingerplay:	**The Kite.** (Source: *Finger Frolics—Revised*, Liz Cromwell, Dixie Hibner, and John R. Faitel)
Crafts:	**Chinese Kite.** This is a simple kite that may be constructed using a large, clear freezer bag. Distribute these to the children along with stickers and stars that they may put on the exterior of the bag. To make a tail for the kite, staple a length of colored ribbon to the unopened portion of the bag to give it balance. A small length of kite string taped to each side of the open section of the bag will allow it to fill up with air and open when the child runs with it. With younger children (two years) you may wish to use a lunch bag instead of a freezer bag. Although it does give a different effect, some younger children may put the freezer bag over their heads if unattended. (Source: *More Beginning Crafts for Beginning Readers*, Alice Gilbreath)

A Diamond Kite.
Recycled plastic bags can make a colorful diamond kite. With the youngest of children you may need to precut the shape, while older children can learn to measure for the correct shape. For the best results use acrylic paints for colorful artwork. If that is unavailable this source gives alternatives when using poster paint.

(Source: *My First Paint Book*, Dawn Sirett)

Activities: **Kite Run.**
The children should be escorted outdoors in order to demonstrate and play with their newly made kites. Whenever possible, children should be given a chance to show off their new creations, and this will give you an opportunity to demonstrate the correct way to use these kites.

Kite Flying.
On a windy day children enjoy trying to get their kites to soar to great heights. This is an activity for non-windy days. Let the children pair up to mimic kite flying with one child actually pretending to be the kite and holding onto a string as he or she is pulled in and out throughout the room.

For a quieter time decorate a number of kite shapes and cut them into two pieces. Mix them up and have a little puzzle matchup activity.

(Source: *Theme-a-saurus II*, Jean Warren)

Songs: (Audio) "Let's Go Fly a Kite"
(Source: *The Disney Collection, Vol. 2*)
(Book) "Let's Go Fly a Kite"
(Source: *The Walt Disney Song Book*, Walt Disney)

97 Libraries

Relate to:	*National Library Week (April 19–25): Celebrates the pleasure of reading and the importance of libraries and librarians to our lives.*

Videos:
Andy and the Lion
Arthur's Lost Library Book
Curious George Goes to the Library (Curious George Goes to Town)
The Library

Books:
The Adventures of Cap'n O.G. Readmore, Fran Manushkin
Alistair in Outer Space, Marilyn Sadler
Author's Day, Daniel Pinkwater
Calico Cat Meets Bookworm, Donald Charles
Edward and the Pirates, David McPhail
How My Library Grew, Martha Alexander
The Librarian from the Black Lagoon, Mike Thaler
Libraries Take Us Far, Lee Sullivan Hill
The Library Dragon, Carmen Agra Deedy
Once Inside the Library, Barbara A. Huff
Quiet! There's a Canary in the Library, Don Freeman
Red Light, Green Light, Mama and Me, Cari Best
Sophie and Sammy's Library Sleepover, Judith Caseley
Storyhour—Starring Megan!, Julie Brillhart
Tomas and the Library Lady, Pat Mora
Too Many Books!, Caroline Bauer
A Visit to the Sesame Street Library, Deborah Hautzig
Walter's Magic Wand, Eric Houghton

Fingerplay: **I Wiggle.**
(Source: *Finger Frolics—Revised*, Liz Cromwell, Dixie Hibner, and John R. Faitel)

Crafts: **Bookbug Bookmarks.**
As a memento of their library visit, the children can make simple bookmarks using the following materials: colored paper, crayons, large pom-poms, and small eyes. The children can decorate their precut bookmarks as they wish. They will then be given a pom-pom to glue on as the bookbug's head and then eyes to glue on the head.

Bubble-Printed Notebook.
Explain to children how books are purchased and prepared for their use only after they are protected with special covers, due date pockets, etc. Now it's time for the children to design their own book covers for their precious books at home.

Add a large amount of dishwashing liquid to a tub of cold water and swish until you get a great deal of suds. Let the children drip different colors of food colorings over the suds, then place large sheets of typing paper one at a time on top of it. After removing the paper place it aside to dry for the children to use later as colorful book covers.
(Source: *The Ultimate Show-Me-How Activity Book*)

Activities: **A Walking Tour.**
In this activity the following topics will be covered:
- Location of books at the child's level
- Book care
- What's available at the library (besides books)
- Library manners
- Visiting the public library.

Teeny Tiny Tale.
All the children can sit in a circle facing each other for this storytelling event. Have the children use very tiny voices to tell a Teeny Tiny open-ended story such as:
Once upon a time there was a teeny tiny____who lived in a teen tiny ____. She . . .
For a variation use Giant voices to tell giant stories. Later let the children illustrate the tale they created as a group.
(Source: *1–2–3 Games*, Jean Warren)

Songs: (Audio) "At the Library"
(Source: *We're On Our Way*)
(Book) "Member of the Library"
(Source: *The Songs of Sesame Street in Poems and Pictures*, Jeffrey Moss, David Axelrod, Tony Geiss, Bruce Hart, Emily Perl Kingsley, and Jon Stone)

98 Machines

Relate to: *The invention of the first European adding machine (Oct. 11, 1887): This is a machine most children are now familiar with and can lead to inventions of other simple machines.*

Videos: *Big Rigs*
Drummer Hoff
I Wanna Be a Heavy Equipment Operator
Mike Mulligan and the Steam Shovel
Simple Machines

Books: *Alistair's Time Machine*, Marilyn Sadler
Bam, Bam, Bam, Eve Merriam
Big Wheels, Anne Rockwell
The Busy Building Book, Sue Tarsky
Construction Zone, Tana Hoban
The Crazy Crawler Crane and Other Very Short Truck Stories, Mittie Cuetara
The Day Veronica Was Nosy, Elizabeth Laird
Dig, Drill, Dump, Fill, Tana Hoban
I Don't Want to Go to Bed, Astrid Lindgren
Jesse Builds a Road, Laurence Pringle
Machines, Anne and Harlow Rockwell
Machines at Work, Byron Barton
Mowing, Jessie Haas
Road Builders, B. G. Hennessy
Trash Trucks!, Daniel Kirk

Fingerplay: **Pound Goes the Hammer.**
(Source: *Storytimes for Two-Year-Olds*, Judy Nichols)

Crafts: **Machine Sculpture.**
Collect a variety of machine parts in preparation for your class creating their own machine sculpture. Items such as pipes, clock parts, and calculators, will suffice. Using heavy tape let the children connect them as they see fit. You may even want to spray paint it later.

A flat sculpture can be designed using nails, wood, and other flat objects. Let the children name their pieces of art and display them prominently in your classroom.
(Source: *Good Earth Art*, Mary Ann F. Kohl and Cindy Gainer)

Gadget Printing.
Children really enjoy making prints of various items. In this source you will find instructions on creating a paint pad for each child to use. Next allow them to select various gadgets or simple machines (potato mashers, forks, combs, etc.) to dip into the paint pad and press on paper. Their artwork will be the envy of everyone.
(Source: *Crafts: Early Learning Activities*, Jean Warren)

Activities:

Machine Hunt.
Tour your classroom or house with your group in search of a variety of simple machines (typewriters, record player, computers, etc.). If you don't have a lot in your room, hang pictures where children can find them. Once you collect whatever they can find, discuss the machines' many functions.

Electronic People Machine.
Build a human machine with a group of children. Tell them when the music begins, the machine turns on; when the music stops, the machine turns off. Try anything, from a simple machine with only two functions (up and down) to a more complex pinball machine where each part of the machine performs a specific and different action to move the ball along.
(Source: *The Cooperative Sports and Game Book*, Terry Orlick)

Songs:

(Audio) "The 'A' Machine"
(Source: *Bert and Ernie Side by Side*)
(Book) "The Choo-Choo Train"
(Source: *The Fireside Book of Children's Songs*, Marie Winn)

99 Magic

Relate to: *National Magic Week (Oct. 25–31): Let the enjoyment of magic encourage love and understanding among those in hospitals, schools, libraries, and similar venues.*

Videos: *The Amazing Bone*
The Magic Fishbone
Rumpelstiltskin
The Sorcerer's Apprentice
Strega Nonna
Sylvester and the Magic Pebble

Books: *Big Anthony and the Magic Ring*, Tomie dePaola
But Not Kate, Marissa Moss
Cinder Apples, Sandy Nightingale
The Flower Faerie, Frank Asch and Vladimir Vagin
The Frog Princess, Elizabeth Isele
Georgie and the Magician, Robert Bright
Humbug Potion, Lorna Balian
Olive and the Magic Hat, Eileen Christelow
Rabbit Goes to Night School, Judy Delton
Rabbit Surprise, Eric L. Houch, Jr.
Snuggle Piggy and the Magic Blanket, Michele Stepto
Sylvester and the Magic Pebble, William Steig
The Toy Brother, William Steig
Uncle Harold and the Green Hat, Judy Hindley
Walter's Magic Wand, Eric Houghton
A Wizard Came to Visit, Kath Vickers

Fingerplay: **Wait, Wait, Wait a Bit.**
(Source: *Finger Frolics—Revised*, Liz Cromwell, Dixie Hibner, and John R. Faitel)

Crafts: **Magical Crystal Garden.**
The children will be delighted when they get to make their own crystal garden and watch it grow. Since a glass container is needed to grow the garden in, you may want each child to bring in a small baby-food jar.
This will require such items as salt, water, laundry bluing, food coloring, charcoal, and ammonia (do not leave children unsupervised during this since ammonia is used). For actual proportions, check in the book listed here.

(Source: *Craft Fun: Easy-to-Do Projects with Simple Materials*, Janet R. McCarty and Betty J. Peterson)

Flower Garden.
Have the children make a bouquet or a wall of flowers that could be displayed in the library that week, or begin your own garden in the classroom. Use paper petals and centers out of cupcake cups. Relate the craft to the book *The Flower Faerie* by Frank Asch.

Activities: **The Magic Feather.**
This game is essentially to develop body awareness and relaxation. While the children sit in a circle with their eyes closed, someone touches them with the magic feather. The children must, with eyes still closed, touch the same part of the body that was touched by the feather. If they succeed they may get to use the feather next.
(Source: *Teacher's Handbook of Children's Games*, Marian Jenks Wirth)

Magic Carpet Race.
Take Aladdin's magic carpet and develop it into relay races for the children. Let those carpets fly across the floor with one child pulling and the other teammate riding. For more details on this delightful game and others see the source.
(Source: *The Disney Party Handbook*, Alison Boteler)

Songs: (Audio) "Magical Music" or "Make Believe"
(Source: *Imagine That!*, Jim Valley and friends)
(Book) "Puff the Magic Dragon"
(Source: *The Reader's Digest Children's Songbook*, William L. Simon)

100 Manners and Etiquette

Relate to:	*International Thank You Days (Jan. 11–18): A time to thank someone who has done something special for you now or in the past.*
	Children's Good Manners Month (Sept.)

Videos:	*Barney's Best Manners*
	Circus Baby
	The Selfish Giant
	Time for Table Manners

Books:	*The Bad Good Manners Book,* Babette Cole
	Big Black Bear, Wong Herbert Yee
	The Child's World of Manners, Sandra Ziegler
	Dinner at Alberta's, Russell Hoban
	Manners, Aliki
	Mind Your Manners, Peggy Parish
	Monster Manners, Bethany Roberts
	Pass the Fritters, Critters, Cheryl Chapman
	Perfect Pig, Marc Brown
	Periwinkle, Roger Duvoisin
	A Proper Little Lady, Nette Hilton
	Richard Scarry's Please and Thank You Book, Richard Scarry
	Say Please, Virginia Austin
	Time for Bed, the Babysitter Said, Peggy Perry Anderson
	Wipe Your Feet!, Daniel Lehan

Fingerplay:	**Sometimes My Hands Are Naughty.** (Source: *Finger Frolics—Revised,* Liz Cromwell, Dixie Hibner, and John R. Faitel)

Crafts:	**Helping Hands.** Have each child make a paint print of their hands to be framed and labeled "____'s HELPING HANDS." Have all the children recite the following pledge and present the hands to their parents:

> I promise to help friends whenever I can and to remember to say thank you when someone helps me.

Thank-you Window Greeting Cards.
Our moms have always told us, "Don't forget to say please and thank-you." Well, sometimes the people we wish to say

thank you to don't live close enough for us to talk to them directly. When that's the case we can still remember our manners by sending our own personal thank-you cards.

The directions in this source guide us in constructing various types of window peek-a-boo cards. Let the children cut attractive illustrations from magazines to glue inside and let the pictures peek through the cards' windows.
(Source: *Make and Play Cards*, Clare Beaton)

Activities:

Mother, May I?
This game is one that is familiar to most children. The leader may be another child or the teacher. The children begin at one end of the room and try to reach the leader by taking the amount of steps that the leader says they may take. The child must first remember to say "Mother, may I?" before taking those steps or he or she will have to return to the beginning of the course. The child who reaches the leader first becomes the new leader.

"May I?" Hopscotch.
Supplies needed for this game are limited to a piece of chalk and some sort of pavement. Great! It saves on money. Draw a large square divided into six boxes (3 next to each other) numbered for the children. The object is to hop from one square to the next, getting all the way to the end without landing on any of the lines. The children must look up at the sky as they jump and stop after each try to ask "May I?" If they are successful in reaching their goal they will be given permission to proceed.

Different variations are suggested such as hopping backwards, etc. Try this and many other children's action games explained in detail in this source.
(Source: *Children's Traditional Games*, Judy Sierra and Robert Kaminski)

Songs:

(Audio) "Always Say Please and Thank You"
(Source: *Meet the Dinner Dogs*)
(Book) "A Child's Prayer of Thanks"
(Source: *God's Wonderful World*, Agnes Leckie Mason and Phyllis Brown Ohanian)

101 Mixed-up Creatures

Relate to:	*Birth of Dr. Seuss (March 2): Celebrate the birth of this author/illustrator and his crazy mixed-up characters.*

Videos:
The Lorax
The Pig's Picnic
The Zax (Cat in the Hat/ Dr. Seuss on the Loose)

Books:
The Bunyip of Berkeley's Creek, Jenny Wagner
Casey in the Bath, Cynthia DeFelice
Cynthia and the Unicorn, Jean Freeman
Hansy's Mermaid, Trinka Noble
I Love You, Stinky Face, Lisa McCourt
I Wish I Had Duck Feet, Theo LeSieg
Monkey Face, Frank Asch
Morton and Sidney, Christ DeMarest
A Most Unusual Lunch, Robert Bender
A Mother for Choco, Keiko Kasza
No Such Things, Bill Peet
The Pig's Picnic, Keiko Kasza
"You Look Ridiculous," Said the Rhinoceros, Bernard Waber
Zoodles, Bernard Most

Fingerplay:
The Centaur.
(Source: *Finger Frolics—Revised*, Liz Cromwell, Dixie Hibner, and John R. Faitel)

Crafts:
Imaginary Creatures.
With the popularity of the Wuzzles, a simple mix-up of animals' parts can make a popular craft. Cut up illustrations of different types of animals and allow the children to mix and match the parts to create their own characters.

When they've selected the parts they want to match help them mount them on large construction paper. They can then color them if needed or leave them as they are. Ask each child to identify what animal each part really belongs to.

Mixed-up Magazine.
A variation of the first craft suggestion is this one in which the children cut various pictures from magazines. You will need a head and body to identify your creature but his limbs and other

parts may even be made of odd items, such as baseball bats, clubs, etc.

Younger children love to mix and match and cut and paste. This is sure to be a success.

(Source: *Preschool Art*, Mary Ann Kohl)

Activities: **The Hopfly Bird.**
A small verse in this game describes the hopfly bird as a bird that must hop high to be able to fly.

Make a mark high on the wall that the children cannot reach by standing but may be able to reach by hopping high. The children line up to pretend to be hopfly birds. They each get to hop three times to try to reach the spot. The child who reaches it in the least amount of hops is the winner and is the best hopfly bird.

Children may later attempt to imitate other mixed-up animals by having their actions and voices do different things (e.g., a frog that meows—hop like a frog while meowing like a cat).

(Source: *New Games to Play*, Juel Krisvoy)

Backward Party.
People can be pretty mixed-up creatures sometimes just as other creations can be. Try celebrating the art of silliness by having your own backwards party. Do everything in reverse. This very useful source will give you everything you need from backward invitations, straws and crafts to such games as Goose, Goose, Duck and Backward Pulling Races. So come one and all to a great party but don't forget: "Come in backwards."

(Source: *Hit of the Party*, Amy Vangsgard)

Songs: (Audio) "We're Gonna Catch a Heffalump"
(Source: *Take My Hand Songs from the Hundred Acre Woods*)
(Book) "The Lion and the Unicorn"
(Source: *Sing Hey Diddle Diddle*, Beatrice Harrop)

102 Money

Relate to:	*National Coin Week (April 19–25): A week to study the hobby of coin collecting and the history of money in this country.*

Videos:	*The Adventures of Two Piggy Banks: Learning to Save* *Alexander, Who Used to Be Rich Last Sunday* *Sam and the Lucky Money*
Books:	*Alexander, Who Used to Be Rich Last Sunday*, Judith Viorst *Argo, You Lucky Dog*, Maggie Smith *Benny's Pennies*, Pat Brisson *Bunny Money*, Rosemary Wells *Dollars and Cents for Harriet*, Betsy and Giulio Maestro *Gia and the Hundred Dollars Worth of Bubblegum*, Frank Asch *The Go-Around Dollar*, Barbara Johnston Adams *How Much Is That Doggie in the Window?*, Iza Trapani *If You Made a Million*, David M. Schwartz *Jelly Bean for Sale*, Bruce McMillan *Mama Bear*, Chyng Feng Sun *The Penny Pot*, Stuart J. Murphy *Pigs Will Be Pigs*, Amy Axelrod *The Purse*, Kathy Caple *Sam and the Lucky Money*, Karen Chinn
Fingerplay:	**Minnie.** (Source: *Move Over, Mother Goose!*, Ruth I. Dowell) **Five Little Pennies.** (Source: *Mitt Magic: Fingerplays for Finger Puppets*, Lynda Roberts)
Crafts:	**Dangling Coin Saver.** This is a very special bank that children can use to save their money for the Christmas holidays. Shaped like a turkey it could be made before the Thanksgiving holiday and used for decoration as well as a bank. The body is constructed of a toilet paper tube with the various features added. For preschoolers you will need to precut most materials. (Source: *Holiday Paper Projects*, E. Richard Churchill) **Penny Rubbings.** Relate this to Lincoln's Birthday; have the children make special posters or greeting cards with decorations from penny

rubbings. The children can use pencils to rub both front and backs of the pennies on lightweight paper.

Design Your Own Dollar.
Older children can create their own dollar on paper (9″ × 4″). After discussing the meanings of the symbols on a dollar bill let the children design their own with words and pictures they believe should be on our American money.
(Source: *Kids Celebrate!*, Maria Bonfanti Esche and Clare Bonfanti Braham)

Activities: **Musical Money.**
A variation of the Musical Chairs game with children passing around little cups with coins in them. When the music stops, the children left holding the cups need to identify the coin they have in their cup. A nice educational, yet fun, game with no losers. It lends itself to many variations and some more of these games can be found in the source where this was located.
(Source: *The Giant Encyclopedia of Theme Activities for Children 2 to 5*, Kathy Charner)

Stolen Money.
Hide a set number of coins (pennies and nickels) throughout the room before your group arrives. Gather the children and allow them to search for the coins with specific instructions to remember the coins' location but not to touch them. The children should gather with their groups to discuss where they found the coins. The group that locates the most coins wins the game.
(Source: *Great Theme Parties for Children*, Irene N. Watts)

Songs: (Audio) "A Penny"
(Source: *Disney's Children's Favorite Silly Songs*)
(Book) "The Money Came in, Came in . . ."
(Source: *Early in the Morning*, Charles Causley)

103 Monsters

Relate to:	*Birthday of Mary Shelley (Aug. 30): Author and creator of one of the most famous, popular monsters in literature, Frankenstein's Monster.*

Videos:	*Leo, The See-Through Crumbpicker* *Monster Mama* *Tailypo* *There's a Nightmare in My Closet*
Books:	*After-School Monster*, Marissa Moss *Annie and the Mud Monster*, Dick Gackenbach *Donovan Scares the Monsters*, Susan Love Whitlock *The Ghost Family Meets Its Match*, Nicola Rubel *Go Away Big Green Monster!*, Ed Emberley *Harry (the Monster)*, Ann Cameron *The House that Jack Built*, Judy Sierra *I Was a Second Grade Werewolf*, Daniel Pinkwater *Love from Aunt Betty*, Nancy Parker *The Marigold Monster*, M. C. Delaney *Monster Brother*, Mary Jane Auch *The Monsters' Test*, Brian J. Heinz *No Such Thing*, Jackie French Koller *One Hungry Monster*, Susan Heyboer O'Keefe *Three-Star Billy*, Pat Hutchins
Fingerplay:	**Five Little Monsters.** (Source: *Finger Frolics—Revised*, Liz Cromwell, Dixie Hibner, and John R. Faitel)
Crafts:	**Egg Carton Creature.** Begin with the bottom of an egg carton turned upside down. Add a string to the face of the creature to pull it along. The child may use paper to put on legs, wings, and so forth as desired. A beautiful illustration sample is available in the source below. (Source: *Lollipop, Grapes and Clothespin Critters: Quick, On-the-Spot Remedies for Restless Children 2–10*, Robyn Freedman Spizman) **Hairy Monster** Children love to pretend to be monsters, the goofier the better.

Here's a hairy creation the children can wear in their next performance of a monster story. It's made very simply using large, brown grocery bags cut up in strips. Attach toilet tissue tubes for two-inch eyes that bug out. The more curled strips you add to your monster's body the hairier he will look. Check this source for a reliable illustration of the final craft.

(Source: *Fun with Paper Bags and Cardboard Tubes*, F. Virginia Walter)

Activities:

Costume Party.
Have a "Worst Monster Competition." Allow the children to come dressed as a scary or humorous monster. Let them parade for the group to any eerie music available and award paper ribbons in various categories. (Suggestion: At this age all should get some type of award.)

Following Footsteps Game.
Let the children list for you all the different types of monsters that they know from their limited experience. Next introduce some folklore monsters to them, including the fabulous Bigfoot. Along with this introduction have each child cut out paper Bigfoot feet by tracing large boots that you have available. With these footprints spread throughout the room and some large dice the children can show their skills in jumping, hopping, counting, and so on while following in the steps of Bigfoot.

(Source: *Teachables from Trashables*, C. Emma Linderman)

Songs:

(Audio) "The Monster Rap"
(Source: *Halloween Fun*)
(Book) "The Ghost of John"
(Source: *Rounds About Rounds*, Jane Yolen)

104 Moving

Relate to:	*National Moving Month (May): To kick off the busiest season (Memorial Day to Labor Day) of Americans moving their families to new locations and how to do it efficiently.*

Videos:	*A Chair for My Mother* *Ira Says Goodbye*

Books:	*Alexander, Who's Not (Do You Hear Me? I Mean It) Moving*, Judith Viorst *The Best Ever Good-bye Party*, Amy Hest *Good-bye, House*, Robin Ballard *I Want to Go Home*, Alice McLerran *I'm Not Moving, Mama*, Nancy Carlstrom *Jamaica's Blue Marker*, Juanita Havill *Leaving Home with a Pickle Jar*, Barbara Dugan *The Leaving Morning*, Angela Johnson *Little Lost Dog*, Inga Moore *Mary Ann*, Betsy James *Moving Day*, Robert Kalan *Mr. Chips*, Laura Kvasnosky *Red Fox on the Move*, Hannah Giffard *Seeds*, George Shannon *To Annabella Pelican from Thomas Hippopotamus*, Nancy Patz

Fingerplay:	**Everybody Out the Door.** (Source: *Move Over, Mother Goose!*, Ruth I. Dowell)

Crafts:	**Personal Carryall.** Show the children how to design their own personal carryalls to carry their most precious items in the car during the move. Gather a number of cardboard bottle carriers from your local supermarket. Supply the children with paints, markers, scraps, and stickers to decorate their new carriers. (Source: *Gifts Galore!*, Ireene Robbins) **Welcome Wagon.** Perhaps you are not the one moving but you've noticed a new child has come to your neighborhood or class. It is time to welcome this person and make him or her feel comfortable. Discuss the concept of welcome wagons with the children and help them make their own. Let the children decorate boxes

and fill them with items they think a newcomer to their neighborhood might need. You'd be surprised what they will feel should be on that list. Encourage the children to save their boxes until they find just such a newcomer to give it to.

(Source: *Purple Cow to the Rescue*, Ann Cole, Carolyn Haas, and Betty Weinberger)

Activities: **I'm Home Now.**
Sometimes moving from one home to another can be difficult for a child. Here's a clever little game about moving from house to house. If you can collect enough boxes you might have the children build and decorate their own residences for this activity. This resembles Musical Chairs except that the children try to find their own home and no one is left out. When a child is ready to move you can try a variation in which the child goes to another house. Call out a name and the other children attempt to discover where this child moved.

(Source: *Purple Cow to the Rescue*, Ann Cole, Carolyn Haas, and Betty Weinberger)

Junk Shop Relay.
When preparing to move from one house to another we usually find we've collected a large amount of junk, as well as treasures. Tell the children we will be practicing moving all that junk and treasure so we will be able to help Mom and Dad if we ever need to move to another house or just from one room to another.

For this ridiculous relay you will need two of each item (hat, toy, cup, etc.). Line up the children and start them passing the items. At intervals the leader can call out wacky commands to slow things down, such as "Put the hat on your head," "Feather—tickle someone," and more.

(Source: *World's Best Outdoor Games*, Glen Vecchione)

Song: (Book) "So Long, It's Been Good to Know You"
(Source: *Gonna Sing My Head Off!*, Kathleen Krull)

105 Music

Relate to:	*Music for Life Week (first full week in July): A week to encourage the use of music for a variety of reasons including recreation, comfort, and pleasure.*

Videos:
The Bremen Town Musicians
Frog Went A-Courtin'
Lentil
Musical Max
Really Rosie

Books:
Anatole and the Piano, Eve Titus
Ben's Trumpet, Rachel Isadora
Bravo, Tanya, Satomi Ichikawa
Brother Billy Bronto's Bygone Blues Band, David F. Birchman
Fog, Susi L. Fowler
The Frog Who Wanted to Be a Singer, Linda Goss
Geraldine, the Music Mouse, Leo Lionni
The Heart of the Wood, Marquerite Davol
J. B.'s Harmonica, John Sebastian
Mama Don't Allow, Thacher Hurd
Mixed-up Magic, Joanna Cole
Music in the Night, Etta Wilson
Musical Max, Robert Kraus
Really Rosie, Maurice Sendak
There's a Hole in the Bucket, Nadine Bernard Westcott

Fingerplay:
If I Could Play.
(Source: *Finger Frolics—Revised*, Liz Cromwell, Dixie Hibner, and John R. Faitel)

Crafts:
Musical Band.
Let the children create their own musical instruments including a tissue box ukulele, a musical comb humdinger, maracas, a one-string base fiddle, a straw tooter, or cymbal crashers from simple, easily accessible supplies.

Follow the simple directions given on pages 24–29 of McCarty and Peterson's book, and your group can create their own band. Illustrations are accompanied by a clear set of instructions to follow.
(Source: *Craft Fun: Easy-to-Do Projects with Simple Materials*, Janet R. McCarty and Betty J. Peterson)

Pan Pipes.
Here's a musical instrument even your three year olds can handle. Supply the children with four cardboard tubes, each one inch shorter than the other. Allow them to paint the tubes different colors and let them dry while you tell other stories. When they are dry tape them together in a row with colorful tape. Plug one end with plasticine. Now the children are ready to play their pipes by blowing into the open ends.
(Source: *Fun with Paper Bags and Cardboard Tubes*, F. Virginia Walter)

Activities:

Bash and Bang Band.
This is a parading song and activity to allow the children to use their newly made instruments or to just pretend they have their favorite instruments with them. Sheet music is made available on a two-page spread. This song will also allow the children to call out and identify their particular instruments.
(Source: *Game-Songs with Prof. Dogg's Troupe*, Harriet Powell)

Christmas Match to Music.
Although this is written as a Christmas game it can easily be altered for other holidays or events. Cut out paper Christmas ornaments and cut them in half. Distribute the portions among the children sitting in the circle. One child is selected to sit in the center of the circle with his or her portion of an ornament and will try to locate the matching portion before the group finishes singing the Christmas song (or other song) that they chose.
    This and many comparable games are offered in this excellent source.
(Source: *The Best of the Mailbox, Book 1: Preschool/Kindergarten edition*, Margaret Michel)

Songs:

(Audio) "One Note March"
    (Source: *Dance in Your Pants*)
(Book) "Brother, Come and Dance with Me"
    (Source: *Eye Winker, Tom Tinker, Chin Chopper*, Tom Glazer)

106 Mythical Creatures

Relate to:	*The first reported sighting of the mythical Loch Ness monster by D. MacKenzie (Oct. 1871).*

Videos:
The Elves and the Shoemaker
Little Toot and the Loch Ness Monster
Pegasus
The Three Billy Goats Gruff

Books:
Bernard's Boring Day, Ron Maris
Cupid, Babette Cole
Feliciana Meets d'Loop Garou, Tynia Thomassie
Franklin and the Tooth Fairy, Paulette Bourgeois
The Ghosts' Trip to Loch Ness, Jacques DuQuennoy
Goblin Walk, Tony Johnston and Bruce Degen
Hansy's Mermaid, Trinka Hakes Noble
Little Toot and the Loch Ness Monster, Hardie Gramatky
Max and Ruby's First Greek Myth: Pandora's Box, Rosemary Wells
The Mystery in the Bottle, Val Willis
Princess Jessica Rescues a Prince, Jennifer Brooks
Runnery Granary, Nancy Farmer
Trouble with Trolls, Jan Brett
Unicorn Dreams, Dyan Sheldon and Neil Reed
Unicorns! Unicorns!, Geraldine McCaughrean

Fingerplay:
The Elf's Coat.
(Source: *Rhymes for Fingers and Flannelboards*, Louise Binder Scott and J. J.Thompson)

Crafts:
Torn Paper Mermaid.
Locate a reproducible picture of a mermaid and give the children their own copies. After the children color their pictures give them green tissue paper to create scales for the mermaid's tail. Have them simply tear small pieces and glue them overlapping to give the effect of scales on a fish.

Silly Sea Serpent.
Break out those egg cartons you've been saving to use for a craft one day. This is the one you've been saving them for. Using the center, spiny portion of the carton for the body and a small section from another carton for the head you can build your own Loch Ness monster.
(Source: *Kitchen Carton Crafts*, Helen Roney Sattler)

Activities:

Stalking Bigfoot.
Select two players, one to be the hunter and the other Bigfoot. Let both stand on opposite ends of a table to begin and blindfold both the hunter and Bigfoot. Since the children can feel the table as they move it's not as scary. Bigfoot attempts to avoid the hunter, while the hunter pursues him. Let the group call out suggestions to each player.
(Source: *The World's Best Party Games*, Sheila Anne Barry)

Mr. Elf.
Arrange the class in a circle with one child (the elf) on a chair in the center. Place a bag of elf gold under the elf's chair while he or she pretends to be asleep. Another child is chosen to sneak up and steal the elf's gold and return to his or her seat shouting "I've got your gold!" The elf must now try to determine who the thief is; the elf then change places with the thief.
(Source: *Classroom Parties*, Susan Spaete)

Songs:

(Audio) "The Unicorn"
(Source: *The Child's Collection of the World*)
(Book) "The Mermaid"
(Source: *Strawberry Fair*)

107 Names

Relate to:	*Get a Different Name Day (Feb. 13): Here's a day when you get to choose your own name. Bored with your current name? Try another one for a day.*

Videos:
Chrysanthemum
Rumpelstiltskin
Tikki Tikki Tembo

Books:
Andy (That's My Name), Tomie dePaola
But Names Will Never Hurt Me, Bernard Waber
Chrysanthemum, Kevin Henkes
From Anne to Zach, Mary Jane Martin
How I Named the Baby, Linda Shute
I Wish I Had Another Name, Jay Williams and Winifred Lubell
Josephina Hates Her Name, Diana Engel
A Lion Named Shirley Williamson, Bernard Waber
The Name of the Tree, Celia Barker Lottridge
Nothing, Mick Inkpen
The Old Woman Who Named Things, Cynthia Rylant
The Other Emily, Gibbs Davis
Paco and the Witch, Felix Pitre
Sabrina, Martha Alexander
Wind Rose, Crescent Dragonwagon

Fingerplay:
Two Little Dickybirds.
     (Source: *Little Boy Blue*, Daphne Hogstrom)

Crafts:
Nameplates.
Have the children make their own special nameplates to be hung on their bedroom door, toybox, or other special places. Four methods are described in the source cited. For those children who still don't recognize their names, have it written on a card for them to copy or make the letters available by having them already cut out of magazines.
     (Source: *Purple Cow to the Rescue*, Ann Cole, Carolyn Haas, and Betty Weinberger)

Name Sculptures.
Let children generate their own creative nameplate for their door. This source gives wonderful instructions for making salt clay or baker's dough. These require no baking, but simply

harden as they dry in the air. Acrylic paints make the best use of color for this craft. An easy and colorful activity that the children will want to do again and again.
(Source: *Make Gifts!*, Kim Solga)

Activities: **New-Neighbor Games.**
These games are particularly good when new children join the group. In Trade a Name the children print their names on many strips of paper. The children may trade their strips with their newly made friends and create a friendship chain with these strips. They should try to get one strip from everyone in the room by trading off one of theirs. They should be sure to keep trading until they are sure they don't have any duplicate names in their possession. The first to do this is the winner.

They can then chain them together with glue or tape to create their own chain friendship belt.

Name Ball.
This is a simple game that requires the children to pay close attention. They should form a circle with one child in the center. The center child will toss a ball in the air while calling the name of a child in the circle. That child will attempt to catch the ball before it hits the ground.
(Source: *Making Children's Parties Click*, Virginia W. Musselman)

Songs: (Audio) "John Jacob Jingleheimer Schmidt"
(Source: *Six Little Ducks: Classic Children's Songs*)
(Book) "Bingo"
(Source: *Reader's Digest Children's Songbook*, William L. Simon)

108 Night

Relate to: *Night of the Shooting Stars (Aug. 11): Since the year 830 a meteor shower known as "The Perseids" (because it begins in the constellation Perseus) arrives every year on this night. Watchers can see as many as 60 meteors an hour cross the sky.*

Videos: *The Berenstain Bears in the Dark*
Goodnight, Gorilla
Moon Man
Owl Moon

Books: *And if the Moon Could Talk*, Kate Banks
Bayou Lullaby, Kathi Appelt
The Deep Blue Sky Twinkles with Stars, Cindy Szekeres
Dreams, Ezra Jack Keats
Lights Out!, John Himmelman
Little Rabbit Goes to Sleep, Tony Johnston
Moon Man, Tomi Ungerer
Moonfall, Susan Whitcher
The Night We Slept Outside, Anne and Harlow Rockwell
Owl Moon, Jane Yolen
Papa, Please Get the Moon for Me, Eric Carle
The Story of the Milky Way, Joseph Bruchac and Gayle Ross
Ten Flashing Fireflies, Philmon Sturges
Twinkle, Twinkle, Little Star, Iza Trapani
What's in the Dark?, Carl Memling

Fingerplay: **The Moon.**
(Source: *Once upon a Childhood: Fingerplays, Action Rhymes, and Fun Times for the Very Young*, Dolores Chupela)

Crafts: **Sun and Moon Masks.**
This is an easy paper craft that children can do and later use to act out stories about the sun and the moon, who are a pair of characters that always belong together. These stories can lead to a great discussion on other pairs the children are familiar with (cat and dog, stars and stripes, etc.).
(Source: *Paper Fun for Kids*, Marion Elliot)

Nighttime Surprises.
Allow the night stars to pop out right in front of the children. Before the children arrive take a white crayon and draw stars

on their construction paper. Supply them with black tempera paint (thinned with water) and brushes and watch their faces as they paint their paper and see the stars appear before them.
(Source: *Theme-a-saurus*, Jean Warren)

Activities:

Musical Sleeping Bags.
Remember Musical Chairs? Try Musical Sleeping Bags. The same rules apply with all sleeping bags (or beach towels, etc.) in a circle. Try this game as a preview to setting down for a nighttime story.
(Source: *Super Slumber Parties*, Brooks Whitney)

Midnight.
A game that requires no equipment but does require the children to stay aware. This game helps the children to understand terms of time such as twelve o'clock, midnight, two o'clock, etc.

Two areas on opposite sides of the room are designated to represent the fox's den and the chicken coop. One player is the fox and the other the mother hen. The remainder of the group are baby chicks traveling with their mother. As the chicks get close to the fox's den the mother hen will ask the fox what time it is. As long as the fox replies anything other than "twelve o'clock or midnight" they are all safe; if he does say this time they must all try to get home safely. Those caught are taken to the den to be eaten, with the last chick caught becoming the next fox.
(Source: *Games for Girl Scouts, 2nd edition*, Joan McEniry)

Songs:

(Audio) "God Bless the Moon"
(Source: *Mommy and Me: Rock-a-Bye Baby)*
(Book) "Roll Over, Roll Over"
(Source: *If You're Happy and You Know it*, Nicki Weiss)

109 Noise/Sounds

Relate to:	*First official flight to break the sound barrier (Oct. 14, 1947): Discuss with the children the effects sound can have on various items.*

Videos:
Lentil
Mr. Brown Can Moo! Can You? (Dr. Seuss's ABC)
Musical Max
Noisy Nora

Books:
As Quiet as a Mouse, Hilda Offen
Bumps in the Night, Harry Allard
Do Monkeys Tweet?, Melanie Walsh
Granny Greenteeth and the Noise in the Night, Kenn and Joanne Compton
Katie and the Sad Noise, Ruth Gannett
Let's Go Home, Little Bear, Martin Waddell
The Listening Walk, Paul Showers
Meow!, Katya Arnold
The Noise Lullaby, Jacqueline K. Ogburn
Oh, What a Noisy Farm, Harriet Ziefert
Petunia and the Song, Roger Duvoisin
Possum and Peeper, Anne Hunter
Shhhh!, Suzy Kline
The Spooky Eerie Night Noise, Mona Rabun Reeves
Too Much Noise!, Ann McGovern

Fingerplay:
Tap and Clap.
(Source: *Children's Counting-out Rhymes, Fingerplays, Jump-Rope and Bounce-Ball Chants and Other Rhythms*, Gloria T. Delamar)

Crafts:
Noisy Goblin.
A noisy little goblin for Halloween celebrations or simply to use for musical activities can be created out of small milk cartons. Place some dried beans inside the cartons and seal and attach a Popsicle stick handle. The exterior of the box can be decorated as a goblin (depicted in this source) or any other character you may wish during the year.
(Source: *175 Easy-to-Do Halloween Crafts*, Sharon Dunn Umnik)

**Craft and
Activity:**   **Maraca Rhythm Maker.**
Music can be made by the simple use of tongue depressors, beans or macaroni, and small paper cups. Have the children create their own maracas.
     Also have other rhythm instruments available for the children to experiment with. Simple lessons in rhythm using these instruments will be enjoyed by all.
     (Source: *Craft Fun: Easy-to-Do Projects with Simple Materials*, Janet R. McCarty and Betty J. Peterson)

Activity: **Rice Balloons.**
Children can make music in a number of ways. Here's a simple method of creating sound. Fill balloons with uncooked rice and let the children try making soft and loud sounds with their balloons. Have other balloons filled with items such as pennies, beans, etc. The children will enjoy exploring the variety of sounds they can get.
     (Source: *Teaching Terrific Twos and Other Toddlers*, Terry Lynne Graham and Lind Camp)

Songs: (Audio) "That Bear Snores"
     (Source: *UnBearable Bears*)
(Book) "Listen to the Noises"
     (Source: *Music for Ones and Twos*, Tom Glazer)

110 Old Age

Relate to:	*As Young as You Feel Day (March 22): Stop acting your real age and try acting as young as you feel in order to enjoy life.*

Videos:	*Alejandro's Gift* *The Bremen Town Musicians* *Cloudy with a Chance of Meatballs* *Wilfrid Gordon McDonald Patridge*
Books:	*Could Be Worse!*, James Stevenson *Fish for Supper*, M. B. Goffstein *A Fruit and Vegetable Man*, Roni Schotter *Great Aunt Martha*, Rebecca C. Jones *It's So Nice to Have a Wolf Around the House*, Harry Allard *Mrs. Peachtree's Bicycle*, Erica Silverman *Mrs. Periwinkle's Groceries*, Pegeen Snow *Remember That*, Leslea Newman *The Snow Child*, Freya Littledale *Stranger in the Mirror*, Allen Say *Sunshine Home*, Eve Bunting *Verdi*, Janell Cannon *When I Am Old with You*, Angela Johnson *William's Ninth Life*, Minna Jung *The Woman Who Saved Things*, Phyllis Krasilousky
Fingerplay:	**Grandma.** (Source: *Finger Frolics—Revised*, Liz Cromwell, Dixie Hibner, and John R. Faitel)
Crafts:	**The Old Woman in the Shoe.** Make the old woman's shoe home using construction paper, crayons, and tape or staples. The children's conception of the old woman's shoe may vary with what they think the shoe should look like. Patterns of various types of shoes can be made available for tracing. After the completion of the craft, show the children the illustrations of this story. **Face Fuzz.** When children think of old people they often think of old men with long white beards. Help the children become that old man in the fairy tales or songs that they are familiar with. Mr. Fuzz Face can be made by using cotton wool to make a long, long

beard, yarn for a mustache, and curtain fringe for heavy eye-brows. Let the children playact such stories or songs as "This Old Man," etc.

(Source: *Children's Crafts: Fun and Creativity for Ages 5–12*, Sunset)

Activities: **This Old Man.**
Children may act out this song in any number of ways:
- act out the numbers by holding up fingers
- act out objects mentioned
- clap the rhythm of the song
- use instruments to beat out the measure

(Source: *Teacher's Handbook of Children's Games*, Marian Jenks Wirth)

Catch the Cane.
Take an item that children normally associate with elderly people, the cane, and turn it into an easy catch-it-if-you-can game. While everyone forms a circle let one child remain in the center holding the cane upright on the floor. When the child is ready he or she will call out a number and release the cane for that other person to catch.

(Source: *Making Children's Parties Click*, Virginia W. Musselman)

Songs: (Audio) "I Know an Old Lady"
(Source: *Disney's Children's Favorites, Vol. 2*)
(Book) "Grandma's Spectacles"
(Source: *Eye Winker, Tom Tinker, Chin Chopper*, Tom Glazer)

111 Parties

Relate to:	*Don't Wait—Celebrate! Week (Aug. 8–14): To encourage having frequent parties celebrating small but important accomplishments such as good grades, etc.*

Videos: *The Berenstain Bears and Too Much Birthday*
Little Bear: Parties and Picnics
Spot Goes to a Party

Books: *Andrew's Amazing Monsters*, Kathryn Hook Berlan
Badger's Bring Something Party, Hiawyn Oram
Brave Horace, Holly Keller
Cassandra Who?, Iris Hiskey
Halloween Party, Linda Shute
Happy Birthday, Dolores, Barbara Samuels
The Hippo Hop, Christine Loomis
Jeremy Bean's St. Patrick's Day, Alice Schertle
Jeremy's Tail, Duncan Ball
Miss Spider's Tea Party, David Kirk
The Pink Party, Maryann MacDonald
Slumber Party, Judith Caseley
Some Birthday!, Patricia Polacco
The Spaghetti Party, Doris Orgel
Spring Green, Valerie M. Selkowe

Fingerplay: **Tea Party.**
(Source: *The Everything Book*, Eleanor Graham Vance)

Crafts: **Pretty Party Plates.**
Planning a classroom party? Have the children help you with the decorations and also create their own party plates. Using paper plates for the center have the children actually create decorative placemats attached to the back of the plates. One example offered by the author is flower petals with the plate as the center of the flower. This book is a must-see for examples of art for the very young when budgets are tight. When aren't they!
(Source: *My Party Book*, Marion Elliot)

Party Hats.
Party hats are traditional in children's parties. Try some of these colorful hats in simple designs forged from paper, glitter, feath-

ers, etc. This is a simple craft that can be completed by even the youngest of children. Bright color illustrations are offered in this source to guide you.

(Source: *The Grolier Kids Craft Paper Craft Book*, David Hancock, Jill Hancock, Ann Murray, Lyn Orton, Cheryl Owen, and Lynda Watts)

Activities:

Paper Plate Paddle Ball.

Looking for some different type of game for a party? Children like ball sports. A simple way for the group to play paddle ball is to stretch a cord across two chairs for a substitute net. Have them make their paddles from two paper plates stapled together, but leave a hole for them to insert their four fingers for control.

A ball can simply be a wad of paper rolled with elastic. See this source for details and rules.

(Source: *Great Indoor Games from Trash and Other Things*, Judith Conaway)

Mardi Gras.

This source offers some wonderful thoughts on a different type of party event. Try having your own Mardi Gras festival. Begin with the "Battle of the Flowers" and end with a costume celebration and fireworks. Numerous suggestions are made, such as crowning the queen of the Mardi Gras.

(Source: *Children Are Children Are Children*, Ann Cole, Carolyn Haas, Elizabeth Heller, and Betty Weinberger)

Songs:

(Audio) "The Bug Party"
(Source: *Chickens in My Hair*)
(Book) "The More We Get Together"
(Source: *The Raffi Singable Songbook*, Raffi)

112 Pets

Relate to:	*Be Kind to Animals Week (first full week in May): Declared by the American Humane Association to encourage people to care for animals.*

Videos:	*Arthur's Pet Business* *Frog Goes to Dinner* *Jim's Dog, Muffins* *The Mysterious Tadpole* *Pet Show!*
Books:	*Any Kind of Dog*, Lynn Reiser *Be Gentle!*, Virginia Miller *Daddy, Could I Have an Elephant?*, Jake Wolf *Furry*, Holly Keller *The Great Hamster Hunt*, Lenore Blegvad *The Habits of Rabbits*, Virginia Kahl *I Took My Frog to the Library*, Eric A. Kimmel *Moonbear's Pet*, Frank Asch *Mr. Green Peas*, Judith Caseley *The New Puppy*, Lawrence Anholt *No Ducks in Our Bathtub*, Martha Alexander *An Octopus Followed Me Home*, Dan Yaccarino *Pet Show*, Ezra Jack Keats *Positively No Pets Allowed*, Nathan Zimelman *The Queen's Goat*, Margaret Mahy
Fingerplay:	**A Kitten.** (Source: *Finger Frolics—Revised*, Liz Cromwell, Dixie Hibner, and John R. Faitel)
Crafts:	**Kitten Bank.** A small cardboard box (tissue box, oatmeal box, etc.) can be transferred into a delightful cat bank with whiskers and all. With construction paper you can make a head and tail to add to the box ends. Use pipe cleaners for whiskers. Paint the box itself to match the color of the head. Cut a small opening for the money. (Source: *Highlights Magazine for Children* [April, 1984], Barbara Bell)

Pebble Pets.
Collect as many smooth stones of various sizes as you can find because once the children begin they may want to make several pets to take home. This is reminiscent of the "Pet Rock" craze of earlier years. Want some suggestions on how to color them just see this source.
   (Source: *The Grolier Kids Crafts Book*, Cheryl Owen and Anna Murray)

Activities: **A 4–H Pet Show.**
Invite your local 4–H group to bring their pets to the program and speak to the children about these animals. These pets may include hamsters, rabbits, ducks, etc. This will allow small children an opportunity to see and touch animals they may have never touched before.

Dog and Flea Game.
Fleas love to hop on a dog. Here's a little game that takes a little skill but children will love to try again and again to succeed. Make your dog from an oatmeal box covered with a brown sock. Add features and floppy ears but leave the top open. The fleas are made of small rubber balls covered in tissues.
   Ready to play? Tell the children to see how many fleas they can get into the dog by bouncing the fleas (balls) on the ground and letting them hop into his top.
   (Source: *Crafts for Kids Who Are Wild About Insects*, Kathy Ross)

Songs: (Audio) "My Dog Rags"
   (Source: *If You're Happy and You Know It: Sing Along with Bob McGrath, Vol. 1*)
(Book) "I Love Little Pussy"
   (Source: *Songs and Rhymes for Little Children*)

113 Pirates

Relate to:	*The capture of Blackbeard the Pirate (Nov. 21, 1718): This is the day known for the capture of one of the most famous pirates of all time, Edward Teach, better known as Blackbeard.*
Videos:	*The Pirate Adventure* (Raggedy Ann and Andy) *Pirate Island*
Books:	*Alvin the Pirate*, Ulf Lofgren *Andy's Pirate Ship: A Spot the Difference Book*, Philippe Dupasquier *Do Pirates Take Baths?*, Kathy Tucker *Edward and the Pirates*, David McPhail *Emily and the Golden Acorn*, Ian Beck *Mimi and Gustav in Pirates!*, Denis Woychuk *Pigasus*, Pat Murphy *Pirates in the Park*, Thom Roberts *The Pirates of Bedford Street*, Rachel Isadora *Pirates: Robbers of the High Seas*, Gail Gibbons *The Pirate Who Tried to Capture the Moon*, Dennis Haseley *To Capture the Wind*, Sheila MacGill-Callahan *Tough Boris*, Mem Fox *The Trouble with Uncle*, Babette Cole *Wild Will*, Ingrid and Dicter Schubert
Fingerplay:	**One-Eyed Pirate; Parrots on a Pirate.** (Source: *52 Programs for Preschoolers: The Librarians Year Round Planner*, Dianne Briggs)
Crafts:	**Parrot Puppet.** What is a pirate without his trusty parrot sitting on his shoulder? Create your own pirate's friend from toilet paper tubes, feathers, and more. Patterns for the parrot's features are supplied in this source and can be reproduced on colored paper to make the results more realistic. (Source: *Hit of the Party*, Amy Vangsgard) **The Pirate.** Hit the high seas with your new pirate mask. Children love to pretend and this uncomplicated craft will allow them to begin in no time. This book will guide you through the steps of making a colorful pirate's mask from only paper plates and con-

struction paper. And, of course, what's a pirate without a beard and eye patch?—these items are also created.
(Source: *Great Masks to Make*, Robyn Supraner)

Activities: **Captain Hook Relay.**
This is a basic Hot Potato game with the children passing along simple treasures like a bracelet to one another with the use of cardboard hooks. Children are very familiar with Captain Hook of Peter Pan fame and they will enjoy placing the hook on their hand to play this game.
(Source: *Celebrate*)

Save Peter Pan/Tiger Lily from Captain Hook.
The children form a protective circle around the child to be protected (Peter Pan or Tiger Lily). Another child representing Captain Hook attempts to break through this circle to tag Peter Pan and in this way become the new Pan. See this and dozens of other beguiling games in the source.
(Source: *Hit of the Party*, Amy Vangsgard)

Songs: (Audio) "Pirate Story"
(Source: *A Child's Garden of Songs*)
(Book) "Pirate Song"
(Source: *Library Storyhour from A to Z*, Ellen K. Hasbrouck)

114 Plants/Seeds

Relate to: *National Garden Week (second full week in April): A week to honor those gardeners who work each year in the gardens to provide food and improve the environment.*

Videos: *The Empty Pot*
Frog and Toad Together: The Garden (Arnold Lobel Video Showcase)
Harold and His Amazing Green Plants
Jack and the Beanstalk
The Little Red Hen

Books: *The Carrot Seed*, Ruth Krauss
The Enormous Carrot, Vladimir Vagin
Jack's Garden, Henry Cole
The Leaf Men, William Joyce
The Marigold Monster, M. C. Delaney
Mrs. Gaddy and the Fast-Growing Vine, Wilson Gage
A Plant Called Spot, Nancy J. Peteraf
The Plant Sitter, Gene Zion
The Pumpkin Man and the Crafty Creeper, Margaret Mahy
The Remarkable Plant in Apt. 4, Giulio Maestro
Seeds, George Shannon
Something Is Growing, Walter Lyon Krodop
Sunflower, Miela Ford
The Surprise Garden, Zoe Hall
The Tiny Seed, Eric Carle

Fingerplay: **My Garden.**
(Source: *Finger Frolics—Revised*, Liz Cromwell, Dixie Hibner, and John R. Faitel)

Crafts: **Berry Basket Planter.**
Using plastic berry baskets saved from stores, the children can weave a beautiful basket with colorful ribbons. Seeds may be planted within a paper flower made and placed in the dirt temporarily until the children's real flowers grow. Simple scraps can be made into a craft the children will take pride in.
(Source: *ScrapCraft: 50 Easy-to-Make Handicraft Projects*, Judith Choate and Jane Green)

Gaelic Pressed Flower Nosegay.
Design a beautifully constructed floral arrangement to hang in any window. Have children collect flowers they think Mom will like and press them between plastic wrap by using some books. Using cardboard or the outer rim of a paper plate cut two circles with the centers cut out. Place the flowers, still in the plastic wrap, in the center of the circles and decorate the outer rims of the plates. These will make nice wall arrangements or the children might want to hang them in the windows with the sun shining through them.
(Source: *The You and Me Heritage Tree*, Phyllis and Noel Fiarotta)

Activities: **Growing Flowers.**
Calming music may be played while allowing the children to pretend they are seeds all curled up. As the teacher circulates around the room, the child that's touched on the head pretends to grow into a type of flower he or she likes best.
Later have the children tell what kind of flower they are and how it feels to grow like a flower.

Pin the Petal on the Flower.
This is a simple take-off on the old and familiar Pin the Tail on the Donkey game. Design a flower on the wall (minus the petals, of course). Follow the basic rules of the donkey game but substitute petals for the donkey tails.
(Source: *Party Plans for Tots*, Kate Harris)

Songs: (Audio) "The Green Grass Grew All Around"
(Source: *Disney's Children's Favorites, Vol. 1*)
(Book) "I Had a Little Nut Tree"
(Source: *Sing Hey Diddle Diddle*, Beatrice Harrop)

115 Poetry

Relate to:	*Great Poetry Reading Day (April 28): Read some good poetry and learn more about the world.*

Videos:
Beast Feast
Casey at the Bat
McElligot's Pool
Madeline
The Owl and the Pussycat

Books:
The Adventures of Isabel, Ogden Nash
Beneath the Ghost Moon, Jane Yolen
Boo to a Goose, Mem Fox
Casey at the Bat, Ernest Lawrence Thayer
Frances Face-Maker, William Cole
The Lady with the Alligator Purse, Nadine Bernard Westcott
Roll Over!, Mordicai Gerstein
Roses Are Pink, Your Feet Really Stink, Diane deGroat
Rosie's Fishing Trip, Amy Hest
The Tale of Custard the Dragon, Ogden Nash
Ten, Nine, Eight, Molly Bang
To Market, To Market, Anne Miranda
Miss Mary Mack, Mary Ann Hoberman
Who Sank the Boat?, Pamela Allen
Who Wants a Cheap Rhinoceros?, Shel Silverstein

Fingerplay:
Wee Willie Winkle.
(Source: *Children's Counting-out Rhymes, Fingerplays, Jump-Rope and Bounce-Ball Chants and Other Rhythms*, Gloria T. Delamar)

Crafts:
Shadow Box Scene.
Introduce your group to poetry and your favorite poets in a fun way through these shadow box scenes. After a reading of a chosen poem give the children paper plates. Ask them to illustrate their favorite part of the poem using either crayons, markers, or cut-outs glued on the plate.

Add a second plate on top of it facing the opposite way and with the center cut out to give the picture a three-dimensional look. Finally, let the children decorate the frame.
(Source: *Paper Plate Art*, Maxine Kinney)

Craft and Activity:

Monster Poetry.
Children enjoy monsters, as long as they're not too scary. Distribute materials such as construction paper, crayons, sticker dots, and feathers for children to create their own monsters. Attach the creation to a stick and it becomes an easily handled puppet.

Place the monster in a box and have the children bring it out at the end of this old folk rhyme, "In a Dark, Dark Wood." The words for this rhyme can also be found in the book *A Dark, Dark Tale* by Ruth Brown.
(Source: *This Way to Books*, Caroline Feller Bauer)

Activity:

Game of the Poet.
This is for a slightly older group but can be modified for the younger audience by doing it orally instead of writing. Each child states or writes four words that rhyme. Then that player passes it to the next person who needs to make up a poem using these words.

Young children can be encouraged to find pictures of items that rhyme to illustrate their poem.
(Source: *The World's Best Party Games*, Sheila Anne Barry

Songs:

(Audio) "Hug O' War"
(Source: *Where the Sidewalk Ends*)
(Book) "I'm Being Eaten By a Boa Constrictor"
(Source: *The Silly Songbook*, Esther L. Nelson)

116 Pop-Mania

Relate to:	*National Popcorn Poppin' Month (Oct.): Proclaimed by the Popcorn Institute.*

Videos:	*Hot-Air Henry* *The Mole and the Chewing Gum*

Books:	*Gia and the Hundred Dollars Worth of Bubblegum*, Frank Asch *Heatwave*, Helen Ketteman *Jolly Snow*, Jane Hissey *Monster Bubbles*, Dennis Nolan *Pop! Goes the Weasel and Yankee Doodle*, Robert Quackenbush *Popcorn: A Frank Asch Bear Story*, Frank Asch *The Popcorn Book*, Tomie dePaola *Show and Tell*, Elvira Woodruff *Tubtime*, Elvira Woodruff *The Well-Mannered Balloon*, Nancy Willard

Crafts:	**Bubble Makers.** Bubbles are a sure success at any time when dealing with young children. Here you will find methods of making easy bubble wands and pipes from Styrofoam trays, soda bottles, and other throwaway items. Need a recipe for the bubble mixture? That's supplied here too. Fill your room with a cloud of bubbles and this is sure to be a big hit. (Source: *Earth-Friendly Outdoor Fun*, George Pfiffner) **Bubble Pop Art.** Here's a simple art project all children will be crazy about. Mix detergent and water in a container and let the children blow bubbles with straws. Let the other children chase the bubbles and catch them on colored paper. Use crayons or markers to trace the wet circles that appear on the paper. Look for even more exciting variations in this source. (Source: *Good Earth Art*, Mary Ann F. Kohl and Cindy Gainer)

Activities:	**Pop-a-Loony.** Decorate your classroom with various balloons. Place a message in each one describing a loony action each child needs to perform. The children can take turns selecting a balloon, pop-

ping it any way they can, and acting out the loony action it requires. The class can try to guess the mime acted out (monkey eating banana) or the child may simply be required to perform a stunt (close eyes and walk backwards).

(Source: *Everybody Wins!: Non-Competitive Party Games and Activities for Children*, Jody L. Blosser)

Bubble Bop.
Divide the group in two with one group blowing bubbles and the other group popping them. Add a little music but instruct the children to pop the bubbles only according to your called-out instructions. Try "Stomp on them," "Run backwards," "Karate chop," etc., then switch groups.

(Source: *Creative Games for Young Children*, Annetta Dellinger)

Songs: (Audio) "Bubblegum"
(Source: *Peanutbutterjam Incredibly Spreadable*)
(Book) "Pop! Goes the Weasel"
(Source: *Every Child's Book of Nursery Songs*, Donald Mitchell)

117 Problem Solving

Relate to: *Birth of Arthur Conan Doyle (May 22): Celebrate the anniversary of the birth of the creator of Sherlock Holmes, a world-famous problem-solving crusader.*

Videos: *Art Dog*
Have You Seen My Duckling?
Katy No-Pocket
Miss Nelson Is Missing
Whistle for Willie

Books: *Anno's Hat Tricks*, Akihiro Nozaki and Mitsumasa Anno
The Best Vacation Ever, Stuart J. Murphy
Detective Whoo, Dennis Panek
Goggles!, Ezra Jack Keats
Harry and the Lady Next Door, Gene Zion
Henry's Wrong Turn, Harriet Ziefert
The Homework Caper, Syd Hoff
How to Be a Friend, Marc Brown
Jeremy's Tail, Duncan Ball
Jingle Bells, Nick Butterworth
Katy No-Pocket, Emmy Payne
The Preposterous Week, George Keenen
Too Much Noise!, Ann McGovern
The Turnip, Janina Domanska
Whistle for Willie, Ezra Jack Keats

Crafts: **Pizza Puzzles.**
Make your own cardboard puzzle in the shape of a pizza. Add food features on the top with pictures from magazines. Help the children with math puzzles by dividing your pizza in equal parts for the child's math group.
(Source: *Good Earth Art*, Mary Ann F. Kohl and Cindy Gainer)

Snooper.
It takes a great snooper to be able to solve the difficult problems that occur. Here's a little snooper with a big nose that can become a little award to the little snoopers in your class who solve their math problems correctly. Collect those seed balls (stickies) from the trees that fall every season, as well as all the acorns you can get. These seed balls become the body, while

acorn caps are the hat. For a long Snoopy nose try using a peanut. For an illustration of this curious sculpture see the following source.

(Source: *Fun-to-Make Nature Crafts*, Robyn Supraner)

Activities:

Detective Fool.

With everyone seated in a circle, one child is chosen to be Detective Fool. He's taken from the room and blindfolded. When he returns to the circle everyone will have changed seats. When Detective Fool points to someone, that person says, "April Fools" or another appropriate phrase, while disguising his voice. If the detective is able to determine who it is he can change places with him in the circle. A friendly game for all classes.

(Source: *Creative Games for Young Children*, Annetta Dellinger)

The Guessing Game.

Children can use their critical thinking skills in this guessing game. Prepare a large number of envelopes with pictures of items (bus, television, etc.) inside. Write clues to the item on the exterior of the envelope and read the clues one at a time to the group until one little detective calls out the correct answer. Reveal the picture.

(Source: *The Best of the Mailbox, Book 2: Preschool/Kindergarten edition*, Margaret Michel)

Songs:

(Audio) "We'll Do It Together"
(Source: *Sesame Street Monsters*)
(Book) "There's A Hole in My Bucket"
(Source: *The Great Song Book*, Timothy John)

118 Reptiles: Alligators, Crocodiles

Relate to:	*National Wildlife Week (Oct. 10–16): A week set aside to advance awareness of wildlife conservation and land that is provided for this purpose.*

Videos:
Alligator All Around
Cornelius
How the Elephant Got His Trunk
Lyle, Lyle the Crocodile
Mama Don't Allow

Books:
Alligator's Toothache, Diane DeGroat
Bill and Pete to the Rescue, Tomie dePaola
Counting Crocodiles, Judy Sierra
Crocodile Beat, Gail Jorgensen
Dial-a-Croc, Mike Dumbleton
Dinner at Alberta's, Russell Hoban
Five Little Monkeys Sitting in a Tree, Eileen Christelow
I Am a Little Alligator, Francois Crozat
Jerome the Babysitter, Eileen Christelow
Kapoc the Killer Croc, Marcia Vaughan
The Lady with the Alligator Purse, Nadine Bernard Westcott
Millicent Maybe, Ellen Weiss
See You Later, Alligator, Babette McCarthy
There's a Crocodile under My Bed!, Ingrid Schubert
Why Alligator Hates Dog: A Cajun Folktale, J.J. Reneaux

Fingerplay: **The Crocodile.**
(Source: *Do Your Ears Hang Low?*, Tom Glazer)

Crafts: **Egg Carton Crocodile.**
Make a crocodile puppet out of everyday egg cartons. The lower half of an egg carton can even be turned upside down in the puppet's mouth to form the crocodile's teeth. If you want to make the crocodile longer and, at the same time, hide your arm, attach a long piece of green cloth to the crocodile's head.
(Source: *Egg Carton Critters*, Donna Miller)

Make an Alligator Purse.
Create a large construction paper purse in the shape of an alligator. Children can add the features themselves. This can be easily used to demonstrate the story *The Lady with the Alligator*

Purse by Nadine Westcott if you give each child paper versions of the story characters.

(Source: *The Giant Encyclopedia of Theme Activities for Children 2 to 5* , Kathy Charner)

Activities: **Crocodile Hunt.**

One child sits on the floor in the center of the room in the middle of a circle. This child crawls along the floor within the circle (lake) as a crocodile would move. The crocodile suddenly stands up, rising from the water, to spot his or her victim. Other children circulate through the room. When the crocodile rises all must freeze. Those who still move are captured by the crocodile and are out of the game.

(Source: *500 Games*, Peter L. Cave)

Alligator and Fish.

A sliding board is suggested for this game but any type of sliding tools can be used (tubes on a slick surface, skateboard-type items to ride on, etc.) to adapt the activity for use in a gymnasium. Select a person to be the alligator, who is placed one giant step away from the end of the slide (or sliding area marked). Children will slide down the slide or area marked and try not to slide into the arms (jaws) of the alligator. The alligator must never move his or her feet from the area they are planted.

(Source: *The Little Witch's Black Magic Book of Games*, Linda Glovach)

Songs: (Audio) "Never Smile at a Crocodile"

(Source: *Six Little Ducks: Classic Children's Songs*)

(Book) "The Crocodile"

(Source: *Do Your Ears Hang Low?*, Tom Glazer)

119 Reptiles: Snakes

Relate to: *Nag Panchami (Aug. 8): A South Indian festival to honor the sacred serpent Ananta. All snakes were reputed to bring wealth and rain, but unhappy ones can cause ruin in the home. Therefore milk and flowers are offered to snakes in shrines.*

Videos: *A Boy and a Boa*
The Day Jimmy's Boa Ate the Wash

Books: *Baby Rattlesnake*, Te Ala
The Cactus Flower Bakery, Harry Allard
Hide and Snake, Keith Baker
How Snake Got His Hiss, Marguerite W. Davol
Jimmy's Boa and the Big Splash Birthday Bash, Trinka Hakes Noble
Jimmy's Boa Bounces Back, Trinka Noble
Joseph and the Snake, Howard Berson
Mrs. Peloki's Snake, Joanne Oppenheim
Slithers, Syd Hoff
Small Green Snake, Libba Moore Gray
Snake Hunt, Jill Kastner
Snake In, Snake Out, Linda Banchek
To Bathe a Boa, C. Imbior Kudrna
Verdi, Janell Cannon

Crafts: **Snake.**
Children can construct a brightly colored snake with colored felt, scissors, and glue. Simply cut a long strip for the body and small oval shapes to fill it out. Don't forget the tongue.
(Source: *Do a Zoom-Do*, Bernice Chesler)

Slithery Snake.
For children a little older and with more patience try this snake craft made of small plastic cups strung together. Paint it, add eyes and a long tongue, and let it slither across the table as its body swivels back and forth.
(Source: *Why Throw It Away? Making Crazy Animals*, Jen Green)

Activities: **Snake by the Tail.**
This may be played outdoors or indoors in a large room. All players line up behind each other holding their hands on the

waist of the person in front of them. The leader must try to touch the snake's tail (last person) taking everyone else with him. Anyone who breaks the chain is out. If the leader succeeds, he goes to the end of the snake and the new leader takes his place at the head.

(Source: *500 Games*, Peter L. Cave)

Big Snake.
Wriggling snakes can fill your room with this activity. Let the children pair off to make a number of small snakes by lying on their stomachs and having one child hold the other's ankles. Let them practice moving around the room and attempting to connect with other snakes to make a larger one.

Add variety by getting the largest snake to do different tricks, such as rolling over without disconnecting.

(Source: *The Cooperative Sports and Games Book*, Terry Orlick)

Songs: (Audio) "Sally the Swinging Snake"
(Source: *Sally the Swinging Snake*)
(Book) "I'm Being Eaten by a Boa Constrictor"
(Source: *The Silly Songbook*, Esther L. Nelson)

120 Reptiles: Turtles

Relate to:	*Dr. Seuss's birthday (March 2): Author and creator of the* Yertle the Turtle *book.*

Videos:
Franklin is Messy
The Tortoise and the Hare
Yertle the Turtle

Books:
Albert's Toothache, Barbara Williams
Ananse's Feast: An Ashanti Tale, Tololwa M. Mollel
Harry and Shelburt, Dorothy VanWoerkom
How Honu the Turtle Got his Shell, Casey A. McGuire-Turcotte
I Can't Get My Turtle to Move, Elizabeth Lee O'Donnell
The Name of the Tree, Celia Barker Lottridge
Timothy Turtle, Al Graham
Tomorrow, Up and Away!, Pat Lowery Collins
The Turtle and the Monkey, Paul Galdone
The Turtle and the Moon, Charles Turner
Turtle Bay, Saviour Pirotta
Turtle Day, Douglas Florian
Turtle Spring, Lillian Hoban
Turtle Tale, Frank Asch
What Newt Could Do for Turtle, Jonathan London

Fingerplay:
I Had a Little Turtle.
   (Source: *Reaching the Special Learner Through Music*)

Crafts:
Paper Turtle.
Using the large format shown in the book listed below, which is appropriate for the manual dexterity of this age, children can color and glue together the parts of a turtle. Large pieces make it easy for the children to handle the work they're doing. The illustrations in this book can be easily duplicated for use.
   (Source: *Big and Easy Art*, Teacher Created Materials, Inc.)

Ornate Box Turtle Wall Hanging.
Using easily obtainable supplies the children can make a box turtle with features to easily identify it. With a paper plate base and another plate for a shell, the children can add depth to their turtle by gluing bottom pieces from an egg carton in a pattern to design the turtle's back. Paint all of it green. Glue

macaroni claws on the feet as an extra feature and hang it from a string on the wall or door of your bedroom.
(Source: *Crafts for Kids Who Are Wild about Reptiles*, Kathy Ross)

Activities: **Great Turtle Race.**
The turtles constructed in the previous crafts can be attached to a string going through a hole. Attach one end of the string to a stationary object, while the child holds the other end parallel to the floor. The player should then ease up on the string and quickly pull it tight again. This continuous motion will move the turtle to the opposite end of the string.
(Source: *Steven Caney's Toy Book*, Steven Caney)

Big Turtle.
Entice the children into creating a giant turtle by cooperating with each other. Get seven or eight children at a time to kneel together and place some object (gym mat, blanket, etc.) over them for a shell. It may take the children a while to get the idea of moving in the same direction in unison, but once they do they will really enjoy the event. Try racing your turtles across the room.
(Source: *The Cooperative Sports and Games Book*, Terry Orlick)

Songs: (Audio) "Turtle"
(Source: *Animal Alphabet Songs*)
(Book) "I Had a Little Turtle"
(Source: *Reaching the Special Learner Through Music*)

121 Royalty

Relate to:	*Anniversary of the discovery of King Tut's Tomb (Nov. 4): Here's a different type of royalty than most children are familiar with today. Discuss the various rituals of Egyptian royalty.*

Videos:
The Emperor's New Clothes
King Midas and the Golden Touch
The Most Wonderful Egg in the World
One Monday Morning
Rumpelstiltskin

Books:
Caterina: The Clever Farm Girl, Julienne Peterson
The Emperor and the Nightingale, Meilo So
The Frog Prince, Jane Canfield
If I Were Queen of the World, Fred Hiatt
King Bidgood's in the Bathtub, Audrey Wood
King Henry's Palace, Pat Hutchins
King of Another Country, Fiona French
Our King Has Horns!, Richard Pevear
The Practical Princess, Jay Williams
The Princess and the Pea, H. C. Andersen
Princess Bee and the Royal Good-night Story, Sandy Asher
Princess Penelope's Parrot, Helen Lester
The Queen's Goat, Margaret Mahy
The Queen's Holiday, Margaret Wild
Rumpelstiltskin, Jacob Grimm

Fingerplay:
Sing a Song of Sixpence.
(Source: *Finger Frolics—Revised*, Liz Cromwell, Dixie Hibner, and John R. Faitel)

Crafts:
King's Crown.
A regal king's crown can be constructed with nothing more than construction paper and staples or tape. Cut a band of paper the circumference of the child's head. Fold strips of an alternate color in loops and attach them all around the band. More suggestions for decorating the band and making a queen's crown can be found in the book listed here.
(Source: *Rainy Day Magic*, Margaret Perry)

Graham Cracker Castles.
Castles are an integral part of the medieval theme when

knights, dragons, kings, and queens roamed the landscape. Help the children build up those castle walls against attack by using basic materials at hand (graham crackers, marshmallows, peanut butter, and animal crackers). Finished the lesson? Maybe it's time for a snack, so let the children storm the castle and eat it down.

(Source: *Bubble Monster and Other Science Fun*, John H. Falk, Robert L. Pruitt II, Kristi S. Rosenberg, and Tali A. Katz)

Activities:

Throne Game.
The Queen of Hearts sits on her throne while the knave tries to steal a tart. The other guests stand on paper squares (the tarts). When the Queen says all change places, each guest tries to get a new tart with the knave trying to steal one. If one is stolen, the person left out becomes the knave.

(Source: *A Pumpkin in a Pear Tree*, Ann Cole, Carolyn Haas, Elizabeth Heller, and Betty Weinberger)

Good Morning Your Majesty.
A nice little greeting activity. Select one child to be the King (or Queen) who sits blindfolded on the throne. As each child enters let him or her bow and greet the King properly and the King will attempt to determine who is speaking to him.

(Source: *50 Fabulous Parties for Kids*, Linda Hetzer)

Treasure Hunt.
Hide the Queen's treasure (a variety of small items) throughout the room or house. As the children enter give the first child a clue. With each find, the children get a clue to the location of the next prize.

(Source: *50 Fabulous Parties for Kids*, Linda Hetzer)

Songs:

(Audio) "I Just Can't Wait to be King"
(Source: *Classic Disney, Vol. 1*)
(Book) "Old King Cole"
(Source: *Singing Bee!: A Collection of Favorite Children's Songs*, Jane Hart)

122 Safety

Relate to:	*National Safety Month (June): A month to practice practical safety techniques in all aspects of our lives.*

Videos:
D. W. Rides Again
Fire Safety for Kids
Meeting Strangers: Red Light, Green Light
Mickey Mouse: Safety Belt Expert
The Rescue Rangers' Fire Safety Adventure

Books:
The Bike Lesson, Stan and Jan Berenstain
Blue Bug's Safety Book, Virginia Poulet
Dinosaurs, Beware!, Marc Brown and Stephen Krensky
D. W. Rides Again!, Marc Brown
Fire Safety, Nancy Loewen
If I Cross the Street, Stephen Kroninger
The Look Out! Book: A Child's Guide to Street Safety, Cindy Blakely
    and Suzanne Drinkwater
Matches, Lighters, and Firecrackers Are Not Toys, Dorothy Chlad
No! No!, Lois Myller
Officer Buckle and Gloria, Peggy Rathmann
Playing Outdoors in Winter, Dorothy Chlad
Red Light! Green Light!, Margaret Wise Brown
Safety Can Be Fun, Munro Leaf
Traffic Safety, Nancy Loewen
Try it Again, Sam, Judith Viorst

Fingerplay: **At the Curb.**
(Source: *Finger Frolics—Revised*, Liz Cromwell, Dixie Hibner, and John R. Faitel)

Craft: **The Traffic Light.**
The source below gives a page to duplicate a traffic light on strong poster board. Have the children fill in the proper colors. By putting the colors on removable strips they can be used for traffic games later.

Children can place it on their bedroom doors to indicate whether or not they want people to be allowed to enter the room.
(Source: *101 Easy Art Activities*, Trudy Aarons and Francine Koelsch)

Craft and Activity:

Felt Board Safety Signs.

Safety signs are in front of us day and night and it's of utmost importance that young children become familiar with some of these as early in life as possible. Here we are presented with an enjoyable method of getting this safety lesson across.

Have a number of signs (yield, exit, stop, etc.) made of felt and displayed on a board. After a discussion of the meanings of each, mix them up and begin the game with "I'm thinking of a sign that means____." Select a child to choose the correct sign.

Later have the children make their own signs of paper. Glue the proper words to their signs using beans or other materials.
(Source: *Everyday Circle Times*, Liz and Dick Wilmes)

Activity:

Red Light, Green Light.

Children must run slowly on the word "green," walk on "yellow," and freeze on "red." A tom-tom can be used to indicate the type of motion, too. This game develops the ability to stop and start with quick reactions.
(Source: *Teacher's Handbook of Children's Games*, Marian Jenks Wirth)

Songs:

(Audio) "9–1–1"
(Source: *Kindergarten Sing and Learn*)
(Book) "The Traffic Cop"
(Source: *This Is Music*, William R. Sur, Mary R. Tolbert, William R. Fisher, and Adeline McCall)

123 School

Relate to:	*American Education Week (the week preceding Thanksgiving): Places attention on the importance of obtaining a good education.*

Videos:	*Louis James Hates School* *Mister Rogers' Neighborhood: Going to School* *Morris Goes to School* *Spot Goes to School* *Starring First Grade*

Books:	*Alice Ann Gets Ready for School*, Cynthia Jabar *Back to School for Rotten Ralph*, Jack Gantos and Nicole Rubel *Beginning School*, Irene Smalls *Betsy's First Day at Nursery School*, Gunilla Wolde *Debbie Goes to Nursery School*, Lois Lenski *I'll Go to School If . . .* , Bo Flood *Little Bunny's Preschool Countdown*, Maribeth Boelts *Lunch Bunnies*, Kathryn Lasky *Minerva Louise at School*, Janet Morgan Stoeke *My First Day at Preschool*, Edwina Riddell *My Nursery School*, Harlow Rockwell *The New Teacher*, Miriam Cohen *School Days*, B. G. Hennessy *Something Special*, Nicola Moon *A Trip Through a School*, Jeanne Rowe

Fingerplay:	**Ready for School.** (Source: *Finger Frolics—Revised*, Liz Cromwell, Dixie Hibner, and John R. Faitel)

Crafts:	**Bear Crayon Box.** Simple and useful crayon-holder boxes can be constructed using crayons, paint, and a cupcake liner box. These boxes can be used by the children when they begin school. (Source: *Beginning Crafts for Beginning Readers*, Alice Gilbreath) **See, What I Did! Clothespin.** When children begin school they take great pride in displaying their accomplishments for the entire family to see. Assist the children in making their own clips to hold their papers. You will need spring-type clothespins, magnets, and construc-

tion paper. Trace the faces supplied to show a little face peering over the papers with pride.

(Source: *Rainy Day Projects for Children*, Gerri Jenny and Sherrie Gould)

Activities:

Who Stole the Cookie from the Cookie Jar?

This is a simple game done with a chant that goes as follows:

All: Who stole the cookie from the cookie jar?

Leader: (Pointing to one child) Did you steal the cookie from the cookie jar?

Child: Who, me?

All: YES, you!

Child: Not me!

All: Not you? Then who? (Pause)

Repeat this chant substituting items found at school for the cookie and selecting a new child each time.

Sour Puss.

When children begin a new year at school they are normally a little frightened and cautious when meeting their new classmates. In this source you will locate this and other fun ice breakers.

Organize the children in a circle and select one child to be It. All the children are instructed to show sour faces and not to smile or laugh. The child who is It will wander the circle until choosing a sour puss whom he or she will try to make laugh. Remember, no touching.

(Source: *Classroom Parties*, Susan Spaete)

Songs:

(Audio) "I Go to School"

(Source: *Put Down the Duckie!*)

(Book) "Mary Had a Little Lamb"

(Source: *Sing Hey Diddle, Diddle*, Beatrice Harrop)

124 Sea and Seashore

Relate to:	*National Week of the Ocean (April 12–18): A time to center our attention on protecting our oceans and their inhabitants.*

Videos:	*Burt Dow: Deep-Water Man* *Little Tim and the Brave Sea Captain* *Swimmy*

Books:	*Beach Bunny*, Jennifer Selby *A Beach Day*, Douglas Florian *Beach Play*, Marsha Hayles *Famous Seaweed Soup*, Antoinette Truglio Martin *A House by the Sea*, Joanne Ryder *I Was All Thumbs*, Bernard Waber *The Mystery in the Bottle*, Val Willis *Pigs on a Blanket*, Amy Axelrod *The Queen's Holiday*, Margaret Wild *Sally and the Limpet*, Simon James *Sand Cake*, Frank Asch *The Seashore Noisy Book*, Margaret Wise Brown *Starfish*, Edith Hurd *Teddy at the Seashore*, Amanda Davidson *The Twelve Days of Summer*, Elizabeth Lee O'Donnell

Fingerplay:	**Five Little Seashells.** (Source: *Finger Frolics—Revised*, Liz Cromwell, Dixie Hibner, and John R. Faitel)

Crafts:	**Shell Necklace or Belt.** With a collection of small shells and some kite string, children can make their own necklaces or belts. Holes in the shells should be done before the program. The shells may be left natural (or painted if time permits). **Paper-Plate Crab.** Children see many creatures from the sea when visiting the seashore and one of the most familiar is the crab. Here they can create their own crab puppet using paper plates and construction paper. You can even have realistic movable claws using paper fasteners. 　This is a craft that can lend itself to further stories on sea

creatures and now the children can participate in the telling using their new puppets.
(Source: *Year-Round Crafts for Kids*, Barbara L. Don Diego)

Activities: **Fishing.**
Set up a small child's pool in the room (no water, please). Inside have numerous small paper fish with small metal tabs glued near the mouth portion. Give each child a small fishing pole (string and stick with a magnet on it) and have them catch as many fish as they can in a given period of time.

Beach Ball Balance.
Beach balls are familiar objects to children at the beach. Try a little cooperative adventure here by having the children team up. Tell the children they can lift the beach balls and pass them along in any way they wish without using their hands. Watch the ingenuity the children demonstrate and the uproarious laughter that you hear as they try.
(Source: *The Cooperative Sports and Games Books*, Terry Orlick)

Songs: (Audio) "There's a Hole in the Bottom of the Sea"
(Source: *Disney's Children's Favorite Silly Songs*)
(Book) "She Waded in the Water"
(Source: *Do Your Ears Hang Low?*, Tom Glazer)

125 Seasons: Fall

Relate to:	*Autumn (Sept. 23–Dec.21): Celebrate the beginning of autumn with the autumnal equinox on September 23.*

Videos: *Winnie the Pooh and the Blustery Day*

Books: *All Ready for School*, Leone Adelson
Autumn, Colin McNaughton
Autumn Days, Ann Schweninger
Caps, Hats, Socks and Mittens, Louise Borden
The Cinnamon Hen's Autumn Day, Sandra Dutton
Clifford's First Autumn, Norman Bridwell
Emily's Autumn, Janice Udry
Every Autumn Comes the Bear, Jim Arnosky
Fall, Chris L. Demarest
Henry Explores the Mountains, Mark Taylor
Marmalade's Yellow Leaf, Cindy Wheeler
Now It's Fall, Lois Lenski
Possum's Harvest Moon, Anne Hunter
Ska-tat!, Kimberley Knutson
Word Bird's Fall Words, Jane Belk Moncure

Fingerplay: **Leaves Are Floating Down.**
(Source: *Finger Frolics—Revised*, Liz Cromwell, Dixie Hibner, and John R. Faitel)

Crafts: **Nature Mobile.**
While the children are outside for the fall activity games, have them collect leaves, pine cones, seed pods, and so forth from the area. With these items, string, and a hanger a simple mobile can be created.
(Source: *Something to Make, Something to Think About*, Martha Olson Condit)

Leaf Place Mat.
Take the children on a scavenger hunt through the schoolyard and instruct them to gather as many different leaves as they can locate. Return to the classroom and give the children a large piece of construction paper to place over their leaves. Demonstrate the method of creating leaf impressions through crayon rubbing using fall colors.

You may want to put clear contact paper over the children's final products so that they can use then over and over again.
(Source: *Storytime Crafts*, Kathryn Totten)

Activities: **Sparrows and Statues.**
In a game similar to the well-known Freeze Tag, children pretend to be sparrows hopping and flying around until the caller yells stop, then all must freeze in position. Those who do not freeze are out of the game. Prizes may be given for the funniest poses.
(Source: *500 Games*, Peter L. Cave)

Autumn Leaves Are Falling Down.
In this source you will locate a cheerful rhyme sung to "London Bridge." After a lesson on the fall season and discussion of the changing of leaf colors the children can mimic these trees by holding up the numerous colored leaves and letting them fall at the appropriate time in the song. This is an activity children will want to repeat again.
(Source: *The Giant Encyclopedia of Circle Time and Group Activities for Children 3 to 6*, Kathy Charner)

Songs: (Audio) "Bluebird, Bluebird through My Window"
(Source: *Folk Song Carnival*)
(Book) "Pretty Leaves"
(Source: *God's Wonderful World*, Agnes Leckie Mason and Phyllis Brown Ohanian)

126 Seasons: Spring

Relate to:	*Vernal Equinox (March 21): This time denotes the start of Spring and is the one time of the year that day and night are equal in length.*

Videos:	*Frog and Toad Are Friends: Spring* (Arnold Lobel Video Showcase) *Madeline and the Easter Bonnet*

Books:	*Arctic Spring*, Sue Vyner *First Comes Spring*, Anne Rockwell *In the Spring*, Craig Brown *Let's Look at the Seasons: Springtime*, Ann Schweninger *Little Bear's Pancake Party*, Janice *My Spring Robin*, Anne Rockwell *One Bright Monday Morning*, Arline Baum *Really Spring*, Gene Zion *Sleepy Bear*, Lydia Dabcovich *Spring Break at Pokeweed Public School*, John Bianchi *Spring Is Here*, Taro Gomi *The Story of May*, Mordicai Gerstein *Wake Up, Groundhog!*, Carlo Cohen *When Spring Comes*, Robert Maass *When Spring Comes*, Natalie Kinsey-Warnock

Fingerplay:	**Little Brown Seed.** (Source: *Finger Frolics—Revised*, Liz Cromwell, Dixie Hibner, and John R. Faitel)

Crafts:	**Paper Flowers.** With the use of paper, straws, glue, scissors, and a coffee can, children can be guided in making a small flower garden of their own. Try showing the children pictures of different types of flowers so they can have variety in their design. The most popular and easiest of designs is the tulip or the daisy. Precut patterns for the children to trace will save time and frustration at this age level. (Source: *Fun with Paper*, Robyn Supraner) **Fluffy Toy Lamb.** After a talk of events that occur in the spring, help the children create their own spring lamb for puppet shows. Use a simple

black glove as a base. The fingers will be the feet and the thumb the face with a little eye on it. The rest is simple. Just cover the palm and back of the hand area of the glove with cotton balls and tie a ribbon around the lamb's neck. Let the children try them out while singing, "Mary had a little lamb."
(Source: *Crafts to Make in the Spring*, Kathy Ross)

Activities:

The Farmer and His Seeds.
The following activity may be performed while singing the words to the tune "Farmer in the Dell."

> The Farmer plants the seeds.
> The Farmer plants the seeds.
> Hi, Ho, the dairy-o.
> The Farmer plants the seeds. (Bend and pretend to plant)
>
> The sun comes out to shine, etc. (Make circle with arms)
> The rain begins to fall, etc. (Fingers flutter up and down)
> The plant begins to grow, etc. (Slowly raise up)
> The farmer cuts them down, etc. (Cutting motion)
> And now he grinds it up, etc. (Grinding motion)
> And now he bakes the bread, etc. (Put in oven)
> And now we'll have some bread. (Pretend to eat.)

Wind and Flowers: A May Day Game.
Divide the class into two groups, each standing behind a line on opposite ends of the room. One group is called Flowers and they select one flower name to be their secret name. They float, hop, and so forth throughout the room while the other team (Wind) calls out flower names in an attempt to find the secret name. When the name is discovered, the wind tries to tag the flowers. Those tagged join the wind and a new name is chosen.
(Source: *A Pumpkin in a Pear Tree*, Ann Cole, Carolyn Haas, Elizabeth Heller, and Betty Weinberger)

Activity and Song:

Over in the Meadow.
This includes instructions for a short dance, as well as music and lyrics to a song that will help the children identify animals and insects appearing in the spring.
(Source: *Dancing Games for Children of All Ages*, Esther L. Nelson)

Song:

(Audio) "Spring Is Here"
(Source: *Family Playground*)

127 Seasons: Summer

Relate to:	*Summer Solstice (June 21): Note the beginning of the summer season on the longest day of the year.*

Videos:	*Frog and Toad Are Friends: A Swim* (Arnold Lobel Video Showcase) *Summer Picnic*

Books:	*The Berenstain Bears Go to Camp*, Stan Berenstain *Harry by the Sea*, Gene Zion *Hotter than a Hot Dog!*, Stephanie Calmenson *One Hot Summer Day*, Nina Crews *Shooting Star Summer*, Candice Ransom *Summer*, Ron Hirschi *A Summer Day*, Douglas Florian *Summer Is . . .* , Charlotte Zolotow *The Summer Noisy Book*, Margaret Wise Brown *Summer's End*, Maribeth Boelts *A Summery Saturday Morning*, Margaret Mahy *The Swimming Hole*, Jerrold Beim *The Twelve Days of Summer*, Elizabeth Lee O'Donnell *When Summer Comes*, Robert Maass *When Summer Ends*, Susi Gregg Fowler

Fingerplay:	**The Rain.** (Source: *Finger Frolics—Revised*, Liz Cromwell, Dixie Hibner, and John R. Faitel)

Crafts:	**Matchbox Boat.** A simple boat of paper, sticks, foil, clay, and paint can be constructed in minutes. This craft requires minimal skills and provides immediate rewards. Five-step illustrated instructions can be located in Ms. Pitcher's book. Remember: Have a tub available to allow the children to test out their creations. Immediate reward is helpful at this age. (Source: *Cars and Boats*, Caroline Pitcher) **Four Seasons Clipboard.** Here you will find a seasonal clipboard that children can make for their home refrigerators where the entire family may leave messages to each other. On a piece of heavy colored poster

board have the children fashion four trees for the four corners representing each of the seasons and their changes. Glue two spring-type clothespins to the top for attaching important messages.

(Source: *175 Easy-to-Do Everyday Crafts*, Sharon Dunn Umnik)

Activities:

Magnet Fishing.

This activity takes a bit of preparation. It will require a small tub or swimming pool, paper fish cut with metal tabs on them, and sticks with string and magnets at the end.

The game can be played in a number of ways:

- Place number scores on certain fish to allow the children to try to get the highest score by catching fish with the high numbers.
- Have certain teams try to catch designated colored fish. The first to collect all their colors wins.

(Source: *500 Games*, Peter L. Cave)

The Day the Hippo UnZipped His Zipper.

This story and activity is perfect on a hot summer day. It's the story of a hippo and a number of other animals who unzip their skin and step out of it in an effort to cool off. Make masks of the different animal characters so that the children can use them to line up and act out this story.

The full text of the story can be located in this source along with other summertime action rhymes.

(Source: *Glad Rags*, Jan Irving and Robin Currie)

Songs:

(Audio) "I Love Summer"
    (Source: *Summersongs*)
(Book) "Row, Row, Row Your Boat"
    (Source: *Rounds about Rounds*, Jane Yolen)

128 Seasons: Winter

Relate to:	*First Day of Winter (on or about Dec. 21).*

Videos: *Ladybug, Ladybug, Winter Is Coming*
Little Bear: Winter Tales
Madeline's Winter Vacation
The Snow Day

Books: *Dear Rebecca, Winter Is Here*, Jean Craighead George
Frederick, Leo Lionni
Henrietta's First Winter, Rob Lewis
In Wintertime, Kim Howard
Katy and the Big Snow, Virginia Burton
The Last Snow of Winter, Tony Johnston
Old Turtle's Winter Games, Leonard Kessler
Stormy Weather, Amanda Harvey
Warm in Winter, Erica Silverman
Where Does Everyone Go?, Aileen Fisher
A Winter Day, Douglas Florian
The Winter Day, Beverly Komoda
Winter Noisy Book, Margaret Wise Brown
A Winter Walk, Lynne Barasch
A Winter's Tale, Ian Wallace

Fingerplay: **Snowflakes.**
(Source: *Finger Frolics—Revised*, Liz Cromwell, Dixie Hibner, and John R. Faitel)

Crafts: **Paper Plate Penguins.**
Construct a penguin out of paper plates and construction paper. Precut parts are advisable for this craft. Two sizes of plates are needed for each child, a six-inch cake plate for the head and a nine-inch plate for the body. This book gives you true-to-size patterns to trace for the eyes, feet, head, beak, and wings of the penguin.
(Source: *Paper Plate Animals*, Bee Gee Hazell)

Snow Scene.
Make a simple winter scene. Give each child a sheet of black or blue construction paper. Have them cut three different sizes of white circles to glue on to form a snowman. (Precut circles for two- or three-year olds is advisable.) Use real material of

various colors for the scarf and hat. Use chalk to draw the snow on the ground and small, white sticker dots for the snow falling from the sky. Stickers are a popular item in crafts at a young age.

Sleepy Bear Mitten Hanger.
During the winter season the children can always use a place to hang their mittens to dry. Here's a craft that will have them finally wanting to hang them up without arguing with Mom. Create a sleepy little polar bear face out of a paper plate. Give him a wintry appearance with a snow cap and add clothespins on a string at the bottom to hang your mittens to dry.
(Source: *175 Easy-to-Do Everyday Crafts*, Sharon Dun Umnik)

Activity: **Snowball Game.**
Try this simple dexterity activity. Give each child a ruler and cottonball. After a discussion on what cottonballs look like (clouds, snowballs, etc.) have the children balance the cottonball on the ruler while performing various activities called out by the leader. Try such feats as balancing on one foot, holding the ruler above the head, or involve the children in team relay events.
(Source: *Focus on Winter*, Rosie Seaman)

Activity and Song: **Shovel the Snow.**
Allow the children to act out the motions of shoveling snow when this is sung in the song.
Try adapting the song to add other verses on what you can do with snow.
(Source: *God's Wonderful World*, Agnes Leckie Mason and Phyllis Brown Ohanian)

Song: (Audio) "Hello Winter"
(Source: *Diamonds and Dragons*)

129 Secrets/ Mysteries

Relate to:	*Mystery Series Week (first full week in Oct.): This is a time to celebrate characters in continuing mystery books. Introduce such crime stoppers as Nancy Drew and others.*

Videos: *Art Dog*
Franklin and the Secret Club

Books: *The 13th Clue*, Ann Jonas
Albert's Halloween: The Case of the Stolen Pumpkins, Leslie Tryon
Anna's Secret Friend, Yorilo Tsutsui
The Case of the Crooked Candles, Jonathan V. Cann
The Dark at the Top of the Stairs, Sam McBratney
Detective Valentine, Audrey Wood
Ducks Disappearing, Phyllis Reyn Naylor
Gertrude, the Bulldog Detective, Eileen Christelow
Grandpa's Teeth, Rod Clement
Hot Fudge, James Howe
Mousekin's Mystery, Edna Miller
Mystery of the Docks, Thatcher Hurd
The Mystery of King Karfu, Doug Cushman
Secrets, Ellen B. Senisi
The Two O'Clock Secret, Bethany Roberts

Fingerplay: **Pocket Surprise.**
        (Source: *Glad Rags*, Jan Irving and Robin Currie)

Crafts: **Mysterious Tablets.**
        In the ruins of Ur many mysterious tablets were located with messages using the cuneiform alphabet drawn in soft clay tablets by scribes. Here's a chance for children to create their own mysterious tablets and leave secret messages for their friends and family. With the use of soft clay, an aluminum can to roll out their clay tablet, and an ice cream stick to scratch in their message, these special messages can be used for a number of different occasions. Also included in this source are instructions on making a cylinder seal for rolling out the child's signature into the clay tablet.
        (Source: *City Crafts from Secret Cities*, Judith Conaway)

        Crayon Magic.
        Help the children leave secret mystery messages for their

friends and family. Have children leave clues to who they are, using crayons and watercolor paints. Need a clue how to do this? Check out this wonderful source of a variety of crafts.
(Source: *Loo-Loo, Boo, and Art You Can Do*, Denis Roche)

Activities: **Mystery Classmate.**
Take photos of all members of the class individually during the first week of school. Have each picture cut in four puzzle-like pieces and placed in individual envelopes with an accompanying nametag. Have a poster titled "Mystery Classmate" displayed in your room. Each day put up one piece of the puzzle until someone in the room can guess who the person is in the photo. When the identity is discovered move the photo and the nametag to a bulletin board that will eventually hold your whole group. This is a fun way to get to know each other.

Mystery Bundle.
Try wrapping a variety of common objects in tissue paper and tie them securely. Pass these objects around the group and see if the children can determine its contents by the shape they see, the touch, or smell. If you wish to keep score give one point to each child who correctly identifies what's in the bundle.
(Source: *Child Magazine's Book of Children's Parties*, Angela Wilkes)

Songs: (Audio) "We Never Keep a Secret for All Our Lives"
(Source: *I've Got Super Power*)
(Book) "The Riddle Song"
(Source: *The Good Times Songbook*, James Leisy)

130 Self-Reliance

Relate to:	*Self-Improvement Month (Sept.): A month to demonstrate the importance of continual learning and self-improvement.*

Videos:
Do It Yourself (Paddington Bear: Paddington, P.I., Vol. 2)
Have You Seen My Duckling?
Regina's Big Mistake

Books:
All Alone after School, Muriel Stanek
All by Myself, Anna Grossnickle Hines
Annabelle and the Big Slide, Rita Pocock
Bear, John Schoenherr
A Cool Kid—Like Me!, Hans Wilhelm
Emily Just in Time, Jan Stepian
I Can Take a Walk, Shigeo Watanabe
I Like Me, Nancy Carlson
Joey on His Own, Eleanor Schick
Let Me Do It!, Janice Gibala-Broxholm
Little Mo, Martin Waddell
My Own Big Bed, Anna G. Hines
Palm Trees, Nancy Cote
Somebody's Awake, Paul Rogers
Stanley, Syd Hoff

Fingerplay:
I Can, Can You?
(Source: *Successful Children's Parties*, Reeta Bochner Wolfsohm)

Crafts:
All by Myself Skill Chart.
Create a special-skills pocket chart to monitor children's progress in becoming more self-reliant. Children enjoy recognizing their names on display. When children master a skill they may put their name on a craft stick and place it in the pocket. This is a craft that can be adapted for many uses.
(Source: *Teaching Terrific Twos and other Toddlers*, Terry Lynne Graham and Linda Camp)

Overnight Bag.
Little ones like the feeling that they are independent. Showing Mom and Dad that they can do it themselves is a matter of pride. Here's a craft they can really enjoy. Pass out a number of catalogs featuring children's items. After discussing sleep-

ing overnight with a friend let the children cut out items they would need to pack in their suitcase for an overnight stay. (Too young for scissors? Let them point and Mom will cut.) Give them each a file folder with a handle and let them glue the pictures inside the folder.

(Source: *Glad Rags*, Jan Irving and Robin Currie)

Activities:

I Can Do It.

This is a variation of the game King of the Hill that will help children demonstrate what they are capable of doing. It is a wonderful method of illustrating self-reliance and more while having a great deal of fun and laughter.

In a bag, place a large number of papers, each listing activities the children need to perform to show growth in their life (e.g., bounce a ball, tie your shoes, put on your own shirt, etc.). These activities can be physical or verbal acts and often change depending on the age of the group playing the game.

The children sit at the bottom of a flight of stairs. If they are able to perform the action that the leader announces from the paper drawn from the bag, they move up one step. If they are unable to do it, they simply wait for their next turn. The first to reach the top of the hill wins. This is a game children will wish to attempt often.

Stop and Go Game.

This activity helps the children practice their gross motor skills while enjoying themselves immensely. Make a collection of circles: red stop and green go circles. Lay out these game pieces across the floor for the children to follow. Instruct the children to follow the signs on the road created by hopping, skipping, jumping or other skills you mention at that time and remember to stop with both feet on the stop sign.

(Source: *The Giant Encyclopedia of Theme Activities for Children 2 to 5*, Kathy Charner)

Songs:

(Audio) "Feelin' Fine"
(Source: *Dance in Your Pants*)
(Book) "The More We Get Together"
(Source: *Raffi Singable Songbook*, Raffi)

131 Senses

Relate to:	*National Save Your Hearing Day (May 31): A day to demonstrate the importance of having your hearing tested.*

Videos:
Apt. 3
King Midas and the Golden Touch

Books:
The Blind Men and the Elephant, Lillian Quigley
Ears Are for Hearing, Paul Showers
Feeling Things, Allan Fowler
Hearing Things, Allan Fowler
I Can Tell by Touching, Carolyn Otto
King Midas and the Golden Touch, Kathryn Hewitt
My First Look at Touch, Jane Yorke
My Five Senses, Margaret Miller
Polar Bear, Polar Bear, What Do You Hear?, Bill Martin Jr.
Seeing Things, Allan Fowler
Sense Suspense: A Guessing Game for the Five Senses, Bruce McMillan
Seven Blind Mice, Ed Young
Smelling, Henry Arthur Pluckrose
Smelling Things, Allan Fowler
Tasting Things, Allan Fowler

Fingerplay:
Circus Senses Action Verse.
(Source: *Holiday Hoopla: Songs and Finger Plays*, Kathy Darling)

Craft:
Scented Gifts.
The sense of smell is one of the strongest of our senses, especially when we come across a particularly unpleasant odor. Help create some pleasant sensations by giving a scented gift. This source gives you examples of six different designs for sachets, including one for your dog.
(Source: *Make Gifts!*, Kim Solga)

Activities:
Blind Man's Buff.
This game extends back to the fourteenth century. Players form a circle with the "Blindman" in the center. The blindfolded child has a helper that spins him three times. He then attempts to catch any player. Players may tease and tap the blindman in attempts to distract him, but if caught they will have to change

places. An old "Blindman" chant is offered in this source to go along with the game.
(Source: *Classic Children's Games*, Vivienne Sernaque)

Touch Hunt.
Play a simple game in which the leader calls out a texture. The children search the room for an item that feels like the texture called out. If the children can read the simple texture words, pass out a list and have your own scavenger hunt. Add a little more difficulty by calling out a texture and a shape together.
(Source: *Stop, Look and Listen*, Sarah A. Williamson)

House Sounds Guessing Game.
A house is a very busy place with a family in it. Have you ever stopped to just listen and count how many different sounds you hear in your home? Make a recording of sounds from your house and see if the children can guess what they are. For a list of suggestions see this source.
(Source: *More Picture Book Story Hours: From Parties to Pets*, Paula Gaj Sitarz)

Songs: (Audio) "Sing the Sound You Hear"
(Source: *Kindergarten Sing and Learn*)
(Book) "Three Blind Mice"
(Source: *The Golden Songbook*, Katharine Tyler Wessells)

132 Sign Language

Relate to: *Deaf Awareness Week (Sept. 20–26): A celebration to promote deaf culture and American Sign Language.*

Videos: *Say, Sing and Sign: Colors*
Say, Sing and Sign: Songs
Sign Me a Story

Books: *Buffy's Orange Leash*, Stephen Golder and Lise Memling
Dad and Me in the Morning, Pat Lakin
Handtalk Birthday, Remy Charlip, Mary Beth and George Ancona
Handtalk Zoo, George and Mary Beth Ancona
I Can Sign My ABC's, Susan Gibbons Chaplin
Koko's Kitten, Francine Patterson
The Little Green Monster, Sue Johnson
More Simple Signs, Cindy Wheeler
Moses Goes to a Concert, Isaac Millman
A Show of Hands, Mary Beth Sullivan and Linda Bourke
The Ugly Duckling in Signed English, Karen Saulnier
A Very Special Friend, Dorothy Hoffman Levi
What Is the Sign for Friend?, Judith E. Greenberg
Where's Spot?, Eric Hill
Words in Our Hands, Ada B. Litchfield

Fingerplay: **Deaf Donald.**
(Source: *Juba This and Juba That*, Virginia A. Tashjian)

Crafts: **Plaster Casting Hands.**
Try teaching the children the universal sign for "I Love You" in American Sign Language. With this in mind help the children make a plaster cast of their hand in this position. All that's required is clay, plaster of Paris, a rolling pin, and some paints. For useful step-by-step guidelines see this source.
(Source: *101 Things to Make*, Juliet Bawden)

Crazy Helping Hand.
Try this craft that uses up all those single gloves that you've been collecting all these years. I can't stand the way you always lose only one glove and then don't know what to do with the one left behind. Now we have a good use for it. Stuff the fingers of the glove with dry papier-mâché (not mixed with

water). Stuff it so that it has some give but the fingers stand up straight. The base of the glove is going to be constructed out of jar lids from mason jars. This will enable you to stand the glove upright. It can be decorated with ribbon as instructed and set on a side table for you to put your rings and necklaces on during the night.

Try not stuffing the ring finger and middle finger but leaving those flat. This will give you the international sign for "I Love You" in sign language and make the gift even more special.

(Source: *Let's Make it from Junk!*, Eileen Mercer)

Activities:

Finger Spelling Bee.
Have a collection of pictures or words of items cut from a magazine. Let each child draw one item from the bag and spell it in sign language. Players keep going until one person remains. Of course, you are eliminated if you spell incorrectly.
(Source: *Finger Spelling Fun*, David A. Adler)

Finger Spelling Telephone.
Played like the original Telephone game, but in this one the child is given a simple message (one word) to spell in sign language. This is passed along until at the final destination the secret word is revealed, hopefully correct.
(Source: *Finger Spelling Fun*, David A. Adler)

Songs:

(Audio) "Hand Talk"
(Source: *Sesame Road*)
(Book) "Make New Friends"
(Source: *Lift Up Your Hands: Popular Songs in Sign Language*, Donna Gadling Walters, Lottie Riekehof, and Daniel H. Pokorny)

133 Space and Spaceships

Relate to:	*Space Week (the week including July 20): This week is considered Space Week in some towns honoring the first step on the moon.*

Videos:
I Wanna Be an Astronaut
Moon Man

Books:
Alistair and the Alien Invasion, Marilyn Sadler
Alistair in Outer Space, Marilyn Sadler
Dmitri, the Astronaut, Jon Agee
Grandpa Takes Me to the Moon, Timothy R. Gaffney
Harold's Trip to the Sky, Crockett Johnson
I Am an Astronaut, Cynthia Benjamin
I Want to Be an Astronaut, Byron Barton
It Came from Outer Space, Tony Bradman
Man on the Moon, Anastasia Suen
My Brother is from Outer Space (The Book of Proof), Vivian Ostrow
Pigs in Space, Ellen Weiss
Regards to the Man in the Moon, Ezra Jack Keats
Tinker and Tom and the Star Baby, Avid McPhail
A Trip to Mars, Ruth Young
What Next, Baby Bear!, Jill Murphy

Fingerplay:
Ten Little Martians.
(Source: *Finger Frolics—Revised*, Liz Cromwell, Dixie Hibner, and John R. Faitel)

Crafts:
A UFO You Can Fly.
A paper-plate flying saucer can be decorated simply using plates, glue, crayons, and a little imagination. A chance to use these UFOs outside would be welcomed by young children.
Dave Ross's entire book is devoted to showing young children how to make at least eight different types of UFOs out of inexpensive materials.
(Source: *Making UFOs*, Dave Ross)

A Felt Space Picture.
Using a square of dark felt for the sky, some varied colored felt to cut out spaceships, a pole, and string, a delightful banner can be designed. This is an uncomplicated banner that young preschoolers can handle. An illustration is available.
(Source: *Felt Craft*, Florence Temko)

A Roaring Rocket.
Let's make a glittering silver rocket made of a cardboard tube covered in foil. Add side wings and flames shooting from the end made of colored tissue paper. Add some pizzazz by gluing your rocket to black poster board, paint a planet beneath it and some spirals with glitter and glue. This outer space scene will attract a lot of compliments.
(Source: *Making Pictures Out of This World*, Penny King)

Activities: **Space Walk.**
Decorate your room with various colored stars and circles with the names of the planets. Add music to the event as the children walk from star to star and planet to planet. Reward the children with sticker stars and other items as they land on given planets. For further instructions see the source.
(Source: *Celebrate*, Rainbow Publishing Co.)

5–4–3–2–1 Blast Off!
Try a space-age version of Freeze Tag or Statues. An easy game for even the youngest child to enjoy.
(Source: *Celebrate*, Rainbow Publishing Co.)

Activity and Song: **One Little, Two Little, Three Little Spacemen.**
(Source: *I Saw a Purple Cow and 100 Other Recipes for Learning*, Ann Cole, Carolyn Haas, Faith Bushnell, and Betty Weinberger)

Song: (Audio) "Spaceship Ride"
(Source: *Red Pajamas and Purple Shoes*)

134 Sports

Relate to:	*National Sports Trivia Week (March 18–24): Ask your favorite sports trivia questions at this time of overlapping sports events.*

Videos:
Casey at the Bat
Frog and Toad Are Friends: A Swim (Arnold Lobel Video Show-case)
Madeline and the Soccer Star
The Olympic Champ
The Tortoise and the Hare

Books:
Allie's Basketball Dream, Barbara E. Barber
Arthur Goes to Camp, Marc Brown
Baseball, Football, Daddy and Me, David Friend
Bunnies and Their Sports, Nancy Carlson
Dulcie Dando, Soccer Star, Sue Stops
Field Day, Nick Butterworth and Mick Inkpen
Fox under First Base, Jim Latimer
Gone Fishing, Earlene Long
Kick, Pass and Run, Leonard Kessler
The Littlest Leaguer, Syd Hoff
Old Mother Hubbard's Dog Takes Up Sports, John Yeoman and Quentin Blake
Olympics!, B. G. Hennessy
Playing Right Field, Willy Welch
Sam the Zamboni Man, James Stevenson
Swish!, Bill Martin Jr. and Michael Sampson
Wait, Skates!, Mildred Johnson

Fingerplay:
The Bear Hunt.
(Source: *Children's Counting-out Rhymes, Fingerplays, Jump-Rope and Bounce-Ball Chants and Other Rhythms*, Gloria T. Delamar)

Crafts:
Basketball Toss.
Basketball is a game that even the youngest children can play. Construct a backboard out of oaktag or poster board. Attach paper cups with number scores above each to the backboard. Allow the children to score by tossing ping-pong balls (or just crumbled paper) into the cups (baskets).

Olympic Games: The Discus Throw.
Prepare for the Olympic Games with a specially designed "Discus" for the discus throw event. You will need the sturdier paper plates for this craft in order for them to soar farther through the air. Permit the children to decorate their discus with their own unique logo and then glue two together for extra strength. Now let the games begin.
(Source: *Look What You Can Make with Paper Plates*, Margie Hayes Richmond)

Activities: **Magnet Fishing.**
This activity takes a bit of preparation. It will require a small tub or swimming pool, paper fish cut with metal tabs on them, and sticks with string and magnets at the end.
The game can be played in a number of ways:
- Place number scores on certain fish to allow the children to try to get the highest score by catching fish with the high numbers.
- Have the children try to catch designated colored fish. The first to collect all their color wins.
(Source: *500 Games*, Peter L. Cave)

Olympic Events.
After enjoying your favorite sports stories and having children share their glorious experiences with the games they enjoy, put on some music, bring out the torch, and introduce the opening of your own "Library Olympics." Try such events as: 10-yard dash, long jump, Frisbee toss, Olympic obstacle course, Nerfball toss, javelin throw (use a straw), and the three-legged race. And, of course, following the game comes the medal awards ceremony.
(Source: *The Penny Whistle Party Planner*, Meredith Brokaw and Annie Gilbar)

Songs: (Audio) "Take Me Out to the Ballgame"
(Source: *Mommy and Me: Rock-a-Bye Baby*)
(Book) "A-Hunting We Will Go"
(Source: *The Silly Songbook*, Esther L. Nelson)

135 Strangers

Relate to:	*National Missing Children's Day (May 25): To inform people of the serious problem of missing children in this country and to educate children on safe procedures at school, home, and while out playing.*

Videos: *The Berenstain Bears Learn about Strangers*
Learn about Living: Never Talk to Strangers
Little Red Riding Hood
Meeting Strangers: Red Light, Green Light
Wings: A Tale of Two Chickens

Books: *Aunt Skilly and the Stranger*, Kathleen Stevens
Aware and Alert, Patricia Lakin
Benjamin Rabbit and the Stranger Danger, Irene Keller
The Berenstain Bears Learn about Strangers, Stan and Jan Berenstain
The Dangers of Strangers, Carole Vogel
Elizabeth Imagined an Iceberg, Chris Raschka
A Kid's Guide to Staying Safe on the Streets, Maribeth Boelts
The Lady in the Box, Ann McGovern
Little Red Riding Hood, Paul Galdone
Never Talk to Strangers, Irma Joyce
Ruby, Michael Emberley
Strangers, Dorothy Chlad
Who Is a Stranger and What Should I Do?, Linda Walvoord Girard
You Can Say "No," Betty Boegehold

Fingerplay: **The Stranger.**
Two little children walking home from school.
   (Hold up two fingers walking across other hand)
They meet a tall man lookin' so cool
   (Bring pointer finger of other hand over to meet others)
The stranger said, "Have an ice cream cone"
   (Hold out imaginary cone)
"NO" shouted the children.
   (Shout out NO)
And they ran on home.
   (Have two fingers race over palm)

Crafts: **Identification Chart.**
Have the children make a frame for their own special identification chart. Include on the chart the children's fingerprints

and, if possible, use a Polaroid camera to include their picture. The children may present this chart to their parents as a special gift.

Craft and Activity:

Shadow Puppets.

While reviewing with the children all the safety tips concerning strangers, ask the children to describe what a stranger would look like. Of course, the result will be many descriptions and you will have to steer them to the fact that a stranger can look like anyone, so we don't have a picture of him or her.

With this in mind introduce the concept of shadow puppets. Since we don't know what our stranger will look like we'll hide his features. Have the children create their own shadow puppets, then help them create their own scripts of "The Child and the Stranger."

A good guide for helping you with this craft and one that offers some patterns and theatrical suggestions is the following source.

(Source: *The Shadow Puppet Book*, Jane Lynch-Watson)

Activity:

Police Visitation.

Contact the local police department and arrange for an officer to speak to the parents, as well as the children. Have the police do official fingerprints for later identification. Many fingerprints done at home are done incorrectly and become useless when needed for identifying a lost child.

Police will offer the children many suggestions on protecting themselves from strangers, and some departments have films for this age group that you may not be able to get elsewhere.

Some departments might even have a costume of McGruff, the crime dog, and will be able to have an officer come dressed as the dog. This costume is only sold to law enforcement agencies.

Songs:

(Audio) "Stranger Danger"
   (Source: *Kindergarten Sing and Learn*)
"Better Say No"
   (Source: *Family Vacation*)
(Book) "Remember Your Name and Address"
   (Source: *Reader's Digest Children's Songbook*, William L. Simon)

136 Toys

Relate to: *Safe Toys and Gift Month (Dec.): Each December the Prevent Blindness of America group produces a list of toys that are hazardous to children's eyesight. Use this time to help children determine which of their toys are hazardous to their baby siblings and must be put away safely.*

Videos: *Alexander and the Wind-up Mouse* (Leo Lionni's Caldecotts)
Corduroy
Ira Sleeps Over
A Pocket for Corduroy

Books: *Arthur's Honey Bear*, Lillian Hoban
Baba Yaga and the Wise Doll, Hiawyn Oram
Bea's 4 Bears, Martha Weston
Cat and Bear, Carol Greene
Eli and Uncle Dawn, Liz Rosenberg and Susan Gaber
Ellen and Penguin, Clara Vulliamy
Ernest and Celestine, Gabrielle Vincent
Geraldine's Blanket, Holly Keller
Hoot, Jane Hissey
Nothing, Mick Inkpen
Poppy the Panda, Dick Gackenbach
Ten out of Bed, Penny Dale
The Toymaker, Martin Waddell
William the Vehicle King, Laura P. Newton
William's Doll, Charlotte Zolotow

Fingerplay: **Tops.**
(Source: *Rhymes for Learning Times*, Louise Binder Scott)

Crafts: **Italian "Piggy in the Pen."**
This is a toy that tests your skills. The "pig" in this toy is a ping-pong ball, and the goal is to try to get it in the round cylinder while it's still attached with a cord. This is a toy that can be taken anywhere (even the car) to amuse children.
    Phyllis Fiarotta's book will supply you with step-by-step instructions and a full-page illustration of the toy itself.
(Source: *Sticks and Stones and Ice Cream Cones*, Phyllis Fiarotta)

My Toy Box.
Children need a special place to store their favorite toys. This source provides you with step-by-step illustrated guidelines for making your own colorful toybox. Any child three and up would be able to design their own with a little adult supervision. The exterior, and main portion of the box, is covered with torn strips of colored paper dipped in a glue solution and placed on the box overlapping. This will need to be stored overnight to dry so be sure you have the time and storage area to do it, but it's sure worth it.
(Source: *I Can Make Toys*, Mary Wallace)

Activities:

Jack-in-the-Box.
The jack-in-the-box is a familiar toy to most children at this age and can be used in this game. Have all the children crouch low in a row representing the store jack-in-the-boxes. One child enters the store reciting a verse (supplied in the book below) about choosing the best toy. He or she will touch the jack-in-the-boxes' heads, telling them to pop up or pop down, trying to mix them up. Anyone who goes in the wrong direction is out, and the final child is the winner.
(Source: *New Games to Play*, Juel Krisvoy)

The Toy Shop.
This is an imaginative activity that allows the children to act out the actions of their favorite toys. Set up an area to be your class toy store. One child can be the shopkeeper, one the customer, and the remainder of the class will be the toys on the shelf. As the customer waits outside for the store to open, the children decide which toy they will be and how they will be that toy. When the customer enters and asks to buy one of the toys, up pops that toy and performs. This can go on until the customer selects a toy not in the store.
(Source: *The Fun Encyclopedia*, E.O. Harbin)

Songs:

(Audio) "Rag Doll Rag"
(Source: *Dance in Your Pants*)
(Book) "Blocks"; "I Roll the Ball"
(Source: *Music for Ones and Twos*, Tom Glazer)

137 Toys: Balloons

Relate to:	*First U.S. balloon flight (Jan. 9, 1793): This flight was launched by Blanchard Jean Pierre.*

Videos: *Hot-Air Henry*
Teddy Bear's Balloon Trip

Books: *Beaten by a Balloon*, Margaret Mahy
Benjamin's Balloon, Alan Baker
The Blue Balloon, Mick Inkpen
Georgie and the Runaway Balloon, Robert Bright
The Grumpalump, Sarah Hayes
Harvey Potter's Balloon Farm, Jerdine Nolen and Mark Buehner
Hot Air Henry, Mary Calhoun
I Don't Care, Marjorie Sharmat
I'm Flying, Alan Wade
Louella and the Yellow Balloon, Molly Coxe
Mine's the Best, Crosby Bonsall
Miss Eva and the Red Balloon, Karen M. Glennon
Nathan's Balloon Adventure, Lulu Delacre
The Well-Mannered Balloon, Nancy Willard
You Can't Take a Balloon into the Metropolitan Museum, Jacqueline Preiss Weitzman and Robin Preiss Glasser

Fingerplay: **The Young Man from the Moon.**
(Source: *Finger Frolics—Revised*, Liz Cromwell, Dixie Hibner, and John R. Faitel)

Crafts: **Around-the-World Balloon.**
Decorate the lower half of a half-pint container and attach it to a helium-filled balloon. This will make a beautiful hot-air balloon that can be used to play balloon races.
(Source: *Pint-Size Fun*, Betsy Pflug)

Ballimp.
A simple "Great Year" blimp can be constructed using a long-style balloon. Add features such as side wings made of cardboard and attach with rubber cement. Decorate as desired, then see how far you can fly your newly made blimp.
(Source: *How to Make Snop Snappers and Other Fine Things*, Robert Lopshire)

Activities: **Balloon Volleyball.**
No scoring is required for this activity, thus omitting winners and losers. Lay a stick or string across the floor to divide the room. Children may hit the large balloon as many times as needed to get it across the line. This allows children to focus on one object and make use of their large motor skills. Many variations of this game can be found in this source.
(Source: *Teacher's Handbook of Children's Games*, Marian Jenks Wirth)

Match the Balloon.
Collect an equal number of colored balloons and colored buttons. Gather the children in a circle around the pile of balloons with each holding a button. As the music plays, the children circle the balloons. When the music stops, a color is called out and each child with that color will run to match his or her colored button with the same colored balloon. Continue until all have a balloon.
(Source: *Child Magazine's Book of Children's Parties*, Angela Wilkes)

Songs: (Audio) "My Balloon"
(Source: *Take My Hand: Songs from the Hundred Acre Woods*)
(Book) "The Balloon"
(Source: *Music for Ones and Twos*, Tom Glazer)

138 Trains

Relate to:	*Anniversary of Casey Jones's Death (April 29, 1900): The famed engineer of the Illinois Central's Cannonball Express. Enjoy the classic folk song about his well-known train ride.*

Videos:
Casey Jones
Freight Train
The Little Engine that Could
Trains

Books:
The Caboose Who Got Loose, Bill Peet
Cecil Bunions and the Midnight Train, Betty Paraskevas
Engine, Engine Number Nine, Stephanie Calmenson
The Freight Train Book, Jack Pierce
Here Comes the Train, Charlotte Voake
The Little Train, Graham Greene
Mooney B. Finch, the Fastest Draw in the West, David McPhail
The Owl Who Became the Moon, Jonathan London
Shortcut, Donald Crews
The Story of the Little Red Engine, Diana Ross
Toot! Toot!, Steven Kroll
The Train Ride, June Crebbin
The Train to Grandma's, Ivan Gantschev
Window Music, Anastasia Suen

Fingerplay: **Choo-Choo Train.**
(Source: *Finger Frolics—Revised,* Liz Cromwell, Dixie Hibner, and John R. Faitel)

Crafts: **Boxes Can Be Trains.**
Simple milk cartons, cereal boxes, or cookie boxes can be cut open, covered with paper, colored, and strung together with string to create a small train. The number of cars depends on the size of the group and materials available. Instructions for a caboose, engine, flatcar, and passenger and coal cars are available in the source below.

If you want to work as a group on one train, why not try getting larger boxes from the supermarkets and making cars for the train that the children can actually sit in? The same instructions can be used for the larger train.
(Source: *Just a Box?,* Goldie Taub Chernoff)

Wash-off Paint Engine.
This paint craft is one that children will delight in as they see their train form with each layer of paint. A traceable pattern is offered in the book. You will need white typing paper, white poster paint to trace the train with, India ink, and water.

The children will be asked to paint the interior of the train with sponges to give it texture and cover the train entirely with India ink after the original paint is dry.

The step-by-step procedure offered in this source is usable for preschoolers and results in a wonderful effect.

Also offered is a Yarn Engine craft for older groups, a train poem and jumprope rhyme for additional activities.
(Source: *Literature Activities for Young Children*, Dianna Sullivan)

Activities: **Choo-Choo Train.**
As the children recite a given verse, they chug along while other children attach themselves to the train one at a time. When the train is complete, they go under the bridge (a stick going up and down). Those who are touched by the stick are out of the game and must return to the station.
(Source: *New Games to Play*, Juel Krisvoy)

Playing Train.
Look for details on this delightful creative dramatics activity in the source indicated below. Children get the whole train experience with everyone pretending to be ticket agents, conductors, engineers, and passengers. Suggestions for realistic props are given and children actually have to have a destination in mind. During the trip children learn the meanings of "one-way," "round trip," etc.
(Source: *Kid's Celebrate*, Maria Bonfanti Esche and Clare Bonfanti Braham)

Songs: (Audio) "The Little Engine that Could"
(Source: *All Aboard!*)
(Book) "Down by the Station"
(Source: *Singing Time: A Book of Songs for Little Children*, Satis N. Coleman and Alice G. Thom)

139 Transportation

Relate to:	*National Transportation Week (the week including the third Friday in May): A week to honor the transportation industry and the people who run it for their contributions in keeping the country running.*

Videos:
Curious George Rides a Bike
Freight Train
Steamboat Willie
Wings: A Tale of Two Chickens

Books:
Christina Katerina and the Great Bear Train, Patricia Lee Gauch
Daisy's Taxi, Ruth Young
Delivery Van, Betsy and Giulio Maestro
Friday's Journey, Ken Rush
Here Comes the Train, Charlotte Voake
I Fly, Anne Rockwell
In the Driver's Seat, Max Haynes
Maxi, the Hero, Debra and Sal Barracca
A Mouse's Tale, Pamela Johnson
The Neighborhood Trucker, Louise Borden
On the Go, Ann Morris
A Rainbow Balloon, Ann Lenssen
This Is the Way We Go to School, Edith Baer
Train Song, Diane Siebert
Where's That Bus, Eileen Browne
Zip, Whiz, Zoom!, Stephanie Calmenson

Fingerplay: **Here Comes the Choo-Choo Train.**
(Source: *Storytimes for Two-year-olds*, Judy Nichols)

Crafts: **Speeding Along.**
Build your own car stick-puppet to be used in a puppet show. Using cardboard, colored paper, glue, and a hole puncher, you can produce the vehicle of your dreams. Place it on a garden stick and it becomes a puppet to help you tell some of the stories you are fond of.
(Source: *The Grolier Kids Crafts Puppet Book*, Lyn Orton)

Toothpaste Airplane.
This imaginative craft can be used as a vehicle to begin a lesson on transportation or a discussion on brushing your teeth. A special pattern is made available to check the dimensions of

your toothpaste box to ensure that it will work. Patterns are also made available for your propellers, wings, etc.

Let the children use this new airplane to store their own personal toothpaste for brushing each day.

(Source: *Rainy Day Projects for Children*, Gerri Jenny and Sherrie Gould)

Activities:

Stop and Go.
Decorate your room by using masking tape to partition off roadways. Let the children determine which vehicle they want to be. Two variations of this activity are offered in the book. One controls the children's movement by music (slow and fast, stop and go) and the other controls their movement with children holding stop and go signs. The children will automatically add their own special sound effects.

(Source: *The Happiest Birthdays : Great Theme Parties for Young Children*, Michaeline Bresnahan and Joan Gaestel MacFarlane)

A Cable Car Relay.
Introduce the children to a mode of transportation that they may not be familiar with, the cable car. Use the lower portion of a milk carton for the base of your car. Attach the car to a circle of string and wrap it around a doorknob so that the children can move their cable car back and forth.

Begin your own relay race. Supply each team with a collection of items that must be moved by cable car to the other side of the room. The first team to move all their items successfully wins the game.

(Source: *Easy Does it!*, James Razzi)

Songs:

(Audio) "The Bus Song"
(Source: *Activity and Game Songs, Vol. 2*)
(Book) "New River Train"
(Source: *The Raffi Singable Songbook*, Raffi)

140 Trees

Relate to:	*Arbor Day (last Friday in April): A day set aside to celebrate trees and their importance in our lives and to this world.*

Videos:	*Arbor Day* *The Giving Tree* *It's Arbor Day, Charlie Brown* *The Legend of Johnny Appleseed*
Books:	*Be a Friend to Trees*, Patricia Lauber *The Bee Tree*, Patricia Polacco *A Busy Year*, Leo Lionni *The Elephant Tree*, Penny Dale *The Never-Ending Greenness*, Nei Waldman *Night Tree*, Eve Bunting *The Oak Tree*, Laura Jane Coats *A Possible Tree*, Josephine Aldridge *The Seed the Squirrel Dropped*, Haris Petie *Someday a Tree*, Eve Bunting *The Talking Tree or Don't Believe Everything You Hear*, John Himmelman *Ten Tall Oak Trees*, Richard Edwards *Tree of Cranes*, Allen Say *What's So Terrible about Swallowing an Apple Seed?*, Harriet Lerner and Susan Goldhor *Why Do Leaves Change Color?*, Betsy Maestro
Fingerplays:	**Trees or Oak Tree.** (Source: *Everyday Circle Times*, Liz and Dick Wilmes)
Crafts:	**My Friendship Tree.** Family trees are a common craft in many classes. Unfortunately with so many diverse family make-ups this can be a difficult project. Many children may be uncomfortable perhaps only showing one parent or other ways their family is different. Try a variation called a "Friendship Tree" where children can include all types of friends, including family. Hand out poster board with a picture of a tree with many branches and children may cut out numerous colored leaves. On each leaf they can draw a picture of something each friend likes to do. (Source: *Rain Day Play!*, Nancy Fusco Castaldo)

Fruit from Trees.
Talk over with the class the diverse number of fruits that grow on trees. Let the children name as many as they can and supply pictures of the others. Cut out all the fruits named and put string on them to hang on the classroom's fruit tree.
(Source: *Everyday Circle Times*, Liz and Dick Wilmes)

Activities: **Tree Charades.**
Prepare a number of cards depicting sundry activities that children can do with a tree, in a tree, or under a tree. Let each child select a card and attempt to get the class to guess what he or she is mimicking.
(Source: *Theme-a-saurus*, Jean Warren)

Feed the Wildlife Tree.
This source offers some wonderful ideas for making adorable decorations to be hung on outdoor trees for the benefit of our beautiful wildlife. Cookie-cutter shapes from bread, orange halves with seeds sprinkled on them, and other suggestions are offered. Take the class on an excursion outdoors to hang their treats on their own wildlife tree. Let them observe the tree each day and take note of what creatures make an appearance.
(Source: *Great Parties for Kids*, Nancy Flyke, Lynn Nejam, and Vicki Overstreet)

Songs: (Audio) "I'm a Nut"
(Source: *Kids Silly Song Sing-a-Longs*)
(Book) "The Green Grass Grew all Around"
(Source: *Shari Lewis Presents 101 Games and Songs for Kids to Play and Sing*, Shari Lewis)

141 Weather: Rain

Relate to:	*National Umbrella Month (March): Celebrate the invention of a versatile item that's used by many.*

Videos:	*The Cat in the Hat* (Dr. Seuss Showcase II) *Cloudy with a Chance of Meatballs* *A Letter to Amy* *Rain* *A Rainbow of My Own*
Books:	*Bumpa Rumpus and the Rainy Day,* Joanne Reay and Adriano Gon *Cat and Mouse in the Rain,* Tomek Begacki *Down Comes the Rain,* Franklyn Branley *It's Raining, It's Raining,* Kin Eagle *Mushroom in the Rain,* Mirra Ginsburg *The Puddle,* David McPhail *Puddles,* Jonathan London *Rain Drop Splash,* Alvin Tresselt *Rain Makes Applesauce,* Julian Scheer *The Rain Puddle,* Adelaide Holl *The Rains Are Coming,* Sanna Stanley *The Storm Book,* Charlotte Zolotow *That Sky, That Rain,* Carolyn Otto *We Hate Rain!,* James Stevenson *Will It Rain?,* Holly Keller
Fingerplay:	**Eensy Weensy Spider.** (Source: *Rhymes for Fingers and Flannel Boards,* Louise Binder Scott)
Crafts:	**Rainbow Shade Pull.** A small cardboard shade pull can be made using such materials as white cardboard, yarn, glue, and colored paper. By cutting the shape of the rainbow from the cardboard it can be used as a base. The yarn and construction paper can be used to add color and yarn attached to the top. This item can be hung in the home window as a proud result of the child's labor. (Source: *Pack-O-Fun Magazine* [Summer 1984])

Pitter Patter Rain Stick.
Rainsticks have been used in ceremonial rituals by tribes in South America for centuries to bring rain to areas of the desert that needed it. Held by one end and tilted to one side, small pebbles trickle down to make the sound of rain falling from the sky. Today they're also used for anything from music to decorations.

The children can create their own sticks with aluminum foil, uncooked rice, long cardboard tubes, and stickers. Tear off another foil sheet 1 1/2 times the length of the tube and create a snakelike strip that is pushed into the tube along with the rice. Seal the other end and decorate with stickers.
(Source: *Crafts to Make in the Spring*, Kathy Ross)

Activities:

We Dress for the Weather.
Using a purchased collection (see source below) or a home-made felt collection, have the children dress felt figures of boys and girls with clothes that are worn when it's raining.
(Source: *We Dress for the Weather*—kit, published by the Instructo Corporation)

Water Puddle Game.
Spring brings rain and often produces many puddles for kids to play in. Discuss with the children proper dress for this weather. Now try this obstacle game. Place around the room blue paper puddles of various sizes. Encourage the children to make their way through this obstacle course without getting "wet." Add variety by having them hop through, skip, jump, etc.
(Source: *Focus on Spring*, Rosie Seaman)

Songs:

(Audio) "Raindrop Song"
(Source: *Where Is Thumbkin?*)
(Book) "It Ain't Gonna Rain No More"
(Source: *The Reader's Digest Children's Songbook*, William L. Simon)

142 Weather: Snow

Relate to:	*Artificial snow introduced to America (Nov. 14, 1965): This was the first use of artificial snow (bleached cornflakes, white sand, and plastic shavings) by the film industry.*

Videos:
Brave Irene
Frosty the Snowman
The Snowman
The Snowy Day

Books:
Emily's Snowball: The World's Biggest, Elizabeth Keown
Emmett's Snowball, Ned Miller
The Golden Snowflake, Francoise and Frederic Joos
Katy and the Big Snow, Virginia Burton
The Magic Sled, Nathaniel Benchley
Mike's House, Julia Sauer
Ralph's Frozen Tale, Elise Primavera
Snow, Uri Shuevitz
Snow Angel, Jean Marzollo
Snow Country, James Skofield
Snowballs, Lois Ehlert
The Snow Speaks, Nancy White Carlstrom
Snowy Day!, Barbara M. Joosse
When Will it Snow?, Syd Hoff
White Snow, Bright Snow, Alvin Tresselt

Fingerplay:
Snowflakes.
    (Source: *Hand Rhymes*, Marc Brown)

Crafts:
Bottled Snow.
You will need small baby food jars for this, among other items. Children have seen in stores the small toys you shake up and it gives you a beautiful snow scene. Well, how about making your own? It's not that difficult, and the child gets a special feeling of accomplishment.

Silver glitter can make a beautiful snow scene. Let the children draw their own scenery or cut it from a magazine and attach it to the exterior of the jar. Clay on the inside of the jar can let you stick small plastic figures inside.
    (Source: *Purple Cow to the Rescue*, Ann Cole, Carolyn Haas, and Betty Weinberger)

Snow Cones.
Try a little refreshment at your storyhour. If you're able to obtain an ice crusher, have the children make their own snow cones. Use canned juices for flavor.

Wooden Spoon Snowman.
Snowmen are familiar creatures to children during the winter season. Try using old ice cream spoons painted white for the snowman's body, then simply add the scarf, hat and features from felt. Add a string to the top and you have a tree ornament, or add a safety pin to the back and the child can wear it.
(Source: *Christmas Ornaments Kids Can Make*, Kathy Ross)

Activity: **Blizzard.**
This is a great lesson in communication and caring for others. Two children at a time are lost in a snowstorm and one is snow-blind. Have the child who can see lead the snow-blind friend through the storm to safety. Add some extra actions, such as struggling through a tunnel (hoops) or going under a log (bench).
With older children you may even wish to add another obstacle. Tell the children they can't touch their friend but can only give verbal instructions from their airplane. This is a really enjoyable event for all.
(Source: *The Cooperative Sports and Games Book*, Terry Orlick)

Songs: (Audio) "Two Little Snowflakes"
(Source: *Red Pajamas and Purple Shoes*)
(Book) "Frosty, the Snowman"
(Source: *The Reader's Digest Children's Songbook*, William L. Simon)

143 Weather: Storms

Relate to:	*Atlantic, Caribbean, and Gulf Hurricane Season (June 1–Nov. 30): Discuss hurricanes, tornadoes, and other storm-related events and the seasons they are usually most active.*

Videos:　　*Brave Irene*
Cloudy with a Chance of Meatballs
The Old Mill

Books:　　*City Storm*, Mary Jessie Parker
Franklin and the Thunderstorm, Paulette Bourgeois
How Thunder and Lightning Came to Be, Beatrice Orcutt Harrell
Hurricane!, Jonathan London
Hurricane, David Wiesner
Just You and Me, Sam McBratney
One Stormy Night, Ruth Brown
Outside, Inside, Carolyn Crimi
Rain Song, Lezlie Evans
Rainflowers, Ann Turner
Rainy Day Dream, Michael Chesworth
Ruby's Storm, Amy Hest
The Storm, Anne Rockwell
Storm Boy, Paul Owen Lewis
Thunderstorm, Mary Szilagyi

Fingerplay:　　**I Hear Thunder; Pitter Patter.**
　　　(Source: *Mother Goose Time*, Jane Marino)

Crafts:　　**Windchimes.**
Catch the wind with wonderfully simplistic windchimes. On a windy day with storms approaching, children can take comfort in the music their own special windchimes make for them. Gather together all those old keys you don't use anymore or can't even remember what they are for. Don't throw them away. Attach colorful ribbons to them and hang them from a central hoop to make your own windchime.
　　　(Source: *Outdoor Fun*, Catherine Ripley)

Cloudy with a Chance of_____.
After reading the story *Cloudy with a Chance of Meatballs* by Judi Barrett, discuss with the children various storms that they have experienced. Give the children a large piece of construc-

tion paper and let them draw houses and trees and so forth for scenery; then encourage them to create their own type of storm by gluing cups, rice, beans, or whatever in the sky.
(Source: *Literature-Based Art Activities*, Darlene Ritter)

Activities:

Cloud and Hail.
After a discussion of storms and hail, have the children gather ping-pong balls together and bounce them off the floor to simulate the sound of hail hitting the ground.

To make this into a game, glue large amounts of cotton to blue paper to show large clouds and hang it on the wall. Put Velcro on the ping-pong balls and let the children toss the hailstones at the clouds to see if they can get them to stick.
(Source: *Kids and Seasons*, Kathy Darling)

The Ocean Is Stormy—A Danish Game.
Mark a number of circles throughout your room and then have the children pair off, with each pair standing in a circle. One pair does not get a circle and they begin the game by becoming the "whale." Each group of children will pretend to be a sea animal, and the whales will swim around, naming each animal. As the whale does this, the sea animal will follow behind him. When the whale finally shouts, "The ocean is stormy," all scatter for a circle. The remaining pair will be the next whale.
(Source: *Games for Girl Scouts*)

Songs:

(Audio) "It's Raining"
(Source: *Circle Time: Song and Rhymes for the Very Young*)
(Book) "The Wind Blow East"
(Source: *Wake Up and Sing!*, Beatrice Landeck and Elizabeth Crook)

144 Westward Ho!

Relate to:	*Will Rogers's Birthday (Nov. 4): Help celebrate the birthday of one of the nation's most famous and beloved cowboys.*

Videos: *Pecos Bill*
I Wanna Be a Cowboy

Books: *Armadillo Rodeo*, Jan Brett
Boss of the Plains: The Hat that Won the West, Laurie Carlson
A Campfire for Cowboy Billy, Wendy K. Ulmer
Casey's New Hat, Tricia Gardella
The Cowboy and the Black-eyed Pea, Tony Johnston
Cowboy Bunnies, Christine Loomis
Cowboy Rodeo, James Rice
Cowboys, Glen Rounds
Do Cowboys Ride Bikes?, Kathy Tucker
Going West, Jean Van Leeuwen
Mathew the Cowboy, Ruth Hooker
Mooney B. Finch, the Fastest Draw in the West, David McPhail
Tyrannosaurus Tex, Betty G. Birney
Yippee-Yay!: A Book about Cowboys and Cowgirls, Gail Gibbons
The Zebra Riding Cowboy, Angela Shelf Medearis

Fingerplay: **At the Rodeo.**
(Source: *Small World Celebrtions*, Jean Warren and Elizabeth McKinnon)

Crafts: **Cowboy Face Mask.**
Let the children ride the plains with the amusing cowboy face mask in this book. It consists of a large ten-gallon hat and mask all in one piece. Children will be happy with the large size of this hat and be ready to start playing cowboy games almost instantly. This is a surefire hit.
(Source: *Paper Fun for Kids*, Marion Elliot)

Hobby Horse.
Help children build their own hobbyhorses for their westward adventure. All that is required is a large piece of cardboard like the type used in gift wrapping, a paper bag for a head, some markers, and masking tape. You might even wish to get yarn to add reins for the child to hold. Happy Trails!
(Source: *The Month by Month Treasure Box*, Sally Patrick, Vicky Schwartz, and Pat Lo Presti)

Activities:
Wild West Target Practice.
Using a collection of soda cans you can set up an appealing target for the children to aim at. Set it upon a table or your own homemade western fence. Fill small socks with beans to create beanbags and see how many targets a child can topple. This source makes available to the instructor quite a few games, crafts, and reproducible patterns for your own wild west party.
(Source: *Hit of the Party*, Amy Vangsgard)

Pony Express Relay Race.
Discuss with the children the early methods of mail delivery, mainly the pony express. With this knowledge let the children set up stations for the pony express to stop at. Divide the children into two teams, with one player from each team waiting at each location. Give the first player the bag with the letter to be passed along. The final child in the relay will place the letter in the box at the end of the race and ring the bell. Add a little western flavor to this by using stick horses and costumes if you like.
(Source: *Party Plans for Tots*, Kate Harris)

Songs:
(Audio) "Home on the Range"
(Source: *Car Songs*)
(Book) "Sweet Betsy from Pike"
(Source: *Songs of the Wild West*)

145 Witches

Relate to: *Salem Witch Trials (March 12, 1692): The Salem trials began on this date with the first accusation against Martha Corey for practicing witchcraft.*

Videos: *Hansel and Gretal*
Strega Nonna
Teeny-Tiny and the Witch Woman
There's a Witch under the Stairs
The Witch's Hat

Books: *Baba Yaga and the Wise Doll*, Hiawyn Oram
The Boy with Two Shadows, Margaret Mahy
The Candy Witch, Steven Kroll
CinderHazel: The Cinderella of Halloween, Deborah Nourse Lattimore
I Know I'm a Witch, David A. Adler
The Littlest Witch, Jeanne Massey
Meredith the Witch Who Wasn't, Dorothea Lachner
Paco and the Witch, Felix Pitre
A Perfect Pork Stew, Paul Brett Johnson
Snow White and the Seven Dwarfs, Jacob Grimm
Space Witch, Don Freeman
Strega Nona Meets Her Match, Tomie dePaola
The Surprise in the Wardrobe, Val Willis
Witch Bazooza, Dennis Nolan
The Witches' Supermarket, Susan Meddaugh

Fingerplay: **Disappearing Witches.**
(Source: *Rhymes for Learning Times*, Louise Binder Scott)

Crafts: **Witch's Hat.**
A witch cannot be a witch without her easily recognizable black hat. Black oaktag is one of the better materials for this project. When the hats are done, the children can use them in the game listed below.
(Source: *Pin It, Tack It, Hang It*, Phyllis and Noel Fiarotta)

Halloween Stick Puppet.
A stick puppet is something that can be made with construction paper and tongue depressors without too much difficulty. Check this source for some wild Halloween crafts including

this colorful, wild-eyed witch that reminds me of a crazy cartoon witch from old Bugs Bunny cartoons.
(Source: *175 Easy-to-Do Halloween Crafts*, Sharon Dunn Umnik)

Activities:

The Witch's Magic Thimble.
Let the witch, with her newly made hat, sit at the table pretending to be asleep with her thimble on the table. The other children sitting in a safe area are designated as the forest. One by one they attempt to steal the thimble. Whoever succeeds becomes the new witch; whoever fails must sit under the table. The goal is to be the witch who captures the most children.
(Source: *New Games to Play*, Juel Krisvoy)

Witch's Spell.
Let the children form a circle with one child in the center designated as the witch. The witch will spin around, say the magic words, raise her hands, and cast a magic spell on all the children turning them into various animals and back again. The children all get to act out the different animals called out. Each child should be given an opportunity to be the witch as well as the animals.
(Source: *1–2–3 Games*, Jean Warren)

Songs:

(Audio) "Witch Doctor"
(Source: *Funny 50s and Silly 60s*)
(Book) "There Was an Old Witch"
(Source: *This Is Music*, William R. Sur, Mary R. Tolbert, William R. Fisher, and Adeline McCall)

146 Zoos

Relate to:	*Zoo and Aquarium Month (June): A special month dedicated to honoring the role zoos and aquariums play in saving wildlife and the conservation of certain ocean and sea life.*

Videos:
Goodnight Gorilla
Happy Lion's Treasure
If I Ran the Zoo
Leo the See-Through Crumbpicker
The Mole in the Zoo

Books:
Alligator Baby, Robert Munsch
Animals at the Zoo, Rose Greydanus
Anthony and the Aardvark, Lesley Sloss
At the Zoo, Douglas Florian
The Biggest Shadow in the Zoo, Jack Kent
The Day the Teacher Went Bananas, James Howe
Goodnight, Gorilla, Peggy Rathmann
I Was Kissed by a Seal at the Zoo, Helen Palmer
I'm in the Zoo, Too, Brent Ashabranner
Leopold the See-Through Crumbpicker, James Flora
My Visit to the Zoo, Aliki
Sammy the Seal, Syd Hoff
Tarzanna, Babette Cole
Tuscanini, Jim Propp
Zoo Dreams, Cor Hazelaar
Zoo-Looking, Mem Fox

Fingerplay: **The Zoo.**
(Source: *Finger Frolics—Revised*, Liz Cromwell, Dixie Hibner, and John R. Faitel)

Crafts: **A Zoo.**
Help the children make their own little zoo with the use of boxes. Directions for a cage, lion, alligator, or elephant can be found in the source below. These can be made with the use of small boxes (cookies, toothpaste, cakes) that can be gathered quickly and at no expense. A great craft for those groups with small budgets.
(Source: *Just a Box?*, Goldie Taub Chernoff)

Egg Carton Zoo.
This is another method of creating amusing zoo animals. These are constructed from empty egg cartons. Build a zoo full of creatures, such as armadillos, giraffes, crabs, rabbits, crickets, and more.
(Source: *Likeable Recyclables*, Linda Schwartz)

Activities:

We Can Do Anything.
This action or listening game can be adapted by instructors to suit whatever lesson they're teaching at the time. The children dance in a circle imitating the various types of zoo animals the teacher acts out.
If you need a quiet time, turn it into a listening game. Have the children try to identify and then repeat the animal sound that the leader calls out. Sheet music for the song is included and can be used for the guitar or piano.
(Source: *Game-Songs with Prof. Dogg's Troupe*, Harriet Powell)

Zoo Game.
Using the reproducible zoo animals in the source provided here, trace them on black construction paper to create the shadows. Follow the instructions to play your own zoo animal match-up game, matching the animal to his own shadow. Also provided for you are other amusing zoo activities, snacks, crafts, and even a zoo chant.
(Source: *Seasonal Activities for 3 Year Olds*, Carol L. Van Hise)

Songs:

(Audio) "Going to the Zoo"
(Source: *Singable Songs for the Very Young*)
(Book) "The Zoo"
(Source: *Music for Ones and Twos*, Tom Glazer)

Appendix A

Guide to Book Publishers

(Addresses and phone numbers for subsidiaries are given only if they differ from that of the parent company)

A & C Black Publishers Ltd. Dist. by
    Talman Co,
89 Fifth Ave.
Suite 802
New York, NY 10003–3020
800–537–8894
No Web Site

ALA (American Library Association)
50 East Huron St.
Chicago, IL 60611
800–545–2433
www.ala.org

Abelard-Schuman Publishers
P.O. Box 242
Manchester, NH 03101
800–999–4650
No Web Site

Abingdon
Div. of United Methodist Publ. House
201 Eighth Ave. South
Nashville, TN 37202
800–251–3320
www.abingdon.org

Addison-Wesley Publishing Co., Inc.
1 Jacob Way
Reading, MA 01867
800–322–1377
www.awl.com

Alleyside Press
Div. of Highsmith Press
W5527 Highway 106
P.O. Box 800
Fort Atkinson, WI 53538–0800
800–558–2110
www.hpress.highsmith.com

Allyn & Bacon, Inc.
Division of Simon & Schuster
160 Gould St.
Needham Heights, MA 02194
800–223–1360
www.prenhall.com

American Heritage Press
    (Inactive)

American Trust Publications
Dist. by Islamic Book Service
2622 E. Main St.
Plainfield, IN 46168
317–839–8150
No Web Site

Annick Press Ltd
Dist. by Dominie Press Inc.
1949 Kellog Ave.
Carlsbad, CA 92008
800–232–4570
www.dominie.com

Arcade Publ. Co.,
Division of Little, Brown and Co.
212–475–2633
www.littlebrown.com

Arco Publishing Inc.
Imprint of Macmillan Publishing

Astor-Honor, Inc.
530 Fifth Ave.
New York, NY 10036–5701
212–840–8800
No Web Site

Atheneum Publications
Sub. of Scribner Book Co., Inc.
1230 Avenue of the Americas
New York, NY 10020
800–223–2348
www.simonsayskids.com

Atlantic Monthly Press
Imprint of Grove/Atlantic Inc.
841 Broadway
New York, NY 10003
800–521–0178
No Web Site

August House Pub. Inc.
P.O. Box 3223
Little Rock, AR 72203
800–284–8784
e-mail: info@augusthouse.com

Avon Books
1350 Avenue of the Americas
New York, NY 10019
800–238–0658
www.avonbooks.com

Bantam Books, Inc.
Div. of Bantam Doubleday Dell Pub.
  Group
1540 Broadway
New York, NY 10036
800–223–6834
www.randomhouse.com

Barron's Educational Series Inc.
250 Wireless Blvd.
Hauppauge, NY 11788
800–645–3476
www.baronsedu.com

Peter Bedrick Books
Dist. by Harper and Row

Beginner Books
Imprint of Random House, Inc.

Benn Book Collection
Dist. by Nichols Pub. Co.

Better Homes & Gardens
Div. of Meredith Corp.

Beyond Words Publ. Inc.
20827 NW Cornell Rd.
Suite 500
Hillsboro, OR 97124–9809
800–284–9673
www.beyondword.com

Blue Sky Press
Imprint of Scholastic Trade Bk.
  Group
555 Broadway
New York, NY 10012
212–343–6100
www.scholastic.com

Bobbs-Merrill Co. Inc.
Imprint of McGraw-Hill Educational & Prof. Pub. Group
1221 Avenue of the Americas
New York, NY 10020
212–512–2000
www.mcgraw-hill.com

Bonanza Books
Div. of Crown Publishers, Inc.

Bonim Books
Divison of Hebrew Publ. Co.
General Delivery
Spencertown, NY 12165–0222
518–392–3322

Bowmar-Noble Publishing Co.
Imprint of McGraw-Hill Prof. Publ.
    Group
1221 Avenue of the Americas
New York, NY 10020
212–512–2000
www.mcgraw-hill.com

Boyds Mills Press
815 Church St.
Honesdale, PA 18431
800–949–7777
www.boydsmillspress.com

Bradbury Press
Affiliate of Macmillan, Inc.
866 Third Ave.
New York, NY 10022

Bridgestone Books
Imprint of Capstone Press Inc.
151 Good Council Dr.
Mankato, MN 56001
507–388–6650
www.capstonepress.com

Bridgewater Books
Imprint of Troll Assoc., Inc.

Bright Ring Publishing, Inc.
P.O. Box 5768
Bellingham, WA 98227
800–480–4278
www.brightring.com

Brotherstone Publishers
Imprint of Borgo Press
Box 2845
San Bernardino, CA 92406
909–884–5813
www.borgopress.com

Browndeer Press
    see Harcourt Brace & Co.

Building Blocks
38W567 Brindlewood
Elgin, IL 60123
800–233–2448
www.bblockspubl.com

Bungalo Books
Dist. by Firefly Bks. Ltd.
Box 1338
Ellicott Sta.
Buffalo, NY 14205
800–387–5085
www.bungalobooks.com

Camden House Publ.
Dist. by Firefly Bks. Ltd.
Box 1338
Ellicott Sta.
Buffalo, NY 14205
800–387–5085
No Web Site

Candlewick Press
2067 Massachusetts Ave.
Cambridge, MA 02140
800–526–0275
No Web Site

Carol Publishing Co.
120 Enterprise Ave.
Secaucus, NJ 07094
201–866–0490
e-mail: cpg-1@erols.com
No Web Site

Carolrhoda Books, Inc.
Imprint of Lerner Publications Co.
241 First Ave. North
Minneapolis, MN 55401
800–328–4929
www.lernerbooks.com

Carson-Dellosa Publ. Co. Inc.
P.O. Box 35665
Greensboro, NC 27425
800–321–0943
www.carson-dellosa.com

Marshall Cavendish Corp.
99 White Plains Rd.
Tarrytown, NY 10591
914–332–8888
www.marshallcavendish.com

Center for Applied Research in
   Education
Subs. of Prentice-Hall Inc.
Charlesbridge Publishing
85 Main St.
Watertown, MA 02172
617–926–0329
www.charlesbridge.com

Chicago Review Press Inc.
814 North Franklin St.
Chicago, IL 60610
800–888–4741
e-mail: ipgbook@mcs.com
No Web Site

Children's Press
90 Sherman Tpke.
Danbury, CT 06816
203–797–3500
publishing.grolier.com

Children's Universe
Imprint of Universe Publishing
Dist. by St. Martin's Press
300 Park Ave. South
New York, NY 10010
800–221–7945
No Web Site

Chronicle Books
85 Second St.
San Francisco, CA 94103
800–722–6657
www.chroniclebooks.com

Circle Time Publishing
1 Corte DeRey
Orinda, CA 94563
202–347–1091
No Web Site

Clarion Books
Div. of Houghton Mifflin Co.
215 Park Ave. South
New York, NY 10003
212–420–5800
www.hmco.com

Cobblehill Books
Imprint of Dutton's Children's
   Books

B. Collins
   (Inactive)

Communication Skill Builders
Subs. of Harcourt Brace & Co.
555 Academic Ct.
San Antonio, TX 78204
800–211–8378
www.hbtpc.com

Contemporary Books Inc.
Imprint of NTC/Contemporary
   Publ. Co.
4255 West Touhy Ave.
Lincolnwood, IL 60646
800–323–4900
www.ntc-contemporary.com

Cool Hand Communications Inc.
Imprint of Book World Press Inc.
1933 Whittfield Park Loop
Sarasota, FL 34243
800–444–2524
www.bookworld.com

Council Oak Publ. Co. Inc.
1350 E. 15th St.
Tulsa, OK 74120
800–247–8850
www.counciloaksbooks.com

Coward
    see Putnam Publishing Group

Crabtree Publishing Co.
350 Fifth Ave.
Suite 3308
New York, NY 10118
800–387–7650
www.crabtree-pub.com

Crocodile Books USA
Dist. by Kane/Miller Book Publish-
    ers
P.O. Box 31029
Brooklyn, NY 11231–0529
www.kanemiller.com

Crowell
    see Harper & Row

Crown Publications, Inc.
201 E. 5th St.
New York, NY 10022
212–572–6117
www.randomhouse.com

DK Publishers Inc.
95 Madison Ave.
New York, NY 10016
212–213–4800
www.dk.com

Dandelion House
    (Inactive)

David S. Lake Publishers
    see Fearon Teachers

Delacorte Press
Subs. of Dell Publishing
1540 Broadway
New York, NY 10036
800–223–6834
www.bdd.com

Dell Publishing
1540 Broadway
New York, NY 10036
800–223–6834
www.bdd.com

T. S. Denison & Co., Inc.
9601 Newton Ave. South
Minneapolis, MN 55431
800–328–3831
www.instructionalfair.com

Andre Deutsch
    see E. P. Dutton

Dial Books for Young Readers
Dist. by Penguin, Putnam
375 Hudson St.
New York, NY 10014
800–526–0275
www.penguinputnam.com

Dillon Press, Inc.
Imprint of Silver Burdett Press

Disney Press
114 Fifth Ave.
New York, NY 10011–5690
212–633–4400
www.disneybooks.com

Dodd, Mead & Co.
    (Inactive)

Doubleday and Co., Inc.
Div. of Bantam Doubleday Dell Pub.
1540 Broadway
New York, NY 10036
800–223–6834
www.randomhouse.com

Down East Books
Box 679
Camden, ME 04843
800–766–1670
e-mail: adevine@downeast.com
No Web Site

E. P. Dutton
Div. of Penguin Dutton Inc.
375 Hudson St.
New York, NY 10014–3657
212–366–2000
No Web Site

Education Center Inc.
P.O. Box 9753
Greensboro, NC 27429–0753
800–334–0298
www.themailbox.com

Element Books Inc.
160 N. Washington St.
4th Floor
Boston, MA 02114
617–915–9400
e-mail: element@cove.com

Enslow Pub. Inc.
44 Fadem Rd.
Box 699
Springfield, NJ 07081
973–379–8890
www.enslow.com

M. Evans & Co. Inc.
216 East 49th St.
New York, NY 10017
212–688–2810
e-mail: mevans@sprynet.com

Fairview Press
2450 Riverside Ave. South
Minneapolis, MN 55454
800–544–8207
www.Press.Fairview.org

Farrar, Straus & Giroux, Inc.
19 Union Sq. West
New York, NY 10035
888–330–8477
www.acadmkt@fsgee.com

Fearon Teachers Aids
Imprint of K–12 Publishing Group
Dist. by The Perfection Learning
   Corp.
10520 New York Ave.
Des Moines, IA 50322
800–762–29999
www.plconline.com

Follett Corp. Press
2233 West St.
River Grove, IL 60171–1817
708–583–2000
No Web Site

Four Winds Publishing
Imprint of SterlingHouse Publ.
   see Sterling Pub. Co. Inc.

Frances Foster Books
   see Farrar, Straus & Giroux

G & H Publishing Co.
   (Inactive)

Gallaudet University Press
800 Florida Ave. NE
Washington, DC 20002–3695
202–651–5488
www.gupress.gallaudet.edu

Girl Scouts of the USA
420 Fifth Ave.
New York, NY 10018
800–221–6707
www.gsusa.org

Gloucester Press
   (Inactive)

Golden Press
88 Seventh Ave.
New York, NY 10106
800–558–5972
www.goldenbooks.com

Good Year Books
  (Inactive)

Green Tiger Press
Dist. by Simon & Schuster

Stephen Greene Press Inc.
Div. of Greenemont Books Inc.
P.O. Box 1000
Brattleboro, VT 05301
  (Inactive)

Greenwillow Books
Div. of William Morrow & Co., Inc
1350 Avenue of the Americas
New York, NY 10019
800–821–1513
www.williammorrow.com

Grosset & Dunlap
  see Putnam Publ. Group

Groundwood Books
Douglas & McIntyre
Dist. by Publishers Group West
1700 Fourth St.
Berkeley, CA 94710
800–788–3123
www.pgw.com

Gryphon House, Inc.
Box 207
Beltsville, MD 20704–0207
www.ghbooks.com

Gumbs & Thomas Pub., Inc.
Dist. by Bookpeople
P.O. Box 373
New York, NY 10039
800–999–4650
www.bponline.com

Harcourt Brace & Co.
Dist. by The Perfection Learning
  Corp.
10520 New York Ave.
Des Moines, IA 50322
800–762–2999
www.plconline.com

Harper & Row Junior Books
Imprint of McGraw-Hill Educational
  & Professional Publishing Group
1221 Avenue of the Americas
New York, NY 10020
800–442–9655
www.mcgrawhill.com

HarperCollins Publishers
10 E. 53rd St.
New York, NY 10022
800–242–7737
www.harpercollins.com

Hastings House Publishers
Imprint of United Publishers Group
50 Washington St. 7th Floor
Norwalk, CT 06854
203–838–4083
www.upub.com

Henry Holt & Co.
115 W. 18th St.
New York, NY 10011
800–488–5233
No Web Site

Holiday House, Inc.
425 Madison Ave.
New York, NY 10017
212–688–0085
No Web Site

Holt, Rinehart and Winston
Subs. of Harcourt Brace & Co.
1120 S. Capital of Texas Hwy.
Austin, TX 78746
800–225–5425
www.hgschool.com

Houghton Mifflin Co.
222 Berkeley St.
Boston, MA 02116–3764
800–225–3362
www.hmco.com

Humanics Learning
Div. of Humanics Ltd.
Humanics Plaza
1482 Mecaslin St. NW
Atlanta, GA 30309
800–874–8844
www.humanicspub.com

Hyperion Books for Children
Div. of Disney Pub. Inc.
114 Fifth Ave.
New York, NY 10011–5690
800–343–9204
www.littlebrown.com

Incentive Publications, Inc.
3835 Cleghorn Ave.
Nashville, TN 37215
800–421–2830
www.nashville.net/-incentiv

Instructor Books
Imprint of Professional Books
555 Broadway
New York, NY 10012
   (Inactive)

Jalmar Press
Subs. of BL Winch & Assoc.
24426 S. Main St.
Suite 702
Carson, CA 90745
800–662–9662
www.ierc.com/blwinch/

Jewish Publications Society
1930 Chestnut St.
Philadelphia, PA 19103
800–234–3151
www.jewishpub.org

John Day Co. Inc.
   see HarperCollins

Joy Street Books
   see Little, Brown & Co.

Kane/Miller Book Publishers
P.O. Box 31029
Brooklyn, NY 11231–0529
718–624–5120
www.kanemiller.com

Kar-Ben Copies, Inc.
6800 Tildenwood Ln.
Rockville, MD 20852
800–4–KARBEN
www.karben.com

Kendall Green Publ.
   see Gallaudet University Press

Kids Can Press, Ltd.
85 River Rock Dr.
Suite 202
Buffalo, NY 14207
800–265–0884
e-mail: info@kidscan.com
No Web Site

Kingfisher
Imprint of Larousse Kingfisher
   Chambers Inc.
95 Madison Ave.
12th Floor
New York, NY 10016
800–497–1657
No Web Site

Alfred A. Knopf, Inc.
Sub. of Random House, Inc.
201 East 50th St.
New York, NY 10022
800–638–6460
www.randomhouse.com/kids

Lane Publishing Co.
   (Inactive)

Learning Triangle Press
Dist. by McGraw-Hill School Division
800–442–9685
www.mhschool.com

Learning Works, Inc.
P.O. Box 6187
Santa Barbara, CA 93160
800–235–5767
www.thelearningworks.com

Lee and Low Books Inc.
95 Madison Avenue
New York, NY 10016
212–779–4400
www.leeandlow.com

Carl J. Leibel, Inc.
   (Inactive)

Lerner Publications Co.
241 First Avenue N
Minneapolis, MN 55401
800–328–4929
www.lernerbooks.com

Linnet Books
   see Shoe String Press Inc.

J. B. Lippincott Co.
Sub. of Harper & Row Publishers,
   Inc.
227 E. Washington Sq.
Philadelphia, PA 19105
800–638–3030
www.lrpub.com

Little, Brown & Co.
Div. of Time, Inc.
3 Center Plaza
Boston, MA 02108
800–759–0190
www.littlebrown.com

Little Friend Press
28 New Driftway
Scituate, MA 02066
800–617–3734
No Web Site

Lodestar Books
   see E.P. Dutton

Lothrop, Lee & Shepard Books
Div. of William Morrow & Co., Inc.
1350 Avenue of the Americas
New York, NY 10019
800–843–9389
www.williammorrow.com

Lowell House Juvenile
2020 Avenue of the Americas
Suite 300
Los Angeles, CA 90067
310–552–7555
e-mail: lowellhous@aol.com

Margaret K. McElderry Books
Imprint of Simon & Schuster
Children's Pub. Division
1230 Avenue of the Americas
New York, NY 10020
212–698–7200
www.simonsayskids.com

McFarland & Co., Inc.
Box 611
Jefferson, NC 28640
800–253–2187
www.mcfarlandpub.com

McGraw-Hill Book Co.
Div. of McGraw-Hill, Inc.
1221 Avenue of the Americas
New York, NY 10020
800–722–4726
www.mcgraw-hill.com

David McKay, Inc.
Sub. of Random House, Inc.
201 E. 50th St.
New York, NY 10022
212–751–2600
www.randomhouse.com

Macmillan Books
Gale Group
27500 Drake Rd.
Farmington Hills, MI 48331
1–800–877–GALE
www.galegroup.com

Marlowe and Co.
841 Broadway
4th Floor
New York, NY 10003
212–614–7880
www.marlowepub.com

Meadowbrook Press
5451 Smetana Dr.
Minnetonka, MN 55343
800–338–2232
www.meadowbrook.com

Melmont
    see Carl Leibel, Inc.

Meredith Corp.
1716 Locust St.
Des Moines, IA 50309–3123
800–678–8091
www.meredithathome.com

Julian Messner
Imprint of Silver Burdette Press

Millbrook Press Inc.
2 Old New Milford Rd.
Brookfield, CT 06804
800–462–4703
No Web Site

Modern Curriculum Press, Inc.
Div. of Simon & Schuster, Inc.
4350 Equity Dr.
Columbus, OH 43216
800–321–3106
www.mcschool.com

Modern Signs Press, Inc.
P.O. Box 1181
Los Alamitos, CA 90720
800–572–7332
www.modsigns.com

Monday Morning Books Inc.
Box 1680
Palo Alto, CA 94302
800–255–6049
www.mondaymorningbooks.com

Mondo Publishing
One Plaza Rd.
Greenvale, NY 11548
800–242–3650
www.mondopub.com

Morning Glory Press Inc.
6595 San Haroldo Way
Buena Park, CA 90620
714–828–1998
www.morningglorypress.com

William Morrow & Co., Inc.
Sub. of Hearst Corp.
1350 Avenue of the Americas
New York, NY 10019
800–821–1513
www.williammorrow.com

Murdoch Books Inc.
P.O. Box 390
Nazareth, PA 18064
No Phone Available

NADJA Publishing
31021 Hamilton Tr.
Trabuco Canyon, CA 92679
800–795–9750

Neugebauer Press USA, Inc.
  see A & C Black

North-South Books
1123 Broadway
Suite 800
New York, NY 10010
800–282–8257
www.northsouth.com

W. W. Norton & Co., Inc.
500 Fifth Ave.
New York, NY 10110
800–233–4830
www.wwnorton.com

Orchard Books
95 Madison Ave.
New York, NY 10016
800–621–1115
www.grolier.com

Oryx Press
4041 N. Central at Indian School Rd.
Phoenix, AZ 85012–3397
800–279–6799
www.oryxpress.com

Overlook Press
386 W. Broadway
New York, NY 10012
212–965–8400
www.overlookpress.com

Owl Books
Imprint of Henry Holt & Co., Inc.
Dist. by Firefly Books Ltd.
Box 1338
Ellicott Sta.
Buffalo, NY 14205
800–387–5085
e-mail: fireflybooks@globalserve.net
No Web Site

Oxford University Press
198 Madison Ave.
New York, NY 10016
800–451–7556
www.oup-usa.org

Pack-O-Fun, Inc.
Clapper Communications Co.
2400 E. Devon Ave.
Suite 375
Des Plaines, IL 60016
846–635–5800
www.pack-o-fun.com

Pantheon Books
Div. of Random House, Inc.
201 E. 50th St.
New York NY 10022
800–638–6460
www.randomhouse.com

Parents Magazine Press
Div. of Gruner & Jahr, USA,
  Publishing
Penguin Putnam Services
685 Third Ave.
New York, NY 10017
800–331–4624
www.penguinputnam.com

Parker Publishing Co., Inc.
Subs. of Prentice-Hall

Peachtree Pub. Ltd
494 Armour Cir. NE
Atlanta, GA 30324
800–241–0113
www.peachtree-online.com

Pelham Books Ltd
Imprint of Viking Penguin

Pelican Publ. Co. Inc.
Box 3110
Gretna, LA 70054
800–843–1724
www.pelicanpub.com

Penguin Books, Inc.
345 Hudson St.
New York, NY 10014
800–526–0275
www.penguinputnam.com

Willa Perlman Books
Div. of HarperCollins Publishers

Perspectives Press
Dist. by Boys Town Press
14100 Crawford St.
Boys Town, NE 68010
800–282–6657
www.ffbh.boystown.org

Philomel Books
Imprint of G.P. Putnam's Sons
200 Madison Ave.
New York, NY 10016
800–788–6262
www.penguinputnam.com

Picture Book Studios USA
2 Center Plaza
Boston, MA 02108–1906
No Phone Available

Clarkson N. Potter Inc.
Dist. by Crown Publ. Group
201 East 50th St.
New York, NY 10022
212–572–6117
www.randomhouse.com

Powerkids Press
Rosen Publ. Group Inc.
29 E. 21st St.
New York, NY 10010
800–237–9932
No Web Site

Prentice Hall Press
Dist. by APDG
4736 Shady Greens Dr.
Fuquay-Varina, NC 27526
800–227–9681
www.APDG-Inc.com

Price Stern Sloan Inc.
Subs. of Penguin Putnam Inc.

Publications International Ltd.
7373 North Cicero Ave.
Lincolnwood, IL 60646
800–745–9299
No Web Site

Putnam Publishing Group
200 Madison Ave.
New York, NY 10016
www.penguinputnam.com

Rainbow Publishers
P.O. Box 261129
San Diego, CA 92196
800–323–7337
No Web Site

Raintree Steck-Vaughn Co.
310 W. Wisconsin Ave.
Milwaukee, WI 53203
800–531–5015
www.steck-vaughn.com

Random House, Inc.
201 E. 50th St.
New York, NY 10022
800–726–0600
www.randomhouse.com

Rayve Productions Inc.
P.O. Box 726
Windsor, CA 95492
800–852–4890
www.spannet.org/rayve/

Reader's Digest Assoc., Inc.
Reader's Digest Rd.
Pleasantville, NY 10570
800–431–1726
www.readersdigest.com

Redleaf Press
450 N. Syndicate
Suite 5
St. Paul, MN 55104
800–423–8309
No Web Site

Nancy Renfro Studios
3312 Pecan Springs Rd.
Austin, TX 78723
800–933–5512
www.fc.net/~puppets/

Rigby Interactive Library
P.O. Box 1650
Crystal Lake, IL 60039–1650
800–822–8661
www.rigby.com

Rising Moon
Subs. of Northland Publ. Co.
P.O. Box 1389
Flagstaff, AZ 86002–1389
800–346–3257
www.northlandpub.com

Rourke Publishing Group
P.O. Box 3328
Vero Beach, FL 32964
800–394–7055
www.rourkepublishing.com

St. Martin's Press
175 Fifth Ave.
New York, NY 10010
800–221–7945
e-mail: inquires@stmartins.com
No Web Site

Scarecrow Press Inc.
4720 Boston Way
Lanham, MD 20706
800–459–3366
www.scarecrowpress.com

Scholastic Inc.
555 Broadway
New York, NY 10012
800–SCHOLASTIC
www.scholastic.com

Charles Scribner's and Sons
Imprint of McGraw-Hill Educational and Professional Pub.
  Group

Shoe String Press Inc.
P.O. Box 657
2 Linsley St.
North Haven, CT 06473–2517
203–239–2702
e-mail: sspbooks@aol.com
No Web Site

Sierra Club Books for Children
85 Second St.
San Francisco, CA 94105
415–977–5500
www.sierraclub.org/books

Silver Burdett Press
4350 Equity Dr.
Columbus, OH 43228
800–321–3106
www.sselem.com

Simon and Schuster
Children's Book Division
Div. of Simon & Schuster Consumer
  Group
1230 Avenue of the Americas
New York, NY 10020
212–698–7200
www.simonsayskids.com

William Sloane Assoc. Inc.
(Inactive)

Smithmark Publishers, Inc.
Div. of US Media Holdings
115 W. 18th St.
Fifth Floor
New York, NY 10011
800–645–9990
No Web Site

Stackpole Book Co., Inc.
5067 Ritter Rd.
Mechanicsburg, PA 17055
800–732–3669
www.stackpolebooks.com

Steck-Vaughn Co.
Subs. of Harcourt Brace
P.O. Box 26015
Austin, TX 78755
800–531–5015
www.steck-vaughn.com

Sterling Publishing Co. Inc.
The Sterling Building
440 Friday Rd.
Pittsburgh, PA 15209
800–898–7886
www.1stworldmall.com/
sterlinghouse

Gareth Stevens, Inc.
Subs. of Primedia Inc.
1555 N. River Dr.
Milwaukee, WI 53212
800–341–3569
www.gsinc.com

Syracuse University Press
1600 Jamesville Ave.
Syracuse, NY 13244–5160
800–365–8929
www.syr.edu/www-syr/aboutsu-
supress/index.html

TAB Books
Div. of McGraw-Hill, Inc.

Tambourine Books
Imprint of William Morrow & Co.,
Inc.

Teacher Created Materials Inc.
6421 Industry Way
Westminster, CA 92683
800–662–4321
www.teachercreated.com

Teaching & Learning Co.
1204 Buchanan St.
P.O. Box 10
Carthage, IL 62321
217–357–2591
www.teachinglearning.com

Ticknor and Fields
Subs. of Houghton Mifflin
215 Park Ave. S
New York, NY 10003
800–225–3362
www.hmco.com

Totline Press
Warren Publ. House Inc.
11627–F Airport Rd.
Everett, WA 98204
800–421–5565
www.frankschaffer.com

Transatlantic Arts, Inc.
P.O. Box 6086
Albuquerque, NM 87197
505–898–2289
www.transatlantic.com/direct

Tricycle Press
Div. of Ten Speed Press
P.O. Box 7123
Berkeley, CA 04707
800–841–2665
www.tenspeed.com

Troll Associates
Sub. of Educational Reading Services
100 Corporate Dr.
Mahwah, NJ 07430
800–526–5289
www.troll.com

Vanguard Press, Inc.
(Inactive)

Viking Penguin, Inc.
375 Hudson St.
New York, NY 10014–3657
800–331–4624
gopher://
gopherserver.cwis.uci.edu:70/11/
departments/books/PubCat/
VikPeng

Henry Z. Walck
(Inactive)

Walker & Co.
Div. of Walker Publishing Co., Inc.
435 Hudson St.
New York, NY 10014
800–289–2553
No Web Site

Warren Publ. House, Inc.
Div. of Frank Schaffer Publications
11627 F Airport Rd.
Everett, WA 98204
800–421–5565
www.frankschaffer.com

Warwick Press
Dist. by Firefly Books Ltd.
Box 1338
Ellicott Sta.
Buffalo, NY 14205
800–387–5085
e-mail: fireflybooks@globalserve.net
No Web Site

Franklin Watts, Inc.
Sub. of Grolier Inc.
90 Sherman Tpke.
Danbury, CT 06816
203–797–3500
www.publishing.grolier.com

Weidenfeld and Nicolson
Dist. by Trafalgar Square
P.O. Box 257
North Pomfret, VT 05053
800–423–4525
www.trafalgarsquarebooks.com

Western Publishing Co. Inc.
Sub. of Western Publishing Group,
Inc.
850 Third Ave.
7th Floor
New York, NY 10022
800–558–5972
www.goldenbooks.com

Whispering Coyote Press
300 Crescent Ct.
Suite 860
Dallas, TX 75201
800–929–6104
No Web Site

Albert Whitman & Co.
6340 Oakton St.
Morton Grove, IL 60053
800–255–7675
www.awhitmanco.com

John Wiley and Sons Inc.
605 Third Ave.
New York, NY 10158–0012
800–CALL-WILEX
www.wiley.com

Williamson Publishing
Church Hill Rd.
Charlotte, VT 05445
800–234–8791
www.williamsbooks.com

H. W. Wilson
950 University Ave.
Bronx, NY 10452
800–367–6770
www.hwwilson.com

Windmill Books, Inc.
c/o Simon & Schuster
1230 Avenue of the Americas
New York, NY 10020
212–698–7200
www.simonsayskids.com

Windom Books
P.O. Box 329
South Harpswell, ME 04079–0329
   (Inactive)

Workman Publishing Co. Inc.
708 Broadway
New York, NY 10003
800–722–7202
www.workmanweb.com

Zaner-Bloser, Inc.
Subs. of Highlights for Children,
   Inc.
P.O. Box 16764
Columbus, OH 43216
800–421–3018
www.zaner-bloser.com

Appendix B

Guide to Video Distributors

Ambrose Video Publishers, Inc.
28 W. 44th St.
Suite 2100
New York, NY 11036
800–526–4663
www.ambrosevideo.com

Baker & Taylor Video
Corporate Headquarters
8140 N. Lehigh Ave.
Morton Grove, IL 60053
800–775–2600
www.btent.com

Better Book Co.,
916 Norwood St.
Fort Worth, TX 76147
817–335–1853

Brodart Co.
500 Arch St.
Williamsport, PA 17705
800–233–8467
www.brodart.com

Buena Vista Home Video
350 S. Buena Vista St.
Mail Code 7912
Burbank, CA 91521
818–295–5768

Children's Circle
Div. of Weston Woods
265 Post Rd. W
Westport, CT 06880–4702
800–543–7843
No Web Site

Charles Clark Co., Inc.
4540 Preslyn Dr.
Raleigh, NC 27616–3177
800–247–7009
No Web Site

Coronet Films
Div. of Simon & Schuster School
    Group)
Imprint of Coronet, The Multimedia
    Co.
2349 Chaffee Dr.
St. Louis, MO 63346
No Web Site

Disney Educational Productions
105 Terry Dr.
Suite 120
Newtown, PA 18940
800–295–5010
www.disney.com/
    EducationalProductions

Encyclopaedia Britannica Educational Corp.
310 S. Michigan Ave.
Chicago, IL 60604–9839
800–621–3900
www.eb.com

First Run Features
153 Waverly Pl.
New York, NY 10014
212–243–0600
www.firstrunfeatures.com

Fox Video Inc.
P.O. Box 900
Beverly Hills, CA 91013
800–800–2FOX

Golden Book Videos
    see Western Publ., Co. Inc.

Good Times Home Videos
16 E. 40th St.
New York, NY 10016
212–951–3000
www.goodtimes.com

Italtoons Corp.
(Address unavailable)

Kimbo Educational
P.O. Box 477
Long Branch, NJ 07740
800–631–2187
www.kimboed.com

Library Video Co.
P.O. Box 580
Wynnewood, PA 19096
800–843–3620
www.libraryvideo.com

Listening Library
1 Park Ave.
Old Greenwich, CT 06870
800–243–4504
www.listeninglib.com

Live Oak Media
P.O. Box 652
Pine Plains, NY 12567
518–398–1010
www.liveoak.com

The Lyons Group
    see Lyrick Studios

Lyrick Studios
2435 N. Central Expressway
Suite 1600
Richardson, TX 75080
972–390–6000
No Web Site

MCA Family Entertainment Inc.
Universal Home Video
70 Universal City Plaza, No. 435
Universal City, CA 91608
818–733–0226
www.mca.com/index.html

Media Basics Video
Lighthouse Sq.
705 Boston Post Rd.
P.O. Box 449
Guilford, CT 06437–0449
800–542–2505
www.mediabasicsvideo.com

Mulberry Park, Inc.
Dist. by William Morrow & Co. Inc.
1350 Avenue of the Americas
New York, NY 10019
800–821–1512
www.williammorrow.com

Paramount Pictures
5555 Melrose Ave.
Hollywood, CA 90038
213–956–8090

A. W. Peller & Assoc., Inc.
Subs. of Educational Impresions
210 Sixth Ave.
P.O. Box 77
Hawthorne, NJ 07507–0106
800–451–7450
www.awpeller.com

Phoenix Films, Inc.
2349 Chaffee Dr.
Saint Louis, MO 63146
800–221–1274
No Web Site

Plains National Instructional Television
(Inactive)

PolyGram Video
Div. of Polygram Records, Inc.
825 Eighth Ave.
New York, NY 10019
212–333–8000
www.polygram.com/polygram

Rabbit Ears Production, Inc.
One Turkey Hill Rd. S
Westport, CT 06880
www.rabbitears.com

Random House, Miller-Brody Productions
201 E. 50th St.
New York, NY 10022
800–726–0600
www.randomhouse.com

Schlessinger Video Productions
Div. of Library Video Co.

Schoolmasters
745 State Cir.
P. O. Box 1941
Ann Arbor, MI 48106
800–521–2832
www.school-tech.com

Sesame St.
c/o Children's Television Workshop
1 Lincoln Plz.
New York, NY 10023
212–595–3456
www.ctw.org

Society for Visual Education, Inc.
SVE & Churchhill Media
6677 N. Northwest Hwy.
Chicago, IL 60631–1304
800–829–1900
www.svemedia.com

Sony Music Distribution
and Song Wonder
Sony Music Entertainment Inc.
550 Madison Ave.
Rm. 2341
New York, NY 10022–3211
212–833–4548
www.sony.com

Stage Fright Productions
11 South Second St.
Geneva, IL 60134
800–979–6800
pages.prodigy.com/stagefright/
welcome.html

Troll Associates
School and Library Division
100 Corporate Dr.
Mahwah, NJ 07430
800–526–5289
www.troll.com

Western Publishing Co., Inc.
850 Third Ave.
7th Floor
New York, NY 10022
800–558–5972
www.goldenbooks.com

Weston Woods Productions
265 Post Rd. W
Westport , CT 06850–1318
800–243–5020
www.scholastic.com

ABBREVIATIONS OF VIDEO DISTRIBUTORS

AV	Ambrose Video Publishers, Inc.
AWP	A. W. Peller & Assoc., Inc.
BC	Brodart Co.
BET	Better Book Co.
BT	Baker & Taylor Video
BV	Buena Vista Home Video
CC	Children's Circle
CHC	Charles Clark Co., Inc.
CF	Coronet Films
EBEC	Encyclopaedia Britannica Educational Corp.
FR	First Run Features
FV	Fox Video, Inc.
GB	Golden Book Videos
GT	Good Times Home Videos
IC	Italtoons Corp.
KE	Kimbo Educational
LL	Listening Library
LOM	Live Oak Media
LG	Lyons Group
LS	Lyrick Studios
LV	Library Video Co.
MB	Media Basics Video
MCA	MCA Family Entertainment, Inc.
MP	Mulberry Park, Inc.
PF	Phoenix Films, Inc.
PN	Plains Nat. Instructional Television
PP	Paramount Pictures
PV	PolyGram Video
RE	Rabbit Ears Production Inc.
RH/MB	RandomHouse/Miller-Brody Prod.
SCH	Schoolmasters
SS	Sesame Street
SM	Sony Music Distribution
ST	Stage Fright Productions
SVE	Society for Visual Education, Inc.
SVP	Schlessinger Video Productions
TA	Troll Associates
WD	Disney Educational Productions
WP	Western Publishing Co., Inc.
WW	Weston Woods Productions

Guide to Videocassettes

Title	Length	Publisher	Number
Abel's Island	30 min.	IC	14
Adventures of Scamper the Penguin, The	85 min.	LV	31
Adventures of Two Piggy Banks: Learning to Save, The	30 min.	LV	102
Alejandro's Gift	8 min.	CHC	40, 110
Alexander and the Terrible, Horrible, No Good, Very Bad Day	14 min.	CHC	60
Alexander and the Wind-up Mouse	24 min.	MP	1, 14, 136
Alexander, Who Used to Be Rich Last Sunday	14 min.	CHC	102
Alexandria's Clean-up, Fix-up Parade	15 min.	EOHSI	38, 39, 56
Alligators All Around	2 min.	WW	3, 118
Alphabet Dragon, The	16 min.	PF	3, 26
Amazing Bone, The	11 min.	WW	16, 99
American Tall Tale Heroes	15 min.	PF	64
Andy and the Lion	10 min.	WW	13, 40
Angus and the Ducks	12 min.	CHC	29
Angus Lost	11 min.	PF	9
Annie Oakley	30 min.	WW	64
Ant and the Dove, The	8 min.	CF	92
Ant and the Grasshopper, The	11 min.	CHC	41
Apt. 3	19 min.	CHC	77, 131
Arbor Day	30 min.	SVP	140
Are You My Mother?	30 min.	CHC	61
Art Dog	11 min.	CHC	18, 117, 129
Arthur Babysits	11 min.	CHC	20
Arthur's Christmas Cookies	40 min.	RH/MB	79
Arthur's Eyes	30 min.	SM	75
Arthur's Halloween	40 min.	RH/MB	83
Arthur's Lost Library Book	30 min.	LV	97
Arthur's Pet Business	30 min.	SM	112
Aunt Ippy's Museum of Junk	26 min.	MCA	56

Title	Length	Publisher	Number
Barney's Best Manners	30 min.	LG	100
Bear and the Fly, The	5 min.	WW	6
Bear Who Slept through Christmas, The	60 min.	BT	79
Beast Feast	12 min.	WW	115
Bea's Own Good	20 min.	LV	93
Bee My Valentine	8 min.	CHC	86
Beginners Bible: The Story of Easter, The	30 min.	SM	80
Berenstain Bears and the Messy Room, The	30 min.	SM	38
Berenstain Bears and Too Much Birthday, The	30 min.	RH/MB	111
Berenstain Bears in the Dark, The	30 min.	LV	108
Berenstain Bears Learn about Strangers, The	30 min.	LV	135
Berenstain Bears Save the Bees, The	30 min.	RH/MB	93
Best Babysitter Ever, The	25 min.	PV	20
Best Valentine in the World, The	11 min.	CHC	86
Big Red Barn	11 min.	CHC	62
Big Rigs	25 min.	ST	98
Blueberries for Sale	9 min.	WW	6
Boy, a Dog, and a Frog, A	9 min.	PF	9, 70
Boy and a Boa, A	13 min.	PF	119
Boy with Two Shadows, The	11 min.	CHC	82
Brave Irene	12 min.	CHC	142, 143
Bremen Town Musicians, The	11 min.	PF	105, 110
Burt Dow: Deep-Water Man	9 min.	WW	10, 124
Camel Who Took A Walk, The	6 min.	WW	5
Caps for Sale	5 min.	WW	15, 45, 90
Casey at the Bat	9 min.	CHC	115, 134
Casey Jones	11 min.	PF	138
Cat in the Hat, The	51 min.	MP	7, 45, 141
Caterpillar and the Polliwog, The	7 min.	WW	92
Chair for My Mother, A	8 min.	CHC	60, 104
Charlie Needs a Cloak	8 min.	WW	44
Chicken Fat: The Youth Fitness Video	25 min.	LV	58
Chicken Soup with Rice	5 min.	WW	50
Chrysanthemum	15 min.	WW	107
Cinder-Elly	12 min.	CHC	68
Circus Baby	5 min.	WW	11, 42, 100
Clean Your Room, Harvey Moon	6 min.	CHC	38
Clifford's Fun with Shapes	30 min.	SCH	47
Cloudy with a Chance of Meatballs	15 min.	RH/MB	110, 141, 143
Cold Blooded Penguin, The	10 min.	WD	31
Corduroy	16 min.	WW	44, 136
Cornelius	30 min.	CHC	118
Cow Who Fell in the Canal, The	9 min.	WW	8

Title	Length	Publisher	Number
Curious George	83 min.	BT	15, 35
Curious George at the Mini Marathon	20 min.	SM	58
Curious George Goes to the Hospital	15 min.	CHC	88
Curious George Goes to the Library	30 min.	SM	97
Curious George Rides a Bike	10 min.	WW	27, 42, 139
D. W. Rides Again	30 min.	SM	122
Dancing with the Indians	8 min.	LOM	57
Danny and the Dinosaurs	9 min.	WW	51
Day Jimmy's Boa Ate the Wash, The	5 min.	WW	90, 119
Dazzle the Dinosaur	30 min.	SM	51
Disney Presents Mickey Loves Minnie	25 min.	WD	54
Do It Yourself	25 min.	BV	130
Dorothy and the Clock	10 min.	PF	43
Dorothy and the Kite	8 min.	PF	96
Dorothy and the Ostrich	9 min.	PF	28
Dr. DeSoto	10 min.	WW	34
Dr. Seuss's ABC	30 min.	FV	26
Dr. Seuss's Sleep Book	30 min.	CHC	21
Draghetto	12 min.	PF	35, 52
Dragon Stew	13 min.	PF	52, 65
Drummer Hoff	5 min.	WW	98
Dumbo	63 min.	BT	11
Elephant's Child	30 min.	MP	11
Elmocize	30 min.	SS	58
Elves and the Shoemaker, The	6 min.	TA	39, 79, 106
Emperor's New Clothes, The	10 min.	PF	44, 90, 91, 121
Empty Pot, The	7 min.	AWP	114
Everybody Knows That	15 min.	CHC	95
Fire Safety for Kids	23 min.	LV	122
Firehouse Dog	11 min.	PF	35
First Easter Rabbit, The	25 min.	CF	80
Fish Is Fish	30 min.	LL	63
Fisherman and His Wife, The	20 min.	WW	26, 63
Fitness Fun with Goofy	19 min.	WD	58
Five Chinese Brothers, The	10 min.	WW	67
Foot Book, The	15 min.	AWP	4
Franklin and the Secret Club	25 min.	PV	129
Franklin Is Messy	25 min.	PV	38, 120
Frederick	24 min.	MP	14
Freight Train	6 min.	CHC	46, 138, 139
Frog Goes to Dinner	12 min.	PF	65, 112

Title	Length	Publisher	Number
Frog and Toad Are Friends: A Swim	60 min.	RH/MB	127, 134
Frog and Toad Are Friends: Spring	60 min.	RH/MB	126
Frog and Toad Are Friends: The Story	60 min.	RH/MB	69, 70
Frog and Toad Together: Dragons and Giants	60 min.	RH/MB	52, 74
Frog and Toad Together: The Garden	60 min.	RH/MB	114
Frog Prince, The	6 min.	MP	70
Frog Princess, The	6 min.	CF	70
Frog Went A-Courtin'	12 min.	WW	70, 105
Frosty the Snowman	30 min.	LV	142
Fruit: Close Up and Very Personal	30 min.	ST	71
Funny Little Bunnies	7 min.	WD	80
Garbage Day!	25 min.	LV	53
Georgie	6 min.	WW	73, 83
Ghost with the Halloween Hiccups, The	7 min.	CF	73, 83
Giant Devil-Dingo, The	10 min.	WW	74
Gingerbread Boy, The	8 min.	TA	59
Giving Thanks	8 min.	WW	53, 56, 57, 87
Giving Tree, The	10 min.	WW	22, 140
Goggles	11 min.	PF	75
Goodnight, Gorilla!	10 min.	WW	108, 146
Goofy Look at Valentine's Day, A	10 min.	WD	86
Grandfather's Mitten	10 min.	PF	23, 25
Grandpa	27 min.	WW	76
Grasshopper and the Ants, The	11 min.	CF	92
Green Eggs and Ham	51 min.	LL	65
Grey Lady and the Strawberry Snatcher, The	10 min.	CHC	71
Halloween	6.5 min.	LOM	83
Hansel and Gretel	14 min.	RH/MB	145
Hanukkah	12 min.	EBEC	78
Happy Birthday Moon	7 min.	WW	32
Happy Lion	8 min.	WW	69
Happy Lion's Treasure	9 min.	EBEC	13, 146
Happy Owls, The	7 min.	WW	30
Harold and His Amazing Green Plants	13 min.	WD	114
Harold and the Purple Crayon	8 min.	WW	18, 46, 90, 91
Harold's Fairy Tale	8 min.	WW	59
Harry the Dirty Dog	10 min.	WW	9, 38
Hat, The	6 min.	WW	44, 45
Have You Seen My Duckling?	6 min.	CHC	117, 130
Helpful Little Fireman	11 min.	CF	35
Henny Penny	6 min.	TA	5, 59, 62
Hercules	11 min.	WW	35

Title	Length	Publisher	Number
Hiawatha	12 min.	WW	57
Holidays for Children: Kwanzaa	25 min.	LV	84
Holidays for Children: St. Patrick's Day	25 min.	LV	85
Horton Hatches an Egg	30 min.	CHC	11, 28, 39, 40, 41
Hospital, The	10 min.	WD	88
Hot Air Henry	12 min.	CHC	116, 136
Hot Hippo	5 min.	WW	6, 55
How the Rhinoceros Got His Skin	30 min.	LV	55
How the Trollusk Got His Hat	30 min.	MP	45
How the Whale Got His Throat	25 min.	LL	10
How to Exercise	11 min.	WD	58
Hush the Baby	5 min.	WW	19
I Can Read with My Eyes Shut	30 min.	RH/MB	1
I Wanna Be a Cowboy	30 min.	BET	144
I Wanna Be a Heavy Equipment Operator	30 min.	BET	98
I Wanna Be a Police Officer	30 min.	BET	37
I Wanna Be an Astronaut	30 min.	BET	133
If I Ran the Circus	30 min.	LV	42
If I Ran the Zoo	18 min.	LL	146
I'll Fix Anthony	13 min.	WW	60
In the Month of Kislev	12 min.	WW	78
In the Night Kitchen	6 min.	WW	91
In the Tall, Tall Grass	6 min.	WW	92
Independence Day	25 min.	LV	81
Ira Says Goodbye	24 min.	WW	104
Ira Sleeps Over	15 min.	RH/MB	21, 69, 136
Island of the Skag, The	13 min.	WW	33
It's Arbor Day, Charlie Brown	25 min.	LV	140
It's Mine	30 min.	CHC	24
Jack and the Beanstalk	10 min.	PF	74, 114
Jim's Dog Muffins	6.5 min.	CHC	54, 112
Joey Runs Away	8 min.	WW	12
John Henry	18 min.	WW	64
Jonah and the Great Fish	5 min.	WW	63
Joshua's Masai Mask	11 min.	WW	66
Katy No-Pocket	25 min.	LV	12, 117
Kids Can Jump	25 min.	LV	58
King Midas and the Golden Touch	30 min.	WW	26, 121, 131
Knots on a Counting Rope	13 min.	WW	57
Ladybug, Ladybug, Winter Is Coming	10 min.	CF	94, 128

Title	Length	Publisher	Number
Lamb Chop's Special Chanukah	60 min.	LV	78
Learn about Living: Never Talk to Strangers	30 min.	LV	135
Learning to Share	45 min.	BET	25
Legend of Johnny Appleseed, The	20 min.	WD	140
Legend of Sleepy Hollow, The	49 min.	MP	73
Lentil	9 min.	WW	49, 105, 109
Leo on Vacation	11 min.	PF	13
Leo the Late Bloomer	6 min.	WW	22
Leo the See-Through Crumbpicker	9 min.	WW	103, 146
Letter to Amy, A	7 min.	WW	32, 141
Let's Eat! Funny Food Songs	30 min.	BET	65
Liar, Liar Pants on Fire	7 min.	CHC	78
Library, The	6 min.	LOM	97
Lion and the Mouse, The	30 min.	LL	13
Little Bear: Parties and Picnics	30 min.	BET	111
Little Bear: Winter Tales	30 min.	PP	128
Little Dog and the Bees, The	7 min.	PF	93
Little Drummer Boy, The	7 min.	WW	79
Little Engine that Could, The	10 min.	CF	138
Little House, The	8 min.	WD	89
Little Mouse's Big Valentine	10 min.	CHC	86
Little Penguin's Tale	28 min.	MB	31
Little Rabbit Who Wanted Red Wings, The	25 min.	LV	17, 26
Little Red Hen, The	30 min.	MP	28, 39, 41, 62, 114
Little Red Lighthouse and Great Gray Bridge, The	9 min.	WW	33
Little Red Riding Hood	9 min.	PF	59, 135
Little Rooster Who Made the Sun Rise, The	11 min.	CF	62
Little Tim and the Brave Sea Captain	11 min.	WW	33, 124
Little Toot	9 min.	CHC	33
Little Toot and the Loch Ness Monster	25 min.	LV	106
Lorax, The	51 min.	LL	101
Louis James Hates School	11 min.	PF	123
Lyle, Lyle the Crocodile	30 min.	AV	39, 118
Madeline	6.5 min.	RH/MB	2, 88, 115
Madeline and the Easter Bonnet	26 min.	GB	45, 80, 126
Madeline and the New House	25 min.	LV	88
Madeline and the Soccer Star	25 min.	GB	134
Madeline's Winter Vacation	26 min.	GB	128
Magic Fishbone, The	11 min.	PF	99
Make Way for Ducklings	11 min.	WW	29, 37
Mama Don't Allow	9 min.	CHC	118
Max's Chocolate Chicken	5 min.	WW	80
McElligot's Pool	12 min.	CHC	115

Title	Length	Publisher	Number
Meeting Strangers: Red Light, Green Light	19 min.	PF	122, 135
Mickey Mouse: Safety Belt Expert	16 min.	WD	122
Mickey Mouse, The Brave Little Tailor	25 min.	CF	14, 74
Mike Mulligan and His Steam Shovel	11 min.	WW	98
Millions of Cats	10 min.	WW	7
Ming Lo Moves the Mountain	10 min.	CHC	67
Miss Nelson Is Missing	14 min.	WW	24, 117
Mister Rogers' Neighborhood: Going to School	28 min.	FV	95, 123
Mole and the Chewing Gum, The	9 min.	PF	116
Mole and the Christmas Tree, The	6 min.	PF	79
Mole in the Zoo, The	10 min.	PF	146
Mommy's Office	7 min.	CHC	72
Monster Mama	10 min.	CHC	61, 103
Moon Man	9 min.	WW	108, 133
Mop Top	10 min.	WW	4
Morris' Disappearing Bag	6 min.	WW	17, 79
Morris Goes to School	15 min.	CHC	95, 123
Most Wonderful Egg in the World, The	6 min.	WW	28, 121
Mother Duck and the Big Race	11 min.	CF	29
Mountains of Love, The	30 min.	KE	54
Mr. Brown Can Moo! Can You?	30 min.	RH/MB	109
Mufaro's Beautiful Daughters	14 min.	WW	40, 66
Musical Max	8 min.	WW	105, 109
Mysterious Tadpole, The	9 min.	WW	51, 112
Napping House, The	5 min.	WW	21
Noisy Nora	6 min.	WW	109
Norman the Doorman	15 min.	WW	14, 18
Officer Buckle and Gloria	12 min.	WW	37
Old Bear: Lost and Found	30 min.	LV	23
Old Mill, The	9 min.	WD	88, 143
Olympic Champ, The	8 min.	WD	134
One Fish, Two Fish, Red Fish, Blue Fish	30 min.	CHC	63
One Monday Morning	10 min.	WW	50, 91, 121
One Was Johnny	3 min.	WW	49
One Zillion Valentines	6 min.	RH/MB	86
Over in the Meadow	9 min.	WW	49
Owen	9 min.	WW	22, 54
Owl and the Pussycat, The	7 min.	PF	7, 30, 115
Owl Moon	8 min.	CHC	30, 108
Paddington Helps Out: Paddington Dines Out	50 min.	CF	6
Patrick's Dinosaurs	28 min.	MB	51

Title	Length	Publisher	Number
Pecos Bill	30 min.	RE	64, 144
Pegasus	17 min.	CHC	106
Pet Show!	45 min.	CC	112
Peter Rabbit	30 min.	CHC	17, 24
Peter's Chair	6 min.	WW	19, 22, 60, 69
Pete's Dragon	105 min.	BC	52
Petunia	10 min.	WW	1, 69
Picnic	13 min.	WW	23
Picture for Harold's Room, A	6 min.	WW	18, 91
Pierre: A Cautionary Tale	50 min.	CF	6, 24
Pig's Picnic, The	5 min.	CHC	16, 101
Pig's Wedding, The	7 min.	CHC	16
Pilgrims of Plimoth, The	26 min.	WW	87
Pirate Adventure, The	30 min.	LV	113
Pirate Island	30 min.	LV	113
Play, The	9 min.	WD	77
Pocket for Corduroy, A	20 min.	PF	44, 136
Pokey Little Puppy, The	30 min.	MP	9
Police Station, The	11 min.	WD	37
Postman Pat	30 min.	GT	36
Prince Cinders	26 min.	FR	68
Princess Scargo and the Birthday Pumpkin	30 min.	WW	32, 57
Puff the Magic Dragon	45 min.	LL	52
Pumpkin Who Couldn't Smile, The	23 min.	MP	83
Puss in Boots	14 min.	CHC	7
Rain	10 min.	CHC	141
Rainbow Fish, The	30 min.	SM	25
Rainbow of My Own, A	5 min.	LOM	141
Really Rosie	26 min.	WW	49, 50, 105
Recycle Rex	10 min.	WD	53
Regina's Big Mistake	30 min.	PN	18, 130
Relatives Came, The	8 min.	CHC	60
Remarkable Riderless Runaway Tricycle	11 min.	WW	27
Rescue Rangers' Fire Safety Adventure, The	14 min.	WD	122
Richard Scarry's: Sally's First Day at School	25 min.	PV	95
Rip Van Winkle	30 min.	WW	41
Rosie's Walk	5 min.	WW	62, 90
Rumpelstiltskin	10 min.	RH/MB	59, 99, 107, 121
Saggy Baggy Elephant	30 min.	MP	11
Sam and the Lucky Money	11 min.	WW	67, 102
Say, Sing and Sign: Colors	30 min.	SCH	132
Say, Sing and Sign: Songs	30 min.	SCH	132

Title	Length	Publisher	Number
Selfish Giant, The	14 min.	WW	74, 100
Sergeant Murphy's Day Off	25 min.	PV	37
Sesame Street Home Video Visits the Hospital	30 min.	SM	88
Seven Candles for Kwanzaa	9 min.	WW	84
Shalom Sesame: Chanukah	30 min.	SS	78
Shout It Out Alphabet Film, The	12 min.	PF	3
Shout It Out Numbers from 1 to 10	6 min.	PF	49
Sign Me a Story	30 min.	LV	132
Silver Cow, The	13 min.	CHC	8
Simple Machines	30 min.	WD	98
Sing-Along Earth Songs	30 min.	RH/MB	53, 56
Smile for Auntie	5 min.	WW	19
Snow White and the Seven Dwarfs	60 min.	LL	85
Snowman, The	26 min.	WW	142
Snowy Day, The	6 min.	WW	128, 142
Song and Dance Man	9 min.	CHC	76
Sorcerer's Apprentice, The	14 min.	WW	99
Spirit of Punxsutawney: Groundhog Day, The	35 min.	LV	82
Spot Goes to a Party	30 min.	WD	111
Spot Goes to School	30 min.	WD	123
Spot's Lost Bone	30 min.	BV	23
Spot Visits His Grandparents	30 min.	LV	76
Spot's Windy Day	30 min.	BV	96
Star Spangled Banner	5 min.	WW	81
Starring First Grade	15 min.	CHC	123
Steamboat Willie	8 min.	WD	139
Stone Soup	11 min.	WW	64, 65
Story, A Story, A	10 min.	WW	66
Story of Jumping Mouse, The	15 min.	CHC	25, 40
Story of Ping, The	10 min.	WW	29, 67
Story of Puss in Boots, The	89 min.	MP	7
Strega Nonna	9 min.	WW	99, 145
Summer Picnic	30 min.	LV	127
Sweet Dreams, Spot	30 min.	WD	21
Swimmy	24 min.	MP	63, 124
Sylvester and the Magic Pebble	11 min.	WW	5, 99
Tailypo	11 min.	CHC	73, 103
Tale of the Groundhog's Shadow	11 min.	CF	82
Tawny Scrawny Lion	30 min.	MP	13
Teddy Bear's Balloon Trip	14 min.	CF	136
Teeny-Tiny and the Witch Woman	14 min.	WW	145
Thanksgiving Day	6 min.	LOM	87
There's a Nightmare in My Closet	14 min.	WW	103

Title	Length	Publisher	Number
There's a Witch under the Stairs	6 min.	CHC	145
There's Something in My Attic	14 min.	WW	54
Three Billy Goats Gruff, The	6 min.	CHC	106
Three Little Kittens, The	25 min.	SM	23
Three Little Pigs, The	8 min.	TA	5, 16
Three Robbers,The	6 min.	WW	2
Thumbelina	9 min.	PF	48
Tikki Tikki Tembo	9 min.	WW	67, 107
Time for Table Manners	6 min.	WD	100
Tom Thumb	10 min.	CHC	48
Tortoise and the Hare, The	30 min.	LL	17, 120, 134
Trains	14 min.	WD	138
Truth about Mother Goose, The	15 min.	WD	68
Twelve Days of Christmas, The	6 min.	WW	79
Twelve Months, The	11 min.	PF	50
Ugly Duckling, The	30 min.	LL	28, 29, 59
Village of Round and Square Houses, The	12 min.	WW	47, 88
Visit from St. Nicholas, A	4 min.	CF	79
Whales	13 min.	LOM	10, 55
What's under the Bed?	8 min.	WW	76
Where the Garbage Goes	30 min.	LV	53
Where the Wild Things Are	8 min.	WW	24
Whistle for Willie	6 min.	WW	9, 117
White Seal, The	30 min.	LV	55
Who's in Rabbit's House	13 min.	CHC	17
Why Monkeys Live in the Trees	30 min.	KE	15
Why Mosquitoes Buzz in People's Ears	10 min.	WW	66, 92
Wilfrid Gordon McDonald Partridge	9 min.	WW	25, 110
William's Doll	18 min.	PF	72
Willie, the Operatic Whale	8 min.	WD	10
Wings: A Tale of Two Chickens	9 min.	WW	135, 139
Winnie the Pooh and a Day for Eeyore	26 min.	WD	32
Winnie the Pooh and the Blustery Day	25 min.	MP	125
Winnie the Pooh and Tigger, Too!	25 min.	MP	6
Winnie the Witch and the Frightened Ghost	25 min.	SVE	73
Witch's Hat, The	7 min.	CHC	145
Wynken, Blynken, and Nod	4 min.	WW	59
Yankee Doodle	10 min.	WW	81
Yertle the Turtle	46 min.	CHC	120
Z Was Zapped, The	8 min.	CHC	3
Zax, The	51 min.	LL	101

Appendix C
Guide to Suggested Music Cassette and CD Distributors

A & M Records, Inc.
Children's Music Div.
1416 N. LaBrea Ave.
Hollywood, CA 80028
www.amrecords.com

Baby Boom Music, Inc.
P.O. Box 62188
Minneapolis, MN 55426
616–470–1667
e-mail: babyboomms@aol.com

Buena Vista Records
  see Walt Disney Records

Columbia
  see Sony Music Entertainment,
  Inc.

Walt Disney Records
500 South Buena Vista St.
Burbank, CA 9152
800–295–5010
www.disney.com

Disneyland Records
  see Walt Disney Records

Drive Entertainment Inc.
10351 Monica Blvd. Suite 404
Los Angeles, CA 90025
310–553–3490
e-mail: drive@earthlink.net

Educational Activities, Inc.
1937 Grand Ave.
Baldwin, NY 11510
800–645–3739
www.edact.com

Educational Graphics Press
  see Shadow Play Records

Elephant Records
  see A & M Records, Inc.

GMR Records
P.O. Box 651
Brattleboro, VT 05302
802–257–9566

Good Moo's Productions
Dist. by Educational Record Center
3233 Burnt Mill Dr.
Suite 100
Wilmington, NC 28403–2655
800–438–1637
www.erc-inc.com

Guitar Bob
Oak Ridge, NJ
201–208–9435

Hap-Pal Music, Inc.
19424 Mayall St.
Northridge, CA 91324
818–885–0200
www.happalmer.com

Hug Bug Music
Box 58067, Station "L"
Vancouver, B.C.
Canada V6P 6C5

Kids Rhino
Div. of Rhino Records Inc.
2225 Colorado Ave.
Santa Monica, CA 90404
800–432–0020
www.rhino.com

Kids USA Audio
P.O. Box 8
Agoura Hills, CA 91376–0008
818–879–1180

Kimbo Educational
P.O. Box 477, Dept. S
Long Branch, NJ 07740
800–631–2187
www.kimboed.com

Kurtoons
425 Washington Terr.
Leonia, NJ 97605
201–585–9823

Lightyear Entertainment
Dist. by WEA
Empire State Building
350 Fifth Ave.
Suite 5101
New York, NY 10118
800–229–7867
www.lightyear.com

Lizard's Rock Music
Dist. by Baker & Taylor Books
142 Spray Ave.
Monterey, CA 93940
800–775–1500
www.baker-taylor.com

Madacy Entertainment Group, Inc.
P.O. Box 1445
St. Laurent, Quebec
Canada H4L 4Z1

Marlboro Records, Inc.
845 Marlboro Spring Rd.
Kennett Square, PA 19348

Music for Little People
P.O. Box 1460
Redway, CA 95560
800–346–4445
www.mflp.com

Peanutbutterjam (PBJ)
P.O. Box 2687
Hartford, CT 06146–2687

David S. Polansky
P.O. Box 5061
Cochituale, MA 01778
e-mail: davidpolan@aol.com
www.galaxymall.com/stores/
   music.html

Rainbow Planet Tapes
Rainbow Planet,Inc.
5110 Cromwell Dr. Gig
Harbor, WA 98335
206–265–3750

Re-Bop Records
P.O. Box 985
Marshfield, VT 05658
800–443–4727
www.reboprecords.com

Rounder Records Corp.
One Camp St.
Cambridge, MA 02140
800–443–4727
www.rounder.com

Sesame Street Records
c/o Children's Television Workshop
1 Lincoln Plaza
New York, NY 10023
212–595–3456
www.ctw.org

Shadow Play Records
Educational Graphics Press, Inc.
P.O. Box 180476
Austin, TX 78718
800–274–8804
www.hellojoe.com

Shoreline Records
Div. of Troubadour
Dist. by Rounder Records
One Camp St. Cambridge, MA
   02140
800–443–4727
www.rounder.com

Singing Toad Productions
P.O. Box 359
Mineral Point, WI 53565

Sony Kids' Music
Sony Music Entertainment, Inc.
550 Madison Ave.
New York, NY 10022–3211
212–833–4548
www.sony.com

Ta-Dum Productions, Inc.
6552 Via Barona
Carlsbad, CA 92009
619–438–6552

Tickle Tune Typhoon
P.O. Box 15153
Seattle, WA 98115

Troubadour Records, Ltd
   (see Rounder Records Corp.)

Ujima Publishing
P.O. Box 11055
Baltimore, MD 21212
410–435–3936

Warner Bros. Records
3300 Warner Ave.
Burbank, CA 91510–4694
800–274–9700
www.wbr.com

Western Publ. Company, Inc.
Subs. of Western Pub. Group Inc.
850 Third Ave.
7th Floor
New York, NY 10022
800–558–5972
www.goldenbooks.com

Bibliography

Aardema, Verna. *How the Ostrich Got Its Long Neck.* N.Y.: Scholastic, 1995; 32pp., $14.95.

————. *This for That.* N.Y.: Dial Books for Young Readers, 1987; 32pp., $14.99.

Aarons, Trudy, and Francine Koelsch. *101 East Art Activities.* Tucson, Ariz.: Communication Skills Builders, 1985; 151pp., $19.95.

Abercrombie, Barbara. *Michael and the Cats.* N.Y.: Margaret K. McElderry, 1993; 32pp., $13.95.

Adams, Adrienne. *The Easter Egg Artists.* N.Y.: Macmillan, 1976; 32pp., $12.95.

————. *The Great Valentine's Day Balloon Race.* N.Y.: Macmillan, 1986; 32pp., $10.05.

Adams, Barbara Johnston. *The Go-Around Dollar.* N.Y.: Four Winds, 1992; 28pp., $16.00.

Adelson, Leone. *All Ready for School.* N.Y.: McKay, 1957; 24pp., $2.75.

————. *Who Blew That Whistle?* N.Y.: R. Scott, 1946; 45pp., $1.25.

Adler, David A. *Finger Spelling Fun.* N.Y.: Franklin Watts, 1980; 32pp., NA.

————. *I Know I'm a Witch.* N.Y.: Henry Holt, 1988; 32pp., NA.

————. *A Picture Book of Hannukah.* N.Y.: Holiday House, Inc., 1982; 32pp., $12.95.

Aesop. *The Lion and the Mouse.* Mahwah, N.J.: Troll Associates, 1981; 32pp., $9.79.

Afanasyev, Alexander Nikolayevich. *The Fool and the Fish.* N.Y.: Dial, 1990; 32pp., $12.95.

Agee, Jon. *Dmitri, the Astronaut.* N.Y.: HarperCollins, 1996; 32pp., $14.95.

Ahlberg, Allan. *Monkey Do!* Mass.: Candlewick, 1998; 32pp., $15.99.

Alborough, Jez. *Watch Out! Big Bro's Coming!* Mass.: Candlewick, 1997; 32pp., NA.

Aldridge, Josephine. *A Possible Tree.* N.Y.: Macmillan, 1993; 32pp., $16.00.

Aleichem, Sholom. *Hannukah Money.* N.Y.: Greenwillow, 1978; 32pp., $11.75.

Alexander, Martha. *How My Library Grew.* N.Y.: Wilson, 1983; 32pp., $18.00.

————. *No Ducks in Our Bathtub.* N.Y.: Dial Books for Young Readers, 1973; 32pp., $8.95.

————. *Sabrina.* N.Y.: Dial, 1971; 28pp., $5.95.

————. *We're in Big Trouble, Blackboard Bear*. N.Y.: Dial, 1980; 32pp., $6.89.

Alexander, Sally Hobart. *Maggie's Whopper*. N.Y: Macmillan, 1992; 32pp., $14.95.

Aliki. *Manners*. N.Y.: Greenwillow, 1990; 32pp., $15.93.

————. *My Hands*. N.Y.: Thomas Y. Crowell, 1990; 32pp., $12.95.

————. *My Visit to the Zoo*. N.Y.: HarperCollins, 1997; 40pp., $14.95.

Allard, Harry. *Bumps in the Night*. N.Y.: Bantam, 1987; 48pp., $2.25.

————. *The Cactus Flower Bakery*. N.Y.: HarperCollins, 1991; 32pp., $14.89.

————. *It's So Nice to Have a Wolf around the House*. N.Y.: Doubleday, 1977; 28pp., $12.50

————. *Miss Nelson Has a Field Day*. Mass.: Houghton Mifflin, 1985; 32pp., $15.00.

————. *Miss Nelson Is Back*. Mass.: Houghton Mifflin, 1982; 32pp., $15.00.

Allen, Janet. *Exciting Things to Do with Color*. N.Y.: J. B. Lippincott, 1997; 45pp., $4.95.

Allen, Judy. *Whale*. Mass.: Candlewick, 1992; 32pp., $15.95.

Allen, Pamela. *Who Sank the Boat?* N.Y.: Putnam, 1983; 32pp., $10.95.

Ambrus, Victor. *What Time Is It, Dracula?* N.Y.: Crown, 1991; 26pp., NA.

Ancona, George and Mary Beth. *Handtalk Zoo*. N.Y.: Macmillan, 1989, 32pp., $14.95.

Andersen, H.C. *The Princess and the Pea*. Mass.: Houghton Mifflin, 1978; 32pp., $10.95.

Anderson, Peggy Perry. *Time for Bed, the Babysitter Said*. Mass.: Houghton Mifflin, 1987; 32pp., $15.00.

————. *To the Tub*. Mass.: Houghton Mifflin, 1996; 32pp., $13.95.

Andrews, Sylvia. *Rattlebone Rock*. N.Y.: HarperCollins, 1995; 32pp., $13.95.

Anholt, Catherine. *Tom's Rainbow Walk*. Mass.: Little, Brown, 1989; 28pp., $12.95.

————. *When I Was a Baby*. Mass.: Little, Brown, 1989; 32pp., $11.95.

Anholt, Catherine and Laurence. *One, Two, Three Count with Me*. N.Y.: Viking, 1996; 26pp., $4.99.

Anholt, Laurence. *The New Puppy*. Wisc.: Western, 1994; 32pp., $12.95.

Appelt, Kathi. *Bayou Lullaby*. N.Y.: Morrow Junior Books, 1995; 40pp., $16.00.

————. *Watermelon Day*. N.Y.: Henry Holt, 1996; 32pp., $14.95.

Araujo, Frank P. *The Perfect Orange*. Calif.: Rayve Productions, 1994; 32pp., $16.95.

Argent, Kerry. *Happy Birthday, Wombat!* Mass.: Little, Brown, 1989; 21pp., $11.95.

Armstrong, Jennifer. *That Terrible Baby*. N.Y.: Tambourine, 1994; 32pp., $14.00.

————. *Wan Hu Is in the Stars*. N.Y.: Tambourine, 1995; 32pp., $14.93.

Arnold, Katya. *Meow!* N.Y.: Holiday House, 1998; 30pp., $16.95.

Arnold, Tedd. *Green Wilma*. N.Y.: Dial for Young Readers, 1993; 32pp., $13.89.

————. *No More Water in the Tub!* N.Y.: Dial Books for Young Readers, 1995; 32pp., $14.99.

Arnosky, Jim. *Every Autumn Comes the Bear*. N.Y.: G. P. Putnam's Sons, 1993; 32pp., $5.95.

————. *Little Lions*. N.Y.: G. P. Putnam's Sons, 1998; 32pp, $15.99.

————. *Otters under Water*. N.Y.: G. P. Putnam's Sons, 1992; 32pp., $14.95.

————. *Rabbits and Raindrops*. N.Y.: G. P. Putnam's Sons, 1997; 32pp., $15.99.

Arnstein, Helen. *Billy and Our New Baby*. N.Y.: Human Sciences , 1973; 32pp., $13.95.

Asbjornsen, Peter. *The Three Billy Goats Gruff*. Calif.: Harcourt Brace Jovanovich, 1998; 28pp., $9.95.

Asch, Frank. *Barnyard Lullaby*. N.Y.: Simon and Schuster, 1998; 40pp., $15.00.

———. *Bread and Honey*. N.Y.: Parents Magazine, 1982; 48pp., $5.95.

———. *Gia and the Hundred Dollars Worth of Bubblegum*. N.Y.: McGraw-Hill, 1974; 32pp., NA.

———. *Monkey Face*. N.Y.: Parents Magazine, 1977; 32pp., NA

———. *Moon Bear*. N.Y.: Charles Scribner's Sons, 1978; 28pp., $8.95.

———. *Moonbear's Pet*. N.Y.: Simon and Schuster Books for Young Readers, 1997; 32pp., $15.00.

———. *Popcorn*. N.Y.: Parents Magazine, 1979; 48pp., $5.95.

———. *Sand Cake*. N.Y.: Parents Magazine, 1993; 48pp., $19.93

———. *Starbaby*. N.Y.: Charles Scribner's Sons, 1980; 28pp., $9.95.

———. *Turtle Tale*. N.Y.: Dial Books for Young Readers, 1980; 32pp., $2.75.

Asch, Frank and Vladimir Vagin. *The Flower Faerie*. N.Y.: Scholastic, 1992; 28pp., $14.95.

Aseltine, Lorraine. *First Grade Can Wait*. Ill.: Albert Whitman, 1988; 32pp., $10.25.

Ashabranner, Brent. *I'm in the Zoo, Too!* N.Y.: Cobblehill, 1989; 32pp., $12.95.

Asher, Sandy. *Princess Bee and the Royal Good-night Story*. Ill.: Albert Whitman, 1990; 32pp., NA.

Ashforth, Camilla. *Monkey Tricks*. Mass.: Candlewick, 1993; 32pp., $15.95.

Ashley, Bernard. *Cleversticks*. N.Y.: Crown, 1991; 32pp., $10.99.

Ata, Te. *Baby Rattlesnake*. Calif.: Children's Book Press, 1989; 32pp., $14.95.

Auch, Mary Jane. *Monster Brother*. N.Y.: Holiday House, 1994; 32pp., $15.95.

Austin, Virginia. *Say Please*. Mass.: Candlewick, 1994; 28pp., $12.95.

Avi. *The Bird, the Frog, and the Light*. N.Y.: Orchard, 1994; 32pp., NA.

Axelrod, Amy. *Pigs Will Be Pigs*. N.Y.: Simon and Schuster Books for Young Readers, 1994; 32pp., $14.00.

———. *Pigs on a Blanket*. N.Y.: Simon and Schuster, 1996; 32pp., $13.00.

Ayer, Jacqueline. *Nu Dang and His Kite*. Calif.: Harcourt Brace Jovanovich, 1959; 30pp., $3.49.

Aylesworth, Jim. *The Completed Hickory Dickory Dock*. N.Y.: Atheneum, 1990; 32pp., $12.95.

———. *One Crow: A Counting Rhyme*. N.Y.: J. B. Lippincott, 1988; 32pp., $12.89.

———. *Shenandoah Noah*. N.Y.: Holt, Rinehart and Winston, 1985; 30pp., NA.

Baehr, Patricia. *School Isn't Fair!* N.Y.: Simon and Schuster, 1991; 32pp., $13.95.

Baer, Edith. *This Is the Way We Go to School*. N.Y.: Demco Media, 1992; 40pp., $10.80.

Bailey, Donna. *What We Can Do About: Litter*. N.Y.: Franklin Watts, 1991; 32pp., $18.70.

Baker, Alan. *Benjamin's Balloon*. N.Y.: Lothrop, Lee and Shepard, 1990; 32pp., $12.95.

———. *Brown Rabbit's Day*. N.Y.: Kingfisher, 1994; 32pp., $7.95.

———. *Two Tiny Mice*. N.Y.: Dial Books for Young Readers, 1990; 32pp., $12.95.

Baker, Keith. *Hide and Snake*. N.Y.: Harcourt Brace Jovanovich, 1991; 32pp., $12.95.

———. *Who Is the Beast?* N.Y.: Harcourt Brace Jovanovich, 1990; 32pp., $12.95.

Balian, Lorna. *A Garden for a Groundhog*. Tenn.: Abingdon, 1985; 32pp., $13.95.

———. *Humbug Potion*. Tenn.: Abingdon, 1984; 28pp., $12.95.

———. *Humbug Rabbit*. Tenn.: Abingdon, 1997; 32pp., $16.95.

———. *Humbug Witch*. Tenn.: Abingdon, 1994; 32pp., $14.95.

———. *Leprechauns Never Lie*. Tenn.: Abingdon, 1994; 32pp., $14.95.

———. *Sometimes It's Turkey*. Tenn.: Abingdon, 1994; 32pp., $14.95.

Ball, Duncan. *Jeremy's Tail*. N.Y.: Orchard, 1990; 32pp., $14.99.

Ballard, Robin. *Good-bye, House*. N.Y.: Greenwillow, 1994; 24pp., $13.93.

———. *Granny and Me*. N.Y.: Greenwillow, 1992; 24pp., NA.

Baltuck, Naomi. *Crazy Gibberish and Other Storyhour Stretches*. Conn.: Linnet Books, 1993; 152pp., $25.00.

Banchek, Linda. *Snake In, Snake Out*. Calif.: Harcourt Brace Jovanovich, 1978; 29pp., $11.89.

Bancroft, Catherine. *Felix's Hat*. N.Y.: Four Winds, 1993; 32pp., $14.95.

Bang, Molly. *Goose*. N.Y.: Blue Sky, 1996; 32pp., $10.95.

———. *The Paper Crane*. N.Y.: Greenwillow, 1985; 32pp., $10.15

———. *Ten, Nine, Eight*. N.Y.: Greenwillow, 1983; 24pp., $16.00.

Banish, Roslyn. *A Forever Family*. N.Y.: HarperCollins, 1992; 44pp., $14.00.

Banks, Kate. *And If the Moon Could Talk*. N.Y.: Frances Foster, 1998; 34pp., $15.00.

Barasch, Lynne. *A Winter Walk*. N.Y.: Ticknor and Fields, 1993; 32pp., $13.95.

Barber, Barbara E. *Allie's Basketball Dream*. N.Y.: Lee and Low, 1996; 32pp., $14.95.

Barbot, Daniel. *A Bicycle for Rosaura*. NY: Kane/Miller, 1991; 24pp., $9.95.

Bare, Colleen Stanley. *Sammy, Dog Detective*. N.Y.: Cobblehill/Dutton, 1998; 32pp., $15.99.

Barlin, Anne and Paul. *Dance-A-Folk Song*. N.Y.: Bowmar, 1974; 96pp., $11.89.

Barracca, Debra and Sal. *Maxi, the Hero*. N.Y.: Dial Books for Young Readers, 1991; 30pp., $14.99.

Barrett, John. *The Easter Bear*. Ill.: Children's Press, 1981; 32pp., $11.27.

Barrett, Judi. *Animals Should Definitely Not Wear Clothing*. N.Y.: Macmillan, 1989; 32pp., $11.19.

———. *Benjamin's 365 Birthdays*. N.Y.: Macmillan, 1978; 34pp., $4.95.

———. *Cloudy with a Chance of Meatballs*. N.Y.: Macmillan, 1982; 30pp., $10.19.

———. *I'm Too Small, You're Too Big*. N.Y.: Atheneum, 1981; 31pp., $9.95.

———. *A Snake Is Totally Tail*. N.Y.: Atheneum, 1983; 32pp., $9.95.

Barrett, Ron. *Pickles to Pittsburgh*. N.Y.: Atheneum, 1997; 32pp., $16.00.

Barry, Sheila Anne. *The World's Best Party Games*, N.Y.: Sterling, 1987; 128pp., $5.95.

Bartalos, Michael. *Shadowville*. N.Y.: Viking, 1995; 40pp., $13.99.

Bartlett, Alison. *Cat among the Cabbages*. N.Y.: Dutton Children's Books, 1996; 32pp., $9.99.

Barton, Byron. *I Want to Be an Astronaut*. N.Y.: Thomas Y. Crowell, 1988; 32pp., $14.89.

———. *Machines at Work*. N.Y.: Thomas Y. Crowell, 1987; 32pp., $14.89.

Bateman, Teresa. *Leprechaun Gold*. N.Y.: Holiday House, 1998; 32pp., $15.95.

Bauer, Caroline Feller. *This Way to Books*. N.Y.: H. W. Wilson Co., 1983; 363pp., $45.00.

————. *Too Many Books!* N.Y.: Frederick Warne, 1984; 32pp., $11.95.

————. *Valentine's Day: Stories and Poems*. N.Y.: HarperCollins, 1993; 95pp., $15.95.

Baum, Arline. *One Bright Monday Morning*. N.Y.: Random House, 1962; 34pp., $4.99.

Bawden, Juliet. *101 Things to Make*. N.Y.: Sterling, 1981; 102pp., $14.95.

Beaton, Clare. *Make and Play Cards*. N.Y.: Warwick, 1990; 24pp., NA.

Beatty, Hetty. *Little Owl Indian*. Mass.: Houghton Mifflin, 1951; 32pp., $4.23.

Beck, Ian. *Emily and the Golden Apple*. N.Y.: Simon and Schuster Books for Young Readers, 1992; 32pp., $14.00.

————. *Five Little Ducks*. N.Y.: Henry Holt, 1992; 32pp., $14.95.

Becker, Joyce. *Hanukkah Crafts*. N.Y.: Bonim, 1978; 144pp., $6.95.

Beil, Karen M. *Grandma according to Me*. N.Y.: Dell, 1994; 32pp., $4.99.

Beim, Jerrole. *The Swimming Hole*. N.Y.: Morrow, 1950; unpaged, $3.78.

Bell, Barbara, ed. *Highlights Magazine for Children*. April 1984; $2.25.

Bellows, Cathy. *The Grizzly Sisters*. N.Y.; Macmillan, 1991; 32pp., $14.95.

Bemelmans, Ludwig. *Madeline's Rescue*. N.Y.: Viking, 1977; 56pp., $10.19.

————. *Rosebud*. N.Y.: Random House, 1993; 32pp., $8.99.

Benchley, Nathaniel. *A Ghost Named Fred*. N.Y.: Harper and Row, 1968; 64pp., $14.89.

————. *The Magic Sled*. N.Y.: Harper and Row, 1972; 64pp., $11.89.

————. *Red Fox and His Canoe*. N.Y.: Harper and Row, 1964; 64pp., $15.89.

————. *The Several Tricks of Edgar Dolphin*. N.Y.: Harper and Row, 1970; 64pp., NA.

Bender, Robert. *The A to Z Beastly Jamboree*. N.Y.: Lodestar, 1996; 30pp., $14.99.

————. *A Most Unusual Lunch*. N.Y.: Dial Books for Young Readers, 1994; 32pp., $14.89.

Benjamin, Alan. *Ribtickle Town*. N.Y.: Macmillan, 1983; unpaged, $10.95.

Benjamin, Cynthia. *I Am an Astronaut*. N.Y.: Barron's Educational Series, 1996; 32pp., NA.

Bentley, Nancy. *I've Got Your Nose!* N.Y.: Doubleday, 1991; 32pp., NA.

Bently, Anne. *The Groggs' Day Out*. N.Y.: Deutsch, 1981; 33pp., $9.95.

Benton, Robert. *Don't Ever Wish for a 7 Ft. Bear*. N.Y.: Knopf, 1972; 34pp., $5.99.

Berenstain, Stan. *The Berenstain Bears and the Week at Grandma's*. N.Y.: Random House, 1987; $5.99.

————. *The Berenstain Bears Go to Camp*. N.Y.: Random House, 1989; 32pp., $5.95.

————. *The Berenstain Bears Visit the Dentist*. N.Y.: Random House, 1981; 32pp., $8.45.

————. *The Bike Lesson*. N.Y.: Random House, 1966; 64pp., $7.99.

Berenstain, Stan and Jan. *The Berenstain Bears Don't Pollute (Anymore)*. N.Y.: Random House, 1991; 32pp., $8.99.

―――. *The Berenstain Bears Learn about Strangers*. N.Y.: Random House, 1985; 32pp., $8.99.

Berg, Cami. *D Is for Dolphin*. N.M.: Windom, 1991; 32pp., $18.95.

Berlan, Kathryn Hook. *Andrew's Amazing Monsters*. N.Y.: Atheneum, 1993; 32pp., $13.95.

Bernhard, Emery. *Ladybug*. N.Y.: Holiday House, 1992; 32pp., $14.95.

Bernhard, Emery and Durga. *How Snowshoe Hare Rescued the Sun: A Tale from the Arctic*. N.Y.: Holiday House, 1993; 32pp., $15.95.

Berson, Howard. *Joseph and the Snake*. N.Y.: Macmillan, 1979; unpaged, $6.96.

Best, Cari. *Red Light, Green Light, Mama and Me*. N.Y.: Orchard, 1995; 32pp., $16.99.

Bester, Roger. *Fireman Jim*. N.Y.: Crown, 1981; 32pp., $9.95.

Better Homes and Gardens. *Dandy Dinosaurs*. Iowa: Meredith, 1989; 32pp., NA.

Bianchi, John. *Spring Break at Pokeweed Public School*. Ontario: Bungalo Books, 1994; 26pp., $14.95.

Birchman, David Fran. *Brother Billy Brontos Bygone Blues Band*. N.Y.: Lothrop, Lee and Shepard, 1992; 30pp., $13.95.

―――. *The Raggly, Scraggly, No-Soap, No-Scrub Girl*. N.Y.: Lothrop, Lee and Shepard Books, 1995; 32pp., $16.00.

Birney, Betty G. *Tyrannosaurus Tex*. Mass.: Houghton Mifflin, 1994; 32pp., $14.95.

Bishop, Claire. *Twenty-two Bears*. N.Y.: Viking, 1964; 31pp., NA.

Blackwood, Mary. *Derek the Knitting Dinosaur*. Minn: Carolrhoda, 1987; 32pp., $19.95.

Blake, Jon. *Wriggly Pig*. N.Y.: Tambourine, 1992; 30pp., NA.

Blake, Quentin. *Mrs. Armitage on Wheels*. N.Y.: Alfred A. Knopf, 1987; 30pp., NA.

Blakely, Cindy, and Suzanne Drinkwater. *The Lookout! Book: A Child's Guide to Street Safety*. N.Y.: Scholastic, 1986; 32pp., $5.95.

Blanco, Alberto. *Angel's Kite*. Calif.: Children's Book Press, 1994; 32pp., $14.95.

Blegvad, Lenore. *The Great Hamster Hunt*. Calif.: Harcourt Brace Jovanovich, 1969; 32pp., $2.97.

Bloom, Suzanne. *A Family for Jamie: An Adoption Story*. N.Y.: Clarkson N. Potter, 1991; 24pp., $13.99.

Bloome, Enid. *The Air We Breathe!* N.Y.: Doubleday, 1971; 32pp., $4.95.

Blos, Joan W. *Lottie's Circus*. N.Y.: Morrow Junior Books, 1989; 32pp., $13.95.

―――. *Martin's Hats*. N.Y.: Morrow, 1984; 32pp., $10.88.

Blosser, Jody L. *Everybody Wins!: Non-Competitive Party Games and Activities for Children*. N.Y.: Sterling, 1996; 144pp., $16.95.

Boechler, Gwenn, Shirley Charlton, and Alice Traer Wayne. *A Piece of Cake*. N.Y.: Doubleday, 1987; 125pp., $9.95.

Boegehold, Betty. *You Can Say "No."* N.Y.: Golden/Western, 1985; 23pp., $4.95.

Boelts, Maribeth. *Summer's End*. Mass.: Houghton Mifflin, 1995; 32pp., $14.95.

―――. *A Kid's Guide to Staying Safe on the Streets*. N.Y.: Powerkids, 1997; 24pp., $13.95.

―――. *Little Bunny's Preschool Countdown*. Ill.: Albert Whitman, 1996; 32pp., $14.95.

Bogacki, Tomek. *Cat and Mouse in the Rain*. N.Y.: Farrar, Straus, and Giroux, 1997; 32pp., $15.00.

Bond, Felicia. *Poinsettia and the Firefighters*. N.Y.: Thomas Y. Crowell, 1984; 32pp., $16.89.

Bond, Michael. *Paddington Bear and the Christmas Surprise*. N.Y.: HarperCollins, 1997; 32pp., $12.95.

Bonica, Diane. *Hand-Shaped Gifts*. Ill.: Good Apple, 1991; 144pp., $13.99.

Bonsall, Crosby. *Mine's the Best*. N.Y.: Harper and Row Junior Books, 1997; 32pp., $8.95.

Borden, Louise. *Caps, Hats, Socks and Mittens*. N.Y.: Scholastic, 1989; 32pp., $4.99.

———. *The Neighborhood Trucker*. N.Y.: Scholastic, 1997; 28pp., $3.95.

Bornstein, Ruth. *Indian Bunny*. Ill.: Children's Press, 1973; unpaged, $4.33.

Bornstein, Ruth Lercher. *Rabbit's Good News*. N.Y.: Clarion, 1995; 32pp., $13.95.

Boteler, Alison. *The Disney Party Handbook*. N.Y.: Disney, 1998; 208pp., $35.50.

———. *The Children's Party Handbook*. N.Y.: Barron's Educational Series, 1986; 188pp., $12.95.

Bourgeois, Paulette. *Franklin and the Thunderstorm*. N.Y.: Kids Can , 1998; 32pp., $10.95.

———. *Franklin and the Tooth Fairy*. Canada: Kids Can, 1995; 32pp., $10.95.

Bourgeois, Paulette and Brenda Clark. *Franklin Rides a Bike*. N.Y.: Scholastic, 1997; 32pp., $3.99.

Boyd, Lizi. *The Not-So-Wicked Stepmother*. N.Y.: Viking Kestrel, 1987; 32pp., $10.95.

———. *Sam Is My Half Brother*. N.Y.: Viking Kestrel, 1990,; 32pp., $11.95.

Bradby, Marie. *More than Anything Else*. N.Y.: Orchard, 1995; 30pp., $15.95.

Bradman, Tony. *It Came from Outer Space*. N.Y.: Dial Books for Young Readers, 1992; 26pp., $12.00.

Branley, Franklyn. *Down Comes the Rain*. N.Y.: HarperCollins, 1997; 32pp., $14.89.

Brashears, Deya and Sharron Werlin Krull. *Circle Time Activities for Young Children*. Calif.: Circle Time , 1981; 139pp., $16.95.

Breathed, Berkeley. *A Wish for Wings that Work*. Mass.: Little, Brown, 1991; 32pp., $14.95.

Breinburg, Petronella. *Shawn's Red Bike*. N.Y.: Crowell, 1975; 24pp., $6.95.

Bresnahan, Michaeline and Joan Gaestel MacFarlane. *The Happiest Birthdays: Great Theme Parties for Young Children*. Mass.: Stephen Greene, 1988; 145pp., $11.95.

Brett, Jan. *Armadillo Rodeo*. N.Y.: G. P. Putnam's Sons, 1995; 32pp., $15.95.

———. *Christmas Trolls*. N.Y.: G. P. Putnam's Sons, 1993; 32pp., $15.95.

———. *The Hat*. N.Y.: G. P. Putnam's Sons, 1997; 32pp., $16.99.

———. *The Mitten*. N.Y.: G. P. Putnam's Sons, 1989; 32pp., $16.99.

———. *Trouble with Trolls*. N.Y.: G. P. Putnam's Sons, 1992; 32pp., $15.95.

Bridges, Margaret Park. *Will You Take Care of Me?* N.Y.: Morrow Junior Books, 1998; 32pp., $22.95.

Bridwell, Norman. *Clifford at the Circus*. N.Y.: Scholastic, 1985; 32pp., $6.95.

———. *Clifford's First Autumn*. N.Y.: Scholastic, 1997; 32pp., $8.19.

———. *Clifford's Good Deeds*. N.Y.: Scholastic, 1985; 32pp., $2.99.

———. *Clifford's Puppy Days*. N.Y. : Scholastic, 1989; 32pp., $10.95.

———. *Clifford's Thanksgiving Visit*. N.Y.: Scholastic, 1993; 32pp., $2.99.

Briggs, Diane. *52 Programs for Preschoolers: The Librarians Year-Round Planner*. Ill.: ALA, 1997; 217pp., $28.00.

Briggs, Raymond. *The Snowman Clock Book*. N.Y.: Random House, 1991; 32pp., $7.99.

Bright, Robert. *Georgie and the Magician*. N.Y.: Doubleday, 1966; 45 pp., $2.50.

———. *Georgie and the Runaway Balloon*. N.Y.: Doubleday, 1983; 32pp., $3.95.

———. *Georgie's Halloween*. N.Y.: Doubleday, 1958; 30pp., $4.95.

———. *Which Is Willy?* N.Y.: Doubleday, 1962; unpaged, NA.

Brillhart, Julie. *Storyhour—Starring Megan!* Ill.: Albert Whitman , 1992; 32pp., NA.

———. *When Daddy Took Us Camping*. Ill.: Albert Whitman, 1997; 24pp., $13.95.

Brisson, Pat. *Benny's Pennies*. N.Y.: Doubleday Books for Young Readers, 1993; 32pp., $14.95.

Brochac, Joseph, and Gayle Ross. *The Story of the Milky Way*. N.Y.: Dial Books for Young Readers, 1995; 32pp., $14.99.

Brokaw, Meredith, and Annie Gilbar. *The Penny Whistle Birthday Party Book*. N.Y.: Simon and Schuster, 1992; 256pp., $14.00.

———. *The Penny Whistle Party Planner*. N.Y.: Weidenfeld and Nicolson, 1987; 244pp., $12.95.

Brooks, Jennifer. *Princess Jessica Rescues a Prince*. Calif.: NADJA, 1994; 48pp., $15.95.

Brown, Craig. *In the Spring*. N.Y.: Greenwillow, 194; 32pp., $13.95.

Brown, David. *Someone Always Needs a Policeman*. N.Y.: Simon and Schuster, 1972; 40pp., $3.95.

Brown, Jerome. *Holiday Gifts and Decorations Kids Can Make (for Practically Nothing)*. Calif.: Fearon Teacher Aids, 1986; 108pp., $12.99.

Brown, Laurie Krasny and Marc Brown. *Dinosaurs Alive and Well!* Mass.: Little, Brown, 1990; 32pp., $14.95.

———. *How to Be a Friend: A Guide to Making Friends and Keeping Them*. N.Y.: Little, Brown, 1998; 32pp., $14.95.

Brown, Marc. *Arthur's Eyes*. Mass.: Little, Brown, 1979; 32pp., $15.95.

———. *Arthur Goes to Camp*. Mass.: Little, Brown, 1982; 32pp., $15.95.

———. *D. W.'s Lost Blankie*. Mass.: Little, Brown, 1998; 32pp., $13.95.

———. *D. W. Rides Again!* Mass.: Little, Brown, 1993; 32pp., $11.15.

———. *Glasses for D. W.*. N.Y.: Random House, 1996; 32pp., $11.99.

———. *Hand Rhymes*. N.Y.: E. P. Dutton, 1985; 32pp., $14.99.

———. *How to be a Friend*. Mass.: Little, Brown, 1998; 32pp., $14.95.

———. *Perfect Pigs: An Introduction to Manners*. Mass.: Little, Brown, 1983; 29pp., $12.45.

Brown, Marc, and Stephen Krensky. *Dinosaurs, Beware!* Mass.: Little, Brown, 1982; 32pp., $5.95.

Brown, Margaret Wise. *Big Red Barn*. N.Y.: Harper and Row Junior Books, 1965; 13pp., $8.70.

———. *Goodnight, Moon*. N.Y.: Harper and Row Junior Books, 1947; 30pp., $8.89.

————. *Little Donkey Close Your Eyes*. N.Y.: HarperCollins, 1995; 32pp., $13.89.

————. *The Little Fireman*. N.Y.: Harper and Row Junior Books, 1952; 34pp., $9.70.

————. *Red Light! Green Light!* N.Y.: Doubleday, 1944; unpaged, $5.95.

————. *The Seashore Noisy Book*. Mass.: Addison-Wesley, 1941; 40pp., $10.89.

————. *The Sleepy Little Lion*. N.Y.: Harper and Row Junior Books, 1947; 24pp., $6.99.

————. *The Summer Noisy Book*. N.Y.: Harper and Row, 1951; 40pp., $10.89.

————. *Winter Noisy Book*. N.Y.: Harper and Row, 1947; 40pp., $10.89.

Brown, Ruth. *Ladybug, Ladybug*. N.Y.: E. P. Dutton, 1988; 28pp., $12.95.

————. *One Stormy Night*. N.Y.: Dutton Children's Books, 1992; 32pp., $4.99.

————. *Toad*. N.Y.: Dutton Children's Books, 1996; 32pp., $15.99.

————. *The World that Jack Built*. N.Y.: Dutton Children's Books, 1991; 32pp., $13.95.

Browne, Anthony. *Bear Hunt*. N.Y.: Atheneum, 1980; 24pp., $8.95.

Browne, Eileen. *Where's That Bus*. N.Y.: Simon and Schuster Books for Young Readers, 1991; 28pp., $13.95.

Bruchac, Joseph. *The Great Ball Game*. N.Y.: Dial Books for Young Readers, 1994; 32pp., $14.89.

Brunhoff, Laurent de. *Babar and the Ghost*. N.Y.: Random House, 1981; 34pp., $6.99.

Brustlein, Janice. *Little Bear Marches in the St. Patrick's Day Parade*. N.Y.: Lothrop, Lee and Shepard, 1967; 26pp., $3.50.

Buckley, Helen E. *Moonlight Kite*. N.Y.: Lothrop, Lee and Shepard, 1997; 32pp., $16.00.

Bucknall, Caroline. *One Bear in the Hospital*. N.Y.: Dial Books for Young Readers, 1991; 32pp., $11.95.

Bulla, Clyde. *Daniel's Duck*. N.Y.: Harper and Row Junior Books, 1979; 64pp., $11. 95.

Bunting, Eve. *In the Haunted House*. N.Y.: Clarion, 1990; 32pp., $14.95.

————. *Night Tree*. N.Y.: Harcourt Brace Jovanovich, 1991; 32pp., $16.00.

————. *Someday a Tree*. N.Y.: Clarion, 1993; 32pp., $15.00.

————. *St. Patrick's Day in the Morning*. N.Y.: Clarion, 1980; 32pp., $15.00.

————. *Sunflower House*. N.Y.: Harcourt Brace and Co., 1996; 32pp., $15.00.

————. *Sunshine Home*. N.Y.: Clarion, 1994, 32pp., $16.00.

————. *A Turkey for Thanksgiving*. N.Y.: Clarion, 1991; 32pp., $13.95

————. *Twinnies*. N.Y.: Harcourt Brace and Co., 1997; 32pp., $15.00.

————. *The Valentine Bears*. Mass.: Harper and Row Junior Books, 1984; 16pp., $15.00.

————. *The Wednesday Surprise*. N.Y.: Clarion, 1989; 32pp., $15.00.

Burden-Patmon, Denis. *Iwani's Gift at Kwanzaa*. N.Y.: Simon and Schuster Books for Young Readers, 1992; 23pp., $4.95.

Burningham, John. *Hey! Get Off the Train*. N.Y.: Crown, 1989; 48pp., $14.99.

Burrough, Tracy Stephen. *The Big Book of Kids Games*. Conn.: Longmeadow, 1992; 184pp., NA.

Burton, Marilee Burton. *My Best Shoes*. N.Y.: Tambourine, 1994; 32pp., $15.00.

Burton, Marilee Robin. *Tail, Toes, Eyes, Ears, Nose.* N.Y.: Harper and Row, 1989; 32pp, $11.89.

Burton, Virginia. *Katy and the Big Snow.* Mass.: Houghton Mifflin, 1943; 40pp., $11.95.

Butterworth, Nick. *Jingle Bells.* N.Y.: Orchard, 1998; 32pp., $15.95.

———. *My Grandpa Is Amazing.* Mass.: Candlewick, 1992; 32pp., $4.99.

Butterworth, Nick, and Mick Inkpen. *Field Day.* N.Y.: Delacorte, 1988; 32pp., $14.00.

———. *Jasper's Beanstalk.* N.Y.: Bradbury, 1993; 24pp., $5.99.

Byars, Betsy. *Go and Hush the Baby.* N.Y.: Viking Penguin, 1971; 30pp., $11.95.

Cable-Alexander, Jane. *Giving a Children's Party.* London: Pelham, 1983; 80pp., $12.95.

Calhoun, Mary. *Hot Air Henry.* N.Y.: William Morrow, 1981; 40pp., $16.00.

———. *The Hungry Leprechaun.* N.Y.: William Morrow, 1962; 28pp., $11.88.

———. *The Pixy and the Lazy Housewife.* N.Y.: William Morrow and Co., 1969; 32pp., NA.

Calmenson, Stephanie. *Engine, Engine, Number Nine.* N.Y.: Hyperion Books for Children, 1996; 32pp., $14.49.

———. *Hotter than a Hot Dog!* Mass.: Little, Brown, 1994, 32pp., $14.95.

———. *The Principal's New Clothes.* N.Y.: Scholastic, Inc., 1989; 32pp., $13.95.

———. *Zip Whiz, Zoom!* Mass.: Little, Brown, 1992; 30pp., $13.95.

Cameron, Ann. *Harry (the Monster).* N.Y.: Pantheon, 1980; 36pp., $6.99.

Cameron, Polli. *"I Can't," Said the Ant.* N.Y.: Coward, 1961; unpaged, $7.99.

Campbell, Peter. *Harry's Bee.* Ind.: Bobbs-Merrill, 1969; 32pp., NA.

Caney, Steven. *Steven Caney's Toy Book.* N.Y.: Workman, 1972; 176pp., $8.95.

Canfield, Jane. *The Frog Prince.* N.Y.: Harper and Row, 1970; 31pp., $4.79.

Cann, Jonathan V. *The Case of the Crooked Candles.* Tex.: Steck-Vaughn Co., 1997; 32pp., $22.83.

Cannon, Janell. *Stellaluna.* Calif.: Harcourt Brace Jovanovich, 1993; 32pp., $16.95.

———. *Verdi.* Calif.: Harcourt Brace Jovanovich, 1997; 32pp., $16.00.

Cantieni, Benita. *Little Elephant and Big Mouse.* Mass.: Picture Book Studios USA, 1981; 32pp., $13.95.

Caple, Kathy. *The Purse.* Mass.: Houghton Mifflin, 1986; 32pp, $12.95.

Capucilli, Alyssa Satin. *Inside a Barn in the Country.* N.Y.: Scholastic, 1995; 32pp., $10.95.

Carle, Eric. *Do You Want to Be My Friend?* N.Y.: Harper and Row Junior Books, 1971; 31pp., $12.89.

———. *The Grouchy Ladybug.* N.Y.: HarperCollins, 1996; 32pp., $15.90.

———. *Have You Seen My Cat?* Mass.: Picture Book Studios USA, 1996; 21pp., $6.99.

———. *Little Cloud.* N.Y.: Philomel, 1996; 32pp., $16.95.

———. *The Mixed-up Chameleon.* N.Y.: Harper and Row Junior Books, 1998; 32pp., $7.95.

———. *Papa, Please Get the Moon for Me.* Mass.: Picture Book Studio, 1986; 32pp., $16.95.

————. *Secret Birthday Message*. N.Y.: Harper and Row Junior Books, 1986; 24pp., $11.15.

————. *The Tiny Seed*. Mass.: Picture Book Studio USA, 1998; 32pp., $12.95.

————. *The Very Hungry Caterpillar*. N.Y.: Putnam, 1986; 32pp., $12.95.

Carlson, Laurie. *Boss of the Plains: The Hat that Won the West*. N.Y.: DK Publishing, 1998; 32pp., $16.95.

————. *EcoArt!* Vt.: Williamson, 1993; 160pp., $12.95.

Carlson, Nancy. *ABC I Like Me!* N.Y.: Viking, 1997; 32pp., $14.99.

————. *Arnie and the New Kid*. N.Y.: Viking Penguin, 1990; 32pp., $4.99.

————. *Bunnies and Their Sports*. N.Y.: Viking Kestrel, 1987; 32pp, $11.95.

————. *How to Lose All Your Friends*. N.Y.: Viking Kestrel, 1994; 32pp., $14.99.

————. *It's Going to Be Perfect*. N.Y.: Viking, 1998; 32pp., $15.99.

————. *I Like Me*. N.Y.: Viking Penguin, 1988; 32pp., $14.99.

————. *Take Time to Relax*. N.Y.: Viking, 1991; 28pp., $13.95.

Carlstrom, Nancy White. *Barney Is Best*. N.Y.: HarperCollins, 1994; 32pp., $14.89.

————. *Fish and Flamingo*. Mass.: Little, Brown, 1993; 32pp., $14.95.

————. *I'm Not Moving, Mama*. N.Y.: Macmillan, 1990; 28pp., $13.95.

————. *How Do You Say It Today, Jesse Bear?* N.Y.: Macmillan, 1992; 30p., $15.00.

————. *Let's Count It Out, Jesse Bear*. N.Y.: Simon and Schuster Books for Young Readers, 1996; 32pp., $15.00.

————. *No Nap for Benjamin Badger*. N.Y.: Macmillan, 1991; 28pp., $13.95.

————. *The Snow Speaks*. Mass.: Little, Brown, 1992; 32pp., $15.95.

————. *Swim the Silver Sea, Joshie Otter*. N.Y.: Philomel, 1993; 32pp., $5.95.

Carmine, Mary. *Daniel's Dinosaurs*. N.Y.: Scholastic, 1990; 26pp., $12.95.

Carreiro, Carolyn. *Hand-Print Animal Art*. Vt.: Williamson, 1997; 144pp., $14.95.

Carrick, Carol. *What Happened to Patrick's Dinosaurs?* N.Y.: Clarion, 1986; 32pp., $16.00.

————. *Valentine*. N.Y.: Clarion, 1995; 32pp., $14.95.

Carter, Penny. *A New House for the Morrisons*. N.Y.: Viking, 1993; 32pp., $12.99.

Cartwright, Ann and Reg. *In Search of the Last Dodo*. Mass.: Joy Street, 1989; 26pp., $14.95.

Caseley, Judith. *Grandpa's Garden Lunch*. N.Y.: Greenwillow, 1990; 24pp., NA.

————. *Harry and Willy and Carrothead*. N.Y.: Greenwillow, 1991; 24pp., $13.88.

————. *Mr. Green Peas*. N.Y.: Greenwillow, 1995; 32pp., $15.00.

————. *Slumber Party*. N.Y.: Greenwillow, 1996; 32pp., $14.93.

————. *Sophie and Sammy's Library Sleepover*. N.Y.: Greenwillow, 1993; 32pp., $16.00.

————. *Witch Mama*. N.Y.: Greenwillow, 1996; 32pp., $15.00.

Castaldo, Nancy Fusco. *Rainy Day Play!* Vt.: Williamson, 1996; 144pp., $12.95.

Cauley, Lorinda Bryan. *Things to Make and Do for Thanksgiving*. N.Y.: Franklin Watts, 1977; 48pp., NA.

————. *Three Blind Mice*. N.Y.: G. P. Putnam's Sons, 1991; 32pp., $14.95.

Causley, Charles. *Early in the Morning*. N.Y.: Viking Kestrel, 1986, 64pp., $14.95.

Cave, Peter L. *500 Games*. N.Y.: Grosset and Dunlap, 1973; 160pp., $1.95.

Cazet, Denys. *Born in the Gravy*. N.Y.: Orchard, 1993; 32pp., $15.95.

————. *"I'm Not Sleepy."* N.Y.: Orchard, 1992; 32pp., $14.99.

————. *A Fish in His Pocket*. N.Y.: Orchard, 1987; 32pp., $17.00.

Chacon, Rick; illus. *Big and Easy Art*. Calif.: Teacher Created Materials, 1986; 32pp., $1.95.

Chaplin, Susan Gibbons. *I Can Sign My ABC's*. D.C.: Kendall Green, 1986; 57pp., $9.95.

Chapman, Cheryl. *Pass the Fritters, Critters*. N.Y.: Four Winds, 1993; 32pp., $14.95.

Chardiet, Bernice. *C Is for Circus*. N.Y.: Walker, 1971; unpaged, $5.85.

Charles, Donald. *Calico Cat Meets Bookworm*. Ill.: Children's Press, 1978; 32pp., $13.30.

————. *Calico Cat's Exercise Book*. Ill.: Children's Press, 1982; 32pp., NA.

————. *Calico Cat's Sunny Smile*. Ill.: Children's Press, 1990; 32pp., NA.

Charlip, Remy, Mary Beth Anacona and George Ancona. *Handtalk Birthday*. N.Y.: Four Winds, 1987; 32pp., $15.95.

Charner, Kathy. *The Giant Encyclopedia of Circle Time and Group Activities for Children 3 to 6*. Md.: Gryphon House, 1996; 510pp., $29.95.

————. *The Giant Encyclopedia of Theme Activities for Children 2 to 5*. Md.: Gryphon House, 1993; 513pp., $29.95.

Chase, Catherine. *The Mouse in My House*. Ill.: Dandelion, 1979; unpaged, $2.50.

Chernoff, Goldie Taub. *Just a Box?* N.Y.: Walker, 1973; 23pp., $1.75.

Chesler, Bernice. *Do a Zoom-Do*. Mass.: Little, Brown, 1975; 118pp., $7.95.

Chester, Jonathan, and Kirsty Melville. *Splash!: A Penguin Counting Book*. Calif.: Tricycle, 1997; 24pp., $12.95.

Chesworth, Michael. *Rainy Day Dream*. N.Y.: Farrar, Straus and Giroux, 1992; 32pp., $14.00.

Chinn, Karen. *Sam and the Lucky Money*. N.Y.: Lee and Low, 1995; 32pp., $14.95.

Chlad, Dorothy. *Matches, Lightners, and Firecrackers are Not Toys*. Ill.: Children's Press, 1982; 31pp., $11.00.

————. *Playing Outdoors in the Winter*. Ill.: Children's Press, 1991; 32pp., NA.

————. *Strangers*. Ill.: Children's Press, 1982; 31pp., $11.00.

Choate, Judith, and Jane Green. *Scrapcraft: 50 Easy to Make Handicraft Projects*. N.Y.: Doubleday, 1973; 64pp., $4.95.

Chocolate, Deborah M. *Kente Colors*. N.Y.: Walker, 1996; 32pp., $15.95.

————. *Kwanzaa*. Ill.: Children's Press, 1990; 31pp., $17.10.

————. *My First Kwanzaa Book*. N.Y.: Scholastic, 1992; 32pp., $10.95.

Choldenko, Gennifer. *Moonstruck: The True Story of the Cow Who Jumped over the Moon*. N.Y.: Hyperion Books for Children, 1997; 34pp., $14.95.

Christelow, Eileen. *Don't Wake Up Mama*. N.Y.: Clarion, 1992; 32pp., $15.00.

————. *Five Little Monkeys Sitting in a Tree*. N.Y.: Clarion, 1991; 32pp., $15.00.

————. *Gertrude, the Bulldog Detective*. N.Y.: Clarion, 1992; 32pp., $13.95.

————. *Jerome the Babysitter*. Mass.: Houghton Mifflin, 1985; 32pp., $12.95.

————. *Olive and the Magic Hat*. N.Y.: Clarion, 1987; 32pp., $12.95.

Chupela, Dolores. *Once Upon a Childhood: Fingerplays, Action Rhymes, and Fun Times for the Very Young*. Md.: Scarecrow, 1998; 119pp., $19.95.

————. *Ready, Set, Go!: Children's Programming for Bookmobiles and Other Small Spaces*. Wisc.: Alleyside, 1994; 228pp., $19.95.

Churchill, E. Richard. *Holiday Paper Projects*. N.Y.: Sterling, 1992; 128pp., $14.95.

Ciancio, Billie, ed. *Pack-o-Fun.* Spring 1984. Ill.: Pack-O-Fun.

Civardi, Anne, and Penny King. *Festival Decorations.* N.Y.: Crabtree, 1998; 32pp., $8.95.

Clark, Emma Chichester. *Catch that Hat!* Mass.: Little, Brown, 1988; 26pp., $12.95.

———. *I Love You, Blue Kangaroo.* N.Y.: Doubleday Books for Young Readers, 1998; 32pp., $15.95.

Cleary, Beverly. *The Growing-up Feet.* N.Y.: William Morrow, 1987; 32pp., $11.95.

———. *The Hullabaloo ABC.* N.Y.: Morrow Junior Books, 1998; 30pp., $15.93.

Clement, Rod. *Grandpa's Teeth.* N.Y.: HarperCollins, 1997; 32pp., $14.95.

Clifton, Lucille. *Three Wishes.* N.Y.: Viking Penguin, 1974; 26pp., $6.95.

Coats, Laura Jane. *The Oak Tree.* N.Y.: Macmillan, 1987; 32pp., NA.

Coats, Lucy. *One Hungry Baby.* N.Y.: Crown Books for Young Readers, 1994; 32pp., $9.99.

Cohen, Izhar. *A-B-C Discovery.* N.Y.: Dial for Young Children, 1998; 32pp., $17.99.

Cohen, Miriam. *Bee My Valentine!* N.Y.: Greenwillow, 1978; 32pp., $11.88.

———. *The New Teacher.* N.Y.: Macmillan, 1972; 31pp., $3.95.

Cole, Ann, Carolyn Haas, Elizabeth Heller, and Betty Weinberger. *Children and Children and Children.* Mass.: Little, Brown, 1978; 212pp., $9.95.

———. *A Pumpkin in a Pear Tree.* Mass.: Little, Brown, 1982; 160pp., $14.45.

Cole, Ann, Carolyn Haas, Faith Bushnell, and Betty Weinberger. *I Saw a Purple Cow and 100 Other Recipes for Learning.* Mass.: Little, Brown, 1972; 96pp., $14.45.

Cole, Ann, Carolyn Haas, and Betty Weinberger. *Purple Cow to the Rescue.* Mass.: Little, Brown, 1982; 160pp., $12.95.

Cole, Babette. *The Bad Good Manners Book.* N.Y.: Dial Books for Young Readers, 1995; 32pp., $13.99.

Cole, Babette. *Cupid.* N.Y.: G. P. Putnam's Sons, 1989; 32pp., $13.95.

———. *Tarzanna.* N.Y.: G. P. Putnam's Sons, 1992; 30pp., $14.95.

———. *The Trouble with Grandad.* N.Y.: G. P. Putnam's Sons, 1988; 32pp., $13.95.

———. *The Trouble with Uncle.* Mass.: Little, Brown, 1992; 32pp., $14.95.

Cole, Henry. *Jack's Garden.* N.Y.: Greenwillow, 1995; 24pp., $16.00.

Cole, Joanna. *A Fish Hatches.* N.Y.: Morrow, 1978; 39pp., $14.93.

———. *How I Was Adopted.* N.Y.: Morrow Junior Books, 1995; 48pp., $16.00.

———. *The Magic Schoolbus inside a Beehive.* N.Y.: Scholastic Press, 1996; 48pp., $15.95.

———. *Mixed Up Magic.* N.Y.: Scholastic, 1987; 32pp., $9.95.

———. *Norma Jean, Jumping Bean.* N.Y.: Random House, 1987; 48pp., $9.99.

Cole, Joanna and Stephanie Calmenson. *The Eentsy, Weentsy Spider: Fingerplays and Action Rhymes.* N.Y.: Morrow Junior Books, 1991; 64pp., $13.95.

———. *Pin the Tail on the Donkey.* N.Y.: Morrow Junior Books, 1993; 48pp., $15.00.

———. *Rain or Shine Activity Book: Fun Things to Make and Do.* N.Y.: Morrow Junior Books, 1997; 192 pp., $20.00.

Cole, William. *Frances, Face-Maker.* Ohio: William Collins, 1963; unpaged, $3.41.

Coleman, Michael. *Hank the Clank.* Wisc.: Gareth Stevens, 1994; 32pp., $19.95.

Coleman, Satis N., Alice G. Thom. *Singing Time: A Book of Songs for Little Children.* N.Y.: The John Day Co., 1928; 48pp., $3.50.

Collins, Pat Lowery. *Don't Tease the Guppies*. N.Y.: G. P. Putnam's Sons, 1994; 32pp., $14.95.

————. *Tomorrow, Up and Away!* Mass.: Houghton Mifflin, 1990; 32pp., $13.95.

Coman, Carolyn. *Losing Things at Mr. Mudd's*. N.Y.: Farrar, Straus and Giroux, 1992; 32pp., $14.00.

Compton, Ken and Joanne. *Granny Greenteeth and the Noise in the Night*. N.Y.: Holiday House, 1993; 32pp., $14.95.

Conaway, Judith. *City Crafts from Secret Cities*. Ill.: Follett, 1978; 68pp., NA.

————. *Great Indoor Games from Trash and Other Things*. Wisc.: Children's Press, 1977; 47pp., NA.

————. *Springtime Surprises!: Things to Make and Do*. N.J.: Troll Associates, 1986; 48pp., NA.

Condit, Martha Olson. *Something to Make, Something to Think About*. N.Y.: Four Winds, 1975; 39pp., $4.95.

Conklin, Gladys. *Lucky Ladybugs*. N.Y.: Holiday House,1968; 32pp., $5.95.

Cooper, Helen. *The Bear under the Stairs*. N.Y.; Dial Books for Young Readers, 1993; 32pp., $5.99.

————. *The Boy Who Wouldn't Go to Bed*. N.Y.: Dial Books for Young Readers, 1996; 32pp., $14.99.

Cooper, Jason. *Fire Stations*. Fla.: Rourke, 1992; 24pp., $10.95.

————. *Police Stations*. Fla.: Rourke, 1992; 24pp., $10.95.

Cooper, Kay. *Too Many Rabbits and other Fingerplays*. N.Y.: Scholastic, 1995; 48pp., $12.95.

Copage, Eric. V. *Kwanzaa: An African-American Celebration of Culture and Cooking*. N.Y.: William Morrow, 1993; 356pp., $25.00.

Cophen, Carol. *Wake Up, Groundhog!* N.Y.: Crown, 1975; 31pp., $4.95.

Corbett, Pie. *The Playtime Treasury*. N.Y.: Doubleday, 1989; 125pp., $16.95.

Corwin, Judith Hoffman. *My First Riddles*. N.Y.: HarperCollins, 1998; 24pp., $9.95.

————. *Papercrafts*. N.Y.: Franklin Watts, 1988; 48pp., $20.00.

Cote, Nancy. *Palm Trees*. N.Y.: Four Winds, 1993; 40pp., $14.95.

Cottringer, Anne. *Ella and the Naughty Lion*. Mass.: Houghton Mifflin, 1996; 32pp., $14.95.

Coursen, Valerie. *Mordant's Wish*. N.Y.: Henry Holt, 1997; 32pp., $15.95.

Cousins, Lucy. *What Can Rabbit See?* N.Y.: Tambourine, 1991; 16pp., $12.95.

Coville, Bruce. *The Foolish Giant*. N.Y.: Harper and Row Junior Books, 1978; 46pp., $13.89.

Cowcher, Helen. *Jaguar*. N.Y.: Scholastic, 1997; 32pp. , $15.95.

————. *Rain Forest*. N.Y.: Farrar, Straus and Giroux, 1997; 32pp., $16.95.

Cowley, Joy. *Gracias, the Thanksgiving Turkey*. N.Y.: Scholastic, 1996; 32pp., $15.95.

Coxe, Molly. *Louella and the Yellow Balloon*. N.Y.: Thomas Y. Crowell, 1988; 32pp., $12.95.

Craven, Carolyn. *What the Mailman Brought*. N.Y.: G. P. Putnam's Sons, 1987; 40pp., $4.95.

Crebbin, June. *Danny's Duck*. Mass.: Candlewick, 1995; 32pp., $13.95.

————. *The Train Ride*. Mass.: Candlewick, 1995; 32pp., $14.95.

Cressey, James. *Max the Mouse*. N.J.: Prentice-Hall, 1977; unpaged, $4.95.

Cresswell, Helen. *Trouble*. N.Y.: E. P. Dutton, 1987; 28pp., $10.95.

Crews, Donald. *Harbor*. N.Y.: Greenwillow, 1982; 32pp., $14.93.

———. *Shortcut*. N.Y.: Greenwillow, 1992; 32pp., NA.

———. *Ten Black Dots*. N.Y.: Greenwillow, 1986; 32pp., $16.00.

Crews, Nina. *One Hot Summer Day*. N.Y.: Greenwillow, 1988; 30pp., $15.00.

Crimi, Carolyn. *Outside, Inside*. N.Y.: Simon and Schuster Books for Young Readers, 1995; 32pp., $15.00.

Cromwell, Liz, Dixie Hibner, and John R. Faitel. *Finger Frolics—Revised*. Md.: Gryphon House, 1983; 83pp., $14.95.

Cross, Peter. *Dudley Bakes a Cake*. N.Y.: Putnam's , 1988; 26pp., $12.95.

Crozat, Francois. *I Am a Little Alligator*. N.Y.: Barron's Educational Series, 1993; 24pp., $8.95.

Crume, Marion. *Do You See Mouse?* N.J.: Silver, 1995; 32pp., $18.95.

Cuetara, Mittie. *The Crazy Crawler Crane and Other Very Short Truck Stories*. N.Y.: E. P. Dutton, 1998; 32pp., $14.99.

Cummings, Pat. *Clean Your Room, Harvey Room!* N.Y.: Bradbury, 1991; 32pp., $16.00.

Cuneo, Mary Louise. *What Can a Giant Do?* N.Y.: HarperCollins, 1994; 32pp., $14.89.

Cushman, Doug. *The Mystery of King Karfu*. N.Y.: HarperCollins, 1996; 32pp., $14.95.

Cuyler, Margery. *Freckles and Jane*. N.Y.: Henry Holt, 1989; 32pp., $14.95.

Czernecki, Stefan. *The Cricket's Cage*. N.Y.: Hyperion Books for Children, 1997; 32pp., $15.49.

Czernecki, Stefan and Timothy Rhodes. *The Singing Snake*. N.Y.: Hyperion Books for Children, 1993; 40 pp., $14.89.

Dabcovick, Lydia. *Sleepy Bear*. N.Y.: E. P. Dutton, 1985; 32pp., $19.99.

Dale, Elizabeth. *How Long?* N.Y.: Orchard, 1998; 32pp., $14.95.

Dale, Penny. *The Elephant Tree*. N.Y.: G. P. Putnam's Sons, 1991; 32pp., $14.95.

———. *Ten out of Bed*. Mass.: Candlewick, 1996; 26pp., $5.99.

Dalgliesh, Alice. *The Fourth of July Story*. N.Y.: Aladdin Paperbacks, 1995; 32pp., $5.99.

Danrell, Liz. *With the Wind*. N.Y.: Orchard, 1991; 32pp., NA.

Darling, Benjamin. *Valerie and the Silver Pear*. N.Y.: Simon and Schuster,1992; 32pp., $14.95.

Darling, Kathy. *Holiday Hoopla: Songs and Finger Plays*. Ill.: Monday Morning, 1990; 64pp., NA.

———. *Kids and Communities*. Ill.: Monday Morning, 1989; 64pp., NA.

———. *Kids and Seasons*. Illlinois: Monday Morning, 1989; 64pp., NA.

Davidson, Amanda. *Teddy's First Christmas*. N.Y.: Henry Holt, 1982; 24pp., $7.95.

———. *Teddy at the Seashore*. N.Y.: Henry Holt, 1984; 24pp., $7.95.

Davies, Aubrey. *Bone Button Borscht*. N.Y.: Kids Can, 1997; 32pp., $15.95.

Davies, Nicola. *Big Blue Whale*. Mass.: Candlewick, 1997; 32pp., $15.99.

Davis, Carl, and Hiawyn Oram. *A Creepy Crawly Song Book*. N.Y.: Farrar, Straus and Giroux, 1993; 55pp., $17.00.

Davis, Gibbs. *The Other Emily*. Mass.: Houghton Mifflin, 1990; 32pp., $4.95.

Davis, Katie. *Who Hops?* Calif.: Harcourt Brace, 1998; 32pp., $13.00.

Davis, Maggie S. *A Garden of Whales*. N.Y.: Camden House, 1993; 32pp., $16.95.

Davis, Robin Works. *Toddle On Over*. Wisc.: Alleyside, 1998; 95pp., $12.95.

Davison, Martine. *Maggie and the Emergency Room*. N.Y.: Random House, 1992; 32pp., $5.99.

————. *Robby Visits the Doctor*. N.Y.: Random House, 1992; 32pp., $5.99.

Davol, Marguerite. *The Heart of the Wood*. N.Y.: Simon and Schuster Books for Young Readers, 1992; 32pp., $14.00.

————. *How Snake Got His Hiss*. N.Y.: Orchard, 1996; 32pp., $14.95.

DeBourgoing, Pascale, and Gallimard Jeunesse. *The Ladybug and Other Insects*. N.J.: Scholastic, 1989; 24pp., $11.95.

Deed, Carmen Agra. *The Library Dragon*. Ga.: Peachtree, 1994; 32pp., $16.95.

Deetlefs, Rene. *Tabu and the Dancing Elephants*. N.Y.: Dutton Children's Books, 1999; 32pp., NA.

DeFelice, Cynthia. *Casey in the Bath*. N.Y.: Farrar, Straus and Giroux, 1996; 24pp., $14.00.

DeGroat, Diane. *Alligator's Toothache*. N.Y.: Crown, 1977; 30pp., $4.95.

————. *Roses Are Pink, Your Feet Really Stink*. N.Y.: Morrow Junior Books, 1996; 32pp., $15.00.

Delacre, Lulu. *Nathan's Balloon Adventure*. N.Y.: Scholastic, 1991; 32pp., $12.95.

Delamar, Gloria T. *Children's Counting-out Rhymes, Fingerplays, Jump-Rope and Bounce-Ball Chants and Other Rhythms*. N.C.: McFarland, 1983; 206pp., $19.95.

Delaney, M.C. *The Marigold Monster*. N.Y.: E. P. Dutton, 1983; 32pp., $9.95.

Dellinger, Annetta. *Creative Games for Young Children*. Ill.: Children's Press, 1986; 64pp., NA.

Delton, Judy. *Groundhog's Day at the Doctor*. N.Y.: Parents Magazine, 1981; 48pp., $5.95.

————. *Penny Wise, Fun Foolish*. N.Y.: Crown, 1977; 48pp., $6.95.

————. *A Pet for Duck and Bear*. N.Y.: Albert Whitman, 1982; 32pp., $10.25.

————. *Rabbit Goes to Night School*. Ill.: Albert Whitman, 1986; 32pp., NA.

————. *My Mom Made Me Go to School*. N.Y.: Delacorte, 1991; 32pp., $13.99.

DeLuise, Dom. *Charlie the Caterpillar*. N.Y.: Simon and Schuster Books for Young Readers, 1990; 40pp., $15.00.

Demarest, Chris L. *Fall*. Calif.: Harcourt Brace Jovanovich, 1996; 16pp., $4.95.

————. *Morton and Sidney*. N.Y.: Macmillan, 1987; 32pp., $12.95.

Demi. *Dragon Kites and Dragonflies: A Collection of Chinese Nursery Rhymes*. Calif.: Harcourt Brace Jovanovich, 1996; 32pp., $14.95.

————. *The Dragon's Tale: and Other Animal Fables of the Chinese Zodiac*. N.Y.: Henry Holt, 1996; 32pp., $16.95.

DePaola, Tomie. *Andy (That's My Name)*. N.Y.: Prentice-Hall Press, 1973; 30pp., $9.95.

————. *The Art Lesson*. N.Y.: Putnam, 1989; 32pp., $16.99.

————. *Big Anthony and the Magic Ring*. Calif.: Harcourt Brace Jovanovich, 1987; 32pp., $12.95.

———. *Bill and Pete to the Rescue.* N.Y.: G. P. Putnam, 1998; 48pp., $15.99.

———. *Fin M'Coul.* N.Y.: Holiday House, 1981; 29pp., $12.95.

———. *Jamie O'Rourke and the Big Potato.* N.Y.: G. P. Putnam's Sons, 1992; 32pp., $14.95.

———. *The Legend of Blue Bonnet.* N.Y.: Putnam, 1983; 29pp., $10.95.

———. *The Mysterious Giant of Barletta.* Calif.: Harcourt Brace Jovanovich, 1984; 32pp., $13.95.

———. *The Popcorn Book.* N.Y.: Holiday House, 1978; 32pp., $15.95.

———. *Strega Nona Meets Her Match.* N.Y.: G. P. Putnam's Sons, 1993; 32pp., $15.95.

DeRegniers, Beatrice. *May I Bring a Friend?* N.Y.: Macmillan, 1964; 44pp., $12.95.

———. *The Shadow Book.* Calif.: Harcourt Brace Jovanovich, 1960; 27pp., $5.95.

Desimini, Lisa. *My House.* N.Y.: Henry Holt, 1994; 32pp., $15.95.

Diller, Harriett. *The Waiting Day.* N.Y.: Green Tiger, 1994; 32pp., $14.00.

Disney, Walt. *The Walt Disney Song Book.* N.Y.: Golden, 1977; 93pp., $6.95.

Dodds, Dayle Ann. *The Color Box.* Mass.: Little, Brown, 1992; 28pp., $14.95.

Domanska, Janina. *The Turnip.* N.Y.: Macmillan, 1969; 29pp., $5.95.

DonDiego, Barbara L. *Year-Round Crafts for Kids.* Pa.: Tab, 1988; 246; $16.95.

Dowell, Ruth I. *Move Over, Mother Goose!* Md: Gryphon House, 1987; 126pp., $12.95.

Dragonwagaon, Crescent. *Annie Flies the Birthday Bike.* N.Y.: Macmillan, 1993; 32pp., $14.95.

———. *Wind Rose.* N.Y.: Harper and Row, 1976; 30pp., $12.95.

Dubanevich, Arlene. *Calico Cows.* N.Y.: Viking, 1993; 32pp., NA.

———. *Tom's Tail.* N.Y.: Viking, 1990; 32pp., $13.95.

Dugan, Barbara. *Leaving Home with a Pickle Jar.* N.Y.: Greenwillow, 1993; 32pp., NA.

Duke, Kate. *Seven Froggies Went to School.* N.Y.: E. P. Dutton, 1985; 32pp., $11.95.

Dumbleton, Mike. *Dial-a-Croc.* N.Y.: Orchard, 1991; 32pp., $15.00.

Dunbar, Joyce. *Lolopy.* N.Y.: Macmillan , 1991; 32pp., $14.95.

Dupasquier, Philippe. *Andy's Pirate Ship: A Spot-the-Difference Book.* N.Y.: Henry Holt, 1994; 32pp., $11.95.

Duquennoy, Jacques. *The Ghost's Dinner.* Wisc.: Western, 1994; 48pp., $9.95.

———. *The Ghosts' Trip to Loch Ness.* Calif.: Harcourt Brace, 1996; 32pp., $11.00.

Dutton, Sandra. *The Cinnamon Hen's Autumn Day.* N.Y.: Atheneum, 1988; 32pp., $12.95.

Duvoisin, Roger. *Crocus.* N.Y.: Alfred A. Knopf, 1977; 28pp., $6.99.

———. *The Happy Hunter.* N.Y.: Lothrop, Lee and Shepard, 1961; 31pp., $2.83.

———. *Periwinkle.* N.Y.: Alfred A. Knopf, 1976; 29pp., $5.99.

———. *Petunia and the Song.* N.Y.: Alfred A. Knopf, 1951; 31pp., $3.49.

———. *Petunia's Christmas.* N.Y.: Alfred A. Knopf, 1963; 28pp., $8.99.

———. *Veronica and the Birthday Present.* N.Y.: Alfred A. Knopf, 1971; 28pp., $8.99.

Eagle, Kin. *It's Raining, It's Pouring.* Tex.: Whispering Coyote, 1994; 32pp., $15.95.

Eagon, Robynne. *Game for a Game?* Ill.: Teaching and Learning, 1995; 144pp., $13.95.

Edwards, Richard. *Ten Tall Oak Trees*. N.Y.: Tambourine, 1988; 32pp., $15.00.

Egan, Tim. *Chestnut Cove*. Mass.: Houghton Mifflin, 1995; 32pp., $14.95.

Ehlert, Lois. *Feathers for Lunch*. Calif.: Harcourt Brace Jovanovich, 1990; 32pp., $15.00.

————. *Snowballs*. Calif.: Harcourt Brace, 1995; 32pp., $15.00.

Elliot, Marion. *My Party Book*. Mass.: Little, Brown, 1994; 96pp., $14.95.

————. *Paper Fun for Kids*. N.Y.: Smithmark, 1994; 96pp., NA.

Elliott, Dan. *Ernie's Little Lie*. N.Y.: Random House, 1992; 40pp., $4.95.

————. *A Visit to the Sesame Street Firehouse*. N.Y.: Random House, 1983; 32pp., $6.00.

Emberley, Ed. *Go Away Big Green Monster*. Mass.: Little, Brown, 1992; 32pp., $14.45.

Emberley, Michael. *Ruby*. Mass.: Little, Brown, 1990; 32pp., $14.95.

Emberley, Rebecca. *My Mother's Secret Life*. Mass.: Little, Brown, 1998; 32pp., $15.95.

Enderle, Judith Ross. *A Pile of Pigs*. Pa: Bell, Boyds Mills, 1993; 32pp., $10.95.

Enderle, Judith Ross, and Stephanie Gordon Tessler. *Where Are You, Little Zack?* Mass.: Houghton Mifflin, 1997; 32pp., $14.95.

Engel. Diana. *Eleanor, Arthur, and Claire*. N.Y.: Macmillan, 1992; 32pp., $14.95.

————. *Josephina Hates Her Name*. N.Y.: Morrow Junior Books, 1989; 32pp., NA.

Ericsson, Jennifer A. *The Most Beautiful Kid in the World*. N.Y.: Tambourine, 1996; 32pp., $16.00.

Erlbach, Arlene. *Happy Birthday Everywhere*. Conn.: Millbrook, 1997; 48pp., $23.90.

————. *Sidewalk Games Around the World*. Conn.: Millbrook, 1997; 64pp., $23.90.

Ernst, Lisa Campbell. *The Bee*. N.Y.: Lothrop, Lee and Shepard, 1986; 32pp., $11.75.

————. *Bubba and Trixie*. N.Y.: Simon and Schuster, 1997; 32pp., $16.00.

————. *The Letters Are Lost*. N.Y.: Viking, 1996; 32pp., $14.99.

————. *Sam Johnson and the Blue Ribbon Quilt*. N.Y.: Lothrop, Lee and Shepard, 1983; 36p., $15.93.

————. *Walter's Tail*. N.Y.: Bradbury, 1992; 32pp., $14.95.

Esche, Maria Bonfanti, and Clare Bonfanti Braham. *Kids Celebrate!* Ill.: Chicago Review, 1998; 300pp., $16.95.

Etkin, Ruth. *The Rhythm Band Book*. N.Y.: Sterling, 1978; 32pp., $11.88.

Evans, Lezlie. *Rain Song*. Mass.: Houghton Mifflin, 1995; 32pp., $14.95.

Eversole, Robyn. *Flood Fish*. N.Y.: Crown, 1995; 32pp., $17.99.

————. *The Magic House*. N.Y.: Orchard, 1992; 32pp., $13.99.

Falk, John H., Robert L. Pruitt II, Kristi S. Rosenberg, and Tali A. Katz. *Bubble Monster and Other Science Fun*. Ill.: Chicago Review, 1996; 172pp., $17.95.

Farber, Norma. *Never Say Ugh to a Bug*. N.Y.: Greenwillow, 1979; 32pp., $11.88.

————. *Return of the Shadows*. N.Y.: HarperCollins, 1992; 32pp., $15.00.

Farmer, Nancy. *Runnery Granary*. N.Y.: Greenwillow, 1996; 32pp., $14.93.

Farrell, Sue. *To the Post Office with Mama*. N.Y.: Annick, 1994; 24pp., $14.95.

Farris, Diane. *In Dolphin Time*. N.Y.: Four Winds, 1994; 32pp., $14.95.

Fatio, Louise. *The Happy Lion*. N.Y.: McGraw-Hill, 1964; 32pp., $10.95.

————. *The Happy Lion in Africa.* N.Y.: McGraw-Hill, 1955; 28pp., $10.95.

————. *Hector Penguin.* N.Y.: McGraw-Hill, 1973; 29pp., $6.84.

Faulkner, William J. *Brer Tiger and the Big Wind.* N.Y.: Morrow Junior Books, 1995; 32pp., $15.00.

Feder, Paula. *Where Does the Teacher Live?* N.Y.: E. P. Dutton, 1996; 48pp., $9.19.

Feiffer, Jules. *I Lost My Bear.* N.Y.: Morrow Junior Books, 1998; 32pp., $16.00.

Fiarotta, Phyllis. *Snips and Snails and Walnut Whales.* N.Y.: Workman, 1975; 288pp., $9.95.

————. *Sticks and Stones and Ice Cream Cones.* N.Y.: Workman, 1973; 322pp., $10.95.

Fiarotta, Phyllis and Noel. *Be What You Want To Be!: The Complete Dress-up and Pretend Craft Book.* N.Y.: Workman, 1977; 304pp., $5.95.

————. *Confetti: The Kid's Make-It-Yourself, Do-It-Yourself Party Book.* N.Y.: Workman, Inc., 1978; 224pp., $10.95.

————. *Cups and Cans and Paper Plate Fans.* N.Y.: Sterling, 1992; 192pp., $19.95.

————. *Music Crafts for Kids.* N.Y.: Sterling, 1993; 160pp., $19.95.

————. *Pin It, Tack It, Hang It.* N.Y.: Workman Publishing Co. Inc., 1975; 283pp., $9.95.

————. *The You and Me Heritage Tree.* N.Y.: Workman, 1976; 285pp., $10.95.

Fine, Anne. *Poor Monty.* N.Y.: Clarion, 1991; 32pp., $14.95.

Fisher, Aileen Lucia. *Where Does Everyone Go?* N.Y.: Crowell, 1961; 30pp., $3.95.

Fisher, Leonard Everett. *Sailboat Lost.* N.Y.: Macmillan, 1991; 32pp., $15.95.

————. *William Tell.* N.Y.: Farrar, Straus and Giroux, 1996; 32pp., $16.00.

Flack, Marjorie. *Ask Mr. Bear.* N.Y.: Macmillan, 1986; 32pp., $14.00.

Flanagan, Alice K. *Officer Brown Keeps Neighborhoods Safe.* Ill.: Children's Press, 1998; 32pp., $19.50.

————. *Dr. Kranner, Dentist with a Smile.* Ill.: Children's Press, 1997; 32pp., $19.00.

Fleming, Denise. *Lunch.* N.Y.: Henry Holt, 1992; 32pp., $15.95.

————. *Where Once There Was a Wood.* N.Y.: Henry Holt, 1996; 32pp., $15.95.

Fleming, Gerry. *Scrap Craft for Youth Groups.* N.Y.: John Day, 1969; 216pp., $6.95.

Flood, Bo. *I'll Go to School If . . .* Minn.: Fairview Press, 1997; 32pp., $14.95.

Flora, James. *Leopold, The Sea-Through Crumbpicker.* Calif.: Harcourt Brace Jovanovich, 1961; 29pp., $5.95.

Florian, Douglas. *At the Zoo.* N.Y.: Greenwillow, 1992; 32pp., $13.93.

————. *A Beach Day.* N.Y.: Greenwillow, 1990; 32pp., $12.95.

————. *A Chef: How We Work.* N.Y.: Greenwillow, 1992; 32pp., $13.93.

————. *A Painter: How We Work.* N.Y.: Greenwillow, 1993; 32pp., $14.00.

————. *A Summer Day.* N.Y.: Greenwillow, 1988; 24pp., $12.95.

————. *Turtle Day.* N.Y.: Thomas Y. Crowell, 1989; 32pp., $15.90.

————. *A Winter Day.* N.Y.: Greenwillow, 1987; 24pp., $16.00.

Ford, Juwanda G. *K Is for Kwanzaa.* N.Y.: Scholastic, 1997; 32pp., $10.95.

Ford, Miela. *SunFlower.* N.Y.: Greenwillow, 1995; 32pp., $15.93.

————. *What Color Was the Sky Today?* N.Y.: Greenwillow, 1997; 24pp., $15.00.

Forte, Imogene. *The Kid's Stuff Book of Patterns, Projects and Plans.* Tenn.: Incentive Publishing, Inc., 1982; 199pp., $14.95.

Fowler, Allan. *Feeling Things.* Ill.: Children's Press, 1991; 32pp., $17.30.

————. *Hearing Things*. Ill.: Children's Press, 1991; 32pp., $18.00.

————. *Seeing Things*. Ill.: Children's Press, 1991; 32pp., $18.00.

————. *Smelling Things*. Ill.: Children's Press, 1991; 32pp., $18.00.

————. *Tasting Things*. Ill.: Children's Press, 1991; 32pp., $18.00.

Fowler, Susi L. *Fog*. N.Y.: Greenwillow, 1992; 32pp., $13.95.

————. *When Joel Comes Home*. N.Y.: Greenwillow, 1993; 24pp., NA.

————. *When Summer Ends*. N.Y.: Greenwillow, 1989; 32pp., NA.

Fox, Dan. *Songs of the Wild West*. N.Y.: Simon and Schuster Books for Young Readers, 1991; 128pp., $19.95.

Fox, Mem. *Boo to a Goose*. N.Y.: Dial Books for Young Readers, 1998; 32pp., $14.99.

————. *Tough Boris*. N.Y.: Harcourt Brace, 1994; 32pp., $15.00.

————. *Zoo-Looking*. N.Y.: Mondo, 1996; 32pp., $14.95.

Freedman, Sally. *Devin's New Bed*. Ill.: Albert Whitman, 1986; 32pp., $10.75.

Freeman, Don. *Bearymore*. N.Y.: Viking Penguin, 1979; 40pp., $4.99.

————. *The Chalk Box Story*. Pa.: J. B. Lippincott, 1976; 38pp., $13.95.

————. *Quiet! There's a Canary in the Library*. Ill.: Children's Press, 1969; 48pp., $10.60.

————. *The Seal and the Slick*. N.Y.: Viking, 1974; 32pp., $5.95.

————. *Space Witch*. N.Y.: Viking Penguin, 1979; 48pp., $3.95.

Freeman, Dorothy Rhodes, and Dianne M. Macmillan. *Kwanzaa*. N.J.: Enslow, 1992; 48p., $18.95.

Freeman, Jean. *Cynthia and the Unicorn*. N.Y.: W. W. Norton, 1967; unpaged, NA.

French, Fiona. *King of Another Country*. N.Y.: Scholastic, 1992; 32pp., $14.95.

French, Vivian. *A Christmas Star Called Hannah*. Mass.: Candlewick, 1997; 22pp., $9.99.

————. *Oliver's Fruit Salad*. N.Y.: Orchard, 1998; 32pp., $14.95.

————. *Red Hen and Sly Fox*. N.Y.: Simon and Schuster Books for Young Readers, 1994; 32pp., $15.00.

Friedrich, Priscilla and Otto. *The Easter Bunny that Overslept*. N.Y.: Lothrop, Lee and Shepard, 1983; 32pp., $4.93.

Friend, David. *Baseball, Football, Daddy, and Me*. N.Y.: Viking, 1990; 32pp., $12.95.

Fuchshuber, Annegert. *The Wishing Hat*. N.Y.: William Morrow, 1977; 28pp., $5.95.

Fyke, Nancy, Lynn Nejam, and Vicki Overstreet. *Great Parties for Kids*. Vt.: Williamson, 1994; 128pp., $10.95.

Gackenbach, Dick. *Annie and the Mud Monster*. N.Y.: Lothrop, Lee and Shepard, 1982; 29pp., $8.59.

————. *Claude and Pepper*. Mass.: Houghton Mifflin, 1974; 32pp., $10.95.

————. *Harry and the Terrible Whatzit*. Mass.: Houghton Mifflin, 1979; 32pp., $15.00.

————. *Hattie Be Quiet, Hattie Be Good*. N.Y.: Harper and Row Junior Books, 1977; 32pp., $9.89.

————. *The Perfect Mouse*. N.Y.: Macmillan, 1984; 32pp., $10.95.

————. *Poopy the Panda*. Mass.: Houghton Mifflin, 1984; 32pp., $11.95.

Gadsby, David, and Beatrice Harrop. *Flying a Round: 88 Rounds and Partner Songs*. London: A and C Black, 1982; 87pp., $15.95.

Gaffney, Timothy R. *Grandpa Takes Me to the Moon*. N.Y.: Tambourine, 1996; 32pp, $16.00.

Gag, Wanda. *The Funny Thing*. N.Y.: Putnam, 1999; 32pp., $9.98.

———. *Millions of Cats*. N.Y.: Putnam, 1996; 32pp., $12.99.

———. *Mrs. Gaddy and the Fast-Growing Vine*. N.Y.: Greenwillow, 1985; 47pp., NA.

———. *Mrs. Gaddy and the Ghost*. N.Y.: Greenwillow, 1979; 55 pp., $9.00.

Galdone, Paul. *The Gingerbread Boy*. Mass.: Houghton Mifflin, 1975; 40pp., $11.15.

———. *The Little Red Hen*. N.Y.: Seabury, 1973; 32pp., $15.00.

———. *Little Red Riding Hood*. N.Y.: McGraw-Hill, 1974; 32pp., $14.95.

———. *The Magic Porridge Pot*. Mass.: Houghton Mifflin, 1979; 32pp., $16.00.

———. *The Three Little Pigs*. Mass.: Houghton Mifflin, 1998; 32pp., $9.95.

———. *The Turtle and the Monkey*. N.Y.: Clarion, 1983; 32pp., $12.15.

Galdone, Paul and Joanna. *Honeybee's Party*. N.Y.: Franklin Watts, 1973; 32pp., $4.95.

Galef, David. *Tracks*. N.Y.: Morrow Junior Books, 1996; 32pp., $16.00.

Gannett, Ruth. *Katie and the Sad Noise*. N.Y.: Random House, 1961; 62pp., $2.39.

Gantos, Jack, and Nicole Rubel. *Back to School for Rotten Ralph*. N.Y.: HarperCollins, 1998; 32pp., $14.95.

Gantschev. Ivan. *The Train to Grandma's*. Mass.: Picture Book Studio, 1987; 32pp., $15.95.

Gardella, Tricia. *Casey's New Hat*. Mass.: Houghton Mifflin, 1997; 32pp., $14.95.

Garrity, Linda K. *The Gingerbread Guide*. Ill.: Good Year, 1987; 96pp., $9.95.

Gauch, Patricia Lee. *Christina Katerina and the Great Bear Train*. N.Y.: G. P. Putnam's Sons, 1990; 32pp., $14.95.

Gay, Michel. *Bibi Takes Flight*. N.Y.: Morrow Junior Books, 1984; 32pp., $11.88.

Geisel, Theodor. *The 500 Hats of Bartholomew Cubbins*. N.Y.: Vanguard, 1990; 44pp., $14.00.

Geoghegan, Adrienne. *Dogs Don't Wear Glasses*. N.Y.: Crocodile Books, USA, 1996; 32pp., $14.95.

George, Jean Craighead. *Dear Rebecca, Winter Is Here*. N.Y.: HarperCollins, 1993; 32pp., $15.00.

Geraghty, Paul. *Slobcat*. N.Y.: Macmillan, 1991; 32pp., $13.95.

———. *Solo*. N.Y.: Crown, 1995; 32pp., $18.99.

Gershator, Phillis. *Zzzng! Zzzng! Zzzng!: A Yoruba Tale*. N.Y.: Orchard, 1998; 32pp., $15.95.

Gerson, Mary Joan. *People of Corn*. Mass.: Little, Brown, 1995; 32pp., $15.95.

Gerstein, Mordicai. *Arnold of the Ducks*. N.Y.: Harper and Row Junior Books, 1983; 64pp., $12.95.

———. *The Story of May*. N.Y.: HarperCollins, 1993; 48pp., $15.89.

———. *Roll Over!* N.Y.: Crown Publishers, 1988; 32pp., $12.00.

Giannini, Enzo. *Zorina Ballerina*. N.Y.: Simon and Schuster Books for Young Readers, 1993; 32pp., $14.00.

Gibala-Broxholm, Janice. *Let Me Do It!* N.Y.: Bradbury, 1994; 32pp, $14.95.

Gibbons, Gail. *Catch the Wind!: All about Kites*. Mass.: Little, Brown, 1989; 32pp., $10.15.

———. *Fire! Fire!* N.Y.: Harper and Row Junior Books, 1984; 40pp., $11.89.

———. *The Honey Makers*. N.Y.: Morrow Junior Books, 1997; 32pp., $15.95.

———. *Penguins!* N.Y.: Holiday House, 1998; 32pp., $16.95.

———. *Pirates: Robbers of the High Seas*. Mass.: Little, Brown, 1993; 32pp., $15.95.

———. *The Post Office Book: Mail and How It Moves*. N.Y.: Thomas Y. Crowell, 1982; 32pp., $14.89.

———. *St. Patrick's Day*. N.Y.: Holiday House, 1994; 32pp., $15.95.

———. *Thanksgiving Day*. N.Y.: Holiday House, 1983; 32pp., $15.95.

———. *Yippee-Yay!: A Book about Cowboys and Cowgirls*. Mass.: Little, Brown, 1998; 32pp., $14.95.

Giffard, Hannah. *Red Fox on the Move*. N.Y.: Dial Books for Young Readers, 1992; 28pp., $14.00.

Gilbreath, Alice. *Beginning Crafts for Beginning Readers*. Ill.: Follett, 1972; 32pp., $5.97.

———. *Making Toys that Crawl and Slide*. Ill.: Follett, 1978; 32pp., $5.97.

———. *More Beginning Crafts for Beginning Readers*. Ill.: Follett, 1976; 32pp., $5.97.

Ginsburg, Mirra. *Mushroom in the Rain*. N.Y.: Macmillan, 1974; 32pp., $5.99.

Girard, Linda Walvoord. *We Adopted You, Benjamin Koo*. Ill.: Albert Whitman, 1989; 32pp., $14.95.

———. *Who Is a Stranger and What Should I Do?* Ill.: Albert Whitman, 1985; 32pp., $13.95.

Girl Scouts of America. *Games for Girl Scouts*. N.Y.: Girl Scouts of the USA, 1990; 128pp., $6.50.

Givens, Terryl. *Dragon Scales and Willow Leaves*. N.Y.: G. P. Putnam's Sons, 1997; 32pp., $12.95.

Glaser, Linda. *The Borrowed Hanukkah Latkes*. Ill.: Albert Whitman, 1997; 32pp., $15.95.

Glass, Andrew. *Charles Tarzan McBiddle*. N.Y.: Doubleday Books for Young Readers, 1993; 32pp., $15.00.

Glass, Marvin. *What Happened Today, Freddy Groundhog?* N.Y.: Crown, 1989; 32pp., NA.

Glazer, Tom. *Do Your Ears Hang Low?* N.Y.: Doubleday, 1980; 96pp., $12.95.

———. *Eye Winker, Tom Tinker, Chin Chopper*. N.Y.: Doubleday, 1973; 91pp., $10.95.

———. *Music for Ones and Twos*. N.Y.: Doubleday, 1983; 96pp., $7.95.

Gleiter, Jan, and Kathleen Thompson. *Johnny Appleseed*. Wisc.: Raintree Children's Books, 1987; 32pp., NA.

Glennon, Karen M. *Miss Eva and the Red Balloon*. N.Y.: Simon and Schuster Books for Young Readers, 1990; 32pp., $13.95.

Gliori, Debi. *Mr. Bear Babysits*. N.Y.: Western, 1994; 32pp., $13.95.

Glovach, Linda. *The Little Witch's Black Magic Book of Games*. N.J.: Prentice-Hall, 1974; 48pp., $4.95.

Goennel, Heidi. *The Circus*. N.Y.: Tambourine, 1992; 32pp., $15.00.

———. *When I Grow Up . . . .* Mass.: Little, Brown, 1987; 30pp., $12.95.

Goffe, Toni. *Joe Giant's Missing Boot: A Mothergooseville Story.* N.Y.: Lothrop, Lee and Shepard, 1990; 32pp., $12.95.

Goffstein, M.B. *Fish for Supper.* N.Y.: Dial Books for the Young, 1976; 32pp., $5.89.

———. *Laughing Latkes.* N.Y.: Farrar, Straus and Giroux, 1980; 32pp., $6.95.

Gogniat, Maurice. *Indian Toys You Can Make.* N.Y.: Sterling, 1974; 32pp., NA.

Golder, Stephen, and Lise Memling. *Buffy's Orange Leash.* D.C.: Kendall Green, 1988; 32pp., NA.

Goldin, Barbara Diamond. *Cakes and Miracles: A Purim Tale.* N.Y.: Viking, 1991; 32pp., $13.95.

Goldman, Dara. *The Hiccup Cure.* N.Y.: G. P. Putnam's Sons, 1989; 32pp., $9.95.

Goldsmith, Howard. *Sleepy Little Owl.* N.Y.: Learning Triangle, 1997; 32pp., $12.95.

Goldstone, Bruce. *The Feastly Feast.* N.Y.: Henry, Holt and Co., 1998; 32pp., $15.95.

Gomi, Taro. *Spring Is Here.* Calif.: Chronicle, 1989; 34pp., $11.95.

Goodman, Joan Elizabeth. *Bernard's Bath.* Pa.: Boyds Mills, 1996; 32pp., $14.95.

Gordon, Margaret. *The Supermarket Mice.* N.Y.: E. P. Dutton, 1984; 32pp., $10.95.

Goss, Linda. *The Frog Who Wanted to Be a Singer.* N.Y.: Orchard, 1996; 40pp., $15.95.

Goss, Linda and Clay. *It's Kwanzaa Time!* N.Y.: G. P. Putnam's Sons, 1989; 72pp., $19.95.

Gould, Roberta. *Making Cool Crafts and Awesome Art.* Vt.: Williamson, 1998; 158pp., $12.95.

Graham, Al. *Timothy Turtle.* Calif.: Harcourt Brace Jovanovich, 1940; 28pp., $5.95.

Graham, Margaret. *Benjy's Boat Trip.* N.Y.: Harper and Row Junior Books, 1977; 30pp., $13.89.

Graham, Terry Lynne, and Linda Camp. *Teaching Terrific Twos and Other Toddlers.* Ga.: Humanics Learning, 1988; 206pp., $28.95.

Graham, Thomas. *Mr. Bear's Boat.* N.Y.: E. P. Dutton, 1988; 32pp., $3.95.

Gramatky, Hardie. *Little Toot and the Loch Ness Monster.* N.Y.: G. P. Putnam's Sons, 1989; 47pp., $13.95.

Gravois, Jeanne M. *Quickly, Quigley.* N.Y.: Tambourine, 1993; 32pp., $14.00.

Gray, Libba Moore. *Small Green Snake.* N.Y.: Orchard, 1994; 32p., $14.95.

———. *Is there Room on the Feather Bed?* N.Y.: Orchard, 32pp., $16.95.

Green, Jen. *Why Throw it Away? Making Crazy Animals.* N.Y.: Gloucester, 1992; 32pp., NA.

Greenberg, Barbara. *The Bravest Babysitter.* N.Y.: Dial for the Young, 1977; 32pp., $6.46.

Greenberg, Judith. *What Is the Sign for Friend?* N.Y.: Franklin Watts, 1985; 32pp., NA.

Greenblat, Rodney A. *Aunt Ippy's Museum of Junk.* N.Y.: HarperCollins, 1991; 32pp., $14.90.

Greene, Carol. *Cat and Bear.* N.Y.: Hyperion Children's Books, 1998; 32pp., $14.49.

———. *Police Officers Protect People.* N.Y.: The Child's World, 1997; 32pp., $21.36.

Greene, Ellin. *The Pumpkin Giant*. N.Y.: Lothrop, Lee and Shepard, 1970; 40pp., NA.

Greene, Graham. *The Little Train*. N.Y.: Doubleday, 1973; 42pp., $5.95.

Greene, Rhonda Gowler. *When a Line Bends . . . Shape Begins*. N.Y.: Houghton Mifflin, 1997; 32pp., $16.00.

Greenstein, Elaine. *Mrs. Rose's Garden*. N.Y.: Simon and Schuster Books for Young Readers, 1996; 28pp., $15.00.

———. *Emily and the Crows*. Mass.: Picture Book Studio, 1992; 32pp., $14.95.

Gregory, Valiska. *Babysitting for Benjamin*. Mass.: Little, Brown, 1993; 32pp., $13.95.

———. *Kate's Giants*. Mass.: Candlewick, 1995; 40pp., $14.95.

Gretz, Susanna. *It's Your Turn, Roger!* N.Y.: Dial Books for Young Readers, 1985; 32pp., $10.95.

Greydanus, Rose. *Animals at the Zoo*. N.J.: Troll Associates, 1997; 32pp., $2.50.

Grier, Ella. *Seven Days of Kwanzaa*. N.Y.: Viking, 1997; 32pp., $10.99.

Grimm, Jacob. *Rumplestiltskin*. N.Y.: Holiday House, 1983; 32pp., $10.95.

———. *Snow White and the Seven Dwarfs*. Mass.: Picture Book Studio USA, 1985; 40pp., $13.95.

Grossman, Bill. *Donna O'Neeshuck Was Chased by Some Cows*. N.Y.: Harper and Row, Publishers, 1988; 32pp., $12.95.

———. *My Little Sister Ate One Hare*. N.Y.: Crown, 1996; 24pp., $17.99.

Gunson, Christopher. *Over on the Farm*. N.Y.: Scholastic, 1995; 32pp., $15.95.

Guthrie, Woody, and Marjorie Mazia Guthrie. *Woody's 20 Grow Big Songs*. N.Y.: HarperCollins, 1992; 48pp., $16.00.

Guy, Rose. *Mother Crocodile*. N.Y.: Delacorte, 1996; 32pp., $6.50.

Haas, Jessie. *Mowing*. N.Y.: Greenwillow, 1994; 32pp., $14.00.

Habrin, E. O. *The Fun Encyclopedia*. N.Y.: Abingdon, 1968; 1008pp., $6.95.

Hadithi, Mwenye. *Lazy Lion*. Mass.: Little, Brown, 1990; 32pp., $14.95.

Hadithi, Mwenye, and Adrienne Kennaway. *Hungry Hyena*. Mass.: Little, Brown, 1994; 32pp., $15.95.

Hague, Michael. *The Perfect Present*. N.Y.: Morrow Junior Books, 1996; 32pp., $16.00.

Haley, Gail E. *The Post Office Cat*. N.Y.: Charles Scribner's Sons, 1976; 32pp., $6.95.

Hall, Donald. *Lucy's Summer*. Calif.: Browndeer, 1995; 40pp., $15.00.

Hall, Zoe. *The Apple Pie Tree*. N.Y.: Blue Sky, 1996; 32pp., $13.95.

———. *The Surprise Garden*. N.Y.: Blue Sky, 1998; 32pp., $15.95.

Halpern, Shari. *Moving from One to Ten*. N.Y.: Macmillan, 1993; 32pp., $13.95.

Hamm, Diane Johnston. *Rock-a-Bye Farm*. N.Y.: Simon and Schuster Books for Young Readers, 1992; 40pp., $15.00.

Hamsa, Bobbie. *Your Pet Penguin*. Ill.: Children's Press, 1994; 32pp., $17.60.

Hancock, David, Jill Hancock, Anna Murray, Lyn Orton, Cheryl Owen, and Lynda Watts. *The Grolier KidsCrafts Papercraft Book*. Conn.: Grolier Educational, 1997; 48pp., NA.

Hariton, Anca. *Butterfly Story*. N.Y.: Dutton Children's Books, 1995; 32pp., $14.99.

Harper, Anita. *It's Not Fair!* N.Y.: G. P. Putnam's Sons, 1986; 32pp., $9.95.

————. *What Feels Best?* N.Y.: G. P. Putnam's Sons, 1988; 24pp., $11.95.

Harrell, Beatrice Orcutt. *How Thunder and Lightning Came to Be.* N.Y.: Dial Books for Young Readers, 1995; 32pp., $14.89.

Harris, Kate. *Party Plans for Tots.* Ill.: Follett, 1967; 159pp., $2.95.

Harrison, David L. *When Cows Come Home.* Pa.: Boyds Mills Press, 1994; 32pp., $15.95.

Harrop, Beatrice. *Sing Hey Diddle Diddle.* London: A & C Black, 1983; 66pp., $9.95.

Harry, Cindy Groom, and staff. *One-Hour Holiday Crafts for Kids.* Ill.: Publications International, 1994; 64pp., $4.95.

Hart, Jane. *Singing Bee!: A Collection of Favorite Children's Songs.* N.Y.: Lothrop, Lee and Shepard, 1982; 160pp., $17.95.

Harvey, Amanda. *Stormy Weather.* N.Y.: Lothrop, Lee and Shepard, 1991; 32pp., $13.95.

Hasbrouck, Ellen K. *Library Storyhour from A to Z.* N.Y.: The Center for Applied Research in Education, 1998; 269pp., $28.95.

Haseley, Dennis. *The Pirate Who Tried to Capture the Moon.* N.Y.: Harper & Row, Publishers, 1983; 42pp., $8.89.

Hassett, John and Ann. *We Got My Brother at the Zoo.* Mass.: Houghton Mifflin, 1993; 32pp., $14.95.

Hautzig, Deborah. *A Visit to the Sesame Street Hospital.* N.Y.: Random House, 1985; 32pp., $3.25.

————. *A Visit to the Sesame Street Library.* N.Y.: Random House, 1986; 32pp., $3.25.

Haviland, Virginia. *The Talking Pot.* Mass.: Little, Brown, 1971; 32pp., $14.95.

Havill, Juanita. *Jamaica's Blue Marker.* Mass.: Houghton Mifflin, 1995; 28pp., $15.00.

————. *Leroy and the Clock.* Mass.: Houghton Mifflin, 1988; 332pp., $13.95.

Hawes, Judy. *Ladybug, Ladybug, Fly Away Home.* N.Y.: Harper and Row, 1967; 32pp., $10.89.

Hawkes, Kevin. *His Royal Buckliness.* N.Y.: Lothrop, Lee and Shepard, 1992; 32pp., $14.93.

Hayes, Sarah. *Mary, Mary.* N.Y.: Margaret K. McElderry, 1990; 32pp., $13.95.

————. *The Grumpalump.* N.Y.: Clarion, 1990; 32pp., $14.95.

————. *This Is the Bear and the Bad Little Girl.* Mass.: Candlewick, 1995; 26pp., $12.95.

Hayles, Karen, and Charles Fuge. *Whale Is Stuck.* N.Y.: Simon and Schuster Books for Young Readers, 1992; 32pp., $14.00.

Hayles, Marsha. *Beach Play.* N.Y.: Henry Holt, 1998; 32pp., $14.95.

Haynes, Max. *Dinosaur Island.* N.Y.: Lothrop, Lee and Shepard, 1991; 32pp., $13.95.

————. *In the Driver's Seat.* N.Y.: Bantam Doubleday Dell, 1997; 26pp., $12.95.

Hazelaar, Cor. *Zoo Dreams.* N.Y.: Frances Foster, 1997; 32pp., $14.00.

Hazell, Bee Gee. *Paper Plate Animals.* N.Y.: Instructo/McGraw-Hill, 1982; 22pp., $3.95.

Hazen, Barbara. *The Me I See!* Tenn.: Abingdon, 1978; unpaged, $5.21.

Hazen, Barbara Shook. *Mommy's Office*. N.Y.: Atheneum, 1992; 32pp., $13.95.

Healton, Sarah H. *Look What I Made!* Pa.: Tab, 1993; 110pp., $16.95.

Heap, Sue. *Cowboy Baby*. Mass.: Candlewick, 1998; 32pp., $15.99.

Hearn, Diane Dawson. *Dad's Dinosaur Day*. N.Y.: Macmillan, 1993; 32pp., $16.00.

Hebert, Holly. *60 Super Simple Crafts*. Calif.: Lowell House Juvenile, 1996; 80pp., $6.95.

Hedderwick, Mairi. *Katie Morag Delivers the Mail*. Mass.: Little, Brown, 1984; 32pp., $13.95.

Heinz, Brian J. *The Monsters' Test*. Conn.: Millbrook, 1996; 32pp., $14.95.

Hellard, Susan. *Eleanor and the Babysitter*. Mass.: Little, Brown, 1991; 32pp., $13.95.

Heller, Nicholas. *The Giant*. N.Y.: Greenwillow, 1997; 24 pp., $14.93.

———. *Goblins in Green*. N.Y.: Greenwillow, 1995; 32pp., $16.00.

Henderson, Roxanne. *The Picture Rulebook of Kids' Games*. Ill.: Contemporary Books, 1996; 240pp., $14.95.

Hendra, Sue. *Oliver's Wood*. Mass.: Candlewick, 1996; 32pp., $15.99.

Henkes, Kevin. *Chrysanthemum*. N.Y.: Greenwillow, 1991; 32pp., $16.00.

———. *Good-bye, Curtis*. N.Y.: Greenwillow, 1995; 24pp., $14.93.

———. *Jessica*. N.Y.: Greenwillow, 1989; 24pp., $11.95.

Hennessy, B. G. *Olympics!* N.Y.: Viking, 1996; 32pp., $14.99.

———. *Road Builders*. N.Y.: Viking, 1994; 32pp., $14.99.

———. *School Days*. N.Y.: Viking, 1990; 32pp., $13.95.

Henri, Adrian, and Simon Henwood. *The Postman's Palace*. N.Y.: Atheneum, 1990; 32pp., $13.95.

Henry, Sandi. *Cut-Paper Play!* Vt.: Williamson, 1997; 160pp., $12.95.

Herman, Emily. *Hubknuckles*. N.Y.: Crown, 1985; 32pp., $9.95.

Hermann, Helen and Bill. *Jenny's Magic Wand*. N.Y.: Franklin Watts, 1988; 32pp., NA.

Hest, Amy. *The Best Ever Good-bye Party*. N.Y.: Morrow Junior Books, 1989; 30pp, $13.95.

———. *Baby Duck and the Bad Eyeglasses*. Mass.: Candlewick, 1996; 32pp., $16.99.

———. *Rosie's Fishing Trip*. Mass.: Candlewick, 1994; 32pp., $13.95.

———. *Ruby's Storm*. N.Y.: Four Winds, 1994; 32pp., $14.95.

Hetzer, Linda. *50 Fabulous Parties for Kids*. N.Y.: Crown Trade Paperbacks, 1994; 176pp., $10.00.

Hewitt, Kathryn. *King Midas and the Golden Touch*. Calif.: Harcourt Brace Jovanovich, 1987; 29pp., $12.95.

Hiatt, Fred. *If I Were Queen of the World*. N.Y.: Margaret K. McElderry, 1997; 32pp., $16.00.

Hill, Eric. *Good Morning, Baby Bear*. N.Y.: Random House, 1984; 24p., $4.99.

———. *Where's Spot? (Sign Language Edition)*. N.Y.: G. P. Putnam's Sons, 1987; 32pp., $11.95.

Hill, Lee Sullivan. *Libraries Take Us Far*. Minn.: Carolrhoda, 1998; 32pp., $19.95.

Hillert, Margaret. *The Three Bears*. Ohio: Modern Curriculum Press, 1963; 32pp., $7.95.

Hilton, Nette. *Andrew Jessup*. N.Y.: Ticknor and Fields Books for Young Readers, 1993; 32pp., $13.95.

———. *The Long Red Scarf*. Minn.: Carolrhoda Books, Inc., 1987; 32pp., $13.95.

———. *A Proper Little Lady*. N.Y.: Orchard, 1989; 32pp., NA.

Himmelman, John. *A Ladybug's Life*. Conn.: Children's Press, 1998; 32pp., $17.25.

———. *Light's Out!* N.Y.: Bridgewater, 1995; 32pp., $13.95.

———. *The Talking Tree or Don't Believe Everything You Hear*. N.Y.: Viking, 1986; 32pp., $9.95.

Hindley, Judy. *Uncle Harold and the Green Hat*. N.Y.: Farrar, Straus and Giroux, 1991; 26pp., $13.95.

Hines, Anna Grossnickle. *All by Myself*. N.Y.: Clarion, 1985; 32pp., $10.95.

———. *Big Help!* N.Y.: Clarion, 1995; 32pp., $13.95.

———. *Big Like Me*. N.Y.: Greenwillow, 1989; 32pp., $15.93.

———. *Daddy Makes the Best Spaghetti*. N.Y.: Clarion, 1986; 32pp., $15.00.

———. *Even if I Spill My Milk?* N.Y.: Clarion, 1994; 32pp., $13.95.

———. *Keep Your Old Hat*. N.Y.: E. P. Dutton, 1987; 24pp., $8.95.

———. *My Own Big Bed*. N.Y.: Greenwillow, 1998; 24pp., $20.75.

———. *They Really Like Me!* N.Y.: Greenwillow, 1989; 24pp., $11.95.

———. *When the Goblins Came Knocking*. N.Y.: Greenwillow, 1995; 26pp., $14.93.

Hinton, S. E. *Big David, Little David*. N.Y.: Doubleday Books for Young Readers, 1995; 34pp., $15.95.

Hirsch, Marilyn. *I Love Hanukkah*. N.Y.: Holiday House, 1984; 32pp., $12.95.

———. *Potato Pancakes All Around*. Pa.: Jewish Publications Society, 1982; 34pp., $5.95.

Hirschi, Ron. *Summer*. N.Y.: Cobblehill, 1991; 32pp., $15.99.

Hiskey, Iris. *Cassandra Who?* N.Y.: Simon and Schuster Books for Young Readers, 1992; 32pp., $14.00.

Hissey, Jane. *Hoot*. N.Y.: Random House, 1997; 32pp., $18.00.

———. *Jolly Snow*. N.Y.: Philomel, 1991; 32pp., $14.95.

Hoban, Lillian. *Arthur's Honey Bear*. N.Y.: Harper and Row Junior Books, 2000; 64pp., $14.95.

———. *Arthur's Loose Tooth*. N.Y.: HarperCollins Children's Books, 1985; 64pp., $11.95.

———. *Silly Tilly's Thanksgiving Dinner*. N.Y.: Harper and Row, 1990; 64pp., $15.89.

———. *Turtle Spring*. N.Y.: Greenwillow, 1978; 47pp., $5.49.

Hoban, Russell. *A Baby Sitter for Frances*. N.Y.: Harper and Row Junior Books, 1964; 28pp., $11.89.

———. *A Bargain for Frances*. N.Y.: Harper and Row Junior Books, 1970; 64pp., $10.89.

———. *Dinner at Alberta's*. N.Y.: Harper and Row Junior Books, 1975; 40pp., $17.00.

Hoban, Tana. *Circles, Triangles, and Squares*. N.Y.: Macmillan, 1974; 32pp., $15.00.

———. *Construction Zone*. N.Y.: Greenwillow, 1997; 32pp., $15.00.

———. *Dig, Drill, Dump, Fill*. N.Y.: Greenwillow, 1975; 32pp., $15.93.

———. *Is It Red? Is It Yellow? Is It Blue?* N.Y.: Greenwillow, 1987; 32pp., $4.95.

―――. *So Many Circles, So Many Squares*. N.Y.: Greenwillow, 1998; 32pp., $15.00.

―――. *Where Is It?* N.Y.: Macmillan, 1974; 28pp., $15.00.

Hobbie, Holly. *Toot and Puddle*. Mass.: Little, Brown, 1997; 32pp., $12.95.

Hoberman, Mary Ann. *Miss Mary Mack*. Mass.: Little, Brown, 1998; 32pp., $14.95.

―――. *One of Each*. Mass.: Little, Brown, 1997; 32pp., $15.95.

Hoff, Syd. *Duncan the Dancing Duck*. N.Y.: Clarion, 1994; 32pp., $13.95.

―――. *Grizzwold*. N.Y.: Harper and Row Junior Books, 1963; 64pp., $14.89.

―――. *Henrietta, Circus Star*. Md.: Garrard, 1978; 32pp., $6.69.

―――. *Henrietta's Fourth of July*. Md.: Garrard, 1981; 32pp., $6.69.

―――. *The Littlest Leaguer*. N.J.: Windmill, 1976; 48pp., $2.50.

―――. *Oliver*. N.Y.: Harper and Row Junior Books, 1960; 64pp., $14.89.

―――. *Sammy the Seal*. N.Y.: Harper and Row Junior Books, 1959; 64pp., $10.89.

―――. *Stanley*. N.Y.: Harper and Row, 1962; 64pp., $13.00.

―――. *Slithers*. N.Y.: Putnam, 1968; 48pp., $15.89.

―――. *When Will It Snow?* N.Y.: Harper and Row Junior Books, 1971; 32pp., $11.89.

Hoffman, Mary. *Amazing Grace*. N.Y.: Dial Books for Young Readers, 1991; 32pp., $15.99.

―――. *Henry's Baby*. N.Y.: Dorling Kindersley, 1993; 32pp., $13.95.

Hofmeyr, Dianne. *Do the Whales Still Sing?* N.Y.: Dial Books for Young Readers, 1995; 28pp., NA.

Hogan, Paula Z. *The Honeybee*. Milwaukee: Raintree Children's Books, 1979; 32pp., $14.95.

Hogrogian, Nonny. *Carrot Cake*. N.Y.: Greenwillow, 1977; 27pp., $10.51.

Hogstrom, Daphne. *Little Boy Blue: Finger Plays for Old and New*. Wisc.: Golden, 1966; 23pp., $3.95.

Hoguet, Susan. *I Unpacked My Grandmother's Trunk*. N.Y.: E. P. Dutton, 1983; 58pp., $10.95.

Hol, Coby. *Henrietta Saves the Show*. N.Y.: North-South, 1991; 28pp., $14.95.

Holabird, Katharine. *Alexander and the Magic Boat*. N.Y.: Clarkson N. Potter, 1990; 32p., $11.95.

Holl, Adelaide. *The Rain Puddle*. N.Y.: Lothrop, Lee and Shepard, 1965; 64pp., $11.88.

Holley, Cynthia, and Jane Walkup. *First Time, Circle Time*. Calif.: Fearon Teachers Aids, 1993; 287pp., $20.99.

Hooker, Ruth. *Matthew the Cowboy*. Ill.: Albert Whitman, 1990; 32pp., $14.95.

Hooks, William H. *Rough Tough Rowdy*. N.Y.: Viking, 1992; 32pp., $12.50.

Houck, Eric L. Jr., *Rabbit Surprise*. N.Y.: Crown, 1993; 28; $15.00.

Houghton, Eric. *The Backwards Watch*. N.Y.: Orchard, 1991; 30pp., NA.

―――. *Walter's Magic Wand*. N.Y.: Orchard, 1989; 32pp., NA.

Howard, Ellen. *The Big Seed*. N.Y.: Simon and Schuster Books for Young Readers, 1993; 32pp., $14.00.

Howard, Kim. *In Wintertime*. N.Y.: Lothrop, Lee and Shepard, 1994; 30pp., $15.95.

Howe, Caroline. *Counting Penguins*. N.Y.: Harper and Row Junior Books, 1983; 32pp., $11.89.

Howe, James. *Creepy-Crawly Birthday*. N.Y.: Morrow Junior Books, 1991; 48pp., $13.95.

⸻. *The Day the Teacher Went Bananas*. N.Y.: E. P. Dutton, 1984; 32pp., $9.95.

⸻. *Hot Fudge*. N.Y.: Morrow Junior Books, 1990; 48pp., $13.88.

⸻. *There's a Dragon in My Sleeping Bag*. N.Y.: Atheneum, 1994; 40pp., $14.95.

Howland, Naomi. *ABCDrive!* N.Y.: Clarion, 1994; 30pp., $13.95.

Hoyt-Goldsmith, Diane. *Celebrating Kwanzaa*. N.Y.: Holiday House, 1993; 32pp., $15.95.

Huff, Barbara A. *Once Inside the Library*. Mass.: Little, Brown, 1985; 32pp., $14.95.

Hughes, Peter. *The Emperor's Oblong Pancake*. N.Y.: Abelard-Schuman, 1961; unpaged, NA.

Hughes, Shirley. *Alfie's ABC*. N.Y.: Lothrop, Lee and Shepard, 1998; 32pp., $16.00.

Hunt, Sarah Ethridge. *Games the World Around*. N.Y.: A. S. Barnes and Company, 1941; 268pp., NA.

Hunt, Tamara. *Pocketful of Puppets*. Tex.: Nancy Renfro, 1984; 80pp., $12.95.

Hunter, Anne. *Possum and the Peeper*. Mass.: Houghton Mifflin, 1998; 32pp., $15.00.

⸻. *Possum's Harvest Moon*. Mass.: Houghton Mifflin, 1996; 32pp., $14.95.

Hurd, Edith. *Johnny Lion's Book*. N.Y.: Harper and Row Junior Books, 1965; 64pp., $15.89.

⸻. *Last One Home is a Green Pig*. N.Y.: Harper and Row Junior Books, 1959; 64pp., $10.89.

⸻. *Starfish*. N.Y.: Harper and Row Junior Books, 1962; 32pp., $12.89.

Hurd, Thacher. *Art Dog*. N.Y.: Harper and Row, 1996; 32pp., $14.95.

⸻. *Little Mouse's Big Valentine*. N.Y.: Harper and Row, 1992; 32pp., $9.90.

⸻. *Mama Don't Allow*. N.Y.: Harper and Row Junior Books, 1985; 40pp., $5.95.

⸻. *Mystery on the Docks*. N.Y.: Harper and Row, 1983; 32pp, $9.95.

Hutchings, Amy and Richard. *Firehouse Dog*. N.Y.: Scholastic, 1993; 32pp., $2.99.

Hutchins, Pat. *Good-night Owl!* N.Y.: Macmillan, 1972; 32pp., $16.00.

⸻. *Happy Birthday, Sam*. N.Y.: Greenwillow, 1992; 32pp., $15.95.

⸻. *King Henry's Palace*. N.Y.: Greenwillow, 1983; 56pp., $10.25.

⸻. *My Best Friend*. N.Y.: Greenwillow, 1993; 32pp., $15.93.

⸻. *Shrinking Mouse*. N.Y.: Greenwillow, 1997; 32pp., $15.00.

⸻. *Three-Star Billy*. N.Y.: Greenwillow, 1994; 32pp., $14.93.

⸻. *Tidy Titch*. N.Y.: Greenwillow, 1991; 32pp., $16.50.

⸻. *What Game Shall We Play?* N.Y.: Greenwillow, 1990; 32pp., $10.15.

⸻. *You'll Soon Grow into Them, Titch*. N.Y.: Greenwillow, 1983; 32pp, $15.93.

Ichikawa, Satomi. *Bravo, Tanya*. N.Y.: Philomel, 1992; 30pp., $14.95.

Inkpen, Mick. *Billy's Beetle*. N.Y.: Harcourt Brace Jovanovich, 1991; 30pp., $13.95.

⸻. *The Blue Balloon*. Mass.: Little, Brown, 1989; 32pp., $14.95.

⸻. *Nothing*. N.Y.: Orchard, 1995; 32pp., $14.95.

Intrater, Roberta Grobel. *Two Eyes, a Nose, and a Mouth*. N.Y.: Scholastic, 1995; 32pp., $12.95.

Ipcar, Dahlov. *The Biggest Fish in the Sea*. N.Y.: Viking Penguin, 1972; unpaged, $4.95.

Irving, Jan, and Robin Currie. *Glad Rags*. Colo.: Libraries Unlimited, 1987; 276pp., NA.

Isadora, Rachel. *Ben's Trumpet*. N.Y.: Greenwillow, 1979; 32pp., $13.00.

———. *The Pirates of Bedford Street*. N.Y.: Greenwillow, 1988; 32pp., $11.88.

———. *A South African Night*. N.Y.: Greenwillow, 1998; 24pp., $15.00.

Isele, Elizabeth. *The Frog Princess: A Russian Tale Retold*. N.Y.: Harper and Row Junior Books, 1984; 32pp., $11.89.

Isenberg, Barbara, and Marjorie Jaffe. *Albert the Running Bear's Exercise Book*. N.Y.: Clarion, 1984; 63pp., $13.95.

Iwamura, Kazuo. *Tan Tan's Hat*. N.Y.: Bradbury, 1983; 40pp., $7.95.

Jabar, Cynthia. *Alice Ann Gets Ready for School*. Mass.: Little, Brown, 1989; 32pp., $13.95.

Jakob, Donna. *Tiny Toes*. N.Y.: Hyperion Books for Children, 1995; 32pp., $14.49.

James, Betsy. *Mary Ann*. N.Y.: Dutton Children's Books, 1994; 32pp., $14.99.

James, Simon. *Sally and the Limpet*. N.Y.: Margaret K. McElderry, 1991; 32pp., $13.95.

Janice. *Harold's Trip to the Sky*. N.Y.: Harper and Row Junior Books, 1957; 64pp., $10.89.

———. *Little Bear's Christmas*. N.Y.: Lothrop, Lee and Shepard, 1964; 26pp., $10.88.

———. *Little Bear's Pancake Party*. N.Y.: Lothrop, Lee and Shepard, 1981; 34pp., $10.88.

———. *Little Bear's Thanksgiving*. N.Y.: Lothrop, Lee and Shepard, 1981; 64pp., $2.50.

Janovitz, Marilyn. *Can I Help?* N.Y.: North-South, 1996; 32pp., $13.95.

———. *What Could Be Keeping Santa?* N.Y.: North-South, 1997; 32pp., $15.90.

Jaramillo, Nelly Palacio. *Grandmother's Nursery Rhymes*. N.Y.: Henry Holt, 1994; 32pp., $14.95.

Jenkins, Jessica. *Thinking about Colors*. N.Y.: Dutton Children's Books, 1992; 32pp., $14.00.

Jenkins, Priscilla Belz. *A Safe Home for Manatees*. N.Y.: HarperCollins, 1997; 32pp., $14.90.

Jenkins, Steve. *Big and Little*. Mass.: Houghton Mifflin, 1996; 32pp., $14.95.

Jennings, Linda. *The Brave Little Bunny*. N.Y.: Dutton Children's Books, 1995; 32pp., $13.99.

———. *Easy Peasy!* N.Y.: Farrar, Straus and Giroux, 1997; 28pp., $14.00.

Jenny, Gerri, and Sherrie Gould. *Rainy Day Projects for Children*. Pa.: Murdock Books, 1990; 121pp., $10.95.

Jeschke, Susan. *Perfect the Pig*. N.Y.: Holt, Rinehart and Winston, 1998; 32pp., $11.15.

John, Timothy. *The Great Song Book*. N.Y.: Benn, 1978; 112pp., $14.95.

Johnson, Angela. *The Leaving Morning*. N.Y.: Orchard, 1992; 28pp., $14.95.

———. *When I Am Old with You*. N.Y.: Orchard, 1990; 32pp., $16.99.

Johnson, Dolores. *What Kind of Baby-sitter Is This?* N.Y.: Macmillan, 1991; 32pp., $13.95.

———. *What Will Mommy Do When I'm at School?* N.Y.: Macmillan, 1990; 32pp., $12.95.

Johnson, Doug. *Never Babysit the Hippopotamuses!* N.Y.: Henry, 1993; 32pp., $14.95.

———. *Never Ride Your Elephant to School.* N.Y.: Henry, 1995; 30pp., $15.95.

Johnson, Mildred. *Wait, Skates!* Ill.: Children's Press, 1983; 32pp., $16.00.

Johnson, Pamela. *A Mouse's Tale.* Calif.: Harcourt Brace Jovanovich, 1991; 32pp., $11.95.

Johnson, Paul Brett. *The Cow Who Wouldn't Come Down.* N.Y.: Orchard, 1993; 32pp., $14.95.

———. *A Perfect Pork Stew.* N.Y.: Orchard, 1998; 32pp., $16.99.

Johnson, Sue. *The Little Green Monster.* Calif.: Modern Signs, 1985; 32pp., $4.50.

Johnston, Marianne. *Let's Talk about Being Shy.* N.Y.: Powerkids, 1996; 24pp., $16.95.

Johnston, Tony. *The Badger and the Magic Fan.* N.Y.: G. P. Putnam's Sons, 1990; 32pp., $13.95.

———. *The Cowboy and the Black-Eyed Pea.* N.Y.: G. P. Putnam's Sons, 1992; 32pp., $15.95.

———. *The Last Snow of Winter.* N.Y.: Tambourine, 1993; 32pp., $13.95.

———. *Little Rabbit Goes to Sleep.* N.Y.: HarperCollins, 1995; 32pp., $10.15.

Johnston, Tony and Bruce Degen. *Goblin Walk.* N.Y.: G. P. Putnam's Sons, 1991; 32pp., $14.95.

Jonas, Ann. *The 13th Clue.* N.Y.: Greenwillow, 1992; 32pp., $14.93.

———. *Where Can it Be?* N.Y.: Greenwillow, 1996; 32pp., $11.75.

Jones, Rebecca C. *Great Aunt Martha.* N.Y.: Dutton Children's Books, 1995; 32pp., $13.99.

Joos, Francoise and Frederic. *The Golden Snowflake.* Mass.: Little, Brown, 1991; 32pp., $14.95.

Joose, Barbara. *Fourth of July.* N.Y.: Alfred A. Knopf, 1985; 46pp., NA.

Joose, Barbara M. *Snow Day!* N.Y.: Clarion, 1995; 32pp., $14.95.

Jorgensen, Gail. *Crocodile Beat.* N.Y.: Bradbury, 1989; 32pp., $13.95.

———. *Gotcha!* N.Y.: Scholastic, 1995; 32pp., $15.95.

Joyce, Irma. *Never Talk to Strangers.* N.Y.: Western, 1985; 32pp., $4.95.

Joyce, William. *George Shrinks.* N.Y.: Harper and Row, 1985; 32pp., $14.89.

———. *The Leaf Men.* N.Y.: HarperCollins, 1996; 40pp., $15.95.

Jung, Minna. *William's Ninth Life.* N.Y.: Orchard, 1993; 32pp., $12.95.

Kadish, Sharona. *Discovering Friendship.* Tex.: Steck-Vaughn Co., 1994; 32pp., NA.

Kahl, Virginia. *The Habits of Rabbits.* N.Y.: Charles Scribner's Sons, 1957; 32pp., $5.99.

Kalan, Robert. *Jump, Frog, Jump.* N.Y.: Greenwillow, 1996; 32pp., $18.95.

———. *Moving Day.* N.Y.: Greenwillow, 1996; 28pp., $15.00.

Kapp, Paul. *Cock-a-Doodle-Doo! Cock-a-Doodle-Dandy: A New Songbook for the Newest Singers.* N.Y.: Harper and Row, 1966; 71pp., $3.95.

Karlin, Nurit. *Little Big Mouse*. N.Y.: HarperCollins, 1991; 32pp., $13.89.

Kastner, Jill. *Barnyard Big Top*. N.Y.: Simon and Schuster, 1997; 32pp., $16.00.

———. *Snake Hunt*. N.Y.: Four Winds, 1993; 32pp., $14.95.

Kasza, Keiko. *Grandpa's Toad's Secrets*. N.Y.: G. P. Putnam's Sons, 1995; 32pp., $15.99.

———. *A Mother for Choco*. N.Y.: G. P. Putnam's Sons, 1992; 32pp., $15.95.

———. *Pig's Picnic*. N.Y.: G. P. Putnam's Sons, 1988; 32pp., $13.95.

———. *The Rat and the Tiger*. N.Y.: G. P. Putnam's Sons, 1993; 32pp., $14.95.

———. *When the Elephant Walks*. N.Y.: G. P. Putnam's Sons, 1990, 32pp., $11.15.

Keats, Ezra Jack. *Dreams*. N.Y.: Macmillan, 1974; 32pp., $11.19.

———. *Goggles!* N.Y.: Macmillan, 1998; 32pp., $15.99.

———. *Jennie's Hat*. N.Y.: Harper and Row Junior Books, 1985; 34pp., $6.95.

———. *Kitten for a Day*. N.Y.: Harper and Row Junior Books, 1993; 32pp., $10.15.

———. *My Dog Is Lost!* N.Y.: Crowell, 1999; 39pp., $5.99.

———. *Pet Show*. N.Y.: Macmillan, 1987; 32pp., $5.99.

———. *Regards to the Man in the Moon*. N.Y.: Macmillan, 1987; 32pp., $10.90.

———. *The Trip*. N.Y.: William Morrow, 1978; 32pp., $15.93.

———. *Whistle for Willie*. N.Y.: Viking Penguin, 1977; 32pp., $14.99.

Keenen, George. *The Preposterous Week*. N.Y.: Dial, 1971; 32pp., $4.95.

Keller, Beverly. *Fiona's Bees*. N.Y.: Coward, McCann and Geoghegen, 1975; 42pp., $4.69.

Keller, Charles. *Glory, Glory, How Peculiar*. N.Y.: Prentice-Hall, 1967; 32pp., $4.95.

Keller, Holly. *The Best Present*. N.Y.: Greenwillow, 1989; 32pp., $11.95.

———. *Brave Horace*. N.Y.: Greenwillow, 1998; 32pp., $15.00.

———. *Cromwell's Glasses*. N.Y.: Greenwillow, 1982; 32pp., NA.

———. *Furry*. N.Y.: Greenwillow, 1992; 24pp., $14.00.

———. *Geraldine's Baby Brother*. N.Y.: Greenwillow, 1994; 24pp., $15.00.

———. *Geraldine's Blanket*. N.Y.: Greenwillow, 1988; 32pp., $9.95.

———. *Grandfather's Dream*. N.Y.: Greenwillow, 1994; 32pp., $15.00.

———. *Harry and Tuck*. N.Y.: Greenwillow, 1993: 24pp., $14.00.

———. *Henry's Happy Birthday*. N.Y.: Greenwillow, 1990; 32pp., $12.88.

———. *Henry's Fourth of July*. N.Y.: Greenwillow, 1985; 32pp., NA.

———. *Horace*. N.Y.: Greenwillow, 1991; 32pp., $13.88.

———. *Merry Christmas, Geraldine*. N.Y.: Greenwillow, 1997; 32pp., $15.00.

———. *What Alvin Wanted*. N.Y.: Greenwillow, 1990; 32pp., $12.95.

———. *Will It Rain?* N.Y.: Greenwillow, 1984; 24pp., $10.88.

Keller, Irene. *Benjamin Rabbit and the Fire Chief*. Ill.: Children's Press, 1986; 32pp., NA.

———. *Benjamin Rabbit and the Stranger Danger*. N.Y.: Dodd, Mead, 1985; 32pp., $8.95.

Kellogg, Steven. *The Mysterious Tadpole*. N.Y.: Dial Books for Young Readers, 1979; 32pp., $19.99.

———. *Paul Bunyan*. N.Y.: William Morrow, 1984; 48pp., $15.90.

———. *Pecos Bill*. N.Y.: William Morrow, 1995; 48pp., $15.00.

Kennaway, Adrienne. *Little Elephant's Walk*. N.Y.: Willa Perlman, 1991; 32pp., $13.89.

Kennedy, Kim. *Mr. Bumble.* N.Y.: Hyperion Books for Children, 1997; 32pp., $15.95.

Kennedy, Richard. *The Leprechaun's Story.* N.Y.: E. P. Dutton, 1979; 32pp., $8.95.

Kent, Jack. *The Biggest Shadow in the Zoo.* N.Y.: Parents Magazine, 1981; 48pp., $5.95.

———. *The Caterpillar and the Polliwog.* N.Y.: Simon and Schuster Books for Young Readers, 1982; 32pp., $14.00.

———. *Clotilda.* N.Y.: Random House, 1978; 36pp., $1.95.

———. *The Fat Cat.* N.Y.: Scholastic, 1972; 32pp., $2.95.

———. *Joey.* N.Y.: Prentice-Hall, 1984; 32pp., $12.95.

———. *The Once-Upon-a-Time Dragon.* Calif.: Harcourt Brace Jovanovich, Inc., 1982; 32pp., $11.95.

———. *Round Robin.* N.Y.: Prentice-Hall, 1982; 32pp., $11.95.

———. *There's No Such Thing as a Dragon.* N.Y.: Western, 1975; 24pp., $1.50.

Keown, Elizabeth. *Emily's Snowball: The World's Biggest.* N.Y.: Atheneum, 1992; 32pp., $13.95.

Kepes, Charles. *Run, Little Monkeys, Run, Run, Run.* N.Y.: Harper and Row Junior Books, 1996; 64pp., $14.89.

Kern, Noris. *I Love You with All My Heart.* Calif.: Chronicle Books, 1998; 32pp., $14.95.

Kesselman, Wendy. *Emma.* N.Y.: Doubleday, 1980; 32pp., $11.19.

———. *Time for Jody.* N.Y.: Harper and Row, 1975; 40pp., $5.79.

Kessler, Leonard. *Kick, Pass, and Run.* N.Y.: Harper and Row Junior Books, 1996; 64pp., $14.89.

———. *Old Turtle's Winter Games.* N.Y.: Greenwillow, 1983; 56pp., $8.88.

———. *Mr. Pine's Purple House.* N.Y.: Grosset and Dunlap, 1965; 64pp., $2.39.

Ketteman, Helen. *Heatwave.* N.Y.: Walker, 1998; 32pp., $15.95.

Kezzeiz, Ediba. *Ramadan Adventure of Fafoose Mouse.* Ind.: American Trust, 1991; 32pp., $3.00.

Khdir, Kate, and Sue Nash. *Little Ghost.* N.Y.: Barron's Educational Series Inc., 1991; 32pp., $12.95.

Kimmel, Eric A. *The Chanukkah Guest.* N.Y.: Holiday House, 1988; 32pp., $15.95.

———. *I Took My Frog to the Library.* N.Y.: Viking, 1992; 32pp., $10.20.

Kimmelman, Leslie. *Hanukkah Lights, Hanukkah Nights.* N.Y.: HarperCollins, 1992; 32pp., $11.15.

King, Bob. *Sitting on the Farm.* N.Y.: Orchard, 1991; 32pp., $13.96.

King, Deborah. *Cloudy.* N.Y.: Philomel, 1989; 32pp., $14.95.

King, Penny, and Clare Roundhill. *Making Pictures: Secrets of the Sea.* Ill.: Rigby Interactive Library, 1997; 29pp., $21.36.

———. *Making Pictures: Spooky Things.* Ill.: Rigby Interactive Library, 1997; 29pp., $21.36.

King-Smith, Dick. *The Spotty Pig.* N.Y.: Farrar, Straus and Giroux, 1997; 32pp., $14.00.

Kinney, Maxine. *Paper Plate Kinney.* Minn.: T. S. Denison and Co., Inc., 1993; 80pp., $8.95.

Kinsey-Warnock, Natalie. *When Spring Comes*. N.Y.: Dutton Children's Books, 1993; 32pp., $14.95.

Kinsey-Warnock, Natalie and Helen Kinsey. *The Bear that Heard Crying*. N.Y.: Cobblehill, 1993; 32pp., $14.99.

Kipling, Rudyard. *The Sing-Song of Old Man Kangaroo*. N.Y.: Pete Bedrick, 1991; 32pp., $14.95.

Kirk, Daniel. *Bigger*. N.Y.: G. P. Putnam's Sons, 1998; 32pp., $15.99.

———. *Trash Trucks!* N.Y.: G. P. Putnam's Sons, 1997; 32pp., $15.95.

———. *Miss Spider's New Car*. N.Y.: Scholastic, 1997; 32pp., $16.95.

———. *Miss Spider's Tea Party*. N.Y.: Scholastic, 1994; 32pp., $15.95.

Kirn, Ann. *The Tale of a Crocodile*. N.Y.: W. W. Norton, 1968; unpaged, $3.95.

Kiser, SuAnn and Kevin. *The Birthday Thing*. N.Y.: Greenwillow, 1989; 24pp., NA.

Kladder, Jeri. *Story Hour: 55 Preschool Programs for Public Libraries*. N.C.: McFarland, 1995; 219pp., $38.50.

Klettenheimer, Ingrid. *Great Paper Craft Projects*. N.Y.: Sterling, 1992; 80pp., NA.

Kline, Suzy. *Shhhhh!* N.Y.: Albert Whitman, 1984; unpaged, $9.25.

Knutson, Kimberley. *Ska-tat!* N.Y.: Macmillan, 1993; 32pp., $14.95.

Kobe, Liz Cromwell, Dixie Hibner, and John R. Faitel. *Finger Frolics 2*. Md.: Gryphon House, 1996; 134pp., $12.95.

Koehler, Rhoebe. *The Day We Met You*. N.Y.: Bradbury, 1990; 40pp., $15.00.

Kohl, MaryAnn. *Preschool Art*. Md.: Gryphon House, 1994; 260pp., $19.95.

Kohl, MaryAnn F., and Cindy Gainer. *Good Earth Art*. Wash.: Bright Ring Publishing, 1991; 224pp., $16.95.

Koller, Jackie French. *No Such Thing*. Pa.: Boyds Mills, 1997; 32pp., $14.95.

Komoda, Beverly. *The Winter Day*. N.Y.: HarperCollins, 1991; 32pp., $13.90.

Konigsburg, E.L. *Samuel Todd's Book of Great Colors*. N.Y.: Atheneum, 1990; 32pp., $13.95.

Kordon, Klaus. *The Big Fish*. N.Y.: Macmillan, 1992; 32pp., $13.95.

Koscielniak, Bruce. *Geoffrey Groundhog Predicts the Weather*. N.Y.: Houghton Mifflin, 1995; 32pp., $13.95.

Kovalski, MaryAnn. *Pizza for Breakfast*. N.Y.: Morrow Junior Books, 1990; 32pp., $13.90.

Krahn, Fernando. *April Fools*. N.Y.: E. P. Dutton, 1974; 32pp., $8.95.

Krasilovsky, Phyllis. *The Man Who Was Too Lazy to Fix Things*. N.Y.: Tambourine, 1992; 32pp., $14.95.

———. *The Woman Who Saved Things*. N.Y.: Tambourine, 1993; 32pp., NA.

Kraus, Charles and Linda. *Charles the Clown's Guide to Children's Parties*. Calif.: Jalmar Press, 1983; 305pp., $9.95.

Kraus, Robert. *Come Out and Play, Little Mouse*. N.Y.: Greenwillow, 1987; 32pp., $11.88.

———. *Eyes, Nose, Fingers, Toes*. N.Y.: Harper and Row Junior Books, 1964; 32pp., NA.

———. *Fables Aesop Never Wrote*. N.Y.: Viking, 1994; 32pp., $14.99.

———. *How Spider Saved Halloween*. N.Y.: Parents Magazine, 1973; 32pp, $8.50.

———. *Ladybug, Ladybug*. N.Y.: Windmill and Dutton, 1957; 32pp., NA.

———. *The Little Giant*. N.Y.: Harper and Row Junior Books, 1989; 24pp., $10.15.

———. *Little Louie the Baby Bloomer*. N.Y.: HarperCollins, 1998; 32pp., $15.95.

———. *Musical Max*. N.Y.: Simon and Schuster Books for Young Readers, 1990; 32pp., $13.95.

Krementz, Jill. *Holly's Farm Animals*. N.Y.: Random House, 1986; 22pp., $3.95.

Krensky, Stephen. *Big Time Bears*. Mass.: Little, Brown, 1989; 32pp., $14.95.

———. *How Santa Got His Job*. N.Y.: Simon and Schuster Books for Young Readers, 1998; 32pp., $15.00.

Krisvoy, Juel. *New Games to Play*. Ill.: Follett, 1968; 111pp., $3.95.

Kroll, Steven. *The Candy Witch*. N.Y.: Holiday House, 1996; 32pp., $7.70.

———. *It's Groundhog Day!* N.Y.: Holiday House, 1991; 32pp., $2.99.

———. *Loose Tooth*. N.Y.: Holiday House, 1984; 32pp., $10.95.

———. *Mary McLean and the St. Patrick's Day Parade*. N.Y.: Scholastic, 1991; 32pp., $15.95.

———. *Oh, What a Thanksgiving!* N.Y.: Scholastic, 1988; 32pp., $12.95.

———. *One Tough Turkey*. N.Y.: Holiday House, 1982; 32pp., $12.95.

———. *Pigs in the House*. N.Y.: Parents Magazine, 1983; 48pp., $5.00.

———. *The Squirrel's Thanksgiving*. N.Y.: Holiday House, 1991; 32pp., $14.95.

———. *Toot! Toot!* N.Y.: Holiday House, 1983; 32pp., $12.95.

———. *Will You Be My Valentine?* N.Y.: Holiday House, 1993; 32pp., $14.95.

Kroll, Virginia. *A Carp for Kimiko*. Mass.: Charlesbridge, 1993; 32pp., $15.00.

———. *Hands!* Pa.: Boyds Mills Press, 1997; 30pp., $7.95.

———. *Masai and I*. N.Y.: Four Winds, 1992; 32pp., $16.00.

Kroninger, Stephen. *If I Crossed the Road*. N.Y.: Atheneum, 1997; 32pp., $16.00.

Krudop, Walter Lyon. *Something Is Growing*. N.Y.: Atheneum, 1995; 32pp., $15.00.

Krull, Kathleen. *Gonna Sing My Head Off!* N.Y.: Alfred A. Knopf, 1992; 147pp., $12.00.

———. *It's My Earth, Too*. N.Y.: Bantam Doubleday Dell, 1992; 32pp., $13.50.

Kudrna, C. Imbior. *To Bathe a Boa*. Minn.: Carolrhoda Books, 1986; 32pp., $19.95.

Kuklin, Susan. *Fighting Fires*. N.Y.: Bradbury, 1993; 32pp., $15.00.

Kunhardt, Edith. *Danny and the Easter Egg*. N.Y.: Greenwillow, 1989; 32pp., $11.90.

———. *I Want to Be a Firefighter*. N.Y.: Grosset and Dunlap, 1989; 32pp., $6.95.

———. *Red Day, Green Day*. N.Y.: Greenwillow, 1992; 32pp., $14.00.

Kvasnosky, Laura. *Mr. Chips*. N.Y.: Farrar, Straus and Giroux, 1996; 32pp., $15.00.

Kwitz, Mary DeBall. *Littlle Chick's Friend, Duckling*. N.Y.: HarperCollins, 1992; 28pp., $12.89.

Lachner, Dorothea. *Meredith, the Witch Who Wasn't*. N.Y.: North-South, 1997; 32pp., $15.95.

Lacoe, Addie. *Just Not the Same*. Mass.: Houghton Mifflin, 1992; 32pp., $14.95.

Lacome, Julie. *I'm a Jolly Farmer*. Mass.: Candlewick, 1994; 24p., $13.95.

LaFontaine, Jean de. *The Hare and the Tortoise*. N.Y.: Golden, 1967; 30pp., $3.95.

Laird, Elizabeth. *The Day Veronica Was Nosy*. N.Y.: Tambourine, 1990; 32pp., $11.90.

Lakin, Pat. *Dad and Me in the Morning*. Ill.: Albert Whitman, 1994; 32pp., $14.95.

———. *Aware and Alert*. Tex.: Steck-Vaughn Co., 1995; 32pp., $19.97.

————. *Don't Touch My Room*. Mass.: Little, Brown, 1985; 32pp., $12.95.

Lamont, Priscilla. *Playtime Rhymes*. N.Y.: DK Publishing, Inc., 1998; 32pp., $12.95.

Lampert, Emily. *A Little Touch of Monster*. N.Y.: Atlantic Monthly, 1986; 32pp., $12.95.

Landeck, Beatrice. *Songs to Grow On*. N.Y.: William Sloane, 1987; 127pp., $13.95.

Landeck, Beatrice, and Elizabeth Crook. *Wake Up and Sing!* N.Y.: William Morrow, 1969; 128pp., $5.95.

Lapp, Carolyn. *The Dentist's Tools*. Minn.: Lerner, 1961; 31pp., $2.95.

Lasker, Joe. *Lentil Soup*. N.Y.: Albert Whitman, 1977; 29pp., $5.75.

Lasky, Kathryn. *Fourth of July Bear*. N.Y.: Morrow Junior Books, 1991; 32pp., $13.95.

————. *Lunch Bunnies*. Mass.: Little, Brown, 1996; 32pp., $14.95.

Lasson, Robert. *Orange Oliver*. N.Y.: David McKay, 1957; 30pp., $2.50.

Latimer, Jim. *Fox under First Base*. N.Y.: Scribner, 1991; 32pp., $13.95.

Lattimore, Deborah Nourse. *CinderHazel: The Cinderella of Halloween*. N.Y.: Blue Sky, 1997; 32pp., $15.95.

Lauber, Patricia. *Be a Friend to Trees*. N.Y.: HarperCollins, 1994; 32pp., $14.89.

Leaf, Munro. *Safety Can be Fun*. N.Y.: J. B. Lippincott, 1961; 32pp., $12.89.

Lee, Jeanne M. *Silent Lotus*. N.Y.: Farrar, Straus and Giroux, 1991; 32pp., $14.95.

Leedy, Loreen. *The Great Trash Bash*. N.Y.: Holiday House, 1991; 32pp., $15.95.

Lehan, Daniel. *Wipe Your Feet!* N.Y.: Dutton's Children's Books, 1992; 26pp., $14.00.

Lehne, Judith Logan. *The Never-Be-Bored Book*. N.Y.: Sterling, 1992; 128pp., $17.95.

Leisy, James. *The Good Times Songbook*. N.Y.: Abingdon, 1974; 432pp., $12.95.

Lember, Barbara Hirsch. *A Book of Fruit*. N.Y.: Ticknor and Fields, 1994; 32pp., $14.95.

Lemieux, Michele. *The Pied Piper of Hamelin*. N.Y.: Morrow Junior Books, 1993; 32pp., $14.95.

Lenski, Lois. *Debbie Goes to Nursery School*. N.Y.: Henry Z. Walck, 1970; 47pp., $3.95.

————. *Now It's Fall*. N.Y.: Henry Z. Walck, 1948; 47pp., $4.95.

————. *Policeman Small*. N.Y.: Henry Z. Walck, 1962; 46pp., $9.95.

Lenssen, Ann. *A Rainbow Balloon*. N.Y.: Cobblehill, 1992; 32pp., $13.50.

Leonard, Marcia. *Little Owl Leaves the Nest*. N.Y.: Bantam, 1984; 32pp., $2.75.

Lerner, Harriet, and Susan Goldhor. *What's So Terrible about Swallowing an Appleseed?* N.Y.: HarperCollins, 1996; 40pp., $14.95.

LeSieg, Theo. *I Wish I Had Duck Feet*. N.Y.: Beginner, 1965; 64pp., $7.99.

Lester, Alison. *Magic Beach*. Mass.: Little, Brown, 1990; 32pp., $13.95.

Lester, Helen. *Tacky the Penguin*. Mass.: Houghton Mifflin, 1988; 32pp., $15.00.

Lester, Julius. *John Henry*. N.Y.: Dial, 1994; 48pp., $16.89.

————. *Princess Penelope's Parrot*. Mass.: Houghton Mifflin, 1996; 32pp., $14.95.

Leuck, Laura. *Teeny, Tiny Mouse: A Book about Colors*. N.Y.: Bridgewater, 1998; 32pp., $15.95.

Levi, Dorothy Hoffman. *A Very Special Friend*. D.C.: Kendall Green, 1989; 32pp., $8.95.

Levine, Abby. *Gretchen Groundhog, It's Your Day!* Ill.: Albert Whitman, 1998; 32pp., $15.95.

———. *This Is the Pumpkin.* Ill.: Albert Whitman, 1997; 32pp., $11.50.

———. *What Did Mommy Do before You?* Ill.: Albert Whitman, 1988; 32pp., $14.95.

Levinson, Nancy Smiler. *Snowshoe Thompson.* N.Y.: HarperCollins, 1992; 64pp., $15.89.

Lewin, Betsy. *Chubbo's Pool.* N.Y.: Clarion, 1996; 32pp., $14.95.

Lewis, Paul Owen. *Storm Boy.* Ore.: Beyond Words, 1995; 32pp., $14.95.

Lewis, Rob. *Henrietta's First Winter.* N.Y.: Farrar, Straus and Giroux, 1990; 32pp., $11.95.

Lewis, Shari. *Shari Lewis Presents 101 Games and Songs for Kids to Play and Sing.* N.Y.: Random House, 1993; 90pp., $9.99.

Lewison, Wendy Cheyette. *The Rooster Who Lost His Crow.* N.Y.: Dial Books for Young Readers, 1995; 32pp., $14.99.

Lexau, Joan. *Finders Keepers, Losers Weepers.* Pa.: J. B. Lippincott, 1967; 28pp., $6.50.

———. *The Homework Caper.* N.Y.: Harper and Row, 1966; 64pp., NA.

———. *Olaf Reads.* N.Y.: Dial for the Young, 1965; 53pp., $6.46.

———. *Who Took the Farmer's Hat?* N.Y.: Harper and Row, 1963; unpaged, $11.89.

Lies, Brian. *Hamlet and the Enormous Chinese Dragon Kite.* Mass.: Houghton Mifflin, 1994; 32pp., $14.95.

Lillegard, Dee. *My Yellow Ball.* N.Y.: Dutton Children's Books, 1993; 32pp., $12.99.

———. *Tortoise Brings the Mail.* N.Y.: Dutton Children's Books, 1997; 32pp., $14.99.

———. *The Wild Bunch.* N.Y.: G. P. Putnam's Sons, 1997; 32pp., $15.95.

Lillie, Patricia. *When the Rooster Crowed.* N.Y.: Greenwillow, 1991; 32pp., NA.

———. *When This Box Is Full.* N.Y.: Greenwillow, 1993; 24pp., $14.00.

Lilly, Melinda. *Eye Spy a Ladybug!* Calif.: Price Stern Sloan, 1997; 10pp., $6.95.

Lindbergh, Reeve. *There's a Cow in the Road.* N.Y.: Dial Books for Young Readers, 1993; 32pp., $13.99.

Linderman, C. Emma. *Teachables from Trashables.* Md.: Gryphon House, 1979; 184pp., NA.

Lindgren, Astrid. *I Don't Want to Go to Bed.* N.Y.: Farrar, Straus and Giroux, 1988; 32pp., $12.95.

———. *I Want a Brother or Sister.* N.Y.: Farrar, Straus and Giroux, 1988; 32pp., $10.95.

Linn, Margot. *A Trip to the Doctor.* N.Y.: Harper and Row, Publishers, 1988; 20pp., $9.95.

Lionni, Leo. *A Busy Year.* N.Y.: Alfred A. Knopf, 1992; 32pp., $10.99.

———. *An Extraordinary Egg.* N.Y.: Alfred A. Knopf, 1994; 40pp., $16.00.

———. *Frederick.* N.Y.: Pantheon, 1967; 32pp., $18.99.

———. *Frederick's Fables.* N.Y.: Knopf Books for Young Readers, 1985; 144pp., $20.00.

———. *Geraldine, the Music Mouse.* N.Y.: Pantheon, 1979; 32pp., $6.95.

———. *It's Mine!* N.Y.: Alfred A. Knopf, 1986; 32pp., $15.99.

———. *Little Blue and Little Yellow*. N.Y.: Astor-Honor, Inc., 1959; 39pp., $14.95.

———. *Matthew's Dream*. N.Y.: Random House, 1995; 32pp., $5.99.

———. *Nicolas, Where Have You Been?* N.Y.: Alfred A. Knopf, 1987; 32pp., NA.

Litchfield, Ada B. *Words in Our Hands*. N.Y.: Albert Whitman Library, 1980; 29pp., $14.95.

Littledale, Freya. *The Snow Child*. N.Y.: Scholastic, 32pp., $1.95.

Lobel, Arnold. *Giant John*. N.Y.: Harper and Row Junior Books,1964; 31pp., $14.89.

———. *Ming Lo Moves the Mountain*. N.Y.: Greenwillow, 1982; 32pp., $11.75.

———. *Owl at Home*. N.Y.: Harper and Row Junior Books, 1975; 64pp., $14.89.

———. *The Rose in My Garden*. N.Y.: Greenwillow, 1984; 40pp., $15.93.

———. *A Treeful of Pigs*. N.Y.: Greenwillow, 1979; 32pp., $15.93.

Loewen, Nancy. *Fire Safety*. N.Y.: Child's World, 1997; 24pp., $12.95.

———. *Traffic Safety*. N.Y.: Child's World, 1997; 24pp., $18.50.

Lofgren, Ulf. *Alvin the Pirate*. Minn.: Carolrhoda Books, 1990; 32pp., $13.95.

Lohf, Sabine. *Building Your Own Toys*. Ill.: Children's Press, 1989; 64pp., NA.

———. *Things I Can Make with Stones*. Calif.: Chronicle, 1989; 32pp., $6.95.

Lonborg, Rosemary. *Helpin' Bugs*. Mass.: Little Friend, 1995; 32pp., $14.95.

London, Jonathan. *Condor's Egg*. Calif.: Chronicle, 1994; 32pp., $13.95.

———. *Froggy's First Kiss*. N.Y.: Viking Penguin, 1998; 32pp., $14.99.

———. *Hurricane!* N.Y.: Lothrop, Lee and Shepard, 1998; 32pp., $16.00.

———. *A Koala for Katie: An Adoption Story*. Ill.: Albert Whitman, 1993; 24pp., $13.95.

———. *Let's Go Froggy*. N.Y.: Viking Penguin, 1994; 30pp., $14.99.

———. *The Owl Who Became the Moon*. N.Y.: Dutton Children's Books, 1993; 32pp., $15.99.

———. *Puddles*. N.Y.: Viking Penguin, 1997; 32pp., $15.99.

———. *What Newt Could Do for Turtle*. Mass.: Candlewick, 1996; 32pp., $16.99.

Long, Earlene. *Gone Fishing*. Mass.: Houghton Mifflin, 1987; 32pp., $5.95.

Long, Jan Freeman. *The Bee and the Dream*. N.Y.: Dutton Children's Books, 1996; 40pp., $15.99.

Long, Teddy Cameron. *Fantastic Paper Holiday Decorations*. N.Y.: Sterling, 1994; 96pp., NA.

Loomis, Christine. *Cowboy Bunnies*. N.Y.: G. P. Putnam's Sons, 1997; 30pp., $15.95.

———. *The Hippo Hop*. Mass.: Houghton Mifflin, 1995; 32pp., $14.95.

Lopez, Loretta. *The Birthday Swap*. N.Y.: Lee and Low, 1997; 32pp., $15.95.

Lopshire, Robert. *How to Make Snop Snappers and Other Fine Things.*, N.Y.: Greenwillow, 1977; 56pp., NA.

———. *Put Me in the Zoo*. N.Y.: Beginner, 1960; 58pp., $7.99.

Lottridge, Celia Barker. *The Name of the Tree*. N.Y.: Margaret K. McElderry, 1989; 32pp., $14.95.

Low, Joseph. *Mice Twice*. N.Y.: Atheneum, 1980; 32pp., $5.99.

Low, William. *Chinatown*. N.Y.: Henry Holt, 1997; 32pp., $15.95.

Lucas, Virginia H., and Walter B. Barbe. *Resource Book for the Kindergarten Teacher*. Ohio: Zaner-Bloser Inc., 1980; 526pp., NA.

Ludwig, Warren. *Old Noah's Elephants.* N.Y.: G. P. Putnam's Sons, 1991; 32pp., $14.95.

Luenn, Nancy. *Mother Earth.* N.Y.: Atheneum, 1992; 32pp., $15.00.

Luttrell, Ida. *Milo's Toothache.* N.Y.: Dial Books for Young Readers, 1992; 40pp., $10.89.

————. *Three Good Blankets.* N.Y.: Atheneum, 1990; 32pp., $13.95.

Lynch-Watson, Janet. *The Shadow Puppet Book.* N.Y.: Sterling, 1980; 128pp., NA.

Lyon, George Ella. *Counting on the Woods.* N.Y.: DK Publishing, Inc., 1998; 32pp., $15.95.

————. *Mama Is a Miner.* N.Y.: Orchard, 1994; 32pp., $15.95.

Maass, Robert. *When Spring Comes.* N.Y.: Henry Holt, 1994; 32pp., $14.95.

————. *When Summer Comes.* N.Y.: Henry Holt, 1993; 32pp., $14.95.

Maccarone, Grace. *The Silly Story of Goldie Locks and the Three Squares.* N.Y.: Scholastic, Inc. 1996; 32pp., $3.50.

MacDonald, Elizabeth. *Mike's Kite.* N.Y.: Orchard, 1990; 32pp., NA.

MacDonald, Maryann. *Little Hippo Gets Glasses.* N.Y.: Dial Books for Young Readers, 1991; 28pp., $11.00.

————. *The Pink Party.* N.Y.: Hyperion Books for Children, 1994; 40pp., $11.49.

————. *Rabbit's Birthday Kite.* N.Y.: A Bantam Little Rooster Book, 1991; 32pp., $9.99.

————. *Rosie and the Poor Rabbits.* N.Y.: Atheneum, 1994; 32pp., $13.95.

————. *Sam's Worries.* N.Y.: Hyperion Books for Children, 1990; 28pp., NA.

MacDonald, Suse. *Peck, Slither, and Slide.* Calif.: Gulliver, 1997; 48pp., $15.00.

MacGill-Callahan, Sheila. *And Still the Turtle Watched.* N.Y.: Dial Books for Young Readers, 1991; 32pp., $14.90.

————. *To Capture the Wind.* N.Y.: Dial Books for Young Readers, 1997; 32pp., $14.99.

Maestro, Betsy. *Big City Port.* N.Y.: Macmillan, 1984; 32pp., $12.95.

————. *Why Do Leaves Change Color?* N.Y.: HarperCollins, 1994; 32pp., $14.89.

Maestro, Betsy and Giulio. *Around the Clock with Harriet.* N.Y.: Crown, 1984; 32pp., NA.

————. *Bike Trip.* N.Y.: HarperCollins Children's Books, 1992; 32pp., $15.89.

————. *Delivery Van.* N.Y.: Clarion, 1990; 32pp., $14.95.

————. *Dollars and Cents for Harriet.* N.Y.: Crown, 1988; 32pp., $12.95.

————. *Harriet Goes to the Circus.* N.Y.: Crown, 1977; 30pp., $12.95.

Maestro, Giulio. *The Remarkable Plant in Apt. 4.* N.Y.: Bradbury, 1973; 32pp., $5.95.

Maguire, Jack. *Hopscotch, Hangman, Hot Potato, and Ha, Ha, Ha.* N.Y.: Prentice Hall, 1990; 304pp., $13.95.

Mahy, Margaret. *Beaten by a Balloon.* N.Y.: Viking, 1997; 32pp., $15.99.

————. *The Boy with Two Shadows.* N.Y.: J. B. Lippincott, 1987; 26pp., $12.89.

————. *A Busy Day for a Good Grandmother.* N.Y.: Margaret McElderry, 1993; 26pp., $14.95.

————. *A Lion in the Meadow.* N.Y.: Overlook, 1986; 32pp., $13.95.

————. *The Pumpkin Man and the Crafty Creeper.* N.Y.: Lothrop, Lee and Shepard, 1990; 28pp., $14.88.

————. *The Queen's Goat*. N.Y.: Dial Books for Young Readers, 1991; 32pp., $12.95.

————. *A Summer Saturday Morning*. N.Y.: Viking, 1998; 32pp., $15.99.

Mainland, Pauline. *A Yoga Parade of Animals*. Mass.: Element, 1998; 32pp., $15.95.

Mandell, Muriel. *Games to Learn By*. N.Y.: Sterling, 1958; 120pp., $3.99.

Manning-Sanders, Ruth. *Festivals*. N.Y.: E. P. Dutton, 1973; 169pp., $8.95.

Manushkin, Fran. *The Adventures of Cap'n O.G. Readamore*. N.Y.: Scholastic, 1984; 32pp., $3.95.

Marino, Jane. *Mother Goose Time*. N.Y.: H. W. Wilson, 1992; 172pp., $30.00.

Maris, Ron. *Better Move On, Frog!* N.Y.: Franklin Watts, 1982; 32pp., $8.90.

————. *Bernard's Boring Day*. N.Y.: Delacorte, 1989; 32pp., $12.95.

————. *I Wish I Could Fly*. N.Y.: Greenwillow, 1986; 32pp., $11.75.

Markle, Sandra. *Exploring Summer*. N.Y.: Atheneum, 1987; 180pp., $2.95.

Markun, Patricia M. *The Little Painter of Sabana Grande*. N.Y.: S & S Children's Books, 1993; 32pp., $14.95.

Marshak, Samuel. *Hail to Mail*. N.Y.: Henry Holt, 1990; 32pp., $9.50.

Marshall, James. *Willis*. Mass.: Houghton Mifflin, 1974; 32pp., NA.

Marston, Hope Irvin. *Fire Trucks*. N.Y.: Cobblehill, 1996; 48pp., $14.99.

Martin, Ann. *Rachel Parker, Kindergarten Show-off*. N.Y.: Holiday House, 1992; 40pp., $15.95.

Martin, Antoinette Truglio. *Famous Seaweed Soup*. Ill.: Albert Whitman, 1993; 32pp., $14.95.

Martin, Bill, Jr. *"Fire! Fire!" said Mrs. McGuire*. Calif.: Harcourt Brace, 1971; 32pp., $15.00.

————. *Old Devil Wind*. Calif.: Harcourt Brace, 1971; 32pp., $13.95.

————. *Polar Bear, Polar Bear, What Do You Hear?* N.Y.: Henry Holt, 1991; 32pp., $15.95.

————. *The Turning of the Year*. N.Y.: Harcourt Brace, 1970; 28pp., $15.00.

Martin, Bill, Jr., and John Archambault. *Knots on a Counting Rope*. N.Y.: Henry HoltInc., 1966; 32pp., $15.95.

Martin, Bill, Jr., and Michael Sampson. *Swish!* N.Y.: Henry Holt, 1997; 32pp., $14.95.

Martin, C.L.G. *The Dragon Nanny*. N.Y.: Macmillan, 1988; 32pp., $14.95.

Martin, David. *Five Little Piggies*. Mass.: Candlewick, 1998; 40pp., $16.99.

Martin, Mary Jane. *From Anne to Zach*. Pa.: Boyds Mills, 1996; 40pp., $14.95.

Martin, Rafe. *The Brave Little Parrot*. N.Y.: G. P. Putnam's Sons, 1998; 32pp., $15.99.

Martin, Toy. *The Pre-School Craft Book*. N.Y.: Sterling, 1984; 64pp., $3.95.

Marzollo, Jean. *Snow Angel*. N.Y.: Scholastic, 1995; 34pp., $14.95.

————. *Ten Cats Have Hats*. N.Y.: Scholastic, 1994; 24pp., $6.95.

Mason, Agnes Leckie, and Phyllis Brown Ohanian. *God's Wonderful World*. N.Y.: Random House, 1954; 173pp., $5.59.

Massey, Jeanne. *The Littlest Witch*. N.Y.: Alfred A. Knopf, 1959; unpaged, $3.54.

Masurel, Claire. *Ten Dogs in the Window*. N.Y.: North-South Trader, 1997; 32pp., $15.95.

Mather, Karen Trella. *Silas the Bookstore Cat*. Me.: Down East, 1994; 32pp., $14.95.

Mathews, Judith and Fay Robinson. *Nathaniel Willy, Scared Silly*. N.Y.: Bradbury, 1994; $15.00.

Mathias, Catherine. *I Can Be a Police Officer*. Mass.: Children's Press, 1984; 32pp., $7.95.

Mathieu, Agnes. *The Easter Bunny*. N.Y.: Dial Books for Young Readers, 1984; 32pp., $7.95.

Matterson, Elizabeth. *Games for the Very Young*. N.Y.: American Heritage, 1969; 206pp., $3.83.

May, Jim. *The Boo Baby Girl Meets the Ghost of Mable's Gable*. Ill.: Brotherstone, 1992; 32pp., $14.95.

Mayer, Mercer. *Liverwurst Is Missing*. N.Y.: Macmillan, 1990; 32pp., $16.00.

Mazer, Anne. *The Salamander Room*. N.Y.: Alfred A. Knopf, 1991; 32pp., $17.99.

McAllister, Angela. *Matepo*. N.Y.: Dial Books for Young Readers, 1991; 32pp., $12.95.

McBratney, Sam. *The Caterpillow Fight*. Mass.: Candlewick, 1996; 24p., $9.99.

———. *The Dark at the Top of the Stairs*. Mass.: Candlewick, 1996; 28pp., $15.99.

———. *Guess How Much I Love You*. Mass.: Candlewick, 1994; 32pp., $15.95.

———. *Just You and Me*. Mass.: Candlewick, 1998; 28pp., $15.99.

McCain, Becky Ray. *Grandmother's Dreamcatcher*. Ill.: Albert Whitman, 1998; 32pp., $15.95.

McCarthy, Bobette. *See You Later, Alligator*. N.Y.: Macmillan Books for Young Readers, 1995; 32pp., $15.00.

McCarty, Janet R., and Betty J. Peterson. *Craft Fun: Easy-to-Do Projects with Simple Materials*. N.Y.: Golden, 1975; 64pp., $4.95.

McCaughrean, Geraldine. *Unicorns! Unicorns!* N.Y.: Holiday House, 1997; 32pp., $15.95.

McCloskey, Robert. *Blueberries for Sal*. N.Y.: Viking Penguin, 1948; 56pp., $11.95.

McCourt, Lisa. *I Love You, Stinky Face*. N.J.: Bridgewater, 1997; 32pp., $15.95.

———. *The Best Night Out with Dad*. Fla.: Health Communications, Inc., 1997; 32pp., $14.95.

McCully, Emily Arnold. *Beautiful Warrior: The Legend of the Nun's Kung Fu*. N.Y.: Scholastic, 1998; 32pp., $16.95.

———. *My Real Family*. N.Y.: Browndeer, 1994; 32pp., $14.00.

McCutcheon, John. *Happy Adoption Day*. Mass.: Little, Brown, 1996; 32pp., $15.95.

McDermott, Gerald. *Anansi the Spider*. N.Y.: Harper and Row Junior Books, 1995; 40pp., $15.95.

———. *Daniel O' Rourke*. N.Y.: Viking Penguin, 1986; 32pp., $12.95.

———. *Tim O'Toole and the Wee Folk*. N.Y.: Viking, 1990; 32pp., $5.99.

———. *Zomo the Rabbit*. Calif.: Harcourt Brace Jovanovich, 1992; 32pp., $14.95.

McDonald, Megan. *Insects Are My Life*. N.Y.: Orchard, 1995; 32pp., $16.99.

———. *Whoo-oo Is It?* N.Y.: Orchard, 1992; 32pp., $16.99.

McDonnell, Flora. *I Love Boats*. Mass.: Candlewick, 1995; 32pp., $16.99.

McDonnell, Janet. *Celebrating Earth Day*. Ill.: Children's Press, 1994; 31pp., $17.50.

———. *Fourth of July*. Ill.: Children's Press, 1994; 32pp., $17.50.

———. *Kangaroo's Adventure in Alphabet Town*. Ill.: Children's Press, 1992; $18.20.

McEniry, Joan. *Games for Girl Scouts, 2nd Edition*. N.Y.: Girl Scouts of the USA, 1969; 96pp., $1.50.

McGeorge, Constance W. *Boomer Goes to School*. Calif.: Chronicle, 1996; 26pp., $13.95.

McGovern, Ann. *The Lady in the Box*. N.Y.: Group West, 1997; 32pp., $14.95.

———. *Too Much Noise!* Mass.: Houghton Mifflin, 1967; 45pp., $16.00.

McGowan, Diane, and Mark Schrooten. *Math Play!: 80 Ways to Count and Learn*. Vt.: Williamson, 1997; 144pp., $12.95.

McGuire, Richard. *The Orange Book*. N.Y.: Children's Universe, 1995; 40pp., $4.99.

McGuire-Turcotte, Casey A. *How Honu the Turtle Got His Shell*. Tex.: Raintree/Steck-Vaughn, 1991; 30pp., $22.83.

McKean, Thomas. *Hooray for Grandma Jo!* N.Y.: Crown, 1994; 32pp., $14.00.

McKee, David. *Elmer*. N.Y.: Lothrop, Lee and Shepard, 1989; 32pp., $14.00.

McKissack, Pat and Frederick. *Constance Stumbles*. Ill.: Children's Press, 1988; 32pp., $13.27.

McKissack, Patricia and Frederick. *Messy Bessey's School Desk*. Ill.: Children's Press, 1998; 31pp., $16.00.

McLeod, Emilie. *The Bear's Bicycle*. Mass.: Little, Brown, 1986; 32pp., $5.95.

McLerran, Alice. *I Want to Go Home*. N.Y.: Tambourine, 1992; 32pp, NA.

McMahan, Patricia. *Listen for the Bus: David's Story*. Pa.: Boyds Mills, 1995; 48pp., $15.95.

McMillan, Bruce. *Jelly Bean for Sale*. N.Y.: Scholastic, 1996; 32pp., $15.95.

———. *Going on a Whale Watch*. N.Y.: Scholastic, 1992; 40pp., $14.95.

———. *Sense Surprise: A Guessing Game for the Five Senses*. N.Y.: Scholastic, 1994; 32pp., $15.95.

———. *Time to . . .* N.Y.: Lothrop, Lee and Shepard, 1989; 30pp., $13.95.

———. *Growing Colors*. N.Y.: Lothrop, Lee and Shepard, 1988; 40pp., $16.00.

McNaughton, Colin. *Autumn*. N.Y.: Dial Books for Young Readers, 1984; 24pp., $4.95.

McPhail, David. *Edward and the Pirates*. Mass: Little, Brown, 1997; 32pp., $15.95.

———. *Mooney B. Finch, the Fastest Draw in the West*. Wisc.: Western, 1994; 32pp., $12.95.

———. *Pigs Ahoy!* N.Y.: Dutton Children's Books, 1995; 32pp., $14.99.

———. *Pigs Aplenty, Pigs Galore!* N.Y.: Dutton Children's Books, 1993; 32pp., $14.99.

———. *The Puddle*. N.Y.: Farrar, Straus and Giroux, 1998; 32pp., $15.00.

———. *Tinker and Tom and the Star Baby*. Mass.: Little, Brown, 1998; 32pp., $14.95.

Meddaugh, Susan. *Cinderella's Rat*. Mass.: Houghton Mifflin, 1997; 32pp., $15.00.

———. *Hog-Eye*. Mass.: Houghton Mifflin, 1995; 32pp., $14.95.

———. *Martha Walks the Dog*. Mass.: Houghton Mifflin, 1998; 32pp., $15.00.

———. *Maude and Claude Go Abroad*. Mass.: Houghton Mifflin, 1980; unpaged, $7.95.

———. *Tree of Birds*. Mass.: Houghton Mifflin, 1990; 32pp., $16.00.

———. *The Witches Supermarket*. Mass.: Houghton Mifflin, 1991; 32pp., $13.95.

Medearis, Angela Shelf. *Dancing with the Indians*. N.Y.: Holiday House, 1991; 32pp., $15.95.

———. *The Zebra-Riding Cowboy*. N.Y.: Henry Holt, 1992; 32pp., $14.95.

Memling, Carl. *What's in the Dark?* N.Y.: Parents Magazine, 1971; 32pp., NA.

Mercer, Eileen. *Let's Make It from Junk*. Pa.: Stackpole, 1976; 160pp., $8.95.

Merriam, Eve. *Bam, Bam, Bam*. N.Y.: Henry Holt, 1994; 32pp., $14.95.

Meshover, Leonard, and Sally Feistel. *The Monkey that Went to School*. Ill.: Follett, 1978; unpaged, $5.97.

Michel, Margaret. *The Best of the Mailbox, Book 1: Preschool/Kindergarten edition*. N.C.: The Education Center, 1993; 192pp., $22.95.

———. *The Best of the Mailbox, Book 2: Preschool/Kindergarten edition*. N.C.: The Education Center, 1996; 192pp., $22.95.

Milgrim, David. *Cows Can't Fly*. N.Y.: Viking , 1998; 32pp., $15.99.

Miller, Donna. *Egg Carton Critters*. N.Y.: Scholastic, 1978; 32pp., $1.95.

Miller, Edna. *Mousekin's Lost Woodland*. N.Y.: Simon and Schuster Books for Young Readers, 1992; 32pp., $13.00.

———. *Mousekin's Mystery*. N.J.: Prentice-Hall Inc., 1983; 32pp., $10.95.

Miller, Kathryn Ann. *Did My First Mother Love Me?: A Story for an Adopted Child*. Calif.: Morning Glory, 1994; 48pp., $12.95.

Miller, Margaret. *Big and Little*. N.Y.: Greenwillow, 1998; 32pp., $15.00.

———. *My Five Senses*. N.Y.: Simon and Schuster Books for Young Readers, 1994; 24pp., $16.00.

———. *Now I'm Big*. N.Y.: Greenwillow, 1996; 32pp., $15.00.

———. *Whose Hat?* N.Y.: Greenwillow, 1988, 40pp., $16.00.

Miller, Ned. *Emmett's Snowball*. N.Y.: Henry Holt, 1990; 32pp., $14.95.

Miller, Virginia. *Be Gentle!* Mass.: Candlewick, 1997; 32pp., $15.99.

Millman, Isaac. *Moses Goes to a Concert*. N.Y.: Farrar, Straus and Giroux, 1998; 32pp., $16.00.

Mills, Claudia. *Phoebe's Parade*. N.Y.: Macmillan, 1994; 32pp., $14.95.

Milne, A.A. *Pooh's Alphabet Book*. N.Y.: E. P. Dutton, 1975; unpaged, $3.27.

Minarik, Else. *Little Bear's Friend*. N..Y.: Harper and Row Junior Books, 1984; 64pp., $8.95.

———. *The Little Girl and the Dragon*. N.Y.: Greenwillow, 1991; 24pp., NA.

Miranda, Anne. *Baby-sit*. Mass.: Little, Brown, 1990; 14pp., $9.95.

———. *To Market, To Market*. N.Y.: Harcourt Brace, 1997; 36pp., $16.00.

Mitchell, Donald. *Every Child's Book of Nursery Songs*. N.Y.: Bonanza, 1968; 175pp., NA.

Mitchell, Rhonda. *The Talking Cloth*. N.Y.: Orchard, 1997; 32pp., $15.95.

Modesitt, Jeanne. *Mama, If You Had a Wish*. N.Y.: Green Tiger, 1993; 40pp., $15.00.

Mogensen, Jan. *Teddy Bear and the Chinese Dragon*. Wisc.: Gareth Stevens, 1985; 32pp., $8.95.

———. *The Tiger's Breakfast*. N.Y.: Crocodile, 1991; 28pp., $14.95.

Molk, Laurel. *Good Job, Oliver!* N.Y.: Crown, 1999; 32pp., $18.99.

Mollel, Tololwa M. *Ananse's Feast: An Ashanti Tale*. N.Y.: Clarion, 1997; 32pp., $14.95.

Moncure. Jane Belk. *Wise Owl's Days of the Week*. Ill.: Children's Press, 1981; 32pp., $10.60.

———. *Word Bird's Fall Words*. Ill.: Children's Press, 1985; 32pp., $21.36.

Monson, A.M. *Wanted: Best Friend*. N.Y.: Dial Books for Young Readers, 1997; 32pp., $14.99.

Moon, Grace. *One Little Indian*. N.Y.: Albert Whitman, 1950; 30pp., $2.00.

Moon, Nicola. *Lucy's Picture*. N.Y.: Dial Books for Young Readers, 1994; 32pp., $15.99.

————. *Something Special*. Ga: Peachtree, 1995; 32pp., $14.95.

Moore, Inga. *Fifty Red Night-caps*. Calif.: Chronicle, 1998; 32pp., $12.95.

————. *Little Dog Lost*. N.Y.: Macmillan, 1991; 28pp., $14.95.

Mora, Pat. *Tomas and the Library Lady*. N.Y.: Alfred A. Knopf, 1997; 32pp., $17.00.

Morgan, Michaela. *Helpful Betty to the Rescue*. Minn.: Carolrhoda Books, Inc., 1993; 32pp., $18.60.

————. *Visitors for Edward*. N.Y.: E. P. Dutton, 1987; 22pp., $8.95.

Morgan, Vanessa, and David West. *Cars and Boats*. N.Y.: Franklin Watts, 1983; 30pp., NA.

Morninghouse, Sundaira. *Habari Gani? What's the News?* N.Y.: Open Hand, 1992; 32pp., $14.95.

Morris, Ann. *The Baby Book*. NJ: Silver, 1996; 32pp., $13.95.

————. *On the Go*. N.Y.: Lothrop, Lee and Shepard, 1990, 28pp., $15.93.

Moss, Jeffrey. *The Sesame Street ABC Storybook*. N.Y.: Random House, 1974; 72pp., $5.99.

Moss, Jeffrey, David Axelro, Tony Reiss, Bruce Hart, Emily Perl Kingsley and Jon Stone. *The Songs of Sesame Street in Poems and Pictures*. N.Y.: Random House/Children's Television Workshop, 1983; 48pp., $6.99.

Moss, Marissa. *After School Monster*. N.Y.: Lothrop, Lee and Shepard, 1991; 32pp., $4.99.

————. *But Not Kate*. N.Y.: Lothrop, Lee and Shepard, 1992; 32pp., $14.00.

————. *Regina's Big Mistake*. N.Y.: Houghton Mifflin, 1990; 28pp., $16.00.

————. *The Ugly Menorah*. N.Y.: Farrar, Straus and Giroux, 1996; 32pp, $14.00.

Most, Bernard. *Cock-a-Doodle-Moo!* N.Y.: Harcourt Brace, 1996; 32pp., $12.00.

————. *The Cow that Went Oink*. N.Y.: Harcourt Brace, 1990; 36pp., $13.00.

————. *Dinosaur Questions*. N.Y: Harcourt Brace, 1995; 36pp., $15.00.

————. *Four and Twenty Dinosaurs*. N.Y.: Harper and Row, 1990; 32pp., $8.95.

————. *If the Dinosaurs Came Back*. Calif.: Harcourt Brace Jovanovich, 1978; 32pp., $15.00.

————. *Zoodles*. N.Y.: Harcourt Brace Jovanovich, 1992; 32pp., $13.95.

Munsch, Robert. *Alligator Baby*. N.Y.: Scholastic, 1997; 32pp., $10.95.

Muntean, Michaela. *Bicycle Bear*. N.Y.: Parents Magazine, 1983; 48pp., $5.95.

Murphy, Jill. *Five Minutes Peace*. N.Y.: G. P. Putnam's Sons, 1995; 32pp., $16.95.

————. *What Next, Baby Bear!* N.Y.: Dial Books for the Young, 1984; 32pp., $11.19.

Murphy, Pat. *Pigasus*. N.Y.: Dial Books for Young Readers, 1996; 32pp., $14.99.

Murphy, Stuart J. *The Best Vacation Ever*. N.Y.: HarperCollins, 1997; 40pp., $14.90.

————. *Get Up and Go!*, N.Y.: HarperCollins, 1996; 40pp, $14.89.

————. *The Penny Pot*. N.Y.: HarperCollins Children's Books, 1998; 32pp., $14.95.

————. *Too Many Kangaroo Things to Do!* N.Y.: HarperCollins Children's Books, 1996; 40pp., $14.89.

Musselman, Virginia W. *Making Children's Parties Click*. Pa.: Stackpole Books, 1967; 140pp., NA.

Myers, Lynne Born. *Turnip Soup*. N.Y.: Hyperion Books for Children, 1994; 32pp., $13.90.

Myers, Walter Dean. *How Mr. Monkey Saw the Whole World*. N.Y.: Doubleday Books for Young Readers, 1996; 32pp., $14.95.

————. *Mr. Monkey and the Gotcha Bird*. N.Y.: Delacorte, 1984; 32pp., $14.95.

Myller, Lois. *No! No!* N.Y.: Simon and Schuster, 1971; 23pp., $3.07.

Nash, Ogden. *The Adventures of Isabel*. Mass.: Little, Brown, 1963; 32pp., $11.15.

————. *The Tale of Custard the Dragon*. Mass.: Little, Brown, 1995; 32pp., $14.95.

Naylor, Phyllis Reynolds. *Ducks Disappearing*. N.Y.: Atheneum Books for Young Readers. 1997; 32pp., $10.00.

————. *Jennifer Jean, the Cross-Eyed Queen*. Minn.: Carolrhoda, 1994; 32pp., NA.

Neeham, Bobbe. *Ecology Crafts for Kids*. N.Y.: Sterling, 1998; 144pp., $24.95.

Neitzel, Shirley. *The House I'll Build for the Wrens*. N.Y.: Greenwillow, 1997; 32pp., $15.00.

————. *The Jacket I Wear in the Snow*. N.Y.: Greenwillow, 1989; 32pp, $15.93.

————. *We're Making Breakfast for Mother*. N.Y.: Greenwillow, 1997; 32pp., $15.00.

Nelson, Esther L. *Dancing Games for Children of All Ages*. N.Y.: Sterling, 1973; 72pp., $16.79.

————. *The Funny Songbook*. N.Y.: Sterling, 1984; 96pp., NA.

————. *The Silly Song-book*. N.Y.: Sterling, 1982; 128pp., $16.79.

————. *Singing and Dancing Games for the Very Young*. N.Y.: Sterling, 1977; 72pp., NA.

Nerlove, Miriam. *Valentine's Day*. Ill.: Albert Whitman, 1992; 32pp., $13.95.

Newcome, Zita. *Toddlerobics*. Mass.: Candlewick, 1996; 32pp., $14.99.

Newman, Leslea. *Remember That*. N.Y.: Clarion, 1993; 32pp., $14.95.

Newman, Nanette. *There' a a Bear in the Bath!* N.Y.: Harcourt Brace, 1994; 32pp., $13.95.

Newton, Laura P. *William the Vehicle King*. N.Y.: Bradbury, 1987; 32pp., $12.95.

Nichols, Judy. *Storytimes for Two-Year-Olds, 2nd edition*. Ill.: American Library Association, 1998; 249pp., $28.00.

Nichols, Cathy. *Tuxedo Sam: A Penguin of a Different Color*. N.Y.: Random House, 1982; unpaged, $3.95.

Nielsen, Laura F. *Jeremy's Muffler*. N.Y.: Atheneum Books for Young Readers, 1995; 32pp., $15.00.

Nightingale, Sandy. *Cider Apples*. N.Y.: Harcourt Brace, 1996; 28pp., $15.00.

Nikola-Lisa, W. *1,2,3 Thanksgiving!* Ill.: Albert Whitman, 1991; 32pp., $24.50.

Noble, Trinka. *Hansy's Mermaid*. N.Y.: Dial Books for the Young, 1983; 32pp., $10.89.

————. *Jimmy's Boa Bounces Back*. N.Y.: Dial Books for the Young, 1984; 32pp., $13.89.

Noble, Trinka Hakes. *Jimmy's Boa and the Big Splash Birthday Bash*. N.Y.: Dial Books for Young Readers, 1989; 32ppp., $13.95.

Nolan, Dennis. *Monster Bubbles*. N.J.: Prentice-Hall, 1976; 32pp., NA.

————. *Witch Bazooza*. N.Y.: Prentice-Hall, 1979; 30pp., $7.95.

Nolen, Jerdine. *Raising Dragons*. Fla.: Harcourt Brace, 1998; 32pp., $16.00.

Nolen, Jerdine and Mark Buchner. *Harvey Potter's Balloon Farm*. N.Y.: Lothrop, Lee and Shepard, 1989; 32pp., $16.00.

Noll, Sally. *I Have a Loose Tooth*. N.Y.: Greenwillow, 1992; 32pp., NA.

Norac, Carl. *I Love You So Much*. N.Y.: Doubleday, 1998; 26pp., $9.95.

Norman, Howard. *The Owl Scatterer*. N.Y.: Atlantic Monthly, 1986; 32pp., $13.95.

Nozaki, Akihiro and Mitsumasa Anno. *Anno's Hat Tricks*. N.Y.: Philomel, 1984; 32pp., $11.95.

Numeroff, Laura. *Chimps Don't Wear Glasses*. N.Y.: Simon and Schuster Books for Young Readers, 1995; 32pp., $14.00.

———. *If You Give a Mouse a Cookie*. N.Y.: Harper and Row Junior Books, 1985; 32pp., $9.89.

———. *If You Give a Pig a Pancake*. N.Y.: HarperCollins, 1998; 32pp., $14.95.

———. *What Mommies Do Best/What Daddies Do Best*. N.Y.: Simon and Schuster Books for Young Readers, 1998; 36pp., $13.00.

Nunes, Susan Miho. *The Last Dragon*. N.Y.: Clarion, 1995; 32pp., $14.95.

Oakley, Ruth. *The Marshall Cavendish Illustrated Guide to Games Children Play Around the World: Ball Games*. N.Y.: Marshall Cavendish, 1989; 48pp., NA.

Oberman, Sheldon. *By the Hanukkah Light*. Pa.: Boyds Mills, 1997; 32pp., $15.95.

Odor, Ruth Shannon, and others. *February Holidays Handbook*. Ill.: Children's Press, 1985; 96pp., $12.95.

Offen, Hilda. *A Fox Got My Socks*. N.Y.: Dutton Children's Books, 1992; 28pp., $10.00.

———. *As Quiet as a Mouse*. N.Y.: Dutton Children's Books, 1994; 32pp., $12.99.

Ogburn, Jacqueline K. *The Noise Lullaby*. N.Y.: Lothrop, Lee and Shepard, 1995; 32pp., $15.00.

Oppenheim, Joanne. *Mrs. Peloki's Snake*. N.Y.: Dodd, Mead, 1980; 32pp., $10.95.

———. *Rooter Remembers*. N.Y.: Viking, 1991; 32pp., $11.95.

Oram, Hiawyn. *Baba Yaga and the Wise Doll*. N.Y.: Dutton's Children's Books, 1997; 32pp., $15.99.

———. *Badger's Bring Something Party*. N.Y.: Lothrop, Lee and Shepard, 1995; 32pp., $15.00.

Orbach, Ruth. *Apple Pigs*. Ohio: William Collins and World, 1976; 32pp., $5.95.

Orgel, Doris. *The Spaghetti Party*. N.Y.: Bantam, 1995; 32pp., $12.95.

Orgel, Doris, and Ellen Schecter. *The Flower of Sheba*. N.Y.: Bantam, 1994; 48pp., $18.60.

Orlick, Terry. *The Cooperative Sports and Games Book*. N.Y.: Pantheon, 1978; 131pp., $7.00.

Ormerod, Jan. *Bend and Stretch*. N.Y.: Lothrop, Lee and Shepard, 1987; 18pp., $5.95.

———. *Ms. MacDonald Has a Class*. N.Y.: Clarion, 1996; 32pp., $15.95.

Orr, Katherine. *Story of a Dolphin*. Minn.: Carolrhoda, 1993; 32pp., $19.95.

Orton, Lyn. *The Grolier KidsCrafts Puppet Book*. Conn.: Grolier Educational, 1997; 48pp., NA.

Osofsky, Audrey. *Dreamcatcher*. N.Y.: Orchard, 1992; 32pp., $16.99.

———. *My Buddy*. N.Y.: Henry Holt, Inc. , 1992; 32pp., $15.95.

Ostheeren, Ingrid. *Coriander's Easter Adventure*. N.Y.: North-South, 1992; 32pp., $14.95.

———. *Martin and the Pumpkin Ghost*. N.Y.: North-South, 1994; 32pp., $14.90.

Ostrow, Vivian. *My Brother Is from Outer Space (The Book of Proof)*. Ill.: Albert Whitman, 1996; 32pp., $14.95.

Otten, Charlotte F. *January Rides the Wind: A Book of Months*. N.Y.: Lothrop, Lee and Shepard, 1997; 32pp., $16.00.

Otto, Carolyn. *I Can Tell by Touching*. N.Y.: HarperCollins, 1994; 32pp., $14.89.

———. *That Sky, That Rain*. N.Y.: Thomas Y. Crowell, 1990; 32pp., $12.95.

Owen, Cheryl, and Anna Murray. *The Grolier KidsCrafts Craft Book*. Conn.: Grolier Educational, 1997; 48pp., NA.

O'Donnell, Elizabeth Lee. *I Can't Get My Turtle to Move*. N.Y.: Morrow Junior Books, 1989; 28pp., $11.95.

———. *Patrick's Day*. N.Y.: Morrow Junior Books, 1994; 32pp., $15.00.

———. *The Twelve Days of Summer*. N.Y.: Morrow Junior Books, 1991; 32pp., $13.95.

O'Keefe, Susan Heyboer. *One Hungry Monster*. Mass.: Little, Brown, 1989; 32pp., $12.95.

O'Malley, Kevin. *Carl Caught a Flying Fish*. N.Y.: Simon and Schuster Books for Young Readers, 1996; 32pp., $13.00.

Packard, Mary. *The Kite*. Ill.: Children's Press, 1990; 28pp., $3.95.

Palatini, Margie. *Elf Help: Http://Www.Falala.Com*. N.Y.: Hyperion Books for Children, 1997; 32pp., $14.95.

Palmer, Hap. *A Fish Out of Water*. N.Y.: Random House, 1961; 32pp., $9.99.

———. *Learning Basic Skills Through Music, Vol. 2*. N.Y.: Creative Movement and Rhythmic Exploration.

Palmer, Helen. *I Was Kissed by a Seal at the Zoo*. N.Y.: Random House, 1962; 62pp., $6.99.

Panek, Dennis. *Detective Whoo*. N.Y.: Bradbury, 1981; 32pp., $.9.95.

Pankake, Marcia and John. *A Prairie Home Companion Folk Song Book*. N.Y.: Viking Penguin, 1988; 316pp., $22.95.

Paraskevas, Betty. *Cecil Bunions and the Midnight Train*. Calif.: Harcourt Brace, 1996; 32pp., $16.00.

Parents and Teachers of First United Nursery School. *Celebrate!: A Sourcebook of Children's Parties and Friendly Traditions*. Ill.: Rainbow, 1987; 180pp., $9.95.

Parish, Peggy. *Let's Celebrate: Holiday Decorations You Can Make*. N.Y.: Greenwillow, 1976; 56pp., $5.95.

———. *Little Indian*. N.Y.: Simon and Schuster, 1968; 32pp., NA.

———. *Mind Your Manners*. N.Y.: Greenwillow, 1994; 56pp., $10.15.

———. *Sheet Magic*. N.Y.: Macmillan, 1971; 96pp., $4.95.

Parker, Mary Jessie. *City Storm*. N.Y.: Scholastic, 1990; 32pp., $12.95.

Parker, Nancy. *Love from Aunt Betty*. N.Y.: Dodd, Mead, 1983; 32pp., $11.95.

Parker, Vic, and Emily Bolam. *Bearobics: A Hip-Hop Counting Story*. N.Y.: Viking, 1997; 26pp., $14.99.

Paterson, Diane. *Soap and Suds*. N.Y.: Alfred A. Knopf, 1984; 46pp., NA.

Patrick, Sally, Vicky Schwartz, and Pat LoPresti. *The Month by Month Treasure Box*. Tenn.: Incentive, 1988; 79pp., $9.95.

Patterson, Francine. *Koko's Kitten*. N.Y.: Scholastic, 1985; 32pp., $10.19.

Patz, Nancy. *To Annabella Pelican from Thomas Hippotamus*. N.Y.: Four Winds, 1991; 32pp., $13.95.

Paul, Ann Whitford. *Hello Toes! Hello Feet!!* N.Y.: DK Publishing, 1998; 32pp., $15.95.

―――. *Shadows Are About*. N.Y.: Scholastic, 1992; 32pp., $13.95.

Paulson, Tim. *Jack and the Beanstalk and the Beanstalk Incident*. N.Y.: Carol, 1996; 32pp., $12.95.

Paxton, Tom. *Engelbert Joins the Circus*. N.Y.: Morrow Junior Books, 1997; 32pp., $15.00.

―――. *Engelbert the Elephant*. N.Y.: Morrow Junior Books, 1990; 32pp., $14.95.

Payne, Emma. *Katy No-Pocket*. Mass.: Houghton Mifflin, 1973; 32pp., $17.00.

Pearson, Susan. *That's Enough for One Day, J.P.!* N.Y.: Dial, 1977; 26pp., $5.95.

Pearson, Tracey Campbell. *The Purple Hat*. N.Y.: Farrar, Straus and Giroux. 1997; 32pp., $16.00.

Peck, Robert. *Hamilton*. Mass.: Little, Brown, 1976; 32pp., $13.45.

Peet, Bill. *The Ant and the Elephant*. Mass.: Houghton Mifflin, 1972; 48pp., $14.95.

―――. *The Caboose Who Got Loose*. Mass.: Houghton Mifflin, 1871; 48pp., $11.95.

―――. *No Such Things*. Mass.: Houghton Mifflin, 1983; 32pp., $14.95.

Pellegrini, Nina. *Families Are Different*. N.Y.: Holiday House, 1991; 30pp., $14.95.

Penn, Malka. *The Miracle of the Potato Latkes*. N.Y.: Holiday House, 1994; 32pp., $15.95.

Peppe, Rodney. *The House that Jack Built*. N.Y.: Delacorte, 1970; 32pp., $13.95.

Perkins, Al. *Tubby and the Lantern*. N.Y.: Random House, 1971; 64pp., $4.00.

Perlman, Janet. *The Emperor Penguin's New Clothes*. N.Y.: Viking, 1994; 32pp., $14.99.

Perrault, Charles. *Puss in Boots*. N.J.: Troll Associates, 1979; 32pp., $9.79.

Perry, Margaret. *Rainy Day Music*. N.Y.: M. Evans, 1970; 160pp., $5.95.

Peteraf, Nancy J. *A Plant Called Spot*. N.Y.: Delacorte, 1994; 32pp., $13.95.

Peters, Lisa Westberg. *When the Fly Flew in . . . .* N.Y.: Dial Books for Young Readers, 1994; 32pp., $15.99.

―――. *October Smiled Back*. N.Y.: Henry Holt, 1996; 32ppp., $14.95.

Petersham, Maud. *The Circus Baby*. N.Y.: Macmillan, 1968; 32pp., $11.95.

Peterson, Carolyn Sue, and Brenny Hall. *Story Programs: A Source Book of Materials*. N.J.: Scarecrow, 1999; 294pp., $29.50.

Peterson, Julienne. *Caterina: The Clever Farm Girl*. N.Y.: Dial Books for Young Readers, 1996; 32pp., $14.99.

Petie, Haris. *The Seed the Squirrel Dropped*. N.J.: Prentice-Hall, 1976; 32pp., $5.95.

Pevear, Richard. *Our King Has Horns!* N.Y.: Macmillan, 1987; 32pp., $14.95.

Pfanner, Louise. *Louise Builds a Boat*. N.Y.: Orchard, 2000; 32pp., $10.95.

Pfeffer, Wendy. *What's it Like to Be a Fish?* N.Y.: HarperCollins, 1996; 32pp., $14.89.

Pfiffner, George. *Earth-Friendly Wearables*. N.Y.: John Wiley and Sons, 1994; 128pp., $12.95.

Pfister, Marcus. *Hopper's Treetop Adventure*. N.Y.: North-South, 1997; 32pp., $15.95.

―――. *How Leo Learned to Be King*. N.Y.: North-South, 1998; 32pp., $15.95.

―――. *Milo and the Magical Stones*. N.Y.: North-South, 1997; 32pp., $18.95.

―――. *Penguin Pete*. N.Y.: North-South, 1987; 32pp., $15.88.

―――. *The Rainbow Fish*. N.Y.: North-South, 1992; 32pp., $18.95.

―――. *Rainbow Fish and the Big Blue Whale*. N.Y.: North-South, 1998; 32pp., $18.95.

Pflug, Betsy. *Pint Size Fun*. N.Y.: J. B. Lippincott, 1972; 38pp., $3.93.

Piankowski, Jan. *Sizes*. N.Y.: Julian Messner, 1983; 32pp., $7.97.

Pierce, Jack. *The Freight Train Book*. Minn.: Carolrhoda, 1980; unpaged, $9.95.

Pilkey, Dav. *'Twas the Night before Thanksgiving*. N.Y.: Orchard, 1990; 32pp., 16.99.

Pinkney, Andrea Davis. *Seven Candles for Kwanzaa*. N.Y.: Dial Books for Young Readers, 1993; 32pp., $14.89.

Pinkwater, Daniel. *Author's Day*. N.Y.: Macmillan, 1993; 32pp., $14.00.

―――. *The Bear's Picture*. N.Y.: E. P. Dutton, 1984; 39pp., $10.95.

―――. *The Big Orange Splot*. N.Y.: Hastings House, 1992; 31pp., $12.95.

―――. *Doodle Flute*. N.Y.: Macmillan Pub., Co., 1991; 32pp., $12.95.

―――. *I Was a Second Grade Werewolf*. N.Y.: E. P. Dutton, 1983; 32pp., $9.66.

Pirotta, Savior. *Turtle Bay*. N.Y.: Farrar, Straus and Giroux, 1997; 32pp., $15.00.

Pitcher, Caroline. *Cars and Boats*. N.Y.: Franklin Watts, 1983; 30pp., $8.90.

―――. *Games*. N.Y.: Franklin Watts, 1984; 30pp., $8.90.

―――. *The Snow Whale*. Calif.: Sierra Club Books for Children, 1996; 24pp., $15.95.

Pitre, Felix. *Paco and the Witch*. N.Y.: Lodestar, 1995; 32pp., $13.99.

Plath, Sylvia. *The Bed Book*. N.Y.: Harper and Row Junior Books, 1976; 40pp., $12.95.

Pluckrose, Henry. *Smelling*. N.Y.: Franklin Watts, 1986; 30pp., NA.

Pocock, Rita. *Annabelle and the Big Slide*. Calif.: Gulliver, 1989; 28pp., $10.95.

Polacco, Patricia. *Aunt Chip and the Great Triple Creek Dam Affair*. N.Y.: Philomel, 1996; 32pp., $15.95.

―――. *Babushka's Mother Goose*. N.Y.: Philomel, 1995; 64pp., $17.95.

―――. *The Bee Tree*. N.Y.: Philomel, 1993; 32pp., $14.95.

―――. *Some Birthday!* N.Y.: Simon and Schuster Books for Young Readers, 1991; 32pp., $15.00.

―――. *The Trees of the Dancing Goats*. N.Y.: Simon and Schuster Books for Young Readers, 1996; 32pp., $16.00.

Polhamus, Jean. *Dinosaur Do's and Don'ts*. N.J.: Windmill, 1975; 23pp., $4.95.

Polushkin, Maria. *The Little Hen and the Giant*. N.Y.: Harper and Row, 1977; 32pp., NA.

―――. *Mother, Mother I Want Another*. N.Y.: Crown, 1988; 32pp., $5.99.

Pomerantz, Charlotte. *You're Not My Best Friend Anymore*. N.Y.: Dial Books for Young Readers, 1998; 32pp., $15.89.

Porter, A. P. *Kwanzaa*. Minn.: Carolrhoda, 1991; 56pp., $18.60.

Poulet, Virginia. *Blue Bug's Safety Book*. Ill.: Children's Press, 1973; 32pp., $15.00.

Poulin, Stephanie. *Could You Stop Josephine?* N.Y.: Tundra Books, 1988; 32pp., $12.95.

Powell, Harriet. *Games-Songs with Prof. Dogg's Troupe.* London: A and C Black, 1983; 56pp., $7.95.

Powers, Mary Ellen. *Our Teacher's in a Wheelchair.* Ill.: Albert Whitman, 1986; 32pp., $12.95.

Prater, John. *The Greatest Show on Earth.* Mass.: Candlewick, 1995; 32pp., $14.95.
———. *Once Upon a Time.* Mass.: Candlewick, 1993; 32pp., $14.95.

Prelutsky, Jack. *The Terrible Tiger.* N.Y.: Macmillan, 1989; 28pp., $3.95.

Press, Judy. *Alphabet Art.* Vt.: Williamson, 1998; 144pp., $12.95.
———. *Creative Fun for 2- to 6-Year-Olds: The Little Hands Big Fun Craft Book.* Vt.: Williamson, 1996; 144pp., $12.95.

Priddy, Roger. *Baby's Book of the Body.* N.Y.: DK Publishing, 1996; 18pp., $9.95.

Primavera, Elise. *Plantpet.* N.Y.: G. P. Putnam's Sons, 1994; 32pp., $15.95.
———. *Ralph's Frozen Tale.* N.Y.: G. P. Putnam's Sons, 1991; 32pp., NA.

Pringle, Laurence. *Jesse Builds a Road.* N.Y.: Macmillan, 1989; 32pp., $13.95.
———. *Octopus Hug.* Pa.: Boyds Mills, 1996; 32pp., $6.95.

Propp, Jim. *Tuscanini.* N.Y.: Bradbury, 1992; 32pp., NA.

Pryor, Bonnie. *Birthday Blizzard.* N.Y.: Morrow Junior Books, 1993; 32pp., $12.95.

Pulver, Robin. *Mrs. Toggle's Beautiful Blue Shoe.* N.Y.: Four Winds, 1994; 32pp., $13.95.

Quackenbush, Robert. *The Holiday Song Book.* N.Y.: Lothrop, Lee and Shepard Co., 1977; 128pp., $9.20.
———. *The Man on the Flying Trapeze.* N.Y.: J. B. Lippincott, 1975; 40pp., $10.70.
———. *Pop! Goes the Weasel and Yankee Doodle.* N.Y.: J. B. Lippincott Co., 1976; 32p., $13.89.

Quigley, Lillian. *The Blind Men and the Elephant.* N.Y.: Charles Scribner's Sons, 1959; 32pp., NA.

Radcliffe, Theresa. *Bashi, Elephant Baby.* N.Y.: Viking, 1997; 32pp., $13.99.
———. *Cimru the Seal.* N.Y.: Viking, 1996; 32pp., $12.99.

Rader, Laura, illust. *Mother Hubbard's Cupboard: A Mother Goose Surprise Book.* N.Y.: Tambourine, 1993; 45pp., $12.95.

Raffi. *Baby Beluga.* N.Y.: Crown, 1983; 32pp., $16.00.
———. *Everything Grows.* N.Y.: Crown Publishers Inc., 1989; 32pp., NA.
———. *The Raffi Everything Grows Songbook.* N.Y.: Crown, 1989; 48pp., $13.95.
———. *The Raffi Singable Songbook.* N.Y.: Crown, 1980; 106pp., $14.95.
———. *The Second Raffi Songbook.* N.Y.: Crown, 1986; 104pp., $14.95.

Raney, Ken. *It's Probably Good Dinosaurs Are Extinct.* N.Y.: Green Tiger, 1993; 32pp., $14.00.

Rankin, Joan. *Wow!: It's Great Being a Duck.* N.Y.: Margaret K. McElderry, 1997; 32pp., $16.00.

Rankin, Kim. *Cut and Create! Holidays.* Ill.: Teaching and Learning, 1997; 80pp., $12.43.

Ransom, Candice F. *Shooting Star Summer.* Pa.: Caroline House/Boyds Mills, 1992; 32pp., $14.95.

Raschka, Chris. *Elizabeth Imagined an Iceberg.* N.Y.: Orchard, 1994; 32pp., $15.99.

Rasmussen, Richard and Ronda. *The Kids' Encyclopedia of Things to Make and Do*. Minn.: Redleaf Press, 1981; 244pp., NA.

Rassmus, Jens. *Farmer Enno and His Cow*. N.Y.: Orchard, 1997; 32pp., $14.95.

Rathmann, Peggy. *Goodnight, Gorilla*. N.Y.: G.P. Putnam, 1994; 40pp., $14.99.

———. *Officer Buckle and Gloria*. N.Y.: G.P. Putnam, 1995; 37pp., $15.95.

Rau, Dana Meachen. *The Secret Code*. N.Y.: Children's Press, 1998; 31pp., $17.00.

Rayner, Shoo. *My First Picture Joke Book*. N.Y.: Viking Kestrel, 1989; 32pp., $11.95.

Razzi, James. *Bag of Tricks!* N.Y.: Parents Magazine, 1971; 61pp., NA.

———. *Easy Does It!* N.Y.: Parents Magazine, 1969; 61pp., NA.

———. *Simply Fun! Things to Make and Do*. N.Y.: Parents Magazine, 1968; 61pp., $3.78.

Reaching the Special Learner through Music. N.Y.: Silver Burdett, 1979; 298pp., NA.

Ready, Dee. *Doctors*. Minn.: Bridgestone, 1997; 24pp., $14.00.

Reay, Joanne, and Adriano Gon. *Bumpus Rumpus and the Rainy Day*. Mass.: Houghton Mifflin, 1995; 32pp., $14.95.

Reeves, Mona Rabun. *The Spooky Eerie Night Noise*. N.Y.: Bradbury, 1989; 32pp., $13.95.

Reiser, Lynn. *Any Kind of Dog*. N.Y.: Greenwillow, 1992; 24pp., $14.00.

———. *The Surprise Family*. N.Y.: Greenwillow, 1994; 32pp., $15.93.

Renberg, Dalia Hardof. *King Solomon and the Bee*. N.Y.: HarperCollins, 1994; 32pp., $14.90.

Reneaux, J. J. *Why Alligator Hates Dog: A Cajun Folktale*. Ark.: August House, 1995; 32pp., $15.95.

Repchuk, Caroline. *The Glitter Dragon*. N.Y.: Marlowe, 1995; 32pp., $14.95.

Rey, Hans. *Curious George Rides a Bike*. Mass.: Houghton Mifflin, 1952; 48pp., $11.15.

Rey, Margaret. *Curious George Flies a Kite*. Mass.: Houghton Mifflin, 1997; 80pp., $8.95.

———. *Curious George Goes to the Dentist*. Mass.: Houghton Mifflin, 1989; 32pp., $9.95.

Rey, Margaret, and Alan J. Shalleck. *Curious George Goes to School*. Mass.: Houghton Mifflin, 1989; 30pp., $12.00.

Rey, Margaret and H. A. *Curious George Visits a Police Station*. Mass.: Houghton Mifflin, 1987; 32pp., $8.95.

Rice, James. *Cowboy Rodeo*. La.: Pelican, 1992; 32pp., $14.95.

Richardson, Jean. *Thomas' Sister*. N.Y.: Four Winds, 1991; 32pp., $13.95.

Richardson, Judith Benet. *The Way Home*. N.Y.: Macmillan, 1991; 32pp., NA.

Richmond, Margie Hayes. *Look What You Can Make with Paper Plates*. N.Y.: Boyds Mills, 1997; 48pp., $5.95.

Riddell, Chris. *Bird's New Shoes*. N.Y.: Henry Holt, 1987; 26pp., $12.95.

———. *The Trouble with Elephants*. N.Y.: J. B. Lippincott, 1988; 32pp., $12.90.

Riddell, Edwina. *My First Day at Preschool*. N.Y.: Barron's Educational Series, Inc., 1992; 32pp., $9.95.

Rieheckly, Janet. *Kwanzaa*. Ill.: Children's Press, 1993; 31pp., $17.50.

Riggers, Maxine. *Amazing Alligators and Other Story Hour Friends*. Ill.: Monday Morning, 1990; 208pp., NA.

Riley, Linnea. *Mouse Mess*. N.Y.: Blue Sky, 1997; 32pp., $15.95.

Ripley, Catherine. *Outdoor Fun*. Mass.: Little, Brown, 1989; 32pp., $12.95.

Ritter, Darlene. *Literature-Based Art Activities*. Calif.: Creative Teaching Press, 1991; 104pp., $9.98.

Robbins, Ireene. *Gifts Galore!* N.Y.: Parker, 1980; 222pp., $14.95.

Roberts, Bethany. *Halloween Mice!* N.Y.: Clarion,1995; 32pp., $12.95.

———. *Monster Manners*. N.Y.: Clarion, 1996; 32pp., $15.00.

———. *The Two O'Clock Secret*. Ill.: Albert Whitman, 1993; 32pp., $13.95.

———. *Valentine Mice!* N.Y.: Clarion, 1997; 32pp., $13.00.

Roberts, Lynda. *Mitt Magic: Fingerplays for Finger Puppets*. Md.: Gryphon House, 1985; 89pp., $12.95.

Roberts, Thom. *Pirates in the Park*. N.Y.: Crown Publishers, 1973; 32pp., $4.95.

Roche, Denis. *Loo-Loo, Boo, and Art You Can Do*. Mass.: Houghton Mifflin, 1996; 32pp., $14.95.

Rockwell, Anne. *Bear Child's Book of Hours*. N.Y.: Thomas Y. Crowell Junior Books, 1987; 32pp., $11.89.

———. *Bear Child's Book of Special Days*. N.Y.: E. P. Dutton, 1989; 32pp., $12.95.

———. *Big Wheels*. N.Y.: E. P. Dutton, 1986; 32pp., $9.95.

———. *Boats*. N.Y.: E. P. Dutton, 1993; 32pp., $4.99.

———. *Fire Engines*. N.Y.: E. P. Dutton, 1986; 32pp., $13.99.

———. *First Comes Spring*. N.Y.: Thomas Y. Crowell, 1985; 32pp., $6.95.

———. *Games: (and How to Play Them)*. N.Y.: Thomas Y. Crowell, 1973; 44pp., $10.89.

———. *I Fly*. N.Y.: Crown Publishers Inc., 1997; 36pp., $17.99.

———. *My Spring Robin*. N.Y.: Macmillan, 1989; 24pp., $12.95.

———. *The Storm*. N.Y.: Hyperion Books for Children, 1994; 32pp., $15.95.

———. *Willy Can Count*. N.Y.: Arcade Publishing Inc. 1989; 26pp., $13.95.

Rockwell, Anne, and Harlow. *Machines*. N.Y.: Macmillan, 1972; 32pp., NA.

———. *The Night We Slept Outside*. N.Y.: Macmillan, 1983; 48pp., NA.

Rockwell, Harlow. *My Dentist*. N.Y.: Greenwillow, 1975; 32pp., $15.00.

———. *My Nursery School*. N.Y.: Greenwillow, 1976; 24pp., $11.75.

Rogers, Fred. *Going to the Dentist*. N.Y.: G. P. Putnam's Sons, 1989; 25pp., $12.95.

———. *Let's Talk about It: Adoption*. N.Y.: G. P. Putnam's Sons, 1994; 32pp., $15.95.

Rogers, Paul. *The Shapes Game*. N.Y.: Henry Holt, 1995; 32pp., $12.95.

———. *Somebody's Awake*. N.Y.: Atheneum, 1989; 20pp., $10.95.

Rogers, Paul and Emma. *Quacky Duck*. Mass.: Little, Brown, 1995; 26pp., $14.95.

Rogers, Sally. *Earthsong*. N.Y.: Dutton's Children's Books, 1998; 32pp., $15.99.

Roop, Peter and Connie. *Let's Celebrate Halloween*. Conn.: Millbrook, 1997; 36pp., $19.90.

Root, Phyllis. *Contrary Bear*. N.Y.: Laura Geringer, 1996; 32pp., $13.95.

———. *Moon Tiger*. N.Y.: Holt, Rinehart and Winston, 1985; 32pp., NA.

———. *Mrs. Potter's Pig*. Mass.: Candlewick, 1996; 32pp., $5.99.

———. *One Duck Stuck*. Mass.: Candlewick, 1998; 40pp., $15.99.

Rose, Deborah Lee. *Meredith's Mother Takes the Train*. Ill.: Albert Whitman, 1991; 24pp., NA.

Rosen, Michael. *This Is Our House*. Mass.: Candlewick, 1996; 32pp., $15.99.

Rosenberg, Liz. *Mama Goose: A New Mother Goose*. N.Y.: Philomel, 1994; 32pp., $15.95.

Rosenberg, Liz, and Susan Gaber. *Eli and Uncle Dawn*. Calif.: Harcourt Brace, 1997; 32pp., $15.00.

Ross,Dave. *Making UFOs*. N.Y.: Franklin Watts, 1980; 32pp., $7.90.

Ross, Diana. *The Story of the Little Red Engine*. N.M.: Transatlantic Arts, Inc., 32pp., $11.95.

Ross, Kathy. *Christmas Ornaments Kids Can Make*. Conn.: Millbrook, Inc., 1998; 64pp., $23.40.

———. *Crafts for Easter*. Conn.: Millbrook, 1995; 48pp., $21.90.

———. *Crafts for Hanukkah*. Conn.: Millbrook, 1996; 48pp., $21.90.

———. *Crafts for Kids Who Are Wild about Dinosaurs*. Conn.: Millbrook, 1997; 48pp., $22.40.

———. *Crafts for Kids Who Are Wild about Insects*. Conn.: Millbrook, 1997; 48pp., $22.40.

———. *Crafts for Kids Who Are Wild about Rainforests*. Conn.: Millbrook, 1997; 48pp., $22.40.

———. *Crafts for Kids Who Are Wild about Reptiles*. Conn.: Millbrook, 1998; 48pp., $22.40.

———. *Crafts for Kwanzaa*. Conn.: Millbrook, 1994; 48pp., $21.00.

———. *Crafts for Valentine's Day*. Conn.: Millbrook, 48pp., $21.90.

———. *Crafts from Your Favorite Fairy Tales*. Conn.: Millbrook, 48pp., $22.40.

———. *Crafts to Make in the Spring*. Conn.: Millbrook, 64pp., $23.40.

———. *Crafts to Make in the Fall*. Conn.: Millbrook, 64pp., $23.40.

———. *Every Day Is Earth Day*. Conn.: Millbrook, 48pp., $21.90.

———. *Gifts to Make for Your Favorite Grown-up*. Conn.: Millbrook, 96pp., $24.90.

———. *The Jewish Holiday Craft Book*. Conn.: Millbrook, 96pp., $25.90.

Ross, Tony. *Lazy Jack*. N.Y.: Dial Books for Young Readers, 1986; 32pp., $3.95.

Ross, Wilda. *What Did the Dinosaurs Eat?* N.Y.: Coward, 1972; 47pp., $3.86.

Rothenberg, Joan. *Inside-Out Grandma: A Hanukkah Story*. N.Y.: Hyperion Books for Children, 1995; 32pp., $14.95.

Rotner, Shelley, and Sheila M. Kelly. *Lots of Dads*. N.Y.: Dial Books for Young Readers, 1997; 24pp., $12.99.

Rounds, Glen. *Cowboys*. N.Y.: Holiday House, 1991; 32pp., $15.95.

Rowe, Jeanne. *A Trip Through a School*. N.Y.: Franklin Watts, 1969; 47pp., NA.

Royston, Angela. *Big Machines*. Mass.: Little, Brown, 1994; 32p., $12.95.

Rubel, Nicole. *The Ghost Family Meets Its Match*. N.Y.: Dial Books for Young Readers, 1992; 32pp., $13.89.

Rush, Ken. *Friday's Journey*. N.Y.: Orchard, 1994; 30pp., $15.99.

Russo, Marisabina. *Alex Is My Friend*. N.Y.: Greenwillow, 1992; 30pp., $13.95.

———. *When Mama Gets Home*. N.Y.: Greenwillow, 1998; 32pp., $15.00.

Ryden, Hope. *Joey: The Story of a Baby Kangaroo*. N.Y.: Tambourine, 1994; 40pp., $14.93.

Ryder, Joanne. *A House by the Sea*. N.Y.: Morrow Junior Books, 1994; 32pp., $15.00.

———. *Jaguar in the Rainforest*. N.Y.: Morrow Junior Books, 1996; 32pp., $15.93.

Rylant, Cynthia. *Birthday Presents*. N.Y.: Orchard, 1987; 32pp., $6.95.

———. *The Bookshop Dog*. N.Y.: Blue Sky, 1996; 40pp., $14.95.

———. *Mr. Putter and Tabby Pick the Pears*. N.Y.: Harcourt Brace, 1995; 44pp., $12.00.

———. *The Old Woman Who Named Things*. N.Y.: Harcourt Brace, 1996; 32pp., $15.00.

———. *The Whales*. N.Y.: Blue Sky, 1996; 40pp., $14.95.

Sachnitter, Jane T. *William Is My Brother*. Ind.: Perspectives, 1991; 32pp., $10.95.

Sadler, Marilyn. *Alistair and the Alien Invasion*. N.Y.: Simon and Schuster Books for Young Readers, 1994; 48pp., $15.00.

Sadler, Marilyn. *Alistair's Elephant*. N.Y.: Prentice-Hall, 1983; 32pp., $11.95.

———. *Alistair in Outer Space*. N.Y.: Prentice-Hall, 1984; 48pp., $15.00.

———. *Alistair's Time Machine*. N.J.: Prentice-Hall, 1989; 40pp., $5.95.

Saint-James, Synthia. *The Gifts of Kwanzaa*. Ill.: Albert Whitman, 1994; 32pp., $14.95.

Samton, Sheila White. *Tilly and the Rhinoceros*. N.Y.: Philomel, 1993; 32pp., $14.95.

Samuels, Barbara. *Happy Birthday, Dolores*. N.Y.: Orchard, 1989; 29pp., $13.99.

Sanfield, Steve, and Susan Gaber. *Bit by Bit*. N.Y.: Philomel, 1995; 32pp., $15.95.

Sathre, Vivian. *Three Kind Mice*. Calif.: Harcourt Brace, 1997; 32pp., $13.00.

Sattler, Helen Roney. *Kitchen Carton Crafts*. N.Y.: Lothrop, Lee and Shepard, 1970; 94pp., NA.

Sauer, Julia. *Mike's House*. N.Y.: Viking Penguin, 1954; 32pp., $3.50.

Saulnier, Karen Luczak, Lillian B. Hamilton, and Harry Bornstein. *The Ugly Duckling in Signed English*. D.C. : Kendall Green, 1974; 48pp., $6.50.

Say, Allen. *Allison*. Mass.: Houghton Mifflin, 1997; 32pp., $17.00.

———. *Stranger in the Mirror*. Mass.: Houghton Mifflin, 1995; 32pp., $16.95.

———. *Tree of Cranes*. Mass.: Houghton Mifflin, 1991; 32pp., $17.95.

Scarry, Richard. *Richard Scarry's Please and Thank You Book*. N.Y.: Random House, 1978; 29pp., $4.99.

Scheer, Julian. *Rain Makes Applesauce*. N.Y.: Holiday House, 1964; 36pp., $16.95.

Scherer, Marge, and Pamela Lawson, editors. *Instructor's Artfully Easy!* N.Y.: Instructor's Books, 1983; 160pp., $15.95.

Schertle, Alice. *Jeremy Bean's St. Patrick's Day*. N.Y.: Lothrop, Lee and Shepard, 1987; 32pp., $14.95.

Schick, Eleanor. *Joey on His Own*. N.Y.: Dial, 1982; 56pp., $7.89.

———. *My Navajo Sister*. N.Y.: Simon and Schuster Books for Young Readers, 1996; 32pp., $16.00.

Schlein, Miriam. *Big Talk*. N.Y.: Bradbury, 1990; 32pp., $12.95.

———. *More than One*. N.Y.: Greenwillow, 1996; 24pp., $15.00.

———. *The Way Mothers Are*. Ill.: Albert Whitman, 1993; 32pp., $14.95.

Schneider, Howie. *Uncle Lester's Hat*. N.Y.: G. P. Putnam's Sons, 1993; 32pp., $13.95.

Schneider, Richard. *Why Christmas Trees Aren't Perfect*. Tenn.: Abingdon, 1987; 32pp., $13.95.

Schoenherr, John. *Bear*. N.Y.: Philomel, 1991; 32pp., $14.95.

Schotter, Roni. *A Fruit and Vegetable Man*. Mass.: Little, Brown, 1993; 32pp., $15.95.

Schubert, Ingrid. *There's a Crocodile under My Bed*. N.Y.: McGraw-Hill, 1981; 24pp., $8.95.

Schubert, Ingrid and Dicter. *Wild Will*. Minn.: Carolrhoda, 1992; 32pp., $19.95.

Schwartz, Alvin. *In a Dark, Dark Room and Other Scary Stories*. N.Y.: Harper and Row, 1984; 64pp., $14.95.

Schwartz, David M. *If You Made a Million*. N.Y.: Lothrop, Lee and Shepard, 1989; 32pp., $16.00.

———M. *Supergrandpa*. N.Y.: Lothrop, Lee and Shepard, 1991; 32pp., $16.93.

Schwartz, Henry. *Albert Goes Hollywood*. N.Y.: Orchard, 1992; 32pp., $15.95.

Schwartz, Linda. *Likeable Recyclables*. Calif.: The Learning Works, 1992; 128pp., $9.95.

Schwartz, Roslyn. *Rose and Dorothy*. N.Y.: Orchard, 1990; 32pp., $4.95.

Schweninger, Ann. *Autumn Days*. N.Y.: Viking, 1993; 32pp., $12.95.

———. *The Hunt for Rabbit's Galosh*. N.Y.: Doubleday, 1976; 30pp., $4.95.

———. *Let's Look at the Seasons: Springtime*. N.Y.: Viking, 1993; 32pp., $13.50.

Scieszka, Jon. *The Frog Prince Continued*. N.Y.: Viking, 1991; 32pp., $14.95.

———. *The True Story of the Three Little Pigs!* N.Y.: Viking Kestrel, 1989; 32pp., $15.99.

Scott, Louise Binder. *Rhymes for Learning Times*. Minn.: T. S. Denison, 1984; 145pp., $15.95.

Scott, Louise Binder, and J. J. Thompson. *Rhymes for Fingers and Flannel Boards*. Minn.: T. S. Denison and Co., Inc., 1984; 136pp., NA.

Scott, Ann Herbert. *Hi*. N.Y.: Philomel, 1994; 32pp., $14.95.

Seaman, Rosie. *Focus on Spring*. Ill.: Fearon Teacher Aids, 1992; 79pp., $10.99.

———. *Focus on Winter*. Ill.: Fearon Teacher Aids, 1992; 79pp., $10.99.

Sebastian, John. *J. B.'s Harmonica*. Calif.: Harcourt Brace Jovanovich, 1993; 32p., $13.95.

Sechrist, Elizabeth Hough, and Janette Woolsey. *It's Time for Thanksgiving*. Pa.: Macrae Smith, 1957; 251pp., $4.48.

Seeger, Ruth Crawford. *American FolkSongs for Children in Home, School, and Nursery School*. N.Y.: Doubleday, 1948; 193pp., $17.10.

Seeley, Laura L. *McSpot's Hidden Spots*. Ga.: Peachtree, 1994; 32pp., $16.95.

Seignobosc, Francoise. *Jeanne-Marie Counts Her Sheep*. N.Y.: Charles Scribner's Sons, 1951; 32pp., $9.95.

Selby, Jennifer. *Beach Bunny*. Calif.: Harcourt Brace, 1995; 32pp., $14.00.

Selkowe, Valerie M. *Spring Green*. N.Y.: Lothrop, Lee and Shepard, 1985; 28pp., NA.

Sendak, Maurice. *Maurice Sendak's Really Rosie Starring the Nutshell Kids*. N.Y.: Harper and Row, 1975; 64pp., $16.95.

———. *Really Rosie*. N.Y.: Harper and Row, 1975; 64pp., $5.95.

Senisi, Ellen B. *Secrets*. N.Y.: Dutton Children's Books, 1995; 32pp., $13.99.

Serfozo, Mary. *Benjamin Bigfoot*. N.Y.: Margaret McElderry, 1993; 32pp., $14.95.

———. *There's a Square*. N.Y.: Scholastic, 1996; 32pp., $6.95.

Sernaque, Vivienne. *Classic Children's Games*. N.Y.: Dell Publishing, 1988, 142pp., $7.95.

Seuss, Dr. *And to Think I Saw it On Mulberry Street*. N.Y.: Vanguard, 1989; 32pp., $14.00.

————. *The Cat in the Hat Songbook*. N.Y.: Random House, 1967; 64pp., $12.00.

————. *Horton Hatches the Egg*. N.Y.: Random House, 1940; 32pp., $15.99.

Severn, Bill. *50 Ways to Have Fun with Old Newspapers*. N.Y.: David McKay, 1978; 152pp., $7.95.

Seymour, Tres. *Hunting the White Cow*. N.Y.: Orchard, 1993; 32pp., $17.95.

Shannon, George. *Heart to Heart*. Mass.: Houghton Mifflin, 1995; 32pp., $13.95.

————. *Seeds*. Mass.: Houghton Mifflin, 1994; 28pp., $13.95.

————. *Tomorrow's Alphabet*. N.Y.: Greenwillow, 1996; 52pp., $15.93.

Shannon, Margaret. *Shannon*. N.Y.: Ticknor and Fields, 1991; 32pp., $13.95.

Sharmat, Marjorie. *The Best Valentine in the World*. N.Y.: Holiday House, 1982; 32pp., $12.95.

————. *I Don't Care*. N.Y.: Macmillan, 1977; 309pp., $6.95.

————. *Mitchell Is Moving*. N.Y.: Simon and Schuster, 1996; 47pp., $15.00.

————. *Tiffany Dino Works Out*. N.Y.: Simon and Schuster, 1995; 32pp., $15.00.

————. *The Trip*. N.Y.: Macmillan, 1976; 64pp., $7.95.

Sharratt, Nick. *My Mom and Dad Make Me Laugh*. Mass.: Candlewick, 1994; 26pp., $12.95.

Shaw, Charles. *It Looked Like Spilt Milk*. N.Y.: Harper and Row Junior Books, 1947; 28pp., $13.95.

Shaw, Nancy. *Sheep Out to Eat*. Mass.: Houghton Mifflin, 1992; 32 pp., $14.00.

————. *Sheep Trick or Treat*. Mass.: Houghton Mifflin, 1997; 32pp., $14.00.

Shelby, Anne. *The Someday House*. N.Y.: Orchard, 1996; 32pp., $14.95.

————. *What to do about Pollution. . . .* N.Y.: Orchard, 1993; 32pp., NA.

Sheldon, Dyan, and Neil Reed. *Unicorn Dreams*. N.Y.: Dial Books for Young Readers, 1997; 32pp., $14.99.

Sherman, Eileen. *The Odd Potato*. Md.: Kar-Ben Copies, 1984; 32pp., $10.95.

Shields, Carol Diggory. *I Wish My Brother Was a Dog*. N.Y.: Dutton Children's Books, 1997; 32pp., $14.99.

Shipton, Jonathan. *No Biting, Horrible Crocodile!* Wisc.: Western, 1995; 32pp., $12.95.

Short, Mayo. *Andy and the Wild Ducks*. Calif.: Melmont, 1959; unpaged, NA.

Shortall, Leonard. *One Way: A Trip with Traffic Signs*. N.Y.: Prentice-Hall, 1975; unpaged, $2.95.

Shorto, Russell. *Cinderella and Cinderella: The Untold Story*. N.Y.: Carol, 1997; 32pp., $12.95.

Showers, Paul. *Ears Are for Hearing*. N.Y.: Thomas Y. Crowell, 1990; 32pp., $12.89.

————. *The Listening Walk*. N.Y.: HarperCollins, 1991; 32pp., $14.90.

————. *Where Does the Garbage Go?* N.Y.: HarperCollins, 1994; 32pp., $12.89.

Shub, Elizabeth. *Seeing Is Believing*. N.Y.: Greenwillow, 1994; 64pp., $14.00.

Shulevitz, Uri. *Snow*. N.Y.: Farrar, Straus and Giroux, 1998; 32pp., $16.00.

————. *Toddle Creek Post Office*. N.Y.: Farrar, Straus and Giroux, 1990; 32pp., $14.95.

Schulz, Charles M. *Charlie Brown's Super Book of Things to Do and Collect.* N.Y.: Random House, 1975; 80pp., $5.99.

Shute, Linda. *Halloween Party.* N.Y.: Lothrop, Lee and Shepard, 1994; 32pp., $15.00.

———. *How I Named the Baby.* Ill.: Albert Whitman, 1993; 32pp., $14.95.

Siebert, Diane. *Train Song.* N.Y.: Thomas Crowell Co., 1990; 32pp., $15.89.

Sierra, Judy. *Counting Crocodiles.* Calif.: Gulliver, 1997; 32pp., $15.00.

———. *Good Night Dinosaurs.* N.Y.: Clarion, 1996; 31pp., $15.00.

———. *The House that Drac Built.* N.Y.: Gulliver Books, 1995; 34pp., $14.00.

Sierra, Judy, and Robert Kaminski. *Children's Traditional Games.* Ariz.: Oryx, 1995; 232pp., $26.50.

Silberg, Jackie. *Games to Play with Toddlers.* Md.: Gryphon House, 1993; 285pp., $14.95.

———. *300 Three Minute Games.* Md.: Gryphon House, 1997; 191pp., $12.95.

Silverman, Erica. *Don't Fidget a Feather!* N.Y.: Macmillan, 1994; 32pp., $16.00.

———. *The Halloween House.* N.Y.: Farrar, Straus and Giroux, 1997; 32pp., 15.00.

———. *Mrs. Peachtree's Bicycle.* N.Y.: Simon and Schuster Books for Young Readers, 1996; 32pp., $15.00.

———. *Warm in the Winter.* N.Y.: Macmillan, 1989; 32pp., $13.95.

Silverstein, Shel. *The Missing Piece.* N.Y.: Harper and Row Junior Books, 1976; 112pp., $14.95.

———. *Who Wants a Cheap Rhinoceros?* N.Y.: Macmillan, 1983; 56pp., $15.95.

Simmons, Jane. *Come Along, Daisy!* Mass.: Little, Brown, 1997; 32pp., $12.95.

Simon, Norma. *Firefighters.* N.Y.: Simon and Schuster Books for Young Readers, 1995; 32pp., $13.00.

———. *I Was So Mad!* Ill.: Albert Whitman, 1974; 40pp., $13.95.

Simon, William L., *The Reader's Digest Children's Songbook.* N.Y.: Reader's Digest Association, Inc., 1985; 252pp., $24.95.

Simons, Robin. *Recyclopedia.* Mass.: Houghton Mifflin, 1976; 118pp., $13.95.

Sirett, Dawn. *My First Paint Book.* N.Y.: Dorling Kindersley, 1994; 48pp., $12.95.

Sitarz, Paula Gaj. *More Picture Book Story Hours: From Parties to Pets.* Colo.: Libraries Unlimited, 1990; 166pp., NA.

Skofield, James. *Round and Around.* N.Y.: HarperCollins, 1993; 32pp., $14.89.

———. *Snow Country.* N.Y.: Harper and Row, 1983; 32pp., $11.95.

Skurzynski, Gloria. *Here Comes the Mail.* N.Y.: Bradbury, 1992; 38pp., $13.95.

Slate, Joseph. *Miss Bindergarten Celebrates the 100th Day of Kindergarten.* N.Y.: Dutton, 1998; 32pp., $14.99.

Slepian, Jan. *Emily Just in Time.* N.Y.: Philomel, 1998; 32pp., $15.99.

Slepian, Jan, and Ann Seidler. *The Hungry Thing Returns.* N.Y.: Scholastic, 1990; 32pp., $11.95.

Sloat, Teri. *Sody Sallyratus.* N.Y.: Dutton Children's Books, 1997; 32pp., $15.99.

Slobodkin, Louis. *Wide-Awake Owl.* N.Y.: Macmillan, 1958; 28pp., $2.50.

Slobodkina, Esphyr. *Caps for Sale.* N.Y.: Harper and Row Junior Books, 1947; 48pp., $14.95.

Sloss, Lesley. *Anthony and the Aardvark.* N.Y.: Lothrop, Lee and Shepard, 1991; 25pp., $13.95.

Smalls, Irene. *Beginning School*. N.J.: Silver, 1997; 32pp., $11.95.

Smith, Lane. *Glasses, Who Needs 'em?* N.Y.: Viking, 1991; 32pp., $15.99.

Smith, Maggie. *Argo You Lucky Dog*. N.Y.: Lothrop,Lee and Shepard, 1994; 32pp., $15.00.

————. *My Grandma's Chair*. N.Y.: Lothrop, Lee and Shepard, 1992; 32pp., $13.93.

Snape, Juliet and Charles. *The Boy with Square Eyes: A Tale of Televisionitis*. N.Y.: Prentice-Hall Books for Young Readers, 1987; 32pp., $12.95.

————. *Frog Odyssey*. N.Y.: Simon and Schuster Books for Young Readers, 1991; 28pp., $14.00.

————. *I'm Not Frightened of Ghosts*. N.Y.: Prentice Hall Books for Young Readers, 1986; 32pp., $11.95.

Snow, Pegeen. *Mrs. Periwinkle's Groceries*. Ill.: Children's Press, 1981; 32pp., $2.50.

Snyder, Carol. *One Up, One Down*. N.Y.: Atheneum Books for Young Readers, 1995; 32pp., $15.00.

Snyder, Dianne. *The Boy of the Three-Year Nap*. Mass.: Houghton Mifflin, 1988; 32pp., $16.95.

So, Meilo. *The Emperor and the Nightingale*. N.Y.: Bradbury, 1992; 26pp., $13.95.

Solga, Kim. *Make Gifts!* Conn.: Grolier Educational, 1991; 48pp., $11.99.

Sommer, Elyse. *Make It with Burlap*. N.Y.: Lothrop, Lee and Shepard, 1973; 96pp., $2.99.

————. *Songs and Rhymes for Little Children*. N.Y.: G & H. Publishing, 1976; (no longer active).

Spaete, Susan. *Classroom Parties*. Ill.: Building Blocks, 1987; 114pp., $8.95.

Spier, Peter. *The Star Spangled Banner*. N.Y.: Doubleday, 1973; 48pp., $9.95.

Spinelli, Eileen. *Somebody Loves You, Mr. Hatch*. N.Y.: Bradbury, 1991; 32pp., $15.00.

————. *Thanksgiving at the Tappletons*. Mass.: Addison-Wesley, 1984; 28pp., $15.89.

Spizman, Robyn Freedman. *Lollipops, Grapes, and Clothespin Critters: Quick-on-the-Spot Remedies for Restless Children*. Mass.: Addison-Wesley, 1985; 160pp. $5.95.

Stadler, John. *The Cats of Mrs. Calamari*. N.Y.: Orchard, 1997; 32pp., $15.95.

Stamper, Judith. *Halloween Holiday Grab Bag*. N.Y.: Troll Associates, 1993; 48pp., $11.89.

Stanek, Muriel. *All Alone after School*. Ill.: Albert Whitman, 1985; 32pp., $13.95.

Stanley, Diane. *Rumpelstiltskin's Daughter*. N.Y.: Morrow Junior Books, 1997; 32pp., $14.93.

Stanley, Sanna. *The Rains Are Coming*. N.Y.: Greenwillow, 1993; 32pp., NA.

Steel, Danielle. *Max's Daddy Goes to the Hospital*. N.Y.: Delacorte, 1989; 32pp., $8.95.

Steig, William. *Dr. DeSoto Goes to Africa*. N.Y.: HarperCollins Children's Books, 1994; 32pp., $5.95.

Steig, William. *Pete's a Pizza*. N.Y.: HarperCollins, 1998; 32pp., $13.95.

————. *Sylvester and the Magic Pebble*. N.Y.: Windmill, 1988; 30pp., $11.15.

————. *The Toy Brother*. N.Y.: HarperCollins, 1996; 32pp., $14.89.

Stein, Sara Bonnett. *A Hospital Story*. N.Y.: Walker, 1984; 48pp., $8.95.

Stepto, Michele. *Snuggle Piggy and the Magic Blanket*. N.Y.: E. P. Dutton, 1987; 22pp., $9.95.

Steptoe, John. *Mufaro's Beautiful Daughters: An African Tale*. N.Y.: Lothrop Lee and Shepard, 1987; 32pp., $15.93.

———. *The Story of Jumping Mouse*. N.Y.: Lothrop, Lee and Shepard, 1984; 40pp., $16.00.

Stevens, Janet. *Androcles and the Lion*. N.Y.: Holiday House, 1989; 32pp., $14.95.

Stevens, Kathleen. *Aunt Skilly and the Stranger*. N.Y.: Ticknor and Fields Books for Young Readers, 1994; 32pp., $14.95.

Stevenson, James. *Could Be Worse!* N.Y.: Greenwillow, 1987; 32pp., $4.95.

———. *Howard*. N.Y.: Greenwillow, 1980; 32pp., $11.88.

———. *The Oldest Elf*. N.Y.: Greenwillow, 1996; 32pp., $14.93.

———. *Sam the Zamboni Man*. N.Y.: Greenwillow, 1998; 32pp., $15.00.

———. *We Can't Sleep*. N.Y.: Greenwillow, 1982; 32pp., $11.88.

———. *We Hate Rain!* N.Y.: Greenwillow, 1988; 32pp., $11.95.

———. *Winston, Newton, Elton, and Ed*. N.Y.: Greenwillow, 1978; 56pp., $7.92.

Stevenson, Robert Louis. *My Shadow*. N.Y.: G. P. Putnam's Sons, 1990; 32pp., $4.95.

Stevenson, Sucie. *Jessica the Blue Streak*. N.Y.: Orchard, 1989; 32pp., $12.99.

Stock, Catherine. *Easter Surprise*. N.Y.: Bradbury, 1991; 32pp., $13.00.

Stoeke, Janet Morgan. *Minerva Louise at School*. N.Y.: Dutton Children's Books, 1996; 32pp., $13.95.

Stolz, Mary. *Emmett's Pig*. N.Y.: Harper and Row Junior Books, 1959; 64pp., $15.89.

Stone, Bernard. *Emergency Mouse*. N.Y.: Prentice-Hall, 1978; 32pp., NA.

Stops, Sue. *Dulcie Dando, Soccer Star*. N.Y.: Henry Holt, 1992; 30pp., $14.95.

Stow, Jenny. *Growing Pains*. N.Y.: Bridgewater, 1995; 32pp., $13.95.

Straatviel, Tynne, and Carolyn K. Corl. *Easy Art Lessons, K–6*. N.Y.: Parker, 1971; 154pp., NA.

Strete, Craig Kee. *They Thought They Saw Him*. N.Y.: Greenwillow, 1996; 32pp, $15.00.

Strete, Craig Kee and Michelle Netten Chacon. *How the Indians Bought the Farm*. N.Y.: Greenwillow, 1996; 32pp., $15.00.

Sturges, Philemon. *Ten Flashing Fireflies*. N.Y.: North-South, 1995; 32pp., $15.88.

———. *What's That Sound, Woolly Bear?* Mass.: Little, Brown, 1996; 32pp., $14.95.

Suen, Anastasia. *Man on the Moon*. N.Y.: Viking, 1997; 32pp., $15.99.

———. *Window Music*. N.Y.: Viking, 1998; 32pp., $15.99.

Sullivan, Dianna. *Literature Activities for Young Children*. Calif.: Teacher Created Materials, Inc., 1989; 96pp., NA.

Sullivan, Mary Beth, and Linda Bourke. *A Show of Hands*. Mass.: Addison-Wesley, 1980; 96pp., $13.89.

Sun, Chyng Feng. *Mama Bear*. Mass.: Houghton Mifflin, 1994; 32pp., $14.95.

Sunset. *Children's Crafts: Fun and Creativity for Ages 5–12*. Calif.: Lane, 1976; 96pp., $2.45.

Supraner, Robyn. *Fun-to-Make Nature Crafts*. N.J.: Troll Associates, 48pp., NA.

Supraner, Robyn. *Fun with Paper*. N.J.: Troll Associates, 1981; 48pp., $9.49.

————. *Great Masks to Make.* N.J.: Troll Associates, 48pp., $12.50.

————. *Happy Halloween: Things to Make and Do.* N.J.: Troll Associates, 1981; 48pp., $8.70.

Supraner, Robyn. *Rainy Day Surprises You Can Make.* N.J.: Troll Associates, 1981; 48pp., $9.49.

Sur, William, Mary R. Tolbert, William R. Fischer, and Adeline McCall. *This Is Music: Book 2.* Mass.: Allyn and Bacon, 1967; 136pp., $12.95.

Swamp, Chief Jake. *Giving Thanks: A Native American Good Morning Message.* N.Y.: Lee and Low, 1995; 24pp., $14.95.

Sweat, Lynn, and Louis Phillips. *The Smallest Stegosaurus.* N.Y.: Viking, 1995; 32pp., $4.99.

Szekeres, Cyndy. *The Deep Blue Sky Twinkles with Stars.* N.Y.: Scholastic, 1998; 30pp., $12.95.

Szilagyi, Mary. *Thunderstorm.* N.Y.: Bradbury, 1985; 32pp., $11.95.

Tafuri, Nancy. *Have You Seen My Duckling?* N.Y.: Greenwillow, 1984; 24pp., $16.00.

————. *I Love You, Little One.* N.Y.: Scholastic, 1998; 32pp., $15.95.

————. *This Is the Farmer.* N.Y.: Greenwillow, 1994; 24pp., $14.00.

Talkington, Bruce. *Pooh's Wishing Star.* N.Y.: Disney, 1997; 32pp., $12.95.

Tanis, Joel E., and Jeff Grooters. *The Dragon Pack Snack Attack.* N.Y.: Four Winds, 1993; 32pp., $14.95.

Tapio, Pat. *The Lady Who Saw the Good Side of Everything.* Mass.: Houghton Mifflin, 1975; 32pp., $6.95.

Tarpley, Natasha Anastasia. *I Love My Hair!* Mass.: Little, Brown, 1998; 32pp., $14.95.

Tarsky, Sue. *The Busy Building Book.* N.Y.: G. P. Putnam's Sons, 1997; 32pp., $15.95.

Tashjian, Virginia A. *Juba This and Juba That.* Mass.: Little, Brown, 1969; 116pp., $15.95.

Taylor, Judy. *Sophie and Jack Help Out.* N.Y.: Philomel, 1983; 32pp., $8.95.

Teague, Mark. *Baby Tamer.* N.Y.: Scholastic, 1997; 32pp., $15.95.

————. *Henry Explores the Mountains.* N.Y.: Atheneum, 1975; 47pp., $9.95.

————. *The Lost and Found.* N.Y.: Scholastic, 1998; 32pp., $15.95.

————. *Pigsty.* N.Y.: Scholastic, 1994; 32pp., $13.95.

Temko, Florence. *Felt Craft.* N.Y.: Doubleday, 1973; 64pp., $4.96.

————. *Folk Crafts for World Friendship.* N.Y.: Doubleday, 1976; 143pp., $8.95.

Testa, Fulvio. *Wolf's Favor.* N.Y.: Dial Books for Young Readers, 1986; 32pp., $11.95.

Tews, Susan. *Lizard Sees the World.* N.Y.: Clarion, 1997; 32pp., $15.00.

Thaler, Mike. *The Librarian from the Black Lagoon.* N.Y.: Scholastic, 1997; 32pp., $2.99.

————. *Owly.* N.Y.: Harper and Row, 1982; 32pp., $12.95.

Thayer, Catherine. *Gus Was a Friendly Ghost.* N.Y.: William Morrow, 1962; 30pp., $24.95.

Thayer, Ernest Lawrence. *Casey at the Bat.* N.Y.: Atheneum, 1994; 32pp., $15.00.

Thayer, Jane. *The Popcorn Dragon*. N.Y.: Morrow Junior Books, 1953; 32pp., $17.00.

Thomassie, Tynia. *Feliciana Meets d'Loop Carou*. Mass.: Little, Brown, 1998; 32pp., $15.95.

Thompson, Carol. *Time*. N.Y.: Delacorte, 1989; 28pp., $12.95.

Thompson, Helen Davis. *Let's Celebrate Kwanzaa: An Activity Book for Young Readers*. N.Y.: Gumbs and Thomas, 1992; 28pp., $5.95.

Thompson, Mary. *Gran's Bees*. Conn.: Millbrook, 1996; 32pp., NA.

Thomson, Pat. *Beware of the Aunts!* N.Y.: Margaret McElderry, 1992; 28pp., $14.95.

Thornhill, Jan. *Wild in the City*. Calif.: Sierra Club Books for Children, 1995; 32pp., $16.95.

Tietyen, David E. *The Illustrated Disney Song Book*. N.Y.: Random House, 187pp., $24.95.

Tillstrom, Burr. *The Dragon Who Lived Downstairs*. N.Y.: William Morrow, 1984; 48pp., $11.88.

Titherington, Jeanne. *Baby's Boat*. N.Y.: Greenwillow, 1992; 24p., $16.95.

Titus, Eve. *Anatole and the Piano*. N.Y.: McGraw-Hill, 1966; 32pp., $6.95.

———. *Anatole over Paris*. N.Y.: McGraw-Hill, 1991; 32pp., NA.

Tolhurst, Marilyn. *Somebody and the Three Blairs*. N.Y.: Orchard, 1990; 30pp., $15.95.

Totline Staff. *1001 Rhymes and Fingerplays*. Wash.: Warren, 1994; 312pp., $29.98.

Totten, Kathryn. *Storytime Crafts*. Wisc.: Alleyside, 1998; 101pp., $23.54.

Trapani, Iza. *How Much Is That Doggie in the Window?* Mass.: Whispering Coyote, 1997; 32pp., $15.95.

———. *Oh Where, Oh Where Has My Little Dog Gone?* Mass.: Whispering Coyote, 1996; 32pp., $18.60.

———. *Twinkle, Twinkle, Little Star*. Mass.: Whispering Coyote, 1994; 32pp., $15.95.

Treinen, Sara Jane. *Incredibly Awesome Crafts for Kids*. Iowa: Better Homes and Gardens, 1992; 168pp., NA.

Tresselt, Alvin. *Rain Drop Splash*. N.Y.: Lothrop, Lee and Shepard, 1990; 26pp., $4.95.

———. *Smallest Elephant in the World*. N.Y.: Alfred A. Knopf, 1959; 27pp., $2.95.

———. *White Snow, Bright Snow*. N.Y.: William Morrow, 1988; 33pp., $4.95.

Trivizas, Eugene. *The Three Little Wolves and the Big Bad Pig*. N.Y.: Margaret K. McElderrry Books, 1993; 32pp., $17.00.

Tryon, Leslie. *Albert's Field Trip*. N.Y.: Atheneum, 1993; 32pp., $16.00.

———. *Albert's Halloween: The Case of the Stolen Pumpkins*. N.Y.: Atheneum Books for Young Readers, 1998; 32pp., $16.00.

Tsutsui, Yorkiko. *Anna's Secret Friend*. N.Y.: Viking Kesrel, 1986; 32pp., $10.95.

Tucker, Kathy. *Do Cowboys Ride Bikes?* Ill.: Albert Whitman, 1997; 32pp., $15.95.

———. *Do Pirates Take Baths?* Ill.: Albert Whitman, 1994; 32pp., $15.95.

———. *The Leprechaun in the Basement*. Ill.: Albert Whitman, 1998; 32pp., $15.95.

Tumpert, Ann. *Nothing Sticks Like a Shadow*. Mass.: Houghton Mifflin, 1984; 32pp., $4.95.

Turk, Hanne. *Goodnight Max*. Mass.: Neugebauer Press URS, 1983; unpaged, NA.

Turner, Ann. *Rainflowers*. N.Y.: HarperCollins, 1992; 32pp., $14.00.

———. *Through Moon and Stars and Night Skies*. N.Y.: Harper and Row, 1990; 32pp., $14.89.

Turner, Charles. *The Turtle and the Moon*. N.Y.: Dutton Children's Books, 1991; 30pp., $14.99.

Turner, Gwenda. *Shapes*. N.Y.: Viking, 1991; 32pp., $9.95.

Turner, Priscilla. *The War Between the Vowels and Consonants*. N.Y.: Farrar, Straus and Giroux, 1996; 32pp., $15.00.

Tusa, Tricia. *Libby's New Glasses*. N.Y.: Holiday House, 1984; 32pp., $11.95.

Tyler, Anne. *Tumble Tower*. N.Y.: Orchard, 1993; 32pp., $15.95.

Udry, Janice. *Emily's Autumn*. N.Y.: Albert Whitman, 1969; unpaged, NA.

Udry, Janice May. *Is Susan Here?* N.Y.: HarperCollins, 1993; 32pp., $14.00.

Ulmer, Wendy. *A Campfire for Cowboy Billy*. Ariz.: Rising Moon, 1997; 32pp., $15.95.

The Ultimate Show-Me-How Activity Book. N.Y.: Smithmark, 1997; 256pp., NA.

Umnik, Sharon Dunn. *175 Easy-to-Do Everyday Crafts*. Pa.: Boyds Mills Press, 1995; 63pp., $6.95.

———. *175 Easy-to-Do Halloween Crafts*. Pa.: Boyds Mills Press, 1995; 63pp., $6.95.

———. *175 Easy-to-Do Thanksgiving Crafts*. Pa.: Boyds Mills Press, 1996; 63pp., $6.95.

Ungerer, Tomi. *Moon Man*. N.Y.: Harper and Row, 1967; 32pp., $6.95.

Upham, Elizabeth. *Little Brown Bear Loses His Clothes*. N.Y.: Putnam, 1978; 24pp., $2.50.

Vagin, Vladimir. *The Enormous Carrot*. N.Y.: Scholastic, 1998; 32pp., $15.95.

Van Hise, Carol L. *Seasonal Activities for 3 Year Olds*. N.C.: Carson-Dellosa, 1997; 64pp., $8.95.

Van Rynback, Iris. *Five Little Pumpkins*. Pa.: Boyds Mills, 1995; 34pp., $7.95.

Van Woerkom, Dorothy. *Harry and Shelburt*. N.Y.: Macmillan, 1977; 48pp., $6.95.

VanBlaricom, Colleen. *Crafts from Recyclables*. Pa.: Boyds Mills, 1992; 48pp, $4.95.

Vance, Eleanor Graham. *The Everything Book*. NY: Golden, 1974; 141pp., NA.

VanCleave, Janice. *Play and Find Out about Math*. N.Y.: John Wiley and Sons, 1998; 122pp., $12.95.

Vangsgard, Amy. *Hit of the Party*. Fla.: Cool Hand Communications, 1994; 385pp., NA.

VanLaan, Nancy. *Little Fish, Lost*. N.Y.: Atheneum Books for Young Readers, 1998; 32pp., $15.00.

———. *This Is the Hat*. Mass.: Little, Brown, 1992; 30pp., $14.95.

VanLeeuwen, Jean. *Amanda Pig, Schoolgirl*. N.Y.: Dial Books for Young Readers, 1997; 48pp., $13.99.

———. *A Fourth of July on the Plains*. N.Y.: Dial Books for Young Readers, 1997; 32pp., $14.89.

———. *Going West*. N.Y.: Dial Books for Young Readers, 1992; 48pp., $14.89.

Vaughan, Marcia. *Kapoc the Killer Croc*. N.J.: Silver Burdett, 1995; 32pp., $10.95.

———. *Snap!* N.Y.: Scholastic, 1994; 32pp., $14.95.

Vaughan, Marcia, and Patricia Mullins. *The Sea-Breeze Hotel.* N.Y.: Willa Perlman, 1992; 32pp., $13.89.

Vecchione, Glen. *World's Best Outdoor Games.* N.Y.: Sterling, 1993; 128pp., $5.95.

Vecere, Joel. *A Story of Courage.* Tex.: Raintree Steck Co., 1992; 32pp., NA.

Velthuijs, Max. *Crocodile's Masterpiece.* N.Y.: Farrar, Straus and Giroux, 1991; 32pp., $14.00.

Verboven, Agnes. *Ducks Like to Swim.* N.Y.: Orchard, 1996; 26pp., $13.95.

Vesey, Amanda. *Duncan's Tree House.* Minn.: Carolrhoda Books, Inc., 1993; 32pp., NA.

Vickers, Kath. *A Wizard Came to Visit.* Ill.: Children's Press Choice, 1987; 24pp., $7.45.

Vigna, Judith. *The Little Boy Who Loved Dirt and Almost Became a Superslob.* Ill.: Albert Whitman, 1975; 32pp., NA.

———. *Couldn't We Have a Turtle Instead?* N.Y.: Albert Whitman, 1975; 29pp., $2.81.

Villarejo, Mary. *The Tiger Hunt.* N.Y.: Alfred A. Knopf, 1959; 28pp., $2.75.

Vincent, Gabrielle. *Ernest and Celestine.* N.Y.: Greenwillow, 1985; 16pp., $5.25.

Vinton, Iris. *Folkway's Omnibus of Children's Games.* Pa.: Stackpole, 1970; 320pp., $8.95.

Viorst, Judith. *Alexander, Who's Not (Do You Hear Me? I Mean It) Moving.* N.Y.: Atheneum, 1975; 28pp., $14.00.

———. *Alexander, Who Used to Be Rich Last Sunday.* N.Y.: Atheneum, 1978; 32pp., $15.00.

———. *Try It Again, Sam.* N.Y.: Lothrop, Lee and Shepard, 1970; 38pp., $11.88.

Voake, Charlotte. *Here Comes the Train.* Mass.: Candlewick, 1998; 32pp., $15.99.

Vogel, Carole. *The Dangers of Strangers.* Minn.: Dillon, 1983; 32pp., $10.95.

Vulliamy, Clara. *Ellen and Penguin.* Mass.: Candlewick, 1993; 26pp., $13.95.

———. *Ellen and Penguin and the New Baby.* Mass.: Candlewick, 1996; 32pp., $5.99.

Vyner, Sue. *Arctic Spring.* N.Y.: Viking, 1992; 32pp., $13.99.

Waber, Bernard. *But Names Will Never Hurt Me.* Mass.: Houghton Mifflin, 1976; 32pp., $14.95.

———. *I Was All Thumbs.* Mass.: Houghton Mifflin, 1990; 48pp, $4.95.

———. *A Lion Named Shirley Williamson.* Mass.: Houghton Mifflin, 1996; 40pp., $15.95.

———. *Lorenzo.* Mass.: Houghton Mifflin, 1961; unpaged, $2.70.

———. *Lyle at Christmas.* Mass.: Houghton Mifflin, 1998; 32pp., $16.00.

———. *"You Look Ridiculous," said the Rhinocerous to the Hippopotamus.* Mass.: Houghton Mifflin, 1966; 38p., $17.95.

Waddell, Martin. *Amy Said.* Mass.: Little, Brown, 1989; 32pp., $12.95.

———. *Can't You Sleep, Little Bear?* Mass.: Candlewick, 1988; 32pp., $16.95.

———. *Farmer Duck.* Mass.: Candlewick, 1991; 32pp., $16.99.

———. *Let's Go Home, Little Bear.* Mass.: Candlewick, 1991; 32pp., $14.95.

———. *Little Mo.* Mass.: Candlewick, 1993; 32pp., $14.95.

———. *Once There Were Giants.* N.Y.: Delacorte, 1995; 30pp., $15.99.

————. *Owl Babies*. Mass.: Candlewick, 1992; 32pp., $15.99.

————. *Small Bear Lost*. Mass.: Candlewick, 1996; 32pp., $15.99.

————. *The Toymaker*. Mass.: Candlewick, 1991; 32pp., $13.95.

————. *You and Me, Little Bear*. Mass.: Candlewick, 1996; 32pp., $15.99.

Wade, Alan. *I'm Flying*. N.Y.: Alfred A. Knopf, 1980; 32pp., NA.

Waggoner, Karen. *The Lemonade Babysitter*. Mass.: Little, Brown, 1992; 32pp., $14.95.

Wagner, Jenny. *The Bunyip of Berkeley's Creek*. N.Y.: Bradbury, 1978; 40pp., $9.95.

Wahl, Jan. *Follow Me Cried Bee*. N.Y. : Crown, 1976; 29pp., $5.95.

Waldman, Neil. *The Never-Ending Greenness*. N.Y.: Morrow Junior Books, 1997; 32pp., $16.00.

Wallace, Ian. *A Winter's Tale*. Ontario: Groundwood, 1997; 32pp., $15.95.

Wallace, Mary. *I Can Make Art So Easy to Make!* Ontario: Greeyde Pencier, 1997; 32pp., $17.95.

————. *I Can Make Toys*. Ontario: Greeyde Pencier, 1994; 32 pp., $17.95.

Wallwork, Amanda. *No DoDos: A Counting Book of Endangered Animals*. N.Y.: Scholastic, 1993; 26pp., $14.95.

Walsch, Melanie. *Do Monkeys Tweet?* Mass.: Houghton Mifflin, 1997; 32pp., $15.00.

Walsh, Ellen Stoll. *Mouse Paint*. N.Y.: Harcourt Brace, 1989; 32pp., $12.00.

————. *Pip's Magic*. N.Y.: Harcourt Brace, 1994; 32pp., $13.95.

Walsh, Jill Paton. *Connie Came to Play*. N.Y.: Penguin, 1995; 32pp., $12.99.

Walters, Donna Gadling, Lottie Riekehof, and Daniel M. Pokorny. *Lift Up Your Hands: Popular Songs in Sign Language*. D.C.: The National Grange, 1992; 62pp., NA.

Walter, F. Virginia. *Fun with Paper Bags and Cardboard Tubes*. N.Y.: Sterling, 1992; 80pp., $19.95.

————. *Great Newspaper Crafts*. N.Y.: Sterling/Hyperion, 1991; 80pp., $17.95.

Walton, Rick. *How Many, How Many, How Many*. Mass.: Candlewick, 1993; 32pp., $14.95.

Wandro, Mark, and Joani Blank. *My Daddy Is a Nurse*. Mass.: Addison-Wesley, 1981; 32pp., $7.95.

Ward, Sally G. *Punky Spends the Day*. N.Y.: E. P. Dutton, 1989; 30pp., $11.95.

Warner, Penny. *Happy Birthday Parties!* N.Y.: St. Martin's, 1985; 140pp., $9.95.

————. *Kids' Holiday Fun*. N.Y.: Meadowbrook, 1994; 214pp., $12.00.

Warren, Jean. *1–2–3 Games*. Wash.: Totline, 1986; 80pp., $8.95.

————. *Crafts: Early Learning Activities*. Calif.: Monday Morning, 1996; 80pp., $7.95.

————. *Theme-a-saurus*. Wash.: Warren, 1989; 280pp., $21.95.

————. *Theme-a-saurus II*. Calif.: Warren, 1990; 278pp., $21.95.

Warren, Jean, and Elizabeth McKinnon. *Small World Celebrations*. Wash.: Warren, 1988; 160pp., $14.95.

Warren, Ramona, and others. *Easter Handbook*. Ill.: The Child's World, 1986; 95pp., $12.95.

Washington, Donna L. *The Story of Kwanzaa*. N.Y.: HarperCollins, 1996; 40pp., $15.95.

Watanabe, Shigeo. *I Can Build a House.* N.Y.: Putnam, 1985; 32pp., $8.95.

———. *I Can Take a Walk.* N.Y.: Philomel, 1983; 28pp., $7.95.

Watkins, Sherrin. *Green Snake Ceremony.* Okla.: Council Oak Pub., Co., Inc., 1995; 32pp., $17.95.

Watson, Wendy. *Happy Easter Day!* N.Y.: Clarion, 1993; 32pp., $14.95.

———. *Hurray for the Fourth of July.* N.Y.: Clarion, 1992; 32pp., $14.95.

Watts, Barrie. *Ladybug.* N.J.: Silver Burdett, 1987; 25pp., $15.95.

Watts, Irene N. *Great Theme Parties for Children.* N.Y.: Sterling, 1991; 128pp., $13.95.

Weil, Lisl. *The Candy Egg Bunny.* N.Y.: Holiday House, 1975; 32pp., $4.95.

Weisgard, Leonard. *The Funny Bunny Factory.* N.Y.: Grosset and Dunlap, 1955; unpaged, NA.

Weiss, Ellen. *Millicent Maybe.* N.Y.: Avon, 1980; 29pp., $1.50.

———. *Pigs in Space.* N.Y.: Random House, 1983; unpaged, $1.95.

Weiss, Nicki. *If You're Happy and You Know It.* N.Y.: Greenwillow, 1987; 40pp., $13.00.

Weitzman, Jacqueline Preiss, and Robin Preiss Glasser. *You Can't Take a Balloon into the Metropolitan Museum.* N.Y. Dial Books for Young Readers, 1998; 32pp., $16.99.

Welch, Willy. *Playing Right Field.* N.Y.: Scholastic, 1995; 32pp., $13.95.

Weller, Frances Ward. *I Wonder If I'll See a Whale.* N.Y.: Philomel, 1991; 32pp., $11.15.

Wellington, Monica. *Seasons of Swans.* N.Y.: Dutton Children's Books, 1989; 32pp., $12.95.

———. *The Sheep Follow.* N.Y.: Dutton Children's Books, 1992; 32pp., $13.00.

Wells, Rosemary. *Bunny Money.* N.Y.: Dial Books for Young Readers, 1997; 32pp., $14.99.

———. *Fritz and the Mess Fairy.* N.Y.: Dial Books for Young Readers, 1991; 32pp., $13.89.

———. *The Little Lame Prince.* N.Y.: Dial Books for Young Readers, 1990; 32pp., $12.95.

———. *McDuff and the Baby.* N.Y.: Hyperion Books for Children, 1997; 26pp., $12.95.

———. *McDuff Comes Home.* N.Y.: Hyperion Books for Children, 1997; 24pp., $12.95.

———. *Max and Ruby's First Greek Myth: Pandora's Box.* N.Y.: Dial Books for Young Readers, 1993; 32pp., $11.99.

———. *Max's Chocolate Chicken.* N.Y.: Dial Books for Young Readers, 1989; 32pp., $9.95.

———. *Max's New Suit.* N.Y.: Dial for the Young, 1998; unpaged, $5.99.

———. *Read to Your Bunny.* N.Y.: Scholastic, 1997; 28pp., $7.95.

———. *Shy Charles.* N.Y.: Dial Books for Young Readers, 1988; 32pp., $11.95.

Wenner, Hilda E., and Elizabeth Freilicher. *Here's to the Women.* N.Y.: Syracuse University Press, 1987; 314pp., $19.95.

Wessell, Katharine Tyler. *The Golden Song Book.* N.Y.: Golden, 1981; 45pp., $5.95.

West, Colin. *"Buzz, Buzz, Buzz," Went Bumblebee*. Mass.: Candlewick, 1996; 24pp., $9.99.

———. *"Not Me," Said the Monkey*. N.Y.: J. B. Lippincott, 1987; 24pp., $12.00.

West, Robin. *My Very Own Thanksgiving: A Book of Cooking and Crafts*. Mass.: Carolrhoda, 1993; 64pp., $21.27.

Westcott, Nadine Bernard. *The Lady with the Alligator Purse*. Mass.: Little, Brown, 1988; 28pp., $15.95.

———. *There's a Hole in the Bucket*. N.Y.: Harper and Row, 1990; 26pp., $12.89.

Weston, Martha. *Bea's 4 Bears*. N.Y.: Clarion, 1992; 32pp., $9.95.

———. *Peony's Rainbow*. N.Y.: Lothrop, Lee and Shepard, 1981; 32pp., NA.

———. *Tuck in the Pool*. N.Y.: Clarion, 1995; 32pp., $12.95.

Wheeler, Cindy. *Marmalade's Yellow Leaf*. N.Y.: Alfred A. Knopf, 1982; 24pp., $8.99.

———. *More Simple Signs*. N.Y.: Viking, 1998; 32pp., $14.99.

Whishaw, Iona. *Henry and the Cow Problem*. N.Y.: Annick, 1995; 24pp., $15.95.

Whitcher, Susan. *Moonfall*. N.Y.: Farrar, Straus and Giroux, 1993; 32pp., $14.00.

Whitlock, Susan Love. *Donovan Scares the Monsters*. N.Y.: Greenwillow, 1987; 32pp., NA.

Whitney, Brooks. *Super Slumber Parties*. Wisc.: Pleasant Company Publications, 1997; 64pp., $7.95.

Wiesner, David. *Hurricane*. N.Y.: Clarion, 1990; 32pp., $16.00.

———. *Tuesday*. N.Y.: Clarion, 1991; 32pp., $15.95.

Wild, Margaret. *All the Better to See You With!* Ill.: Albert Whitman, 1992; 32pp., $14.95.

———. *The Queen's Holiday*. N.Y.: Orchard, 1992; 32pp., $13.99.

Wilde, Oscar. *The Selfish Giant*. N.Y.: G. P. Putnam's Sons, 1995; 32pp., $14.99.

Wildsmith, Brian. *Brian Wildsmith's Fishes*. N.Y.: Franklin Watts, 1987; 30pp., $11.95.

———. *The Owl and the Woodpecker*. N.Y.: Franklin Watts, 1972; 29pp. $5.95.

Wildsmith, Brian, and Rebecca. *Jack and the Meanstalk*. N.Y.: Alfred A. Knopf, 1994; 26pp., $15.99.

Wilhelm, Hans. *A Cool Kid—Like Me!* N.Y.: Crown, 1990; 32pp., $3.99.

Wilkes, Angela. *Child Magazine's Book of Children's Parties*. N.Y.: DK Publishing, 1996; 80pp., $18.95.

Willard, Nancy. *The Well-Mannered Balloon*. Calif.: Harcourt Brace Jovanovich, 1991; 28pp., $3.95.

Willey, Margaret. *Thanksgiving with Me*. N.Y.: Laura Geringer Book, 1998; 32pp., $14.95.

Williams, Barbara. *Albert's Toothache*. N.Y.: E. P. Dutton, 1974; 32pp., $3.95.

———. *Someday, Said Mitchell*. N.Y.: E. P. Dutton, 1976; 27pp., $5.95.

Williams, Jay. *Everyone Knows What a Dragon Looks Like*. N.Y.: Macmillan, 1984; 32pp., $6.95.

———. *The Practical Princess*. N.Y.: Parents Magazine, 1969; 40pp., $8.50.

Williams, Jay, and Winifred Lubell. *I Wish I Had Another Name*. N.Y.: Atheneum, 1962; 32pp., NA.

Williams, Karen Lynn. *When Africa Was Home*. N.Y.: Orchard, 1991; 32pp., $16.99.

Williams, Nancy. *A Kwanzaa Celebration*. N.Y.: Simon and Schuster, 1995; 14pp., $11.95.

Williams, Sue, ed. *Strawberry Fair*. London: A and C Black, 1985; 96pp., $14.95.

Williams, Vera B. *Lucky Song*. N.Y.: Greenwillow, 1997; 24pp., $15.00.

Williamson, Sarah. *Stop, Look and Listen*. Vt: Williamson, 1996; 144pp., $12.95.

Willis, Jeanne. *The Tale of Georgie Grub*. N.Y.: Holt, Rinehart and Winston, 1982; 24pp., $9.95.

Willis, Val. *The Mystery in the Bottle*. N.Y.: Farrar, Straus and Giroux, 1991; 32pp., $14.95.

———. *The Surprise in the Wardrobe*. N.Y.: Farrar, Straus and Giroux, 1990; 32pp., $15.00.

Wilmes, Liz and Dick. *Everyday Circle Times*. Ill.: Building Blocks, 1983; 216pp., $16.95.

Wilson, Etta. *Music in the Night*. N.Y.: Cobblehill, 1993; 32pp., $12.99.

Winch, John. *The Old Woman Who Loved to Read*. N.Y.: Holiday House, 1996; 32pp., $15.95.

Winkleman, Katherine K. *Police Patrol*. N.Y.: Walker, 1996; 32pp., $15.95.

Winn, Marie. *The Fireside Book of Children's Songs*. N.Y.: Simon and Schuster, 1966; 192pp., $12.95.

———. *The Fireside Book of Fun and Games Songs*. N.Y.: Simon and Schuster, 1974; 224pp., $14.95.

———. *What Shall We Do and Allee Galloo!* N.Y.: Harper and Row, 1970; 87pp., NA.

Winteringham, Victoria. *Penguin Day*. N.Y.: Harper and Row, 1982; 32pp., NA.

Winters, Kay. *The Teeny Tiny Ghost*. N.Y.: HarperCollins, 1997; 32pp., $14.95.

Winthrop, Elizabeth. *Tough Eddie*. N.Y.: E. P. Dutton, 1985; 32pp., NA.

Wirth, Marian Jenks. *Teacher's Handbook of Children's Games*. N.Y.: Parker, 1976; 272pp. $24.95.

Wiseman, Bernard. *Little New Kangaroo*. N.Y.: Macmillan, 1973; 32pp., $4.95.

Wojciechowski, Susan. *The Best Halloween of All*. Mass.: Candlewick, 1998; 32pp., $9.99.

Wolde, Gunilla. *Betsy and the Doctor*. N.Y.: Random House, 1976; 24pp., $4.99.

———. *Betsy's First Day at Nursery School*. N.Y.: Random House, 1976; 24pp., $4.99.

Wolf, Bernard. *Michael and the Dentist*. N.Y.: Four Winds, 1980; 42pp., $8.95.

Wolf, Jake. *Daddy, Could I Have an Elephant?* N.Y.: Greenwillow, 1996; 32pp., $15.00.

Wolfe, Irving, and Beatrice Perham Krone, and Margaret Fullerton. *Proudly We Sing*. Ill.: Follett, 1958; 240pp., NA.

Wolff, Ferida. *The Emperor's Garden*. N.Y.: Tambourine, 1994; 32pp., $14.95.

Wolfsohn, Reeta Bochner. *Successful Children's Parties*. N.Y.: Arco, 1979; 112pp., $8.95.

Wong, Herbert H., and Mathew F. Vessel. *My Ladybug*. Mass.: Addison-Wesley, 1969; 32pp., $4.35.

Wood, Audrey. *Detective Valentine*. N.Y.: Harper and Row, 1987; 40pp., $12.90.

Wood, Audrey. *King Bidgood's in the Bathtub.* Calif.: Harcourt Brace, 1985; 32pp., $16.00.

————. *Little Penguin's Tale.* N.Y.: Harcourt, Brace Jovanovich, 1989; 32pp., $13.95.

————. *Rude Giants.* N.Y.: Harcourt Brace, 1993; 32pp., $13.95.

————. *Sweet Dream Pie.* N.Y.: Blue Sky, 1998; 32pp., $15.95.

Woodruff, Elvira. *Show-and-Tell.* N.Y.: Holiday House, 32pp., $14.95.

————. *Tubtime.* N.Y.: Holiday House, 1990; 32pp., $14.95.

Woolley, Catherine. *The Horse with the Easter Bonnet.* N.Y.: William Morrow, 1953; 48pp, $2.00.

————. *Quiet on Account of Dinosaur.* N.Y.: William Morrow, 1964; unpaged, $11.88.

Wormell, Mary. *Hilda Hen's Happy Birthday.* Calif.: Harcourt Brace, 1995; 32pp., $14.00.

Woychuk, Denis. *Mimi and Gustav in Pirates!* N.Y.: Lothrop, Lee and Shepard, 1992; 32pp., NA.

Wright, Dare. *Edith and the Little Bear Lend a Hand.* N.Y.: Random House, 1972; 43pp., $2.95.

Wyllie, Stephen. *A Flea in the Ear.* N.Y.: Dutton Children's Books, 1995; 32pp., $14.99.

Yaccarino, Dan. *An Octopus Followed Me Home.* N.Y.: Viking, 1997; 32pp., $15.99.

Yee, Paul. *Sing on New Snow: A Delicious Tale.* N.Y.: Macmillan, 1991; 32pp., $13.95.

Yee, Wong Herbert. *Big Black Bear.* Mass.: Houghton Mifflin, 1993; 32pp., $14.95.

————. *Fireman Small.* Mass.: Houghton Mifflin, 1994; 32pp., $13.95.

————. *Mrs. Brown Went to Town.* Mass.: Houghton Mifflin, 1996; 32pp., $14.95.

————. *The Officers' Ball.* Mass.: Houghton Mifflin, 1987; 32pp., $14.95.

Yeoman, John. *Old Mother Hubbard's Dog Takes Up Sports.* Mass.: Houghton Mifflin, 1989; 18pp., $6.95.

Yeoman, John, and Quentin Blake. *Old Mother Hubbard's Dog Needs a Doctor.* Mass.: Houghton Mifflin, 1990; 32pp., NA.

Yolen, Jane. *Beneath the Ghost Moon.* Mass.: Little, Brown, 1994; 32pp., $14.95.

————. *The Emperor and the Kite.* N.Y.: Putnam, 1998; 27pp., $5.99.

————. *The Fireside Songbook of Birds and Beasts.* N.Y.: Simon and Schuster, 1972; 223pp., $9.95.

————. *Jane Yolen's Old MacDonald Songbook.* Pa.: Boyds Mills Press, 1994; 96pp., $16.95.

————. *No Bath Tonight.* N.Y.: Harper and Row Junior Books, 1978; 31pp., $12.95.

————. *Owl Moon.* N.Y.: Philomel, 1987; 32pp., $16.99.

————. *Rounds and Rounds.* N.Y.: Franklin Watts, 1977; 120pp., $7.90.

————. *Sleeping Ugly.* N.Y.: Coward, McCann and Geoghegan, 1981; 64pp., $5.99.

————. *Welcome to the Greenhouse.* N.Y.: Putnam, 1997; 32pp., $5.95.

Yorinks, Arthur. *Louis the Fish.* N.Y.: Farrar, Straus and Giroux, 1986; 32pp., $5.95.

————. *Ugh.* N.Y.: Farrar, Straus and Giroux, 1990; 32pp., $13.95.

Yorke, Jane. *My First Look at Touch.* N.Y.: Random House, 1990; 18pp., $6.95.

Yoshida, Toshi. *Rhinoceros Mother*. N.Y.: Philomel, 1991; 32pp., $14.95.

Young, Ed. *Seven Blind Mice*. N.Y.: Philomel, 1992; 40pp., $17.99.

Young, Ruth. *Daisy's Taxi*. N.Y.: Smithmark, 1991; 32pp., $4.95.

———. *My Baby-sitter*. N.Y.: Viking Kestrel, 1987; 24pp., $4.95.

———. *A Trip to Mars*. N.Y.: Orchard, 1990; 32pp., $14.95.

Yudell, Lynn. *Make a Face*. Mass.: Little, Brown, 1970; unpaged, $4.95.

Zalben, Jane Breskin. *Beni's First Channukah*. N.Y.: Henry Holt, 1988; $12.95.

Zelinsky, Paul O. *The Maid and the Mouse and the Odd-Shaped House*. N.Y.: Dutton Children's Books, 1981; 32pp., $14.99.

Zemach, Margot. *The Three Wishes*. N.Y.: Farrar, Straus and Giroux; 1986; 32pp., $16.00.

Zidrou. *Ms. Blanche, the Spotless Cow*. N.Y.: Henry Holt, 1992; 32pp., $14.95.

Ziefert, Harriet. *Bigger than a Baby*. N.Y.: HarperCollins, 1991; 32pp., $13.95.

———. *Henry's Wrong Turn*. Mass.: Little, Brown, 1989; 32pp., $13.95.

———. *Oh, What a Noisy Farm!* N.Y.: Tambourine, 1995; 32pp., $15.00.

———. *What Is Hanukkah?* N.Y.: Harper Festival, 1994; 32pp., $5.95.

Ziegler, Sandra. *At the Dentist: What Did Christopher See?* Ill.: Children's Press, 1976; 32pp., $4.50.

———. *The Child's World of Manners*, N.Y.: Child's World, 1998; 23pp., $18.50.

———. *A Visit to the Post Office*. Ill.: Children's Press, 1989; 31pp., NA.

Zimelman, Nathan. *Positively No Pets Allowed*. N.Y.: E. P. Dutton, 1980; 32pp., $7.95.

———. *Treed by a Pride of Irate Lions*. Mass.: Little, Brown, 1990; 30pp., $14.95.

Zimmermann, H. Werner. *A Circle Is Not a Valentine*. Ontario: Oxford University Press, 1990; 32pp., NA.

Zindel, Paul. *I Love My Mother*. N.Y.: Harper and Row Junior Books,1975; 32pp., $12.89.

Zion, Gene. *Harry and the Lady Next Door*. N.Y.: Harper and Row, 1996; 32pp., $14.89.

———. *Harry by the Sea*. N.Y.: Harper and Row Junior Books, 1965; 28pp., $14.00.

———. *Harry the Dirty Dog*. N.Y.: Harper and Row Junior Books, 1956; 28pp., $14.95.

———. *The Plant Sitter*. N.Y.: Harper and Row Junior Books, 1976; 32pp., $1.95.

———. *Really Spring*. N.Y.: Harper and Row Junior Books, 1956; 28pp., $12.89.

———. *The Summer Snowman*. N.Y.: Harper and Row Junior Books, 1955; 30pp., $12.89.

Zolotow, Charlotte. *The Bunny Who Found Easter*. Mass.: Houghton Mifflin, 1998; 32pp., $15.00.

———. *I Know an Old Lady*. N.Y.: Greenwillow, 1986; 24pp., $10.15.

———. *Mr. Rabbit and the Lovely Present*. N.Y.: Harper and Row Junior Books, 1962; 32pp., $14.95.

———. *The Quarreling Book*. N.Y.: Harper and Row Junior Books, 1963; 32pp., $13.00.

———. *The Storm Book*. N.Y.: Harper and Row Junior Books, 1952; 28pp., $6.95.

———. *Summer is. . . .* N.Y.: Harper and Row Junior Books, 1972; 32pp., $10.89.

———. *William's Doll*. N.Y.: Harper and Row Junior Books, 1972; 32pp., $15.89.

Index to Picture Book Titles

Note: Numbers refer to activity numbers, not to page numbers.

Index to Authors of Picture Books

Note: Numbers refer to activity numbers, not to page numbers.

Index to Crafts

Note: Numbers refer to activity numbers, not to page numbers.

Index to Activities

Note: Numbers refer to activity numbers, not to page numbers.

Index to Song Titles

Note: Numbers refer to activity numbers, not to page numbers.

About the Author

Carolyn Cullum has worked as a supervising children's librarian in a public library in New Jersey for the past 18 years. Her past experiences include working with children as an elementary school teacher for five years, as a school librarian, and as a Sunday School teacher with her local church.

She has a B.A. in elementary education, an MLS in library service and an educational media specialist certification. She also has spoken to such groups as local PTA groups, Edison Kindergarten Teacher's Association, Elks group holiday parties, high school parenting classes, local cable television shows in Edison, N.J., New Jersey Association of Kindergarten Teachers Convention, and various elementary school auditorium programs and college events.